Building Smart and Sustainable Businesses With Transformative Technologies

Hamed Nozari
Department of Management, Azad University of the Emirates, Dubai, UAE

IGI Global
PUBLISHER of TIMELY KNOWLEDGE

A volume in the Advances in E-Business Research (AEBR) Book Series

Published in the United States of America by
IGI Global
Business Science Reference (an imprint of IGI Global)
701 E. Chocolate Avenue
Hershey PA, USA 17033
Tel: 717-533-8845
Fax: 717-533-8661
E-mail: cust@igi-global.com
Web site: http://www.igi-global.com

Library of Congress Cataloging-in-Publication Data

Names: Nozari, Hamed, 1984- editor.
Title: Building smart and sustainable businesses with transformative technologies / edited by: Hamed Nozari.
Description: Hershey, PA : Business Science Reference, [2024] | Includes bibliographical references and index. | Summary: "Examining the dimensions, components and key indicators affecting digital businesses in the era of transformative technologies and their effects on sustainable development is one of the most important goals of this book"-- Provided by publisher.
Identifiers: LCCN 2023037436 (print) | LCCN 2023037437 (ebook) | ISBN 9798369302101 (hardcover) | ISBN 9798369302118 (paperback) | ISBN 9798369302125 (ebook)
Subjects: LCSH: Business enterprises--Technological innovations. | Technological innovations--Management. | Sustainable development.
Classification: LCC HD45 .B7935 2024 (print) | LCC HD45 (ebook) | DDC 658.4/063--dc23/eng/20231127
LC record available at https://lccn.loc.gov/2023037436
LC ebook record available at https://lccn.loc.gov/2023037437

This book is published in the IGI Global book series Advances in E-Business Research (AEBR) (ISSN: 1935-2700; eISSN: 1935-2719)

British Cataloguing in Publication Data
A Cataloguing in Publication record for this book is available from the British Library.
All work contributed to this book is new, previously-unpublished material.

For electronic access to this publication, please contact: eresources@igi-global.com.

Advances in E-Business Research (AEBR) Book Series

ISSN:1935-2700
EISSN:1935-2719

Editor-in-Chief: In Lee, Western Illinois University, USA

MISSION

Technology has played a vital role in the emergence of e-business and its applications incorporate strategies. These processes have aided in the use of electronic transactions via telecommunications networks for collaborating with business partners, buying and selling of goods and services, and customer service. Research in this field continues to develop into a wide range of topics, including marketing, psychology, information systems, accounting, economics, and computer science.

The **Advances in E-Business Research (AEBR) Book Series** provides multidisciplinary references for researchers and practitioners in this area. Instructors, researchers, and professionals interested in the most up-to-date research on the concepts, issues, applications, and trends in the e-business field will find this collection, or individual books, extremely useful. This collection contains the highest quality academic books that advance understanding of e-business and addresses the challenges faced by researchers and practitioners.

COVERAGE

- Online Consumer Behavior
- E-procurement methods
- Web 2.0
- Electronic Supply Chain Management
- E-business models and architectures
- Economics of e-business
- Web Service-Based Business Systems
- Mobile Business Models
- Trust, Security, and Privacy
- E-business systems integration

The Advances in E-Business Research (AEBR) Book Series (ISSN 1935-2700) is published by IGI Global, 701 E. Chocolate Avenue, Hershey, PA 17033-1240, USA, www.igi-global.com. This series is composed of titles available for purchase individually; each title is edited to be contextually exclusive from any other title within the series. For pricing and ordering information please visit http://www.igi-global.com/book-series/advances-business-research/37144. Postmaster: Send all address changes to above address.

Titles in this Series

For a list of additional titles in this series, please visit:
http://www.igi-global.com/book-series/advances-business-research/37144

Metaverse Applications for New Business Models and Disruptive Innovation
Muhammad Anshari (Universiti Brunei Darussalam, Brunei) Muhammad Syafrudin (Sejong University, South Korea) and Ganjar Alfian (Universitas Gadjah Mada, Idonesia)
Business Science Reference • © 2023 • 265pp • H/C (ISBN: 9781668460979) • US $250.00

Digital Technologies for Entrepreneurship in Industry 4.0
Elena G. Popkova (MGIMO University, Russia)
Business Science Reference • © 2022 • 270pp • H/C (ISBN: 9781668442654) • US $250.00

Driving Transformative Change in E-Business Through Applied Intelligence and Emerging Technologies
Hamed Taherdoost (University Canada West, Canada)
Business Science Reference • © 2022 • 307pp • H/C (ISBN: 9781668452356) • US $250.00

Virtual Technologies and E-Collaboration for the Future of Global Business
Jingyuan Zhao (University of Toronto, Canada) and Joseph Richards (California State University, Sacramento, USA)
Business Science Reference • © 2022 • 273pp • H/C (ISBN: 9781668450277) • US $250.00

Navigating Digital Communication and Challenges for Organizations
José Gabriel Andrade (University of Minho, Portugal) and Teresa Ruão (CECS, Universidade do Minho, Portugal)
Business Science Reference • © 2022 • 325pp • H/C (ISBN: 9781799897903) • US $230.00

Handbook of Research on Smart Management for Digital Transformation
Belem Barbosa (University of Porto, Portugal) Sandra Filipe (University of Aveiro, Portugal) and Claudia Amaral Santos (University of Aveiro, Portugal)
Business Science Reference • © 2022 • 614pp • H/C (ISBN: 9781799890089) • US $325.00

For an entire list of titles in this series, please visit:
http://www.igi-global.com/book-series/advances-business-research/37144

IGI Global
PUBLISHER of TIMELY KNOWLEDGE

701 East Chocolate Avenue, Hershey, PA 17033, USA
Tel: 717-533-8845 x100 • Fax: 717-533-8661
E-Mail: cust@igi-global.com • www.igi-global.com

Table of Contents

Detailed Table of Contents

Supply Chain 5.0 is the latest change in the continuous management system of procurement and supply chain in the new era. This concept describes the use of transformative technologies such as artificial intelligence (AI), blockchain, the internet of things, and big data analytics to create a continuous network of self-managing supply chain nodes. This system is an ecosystem that combines different technologies simultaneously to create an integrated network and to create a sustainable, resilient, and human-centered process-oriented system. This research has tried to identify the main actors and provide an analytical framework by examining the dimensions and components of this intelligent system. Understanding this framework is always an effective guide for the powerful implementation of this smart system.

Connected devices are physical objects that can communicate with each other and other systems through the internet. They include everything from traditional computing hardware, such as a laptop or desktop, to common mobile devices, such as a smartphone or tablet, to a wide variety of physical devices and objects. The internet of things describes a network of physical objects—"things"—that are embedded with sensors, software, and other technologies to connect and exchange data with other devices and systems over the internet. Internet of things-connected devices create a world where data is exchanged between physical objects such as

chain management. For this reason, it is necessary to know the emerging trends for blockchain technology in smart supply chain management. Therefore, the present study focuses on the blockchain technology on smart supply chain management. Accordingly, the aim is to identify emerging trends for blockchain technology on smart supply chain management by using Vosviewer from systematic literature review perspective.

IoT is about improving trade forms and arrangements using sensors, gadgets, doors, and stages. Utilizing the IoT by collecting all data in one put, producers can make intelligent decisions in their business and design more efficient and optimal processes. Therefore, the IoT can be useful for companies by reducing costs, increasing efficiency, progressing client involvement and fulfillment, and expanding dynamism and adaptability. As a result, by utilizing the IoT in businesses, they have lower upkeep costs and superior disappointment administration. In an inventive trade, an observing framework based on the IoT predicts issues and permits ideal time planning for exercises. By utilizing the IoT, companies can robotize forms and decrease labor costs. It also moves forward benefit conveyance and gives transparency in exchanges to the client. In this respect, this chapter bargains with the essential definition of the IoT, the sorts of IoT gadgets, how to utilize them in businesses, the reason for clever companies, and when it is considered intelligent.

The conventional supply chain framework included smart objects to upgrade intelligence, mechanization capabilities, and intelligent decision-making. Internet of things (IoT) advances give uncommon openings to extend productivity, diminish supply chain framework costs, and optimize energy consumption. Optimizing energy utilization with the IoT makes moving forward operational productivity in any industry conceivable. The applications of IoT within the energy segment have pulled in the extraordinary consideration of customers, businesses, and indeed, governments. For case, joining sun-oriented energy into control checking systems is one of the benefits of IoT within the supply chain, which changes a supply chain administration framework into a green and energy-saving plan. Utilizing daylight as an energy source empowers commerce to spare costs while giving a nonstop control supply to guarantee gadgets work without battery substitutions. Using renewable vitality, an intelligent framework prepared with the IoT transmits less nursery gases than conventional vitality sources.

This study aims to review collaboration in Supply Chain 4.0. For this objective, dimensions and outcomes of collaboration are analyzed based on businesses. An overview of the different dimensions and outcomes of collaboration was created in Industry 4.0 platform. Research data was obtained from literature review and then refined according to SC experts. The findings show that collaboration in Supply Chain 4.0, with the activation of dimensions including information and communication management, resource planning in the production and logistics process, collaborative decisions for business goals, technology and business development, motivational alignment, performance evaluation in integrated processes, marketing and customer orientation can lead to sustainable performance. In this study, a comprehensive approach is made to accessing collaboration concept among business partners in Industry 4.0 by creating a new conceptual framework to achieve economic, social, and environmental performance.

One of the important issues in the field of contract implementation is the security and speed of contract implementation in a way that can gain the trust of the contracting parties. In response to this challenge, one of these tools are smart contracts, which compared to other types of electronic contracts have features such as high speed and security and low cost in forming the contract. Smart contracts are currently used in various fields such as finance, law, banking, stock exchange, blockchain, government, industry, charity, etc. These contracts have many advantages, such as reducing costs, increasing speed, improving security, eliminating intermediaries, and preventing fraud. In simpler terms, smart contracts have taken over the task of making transactions with tools, the most important of which is the blockchain platform. Hence, in this research, the framework of using smart contracts in the field of e-commerce is discussed and the advantages, disadvantages, how to apply, successful experiences, and perspectives for the future of these contracts are presented.

Smart business is the advances and applications that are utilized to gather, coordinate, analyze, and show commerce within the organization. The smart business may be profound and comprehensive information of components such as customers, competitors, financial environment, operations, and organizational processes, which influence the quality of administration choices within the organization. Smart management enables all of an organization's senior managers to make informed decisions about everything from research and development, marketing, and investment tactics to long-term strategies. Therefore, the success of smart businesses in the new era of success depends on various parameters that should be paid special attention to. For this reason, the most important key indicators of success in smart organizations have been evaluated in this research. In order to analyze the results, a fuzzy decision-making method has been used. The results show that adequate budget and infrastructure growth is the most important critical success factor in developing smart businesses.

The integration of IoT in the export market has brought significant benefits such as improved operational efficiency, cost savings, enhanced security, and better customer satisfaction. As the technology continues to advance, we can expect further innovations and advancements in IoT applications within the export industry. On the other hand, empirical knowledge (export experience) about foreign markets is a driving force in the internationalization of companies. This research investigates the possibility of entering and growing exports, emphasizing the role of export experience for young exporters. The statistical population of the research includes all Iranian food manufacturing companies that have had exports between the years 2019 and 2022. The research data has been extracted from the statistical system of the Islamic Republic of Iran Customs Administration and the Trade Development Organization. STATA econometric software has been used for data analysis.

This study examines the feasibility of fostering symbiotic relationships between humans and machines in the hotel industry and explores effective strategies for managing their collaboration to maximize benefits. The chapter follows a rigorous methodology, conducting a systematic literature review using scientific databases, analyzing published and unpublished articles and data from various organizations. Key focus areas include the "hospitality industry," "man and machine," and "machine as co-workers." Findings demonstrate that strategic management and implementation of human-machine relationships can enhance organizational performance and yield substantial benefits. Addressing inherent challenges and intricacies is vital for a favorable outcome. The study presents a theoretical framework elucidating the impact of human-machine interaction on organizational outcomes.

With the expansion of the internet of things (IoT) and its impact on today's life, a significant improvement can be seen in hospital services. The IoT allows patients to take control of their condition. This method can reduce the anxiety of patients to some extent. On the other hand, by collecting the patient's data during the hospital stay, doctors gain clearer views of the patient's body physiology and can provide more specialized and special care plans. With the method provided by the IoT, the interaction between the doctor and the patient increases, and it also helps by monitoring the patient's health remotely and reducing the time spent in the hospital. Storing information from the IoT locally is not only expensive but also brings certain complications for medical centers. For this reason, hospitals are turning to cloud storage of patient information. In this research, in addition to describing the basic features of smart hospitals based on the IoT and cloud computing, a hospital chart based on these technologies is also presented.

Preface

With the expanding development of innovation, the shape of business and the interactions of commerce exercises with clients have changed. Innovation and the Web boom have caused unused businesses to rise and numerous conventional businesses to alter their shape and utilize the Internet.

Business intelligence is application programs and technologies organizations use to collect, integrate, analyze, and present business data. Among the benefits of smart business are facilitating and optimizing the decision-making process, identifying business opportunities, increasing information sharing, more effective communication with customers, increasing the ability to prepare diverse and dynamic reports, and predicting the organization's future conditions.

Digital transformations and transformational technologies play a fundamental role in the implementation and creation of today's businesses and the sustainable development of businesses. For this reason, it is essential to understand the characteristics of these businesses with an emphasis on transformative technologies in today's world. Therefore, this book has made an effort to provide a comprehensive view of sustainable smart businesses based on powerful technologies. The dimensions, components, and indicators affecting these businesses and the cause-and-effect relationships of the actors have also been examined, which can be a practical guide for researchers and enthusiasts.

In this book, the general atmosphere of Industry 4.0 and Industry 5.0 is examined in the first chapters. In parts of the book, the key indicators of success in smart businesses are analyzed. The impact of transformative technologies such as the Internet of Things, big data and blockchain in supply chain and business processes are analyzed, and finally these effects are examined in some industries as a case study.

In Chapter 1, we delve into the revolutionary concept of Supply Chain 5.0, which harnesses transformative technologies like AI, blockchain, IoT, and big data analytics to form an interconnected network of self-managing supply chain nodes. We explore the dimensions and components of this intelligent system, identifying key actors and providing an analytical framework. This knowledge serves as a practical guide for the effective implementation of this cutting-edge system.

Chapter 2 explores the world of connected devices, which can communicate with each other and other systems via the Internet. We discuss the Internet of Things (IoT) and how it forms a network of physical objects embedded with sensors and software. The chapter focuses on the technology enabling communication between IoT devices, highlighting the significance of this exchange of data in modern technology and business.

In Chapter 3, we trace the evolution of the concept of sustainable development from its origins in the biological system to its comprehensive application in various domains, including the economy, society, and the environment. The impact of digital technologies on advancing the Sustainable Development Goals is examined, emphasizing the growth of smart businesses and processes in smart societies as drivers of technological and economic development.

Chapter 4 delves into the integration of digital technologies, particularly blockchain, into traditional supply chain management processes to create a smarter and more efficient system. We explore the growing potential of blockchain in smart supply chain management and the emerging trends in this field. Businesses are encouraged to embrace blockchain technology to enhance their supply chain operations.

Chapter 5 provides insights into how businesses can leverage the Internet of Things (IoT) to streamline their operations, reduce costs, increase efficiency, enhance customer engagement, and adapt to changing dynamics. The chapter discusses the fundamental concepts of IoT, its types of devices, and how it can transform businesses into intelligent enterprises.

In Chapter 6, we explore the use of IoT in optimizing energy consumption within supply chains, offering cost-saving and environmentally friendly solutions. The applications of IoT in the energy sector are discussed, including the integration of solar energy to create green and energy-efficient supply chain management systems.

Chapter 7 delves into the dimensions and outcomes of collaboration within supply chain 4.0. The study highlights various aspects of collaboration and their positive impact on sustainable performance in the Industry 4.0 landscape. A new conceptual framework is presented, emphasizing economic, social, and environmental performance through collaborative efforts.

Chapter 8 explores the significance of smart contracts in ensuring secure and efficient contract implementation, ultimately gaining the trust of contracting parties. It discusses the advantages, disadvantages, and application of smart contracts in various sectors, with a focus on e-commerce. The future prospects of smart contracts are also considered.

Chapter 9 evaluates the critical success factors for smart organizations in the new era. The research emphasizes the importance of budget and infrastructure growth as the most significant factors for success in smart businesses, using a fuzzy decision-making method to analyze the results.

Chapter 10 explores the integration of IoT in the export market and its benefits, including improved operational efficiency, cost savings, security enhancements, and enhanced customer satisfaction. It also highlights the role of export experience in the internationalization of companies, with a focus on young exporters in the Iranian food manufacturing industry.

Chapter 11 investigates the feasibility of fostering symbiotic relationships between humans and machines in the hospitality industry. It offers strategies for managing this collaboration to maximize benefits while addressing challenges. The chapter presents a theoretical framework outlining the impact of human-machine interaction on organizational outcomes.

Chapter 12 explores the impact of the Internet of Things (IoT) on hospital services and the role of cloud computing in storing patient information. It highlights the benefits of IoT in increasing patient engagement and improving healthcare while reducing hospitalization time.

Chapter 13 analyzes the potential benefits of implementing blockchain technology in the automotive supply chain. A case study approach is used to examine a European automotive company's hesitancy to adopt blockchain. The chapter offers strategic recommendations to enhance security, efficiency, and technological advancements within the supply chain.

The final chapter provides an overview of digital disruption and its connection to China's economic leadership, emphasizing the country's integration of digital innovation and sustainability. The impact of the COVID-19 pandemic on accelerating the transition to digital business models is discussed. The chapter highlights China's strategy for smart supply chains, incorporating technologies like big data, AI, IoT, and blockchain to improve supply chain management and promote sustainability.

Hamed Nozari
Department of Management, Azad University of the Emirates, Dubai, UAE

Chapter 1
An Analytical Framework for Smart Supply Chains 5.0

Hamed Nozari
https://orcid.org/0000-0002-6500-6708
Azad University of the Emirates, Dubai, UAE

Agnieszka Szmelter-Jarosz
https://orcid.org/0000-0002-6183-6114
Faculty of Economics, University of Gdańsk, Poland

ABSTRACT

Supply Chain 5.0 is the latest change in the continuous management system of procurement and supply chain in the new era. This concept describes the use of transformative technologies such as artificial intelligence (AI), blockchain, the internet of things, and big data analytics to create a continuous network of self-managing supply chain nodes. This system is an ecosystem that combines different technologies simultaneously to create an integrated network and to create a sustainable, resilient, and human-centered process-oriented system. This research has tried to identify the main actors and provide an analytical framework by examining the dimensions and components of this intelligent system. Understanding this framework is always an effective guide for the powerful implementation of this smart system.

DOI: 10.4018/979-8-3693-0210-1.ch001

1. INTRODUCTION

Also, due to the volume of transactions in the business world, this chain is now much more complicated than in the past and faces more costs. Therefore, today's businesses in many industries are looking for ways to improve their supply chain situation. These new changes have forced industries to act smarter than before.

The supply chain is one of the areas affected by the fourth and fifth industrial revolutions and digital technologies such as the Internet of Things, advanced robotics, and big data analysis. Smart supply chain is the process of supply, warehousing, inventory control, production, and supply of products using smart technology. This method actually replaces the traditional and conventional methods of supply chain management based on the re-engineering of various processes. The main effort is to make a fundamental change in supply chain management by focusing on the possibilities of new technologies (Ivanov, 2023).

Although each of these technologies is capable of creating significant opportunities for businesses, the combination of these technologies together seems to lead to a major transformation in the supply chain. On the one hand, technology such as the Internet of Things, with the help of devices and sensors, leads to an increase in the speed of receiving information in real-time, from the state of the supply chain. On the other hand, big data analysis by processing this large volume of generated data brings identification of patterns and prediction of trends. In addition, artificial intelligence adds high analytical power to this collection. Blockchain is also a valuable solution for data security. Provides transparent and decentralized management. All these factors together provide a supply chain that, in addition to being smart, is sustainable and resilient and cares about people's lives. This intelligent hybrid process based on technology and integrated into the supply chain can lead to the supply chain system, which is called Supply Chain 5.0. Businesses that are able to use the combination of these technologies together will become an information-based business that is able to make decisions based on real and timely data and generally increase business productivity (Kamble, 2023).

Supply Chain 5.0 represents a critical departure from past eras by presenting intelligence, mechanization, and more noteworthy permeability into the whole supply chain organization. In addition, it is a biological system that combines different advances such as artificial intelligence, IoT, mechanical autonomy, blockchain, and big data analytics to make a bond together (Nozari et al., 2021). The utilization of AI is especially pivotal in Supply Chain 5.0. AI calculations can offer assistance in foreseeing requests and optimizing stock levels, progressing operational effectiveness, and diminishing squandering. AI-powered robots can moreover robotize monotonous assignments, such as picking and pressing, and decrease the hazard of human mistakes.

AI too makes a difference in making strides in client encounters, permitting for more precise conveyance times and real-time following of products (Najafi et al., 2022).

Supply Chain 5.0 speaks to the long-term supply chain administration. It can make a completely coordinates, straightforward, and autonomous supply chain organized by combining progressed advances such as counterfeit insights, blockchain, the Internet of Things, and huge information analytics. As a result, it offers critical benefits including expanded effectiveness, decreased costs, progressed client involvement, and more prominent supportability. As businesses proceed to grasp computerized change, Supply Chain 5.0 is likely to end up the unused standard in supply chain administration (Nozari et al., 2019).

Considering the ever-increasing growth of transformative technologies and their significant role in the smartening of supply chain processes, in this research, an analytical framework for supply chains based on transformative technologies in Industry 5.0, i.e. supply chain 5.0, has been presented. A correct understanding of this framework is always a good guide for identifying key players and effective implementation of these intelligent systems in the era of integrated intelligence.

2. INDUSTRY 5.0

During its ten-year period, the fourth-generation industry has focused less on the principles of fairness and social sustainability and has focused more on digitization and artificial intelligence-based technologies in order to increase production efficiency and flexibility. The fifth-generation industry focuses on a different issue, and in fact, the importance of research and innovation to support the industry in its long-term service to humanity at planetary boundaries is emphasized (Nozari, Szmelter-Jarosz & Ghahremani-Nahr, 2021). The fifth-generation industry should be defined in terms of broad objectives that go beyond the production of profitable goods and services. These broader goals include three main elements: human-centeredness, sustainability, and resilience. Figure 1 shows the dimensions of Industry 5.0. Of course, it can be seen that these dimensions were also present in Industry 4.0, but the alignment and overlap of these dimensions with transformational technologies in Industry 4.0 form the concept of Industry 5.0.

Figure 1. The dimensions of Industry 5.0

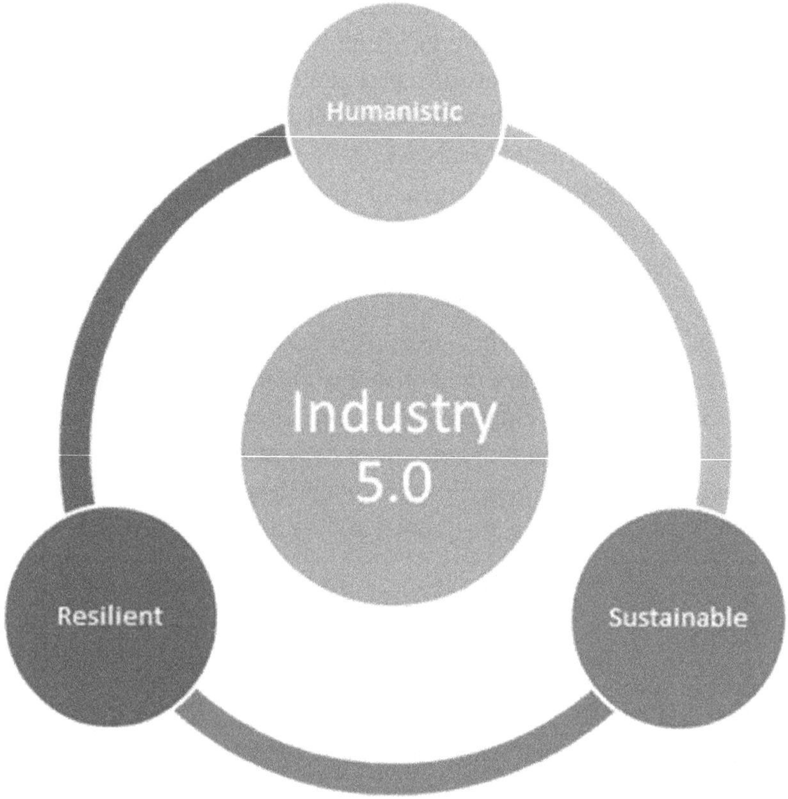

Industry 5.0 or smart industry is a new concept in the field of technology and production, where humans are the center of attention and technologies are designed to respond to their individual and personal needs. In this concept, man, as an active and intelligent agent, is involved in production and service processes and controls the processes according to his needs.

In Industry 5.0, technologies such as artificial intelligence, the Internet of Things, 3D printing, augmented reality, robotics, and automated systems are used. By using these advanced technologies and techniques, production processes are designed in such a way that humans are involved as an important factor in them and can adjust the production process to their liking. Industry 5.0 improves the quality and efficiency of production and service processes. Also, this concept reduces resource wastage and increases productivity and efficiency in production processes. Due to the intelligent capabilities available in Industry 5.0, this concept can be used in various industries such as automotive, electronics, machinery, medicine, etc. (Nayeri et al., 2023). Key enabling technologies of Industry 5.0 are shown in Figure 2.

Figure 2. Key technologies of Industry 5.0

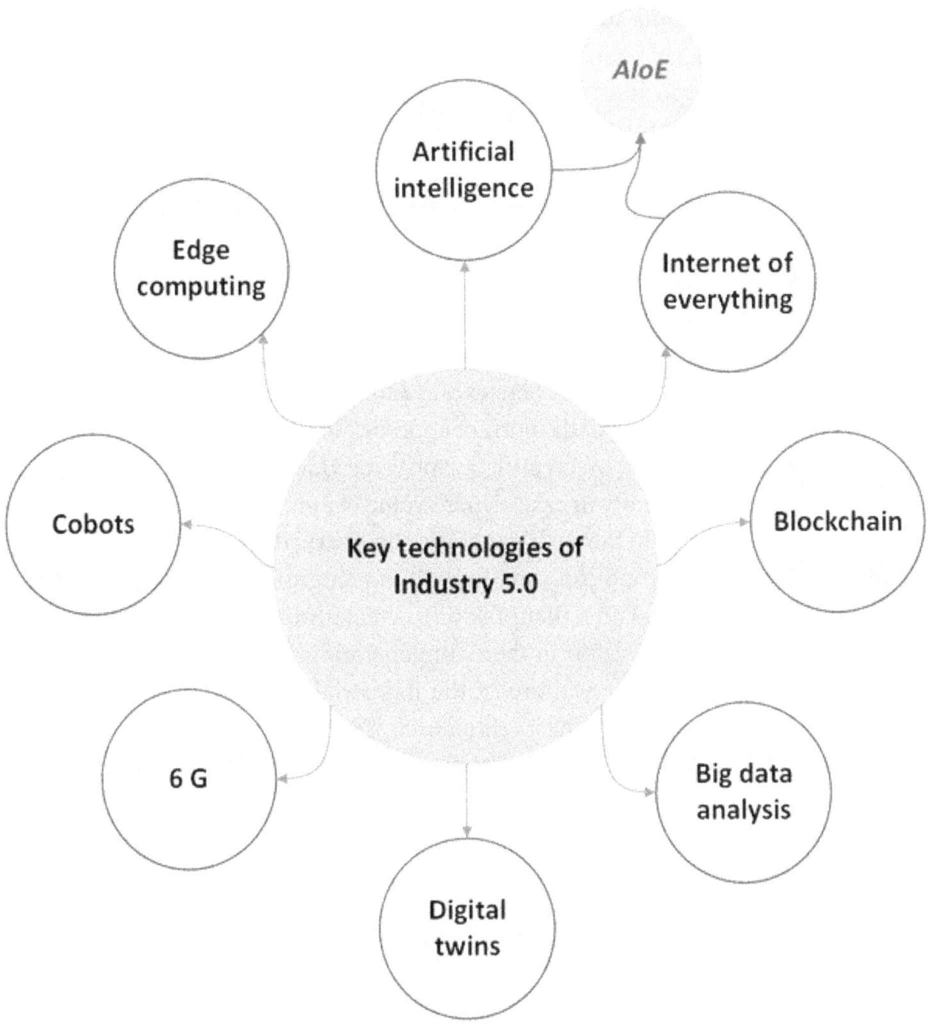

The fifth industrial revolution can be summed up as a combination of human and machine cooperation in the workplace. Although we may not be exactly sure that the fifth industrial revolution will change our personal lives, we should be fully prepared to accept its inevitability. In the fifth generation, the industry will be more resilient, and stable and work more efficiently in the use of resources and talents. In general, sustainability, human-centeredness, and resilience are the distinctive features of the fifth-generation industry (Nozari, Szmelter-Jarosz & Ghahremani-Nahr, 2022). Based on the human-centered approach, instead of Emerging technologies being considered as a starting point and their potential to increase productivity being explored, the main needs and benefits of humans in the production process should be emphasized. According to the latter approach, industry must be sustainable in order to respect planetary boundaries. Industry must develop circular processes that enable the reuse, repurposing, and recycling of natural resources, as well as reducing waste and environmental impact. Sustainability means reducing energy consumption and greenhouse gas emissions in order to avoid the consumption and erosion of natural resources and ensure the needs of today's generations without jeopardizing the needs of future generations (Ghobakhloo et al., 2023). Technologies such as artificial intelligence and additive manufacturing can play an important role in this field by optimizing resource efficiency and minimizing waste. A resilience approach ensures that industrial production is able to provide and support key infrastructure in times of crisis, and geopolitical changes and natural crises such as the COVID-19 pandemic imply a weakening of the current approach to globalized production. This issue can also be moderated by creating adaptive production capacity and flexible business processes, especially in cases where value chains address basic needs such as healthcare or security. In the fifth-generation industry, the ability of the industry to fulfill social goals beyond jobs and growth is recognized and, in fact, the fact that the industry can act as a resilient factor to create prosperity is acknowledged. For this purpose, the production in the fifth generation industry should value the planetary boundaries and the welfare of the industrial workers in the production process should be the main emphasis (Frederico, 2021).

Industry 5.0 can have many benefits for companies. Below are some of the benefits of using Industry 5.0 for companies:

- ***Improving the quality of products***: By using advanced technologies such as artificial intelligence, augmented reality, and 3D printing, companies can improve the quality of their products and produce higher quality products that meet the needs of customers.
- ***Increased productivity***: By using smart technologies, companies can improve their production processes and increase their productivity. For example, the use of robotics in production processes can improve efficiency and reduce human errors.
- ***Reducing costs***: using advanced technologies such as the Internet of Things and artificial intelligence can help reduce production costs and increase the speed of production processes.

- ***Speeding up processes***: Using smart technologies such as the Internet of Things and automated systems can help speed up production and service processes.
- ***Responding to customer needs***: Using smart technologies, companies can respond to customer needs quickly and accurately, and this can help increase customer satisfaction and increase sales.

Overall, the use of Industry 5.0 can help companies improve quality, reduce costs, and increase productivity, helping them to serve the competitive market in the best possible way. The most important application domains of Industry 5.0 are shown in Table 1.

Table 1. The most important scope of Industry 5.0 applications

Smart Supply Chain	Smart Healthcare	Cloud Manufacturing
• Minimize errors • Reduce operating costs • Margin increase • Effective communication between all actors in the supply chain	• Quick and optimal access to facilities • Reduce human errors • Data access speed	• Low cost manufacturing processes • High reliability • Higher quality • Ability to respond to issues at the moment • Delivery on time
Manufacturing and Production	**Disaster Management**	**Smart Education**
• Increase Productivity • Production of innovative and quality products • energy efficiency	• Ability to face multiple crises simultaneously • Increasing the level of cooperation	• Improving visual ability and creativity • Interactive learning • Education independent of time and place

Despite all the benefits that Industry 5.0 brings to businesses, it also has challenges. Figure 3 shows the peninsulas, challenges, and future directions of Industry 5.0.

Figure 3. Peninsulas, challenges, and future paths of Industry 5.0 (Maddikunta et al., 2022)

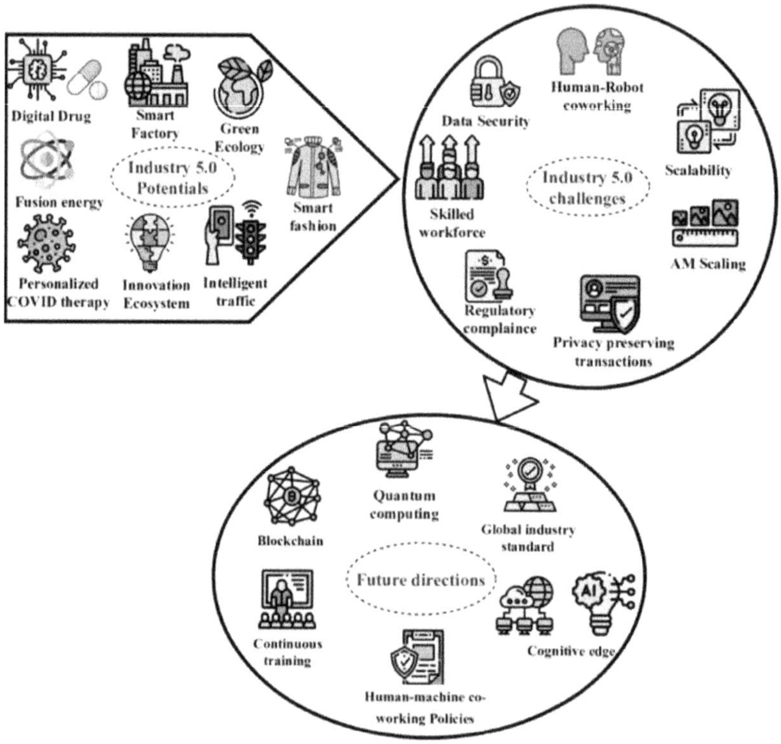

3. SUSTAINABLE AND SMART SUPPLY CHAINS IN INDUSTRY 5.0

The sustainable supply chain is the consideration of social, economic, and environmental issues in all organizational processes. These processes include the entire life cycle of the supply chain, from the purchase of raw materials to product design and development, warehousing, distribution, and delivery of the final product (Nozari, Fallah, Szmelter-Jarosz, & Krzemiński, 2021).

The meaning of sustainability is to focus on the long-term impacts of the company's exercises and the sustainability of assets for future utilization at the same time as today's benefit. Within the writing of organization and administration, sustainability has become an imperative device that ensures competitive advantage and social duty. Presently the sustainability addition has been included in numerous organizational topics. The sustainable supply chain is additionally one of these subjects that's closely related to the concept of a green supply chain. These concepts emerged the significance of social and natural concerns in conjunction with financial components in supply chain arranging (Nozari, Ghahremani-Nahr & Szmelter-Jarosz(*), 2023).

Advances in disruptive technologies enable businesses to provide disruptive forms of reality to support supply chain operations, sustainability, and experience-based learning. Sustainability is one of the increasing concerns of supply chain managers because most of the indirect problems of an organization are caused by its supply chain. Transformative technologies such as artificial intelligence, IoT, big data, and blockchain can help improve supply chain operations to make them greener and more sustainable (Govindan, 2023).

Devices prepared with transformative advances can offer assistance to optimize transportation courses by taking into consideration components such as activity, street closures, and climate to decrease the sum of miles traveled. Since expectations based on these innovations can spare Ideal stock levels can offer assistance to diminish carbon emanations caused by putting away and moving overabundance stock. Keen vitality utilization arrangements can moreover diminish carbon emanations related to stockroom vitality utilization. Artificial intelligence combined with big data can offer assistance to the supply chain to end up not as it were sustainable but moreover adaptable (Aliahmadi and Nozari, 2023).

Blockchain-based technologies have become increasingly popular in recent years as a decentralized technology that enables secure, instant, and low-cost transactions. However, its potential uses extend beyond financial transactions. At its core, these technologies enable safe, transparent, and efficient record-keeping. These technologies can be used to improve the sustainability of supply chain management. One of the main sustainability concerns in supply chain management is the carbon footprint associated with transporting goods from one location to another. Transportation and logistics companies are constantly looking for ways to reduce this carbon footprint, and blockchain could be one solution. By using digital currency, supply chain participants can reduce the need for intermediaries such as banks and financial institutions, which often require long travel times to complete transactions.

Another sustainability concern in supply chain management is ethical sourcing. Companies must ensure that the goods they purchase are ethically and sustainably produced. Cryptocurrency can be used to create transparent and traceable records of every transaction, ensuring that supply chain participants are acting ethically. This can be especially important in industries such as fashion and agriculture where ethical and sustainable sourcing is a priority (Nozari, Ghahremani-Nahr & Szmelter-Jarosz, 2023).

Blockchain can help create a circular economy by enabling the creation of tokenized assets. This means that goods and services can be easily exchanged between participants in a supply chain, which reduces waste and promotes reuse. For example, if a company produces excess inventory, it can tokenize that inventory and offer it to another company that can use it. This reduces waste and promotes a more sustainable economy.

Disruptive technologies have the potential to transform the world of supply chain management and make it more efficient and sustainable. By reducing the carbon footprint of logistics, ensuring ethical sourcing and transactions, and enabling the circular economy, digital currency can help businesses meet their sustainability goals while also improving their bottom line (Kumar, & Mallipeddi, 2022).

As can be seen, these technologies have a tremendous impact on the sustainability of supply chain technologies. Therefore, the integrated combination of these technologies can add multiple sustainability to processes from different dimensions. Therefore, one can understand the powerful effects of Industry 5.0 on the sustainability of supply chains.

4. A FRAMEWORK FOR SUPPLY CHAIN 5.0

Supply Chain 5.0 speaks to a noteworthy flight from past eras by presenting intelligence, computerization, and more noteworthy visibility into the complete supply chain arrangement. In expansion, it is a biological system that combines different innovations such as artificial intelligence, IoT, robotics, blockchain, and big data analytics to form a completely coordinates and coordinated organization.

The utilization of artificial intelligence is particularly critical in Supply Chain 5.0. Artificial intelligence calculations can offer assistance in anticipating requests and optimizing stock levels, moving forward operational productivity, and decreasing squandering. AI-powered robots can also robotize monotonous assignments such as picking and packing, diminishing the risk of human mistakes. AI moreover makes a difference in making strides the client involvement, empowering more exact conveyance times and real-time following of merchandise (Karmaker et al., 2023).

IoT apparatuses are moreover basic in Supply Chain 5.0. They can screen stock levels in genuine time, optimize directing, and diminish shipping costs. They can track the condition of merchandise amid travel, guaranteeing they are kept at the correct temperature and mugginess, lessening the chance of decay or harm.

Big data analytics is another basic component of Supply Chain 5.0. It makes a difference that those within the supply chain filter through mountains of data, recognize patterns and designs, and make educated choices.

Another basic innovation in Supply Chain 5.0 is Blockchain. The utilization of blockchain can offer assistance in making a straightforward and secure supply chain arrangement where all members have access to the same information, guaranteeing tall belief and decreasing the chance of extortion. It too empowers real-time following of merchandise, given they are not misplaced or stolen in travel.

As a result, it offers critical benefits including expanded productivity, decreased costs, made strides in client involvement, and more noteworthy supportability. As businesses proceed to grasp digital transformation, Supply Chain 5.0 is likely to become the unused standard in supply chain administration.

The cross-breed human-machine show of supply chain 5.0 makes a difference in companies withstand disturbance without jeopardizing competitiveness or benefit. To form adaptability within the supply chain without changing personnel or inquiring customers or suppliers to alter forms, digitization, and human collaboration are key (Villar et al., 2023). The most important effects of technologies on Supply Chain 5.0 are:

- ***Customization and Personalization***: Coordinates utilization of disruptive technologies may center on mass customization of items, permitting producers to deliver custom-fitted items at scale. This seems to affect supply chains by requiring more flexible generation forms and dexterous supply systems that are able to reply to personal client requests.
- ***Sustainability***: As sustainability becomes a major concern, Industry 5.0 can coordinate naturally neighborly hones all through the supply chain. This may incorporate utilizing artificial intelligence and data analytics to optimize vitality utilization, diminish waste, and minimize environmental effects.
- ***Real-Time Information Sharing***: Supply Chain 5.0 may advance real-time information sharing over the supply chain, giving superior visibility and transparency. This may increment collaboration, minimize delays, and move forward in general productivity.
- ***Resilience and Risk Management***: Supply chain 5.0 can put more accentuation on making versatile supply chains that can rapidly adjust to disturbances, such as pandemics, geopolitical occasions, or common disasters. This may incorporate methodologies such as double sourcing and scenario arranging.
- ***Cyber Security and Information Security***: As the network increments, there's a requirement for expanded cybersecurity and information protection measures. supply chain 5.0 is likely to require solid security conventions to secure touchy supply chain information from cyber threats.

Despite all the benefits that supply chain 5.0 has, it can also bring challenges such as high implementation costs, security and privacy, resistance to changes, and lack of human skills. In spite of these challenges, the potential benefits of Supply Chain 5.0 are critical for supply chain administration. Businesses that are able to effectively actualize these advances can pick up a competitive advantage and progress their bottom line.

It is imperative to note that the total effect of Supply Chain 5.0 on supply chain administration depends on how it is received and coordinated into businesses. As this concept proceeds to advance, businesses must survey its potential benefits and challenges and alter their techniques to adjust to the changing scene of manufacturing and supply chains (Gamal et al., 2023).

The analytical framework of supply chain 5.0 is shown in Figure 4. In order to develop this framework, the basic elements and components of the intelligent supply chain were extracted from the literature. Then, by using the opinions of experts active in the field of supply chain and familiar with the concepts of information technology (10 experts active in the industry and with related work records and 7 academic experts with related research records), cause and effect relationships have been formed. This framework has been validated and approved using expert opinions.

Figure 4. Framework for Supply Chain 5.0

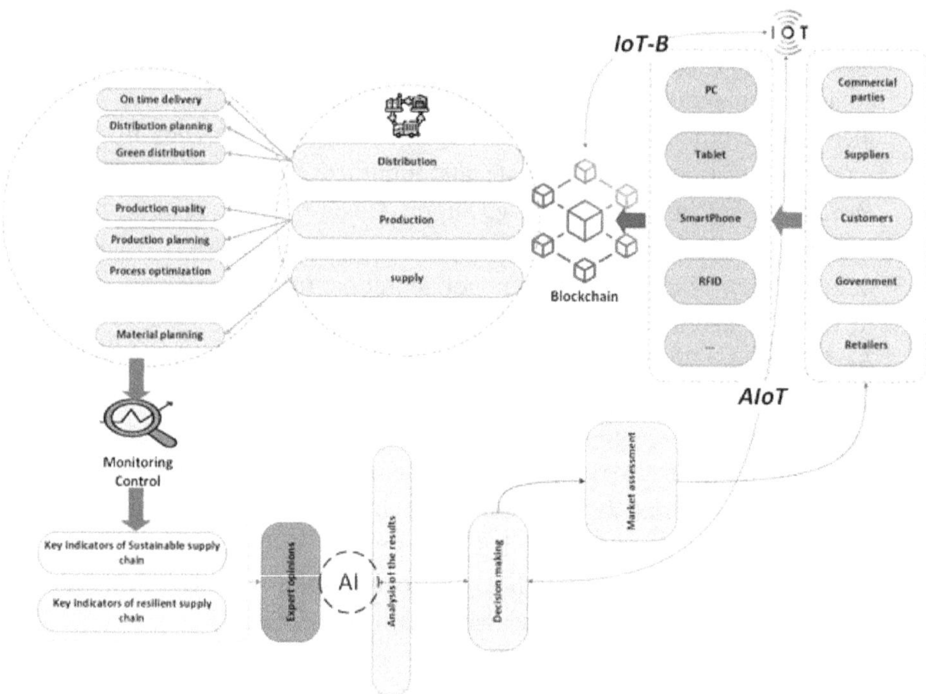

5. CONCLUSION

Quick changes and propels in data innovation have made supply chain administration experience principal changes. Unused innovations and their applications in different businesses and administrations have given different capabilities to companies. Building up different and numerous communications, the combination of capabilities and competencies are of this category. Too, the plausibility of quick and shifted developments, spry exercises and forms, and such things have been given. These capabilities can be shown within the clever supply chain of the organization.

Today's organizations must move from the conventional inactive and moderate state to energetic, quick, and adaptable systems. Supply chain insights give this plausibility for organizations. In this way, organizations can work with straightforward and plenteous get to and without time and put limitations. In this regard, the smart supply chain is the future generation of the supply chain and the only way out of problems.

The next era of commerce victory through customer centricity, maintainability human rights, and digitization presents a transformative time in supply chain administration and presents a groundbreaking trade demonstration that joins these three center components (customer centricity, coordinating solidness, and progressed interaction). Supply Chain 5.0 reacts to the developing request for item customization and personalization, which needs the correct combination of human inventiveness and machine effectiveness. Whereas machines take over the work of work, people can center on inventive assignments and cognitive problem tackling, things that machines cannot do.

One of the objectives of Supply Chain 5.0 is to assist in making flexibility in your supply chain without requiring extreme changes to your organization or your customers' organizations. The human-machine cross-breed demonstrates makes a difference in companies withstand disturbance without jeopardizing competitiveness or productivity.

In this research, an analytical framework for supply chain 5.0 has been presented, which can be an effective guide for understanding the causal and causal relationships of all actors in these smart and sustainable supply chains.

REFERENCES

Aliahmadi, A., & Nozari, H. (2023, January). Evaluation of security metrics in AIoT and blockchain-based supply chain by Neutrosophic decision-making method. *Supply Chain Forum International Journal (Toronto, Ont.)*, *24*(1), 31–42.

Frederico, G. F. (2021). From supply chain 4.0 to supply chain 5.0: Findings from a systematic literature review and research directions. *Logistics*, *5*(3), 49. doi:10.3390/logistics5030049

Gamal, A., Abd El-Gawad, A. F., & Abouhawwash, M. (2023). Towards a Responsive Resilient Supply Chain based on Industry 5.0: A Case Study in Healthcare Systems. *Neutrosophic Systems with Applications*, *2*, 8–24. doi:10.61356/j.nswa.2023.7

Ghobakhloo, M., Iranmanesh, M., Morales, M. E., Nilashi, M., & Amran, A. (2023). Actions and approaches for enabling Industry 5.0-driven sustainable industrial transformation: A strategy roadmap. *Corporate Social Responsibility and Environmental Management*, *30*(3), 1473–1494. doi:10.1002/csr.2431

Govindan, K., Salehian, F., Kian, H., Hosseini, S. T., & Mina, H. (2023). A location-inventory-routing problem to design a circular closed-loop supply chain network with carbon tax policy for achieving circular economy: An augmented epsilon-constraint approach. *International Journal of Production Economics*, *257*, 108771. doi:10.1016/j.ijpe.2023.108771

Ivanov, D. (2023). The Industry 5.0 framework: Viability-based integration of the resilience, sustainability, and human-centricity perspectives. *International Journal of Production Research*, *61*(5), 1683–1695. doi:10.1080/00207543.2022.2118892

Kamble, S. S., Gunasekaran, A., Subramanian, N., Ghadge, A., Belhadi, A., & Venkatesh, M. (2023). Blockchain technology's impact on supply chain integration and sustainable supply chain performance: Evidence from the automotive industry. *Annals of Operations Research*, *327*(1), 575–600. doi:10.100710479-021-04129-6

Karmaker, C. L., Bari, A. M., Anam, M. Z., Ahmed, T., Ali, S. M., de Jesus Pacheco, D. A., & Moktadir, M. A. (2023). Industry 5.0 challenges for post-pandemic supply chain sustainability in an emerging economy. *International Journal of Production Economics*, *258*, 108806. doi:10.1016/j.ijpe.2023.108806

Kumar, S., & Mallipeddi, R. R. (2022). Impact of cybersecurity on operations and supply chain management: Emerging trends and future research directions. *Production and Operations Management*, *31*(12), 4488–4500. doi:10.1111/poms.13859

Maddikunta, P. K. R., Pham, Q. V., Prabadevi, B., Deepa, N., Dev, K., Gadekallu, T. R., ... Liyanage, M. (2022). Industry 5.0: A survey on enabling technologies and potential applications. *Journal of Industrial Information Integration*, *26*, 100257. doi:10.1016/j.jii.2021.100257

Najafi, S. E., Nozari, H., & Edalatpanah, S. A. (2022). Artificial Intelligence of Things (AIoT) and Industry 4.0–Based Supply Chain (FMCG Industry). *A Roadmap for Enabling Industry 4.0 by Artificial Intelligence*, 31-41.

Nayeri, S., Sazvar, Z., & Heydari, J. (2023). Towards a responsive supply chain based on the industry 5.0 dimensions: A novel decision-making method. *Expert Systems with Applications*, *213*, 119267. doi:10.1016/j.eswa.2022.119267

Nozari, H., Fallah, M., Kazemipoor, H., & Najafi, S. E. (2021). Big data analysis of IoT-based supply chain management considering FMCG industries. *Бизнес-информатика*, *15*(1, 1 (eng)), 78–96. doi:10.17323/2587-814X.2021.1.78.96

Nozari, H., Fallah, M., Szmelter-Jarosz, A., & Krzemiński, M. (2021). Analysis of security criteria for IoT-based supply chain: a case study of FMCG industries. *Central European Management Journal, 29*(4).

Nozari, H., Ghahremani-Nahr, J., & Szmelter-Jarosz, A. (2023). AI and machine learning for real-world problems. *Advances In Computers*.

Nozari, H., Ghahremani-Nahr, J., & Szmelter-Jarosz, A. (2023). A multi-stage stochastic inventory management model for transport companies including several different transport modes. *International Journal of Management Science and Engineering Management*, *18*(2), 134–144. doi:10.1080/17509653.2022.2042747

Nozari, H., Najafi, E., Fallah, M., & Hosseinzadeh Lotfi, F. (2019). Quantitative analysis of key performance indicators of green supply chain in FMCG industries using non-linear fuzzy method. *Mathematics*, *7*(11), 1020. doi:10.3390/math7111020

Nozari, H., Szmelter-Jarosz, A., & Ghahremani-Nahr, J. (2021). The Ideas of Sustainable and Green Marketing Based on the Internet of Everything—The Case of the Dairy Industry. *Future Internet*, *13*(10), 266. doi:10.3390/fi13100266

Nozari, H., Szmelter-Jarosz, A., & Ghahremani-Nahr, J. (2022). Analysis of the challenges of artificial intelligence of things (AIoT) for the smart supply chain (case study: FMCG industries). *Sensors (Basel)*, *22*(8), 2931. doi:10.339022082931 PMID:35458916

Villar, A., Paladini, S., & Buckley, O. (2023, July). Towards Supply Chain 5.0: Redesigning Supply Chains as Resilient, Sustainable, and Human-Centric Systems in a Post-pandemic World. *Operations Research Forum*, *4*(3), 60. doi:10.100743069-023-00234-3

Chapter 2
The Future of Devices in Digital Businesses and Improving Productivity

Paria Samadi Parviznejad
Academic Center for Education, Culture, and Research, Iran

ABSTRACT

Connected devices are physical objects that can communicate with each other and other systems through the internet. They include everything from traditional computing hardware, such as a laptop or desktop, to common mobile devices, such as a smartphone or tablet, to a wide variety of physical devices and objects. The internet of things describes a network of physical objects—"things"—that are embedded with sensors, software, and other technologies to connect and exchange data with other devices and systems over the internet. Internet of things-connected devices create a world where data is exchanged between physical objects such as sensors, on-device software, and adjacent technologies with other systems and devices. The essential enabling technology is the communication between internet of things "things" that enables these exchanges.

1. INTRODUCTION

Physical things that can connect online to other systems and other connected devices are referred to as connected devices. They include anything from typical mobile devices like a smartphone or tablet to more and more actual physical objects (Caporuscio & e al., 2020). Connected devices also include traditional computing hardware like a laptop or desktop. Household appliances, heating and cooling units,

DOI: 10.4018/979-8-3693-0210-1.ch002

automobiles, fitness trackers, environmental sensors, and other items are included in this expanding list. These gadgets, which frequently contain sensors, software, and processing chips, gather data and distribute it to other gadgets and systems (Cooke & Zubcsek, 2017). Remote monitoring and control are frequently used with connected devices. They use a variety of wired and wireless networks and protocols, including WiFi, NFC, 3G, and 4G networks, to connect to the internet and one another. When connected devices are properly managed, businesses may benefit greatly from better decision-making utilizing reliable and accurate data, increased cost and energy efficiency, as well as improved safety and security thanks to real-time tracking and monitoring (Goudarzi et al., 2022). Connected gadgets, for instance, present significant potential for new business models and revenue-generating opportunities as part of the IoT (Seydoux & et al., 2017).

A major movement, pattern or trend emerging in the macro environment; an emerging force likely to have a significant impact on the kinds of products and services is as a megatrend. Identifying megatrends helps an organization identify potential threats and opportunities. Because it can then take action to prepare for the potential threats. It can also make the most of the opportunities. So it is necessary to study the different aspects of connected devices as a megatrend.

2. DESIGN AND ENGINEERING OF INTERNET OF THINGS DEVICES

Is it reasonable to claim that the " Internet of Things (IoT)" has gained widespread acceptance at this point, given that practically everyone carries a connected gadget with them at all times? As new "smart" devices are created and people continue to use the internet to entertain themselves, socialize with one another, share information, keep track of things, and stay connected, there are currently about 21.5 billion internet-connected devices in use worldwide (Duraipandian & Vinothkanna, 2019). This number is expected to rise exponentially in the coming years. When a consumer buys a smart device, they anticipate that it will be simple to use and perform as advertised. Unfortunately, IoT devices are not always faultless, just like anything else. How frequently has your smartphone been unable to quickly couple with a system, hub, or application? Most likely more frequently than you would like (Chengoden et al., 2023).

Ideas for new and distinct sorts of linked devices are continuously conceived as the growing technologies that underpin the IoT continue their rapid progress. We all consider smartphones, laptops, and tablets to be "connected devices," but the IoT ecosystem encompasses far more than just items you can buy at your neighborhood Best Buy or Apple Store (Lan et al., 2019). Everything from vehicles, TVs, and refrigerators to thermostats, door locks, and practically every object in between can now be web-enabled due to the fact that connecting various "things" to the internet has very few technical restrictions. Household appliances, heating and cooling systems, automobiles, fitness trackers, environmental and production sensors, and many more items are now included in the growing list of connected devices (Petit & Cambon, 2016). Whether a device is used to track our belongings, monitor our health, safeguard our houses, or unlock and operate our automobiles, homes, and appliances, it must be built and manufactured with connectivity, interoperability, and the end user's experience at the forefront of its design and engineering According to the figure1, Future ports will become "IoT-enabled" and create the so-called "Smart Port". However, the uninterrupted flow of data originating from a multitude of deployed "things" must be integrated into the port's information system. To achieve this, a unified layer that provides interoperability, multi-tenancy and scalability is essential (Bracke et al, 2021).

Figure 1. IoT wireless technologies

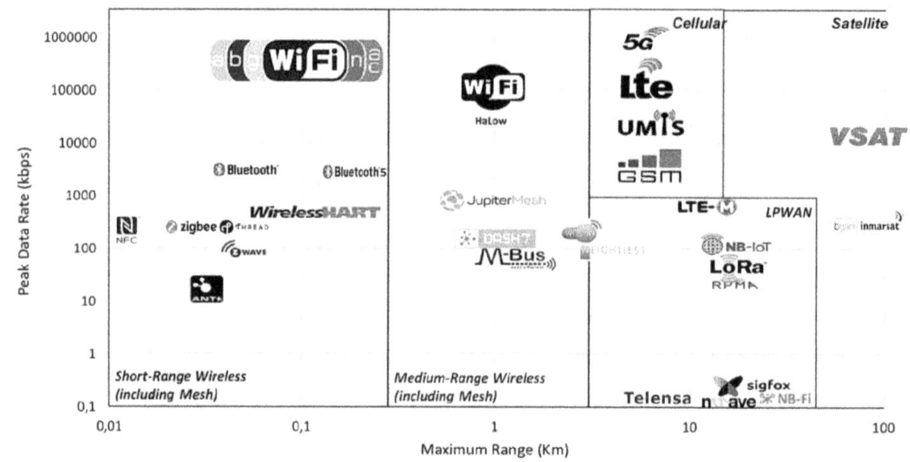

Your product may have the same appearance as it did before to being intelligent and connected, but it is fundamentally changed. These days, connected gadgets are a part of a wider ecosystem that includes a variety of stakeholders, goods, and activities. They communicate with each other within this ecosystem. The engineering of IoT devices is different from the design of other devices in that it involves specialized hardware and software technology that enables connected devices to communicate directly with one another, make decisions together, and exchange data frequently without the need for the cloud or servers (Rath et al., 2022). In addition, a lot of these devices lack the space necessary for a keyboard or other human interface for entering passwords or other settings, necessitating engineering to enable human input at least during setup. Therefore, IoT device engineering also encompasses the systems — such as a cloud application and an end-user mobile or web application, for example to which the device is communicating, unlike linked device design, which concentrates on the gadget itself, including mechanical and electrical designs as well as embedded software.

2.1. Develop Embedded Software

The interaction that IoT apps have with physical linked devices is the key distinction between IoT apps and other applications when it comes to IoT app development. For command and control, onboarding, and OTA embedded software upgrades, IoT apps need to communicate with products. However, developers who haven't worked with hardware before frequently don't comprehend the challenges of developing embedded systems well. The difficulties in designing IoT apps might range from diverse states and behaviors to the time it takes for hardware devices to conduct an operation and OTA updates that necessitate extra care to change the code (Lee, 2019).

Our skilled and knowledgeable engineers and architects at Cardinal Peak assist businesses from a variety of sectors in creating and maintaining connected goods and devices. We focus on all facets of connected device design, including the cloud, hardware, and embedded software, and we know how to cut down on both the short- and long-term costs associated with the cloud. With this degree of proficiency, we are able to design and create linked devices that can thrive in the networked ecosystems of today (Ogudo et al., 2019).

Figure 2, hereafter detailed, illustrates a high-level representation of the functional architecture of the PortForward project with, in blue, the components discussed in following sections. The typical data-flow is initiated at 'data producers' side (on the very left of the diagram), that in an IoT context typically consists of connected devices. Nevertheless, more traditional Information Systems may complement this category as well (e.g., a weather forecast Application Programming Interface (API), a cruise line company API, the Information System of the municipality).

Figure 2. IoT Software architecture
Source: Bracke et al. (2021)

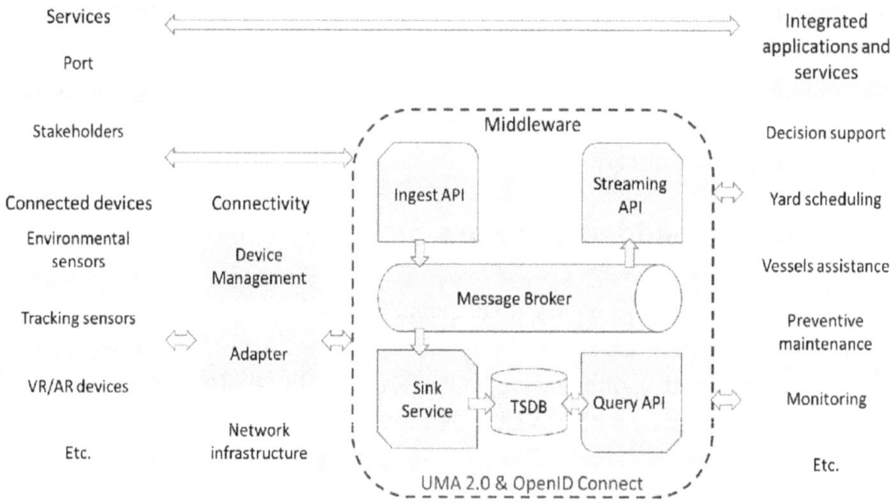

2.2. Key Insights From the Data

Nearly three-quarters of feld service organizations (71%) have a 24/7 view of equipment data using connected devices. Most feld service organizations consider their ability to leverage data from connected devices in the feld for predictive insights as either good (44%) or exceptional (19%) compared to their competitors. Even so, most feld service organizations cite either business agility (28%) or customer dissatisfaction (27%) as their biggest business pains. Most feld service organizations cite anticipating vulnerabilities (54%) and driving customer satisfaction (53%) as real accomplishments for their company thanks to the use of connected devices. 73% of respondents claim their customers demand rapid responses, and they are delivering on those expectations. Nearly half of feld service organizations (47%) indicate connected devices increase team productivity, and over half (58%) claim mobile technologies for their technician's leverage data from connected devices to support their successful rapid responses to customers in the feld. Most feld service organizations (54%) claim a revamped customer engagement solution to help maintain or enhance relationships with customers is a priority for their next software initiative. In each case, nearly half cite one connected, automated system from feld to back ofce (49%) and a fully automated, dynamic scheduling solution to manage dispatching and feld staf (49%) as priorities as well. Nearly half of feld service organizations plan on selecting a new service software within the next three months (4%) or in the next 3 -12 months (40%). Only 17% are happy with their current solution to the extent that they do not plan on selecting a new service software (Rafique et al., 2020).

2.3. Engineering of Devices

- *Technologies*

To link with other systems and other connected devices through the internet, connected devices must smoothly interact with mobile applications and cloud services. By its very nature, connected device development is complex and calls for a thorough understanding of wireless networks and communications protocols, including Wi-Fi, NFC, Zigbee, LoRa, and 5G networks, as well as security norms, data gathering, artificial intelligence (AI)/machine learning (ML), and analytics.

Connected devices need connectivity, data processing, and an intuitive user interface to gather data and communicate information with other devices and systems. They are embedded with processing chips, software, and sensors. Although the IoT concept has been around for a while, current technology developments have made it a reality.

- *Sensors*

The availability of low-cost, low-power sensor technology enables manufacturers to include information-detection and measurement capabilities into their products.

- *Connectivity*

A wide range of internet network protocols make it feasible to connect sensors to the cloud and other "things" for effective data transfer. The cloud is the platform that allows sensors and devices to communicate with one another, boosting connectivity as cloud computing platforms spread over more and more devices. The underlying infrastructure, servers, and storage required for real-time operations and processing are accessible through the cloud, which also stores IoT data.

- *App development*

Consumers can control their devices and settings, as well as monitor any outputs or data generated, using an end-user app.

- *ML and data analytics*

As AI develops, ML algorithms are able to learn and automatically improve via experience and by using data, making it faster and easier than ever to acquire the insights produced by connected devices.

There are a few more technological issues that engineers need to be aware of when it comes to linked device design and engineering. The device's power source and energy consumption should be prioritized first. The use of wired electricity is just not an option for many connected devices. Imagine having to send a cable from a widely dispersed system to a sensor a mile away in order to gather data and relay it in real time to the central system. As a result, IoT gadget battery life is still a problem. A smartphone and its applications are virtually useless if the battery life is unstable and brief. Thanks to improvements in wireless sensing, the IoT may now be continuously monitored remotely.

3. EXAMPLES OF CONNECTED DEVICE

The IoT refers to the rapidly growing network of connected objects able to collect and exchange data using embedded sensors. Insider Intelligence has outlined some applications for the IoT, along with some specific devices and examples below:

Figure 3. Examples of IoT devices

- ***Wearable***

Watches are no longer just for telling time. The Apple Watch and other smartwatches on the market have turned our wrists into smartphone holsters by enabling text messaging, phone calls, and more. And devices such as Fitbit and Jawbone have helped revolutionize the fitness world by giving people more data about their workouts (Vijayan et al., 2021).

- ***Smart Cities***

The IoT has the potential to transform entire cities by solving real problems citizens face each day. With the proper connections and data, the IoT can solve traffic congestion issues and reduce noise, crime, and pollution (Haque et al., 2022).

- ***Connected Car***

These vehicles are equipped with Internet access and can share that access with others, just like connecting to a wireless network in a home or office. More vehicles are starting to come equipped with fobs in lieu of physical keys, which use sensors to do everything from remote start and setting off the alarm to popping the trunk and unlocking the vehicle with smart locks (Coutinho & Boukerche, 2019).

- ***Smart Home***

A smart home is a group of programmable, connected IoT devices that use Wi-Fi, Bluetooth, Zigbee, or Z-Wave technology for communication. You can remotely control these devices using a touch-screen control panel or smartphone. Smart home systems using AI can monitor appliances, predict how much energy they will consume, and then adjust their usage so that energy consumption stays within a specified range. This can be beneficial for reducing energy bills while still maintaining the comfort of living spaces. A part of the IoT, smart home systems and devices often operate together, sharing consumer usage data among themselves and automating actions based on the homeowners' preferences. Smart home is a significant part of IoT, where internet-connected appliances and devices are automatically controlled, often with a mobile phone. Dishwashers, refrigerators, smart TVs, smart watches, cars and trucks, heating and cooling systems, fitness machines and trackers are examples of IoT-enabled products with which you may have personal experience are examples of IoT at homes (Hammi et al., 2022).

- ***Applications of IoT in Smart Homes***

A smart home app, sometimes referred to as a home automation app or a smart home automation app, is an application used to remotely control and manage connected non-computing devices in the home, typically from a smartphone or tablet. Lighting (Today, home lighting can automatically adjust to personal needs), Bathrooms (IoT technologies in the bathroom can make your home routine more entertaining and convenient), Gardens, Kitchen, Security Systems, Safety Sensors, Temperature Control and doors (Choi et al., 2022). Home automation systems that incorporate the IoT can automate a variety of tasks, such as heating and cooling your home, feeding your pets, and controlling lights and other appliances. Using the IoT, all of these devices can be connected to a single network and controlled remotely (khan et al., 2022).

- ***Connected Health Devices***

It only makes logical that the healthcare sector is seeing a lot of linked health equipment and remote patient monitoring (RPM) technology in an era where practically everyone is digitally connected in some way, even many senior folks who are frequently classified as technophobic (Holko et al., 2022). The range of connected health gadgets includes Fitbits, Bluetooth-enabled scales, wearable heart monitors, and more. To enable healthcare decisions to be made remotely, they offer health measurements of patients and communicate them back to physicians or, in certain situations, are reported back to providers. Technologies for remote patient monitoring are similar to telemedicine because they automatically monitor and report on patients, frequently those with chronic illnesses, allowing caregivers to monitor patients from a distance. Connected health and RPM are more crucial than ever during the COVID-19 pandemic because they let doctors to monitor patients without having to physically interact with them, halting the spread of the novel coronavirus (Steenwinckel et sl., 2022). Additionally, they keep patients with less serious conditions out of hospitals, saving valuable bed space for patients with serious conditions. During the pandemic, hospitals all over the country have found significant success with connected health and RPM.

Healthcare IT News has collected this extensive list of vendors to assist healthcare CIOs, CMOs, and other professionals in locating connected health devices and RPM technologies. Short summaries of the businesses and their goods can be found here. Additionally, the list will keep getting updated. Medical devices used in connected health solutions use sensors and wireless connectivity to collect and transmit patient data, such as biometric readings, and that data is made available to healthcare providers or patients themselves in a cloud-based platform or application programming interface. Connected health often includes programs such as telehealth, remote care (such as home care) and disease and lifestyle management. Incorporating the above definitions, "smart medical devices" has defined as those that can be controlled by users or other devices, and connect to the internet. An example of technology is a smart watch with a user-friendly interface. This watch collects a patient's heartrate data, then uploads this data to the cloud. It can be defined as connecting clinicians to clinicians, patients to clinicians, and even patients to other patients through various technological modalities. This technology facilitates exchange of information, remote diagnosis and treatment, continuous and intermittent monitoring, and ongoing health management (Chouvarda et al., 2019).

4. CHALLENGES OF CONNECTED DEVICES

The most frequent security problem is misconfiguration. It's crucial to keep in mind that you're not just protecting a single program or application when it comes to connected device product security—you're protecting a complete ecosystem. When creating this system, you are in charge of both the system's overall security as well as the caliber of the first-party software you design (Williams & McCauley, 2016). To guarantee that the device is configured securely, your product development teams and product security teams in particular need to collaborate. The operating system, boot order, peripheral firmware, network services, and third-party software are all configured securely. Configuration problems may appear and have detrimental effects. Shipment of a product with hardcoded service account credentials, for instance, may result in reputational harm or legal penalties (Kos et al., 2019). These parameters are frequently found in configuration files or unofficial binaries, which are frequently disregarded:

- As soon as the goods is dispatched, your control is reduced. Even if you create a secure gadget, it can still be attacked if the end user doesn't configure it correctly. Since you are transferring ownership of these devices to your clients, it is up to them to set them up correctly, ensure that they are getting the most recent firmware upgrades, and report any security flaws to your team so that they may be fixed.
- Some device manufacturers have made an effort to address this problem by spending money to send out specialized teams to service and configure devices so that they are properly secured. This kind of investment can be quite time-consuming and expensive. However, the alternative would be to take a chance on misconfiguration and leave the door open for a breach or assault without device-specific tooling. Such an attack's results could have a significant influence on the device manufacturer.

- Your supply chain has become more susceptible, opaque, and complicated. Hardware and software components, which are occasionally closely integrated with one another, are provided by many suppliers. You must be aware of the dangers and vulnerabilities that might be introduced into your products through those channels because of the large number of vendors that are participating in the supply chain, both from a hardware and software standpoint. While each of your vendors is employing a DevOps approach of their own, preferably with security integrated, without the proper tools, you are unable to properly understand the contents of the software that is integrated into your development process.
- This means that since you have no control over the security practices of your vendors, it is up to your team to find and fix any vulnerabilities they create. The less chance there is of passing these security concerns on to your consumers, the earlier you may accomplish this in the development process. But in order to achieve this, you must be able to decipher the binary files contained in the firmware of your device.
- Threats and vulnerabilities can emerge late in the development process. Even though you take every precaution during the development process to ensure the security of every component of your device, it is crucial that you continue to examine final firmware images. In the last stages of development, some of the most significant flaws (such problems with credentials) and sophisticated threats can be added. These kinds of connected device assaults have already occurred, along with well-known events like the Solar Winds breach.

Figure 4. Challenges of connected devices

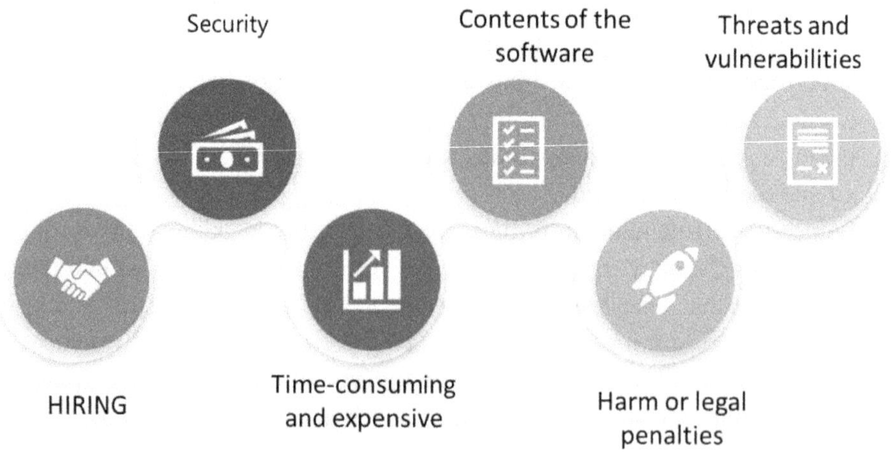

You don't have the proper equipment. If you've tried to address the linked device security issue, you've probably discovered that there aren't many or any safe embedded programming tools available. As a result, it is up to your team to create custom toolkits to confirm the product security. You might not have the time or specialized, knowledgeable team members needed for this. Many people are aware that they should set anti-virus (AV) software on their computers and exercise caution when downloading or visiting websites. Unfortunately, the majority of individuals undoubtedly do not think that the security of their IoT devices is at risk. Although these new technologies increase accessibility and integrate more seamlessly into our lives, many of the corporations who created them do not build them with security in mind. For instance, the default passwords on many IoT devices are generally known, cannot be changed, or are difficult to change. In order to address known vulnerabilities, they may also be difficult or impossible to update, or they may lack features that allow for security customization. Our reliance on Internet-connected gadgets has increased more quickly than we have the tools or knowledge to secure them. As with any Internet-connected device, leaving IoT devices open is like leaving your front door unlocked. It allows attackers access to your private data and gives them the chance to further breach other networked devices (Sobin, 2020).

4.1. Security for IoT Devices

Next, practically all IoT devices have some security vulnerabilities, as is the case with most technology. In order to prevent hackers from stealing data, spying on device owners/operators, or doing anything else that could have disastrous repercussions, it is crucial that these devices are safe given that the number of internet-connected devices is more than two times the size of the world's population. Let's talk about over-the-air (OTA) upgrades. OTA updates have a number of advantages for connected devices since they allow for remote repair of bugs or security problems. While OTA updates can improve security, they also have the potential to brick a device, which is very unpleasant for users and can harm the reputation of the brand of the device manufacturer (Williams & McCauley, 2016). As these technologies advance, the IoT has become one of the most significant inventions of the twenty-first century because seamless communication between people, processes, and objects is now conceivable (Tawalbeh et al., 2020).

4.2. How Can We Protect IoT Devices?

What can you do, then, to take advantage of IoT device capabilities while also maintaining your security? You may find the following advice useful in these efforts (Tawalbeh et al., 2020):

- Be aware of the IoT devices that are plugged into your network. It's possible that your network has gadgets linked that you are unaware of.
- Only invest in the equipment you actually need. Some Internet-enabled devices can be convenient to have, but they offer little value and compromise your security.
- Establish a unique Wi-Fi network just for IoT devices to keep them apart from other devices on your network. If one of your connected IoT devices is compromised, this safeguards your other devices.
- If at all possible, update the device's software. Regular gadget updates will lessen the likelihood of a successful attack.
- Change the preset passwords with your own strong, unique ones. Passwords should have a minimum of 10 characters, including capital and lowercase letters, digits, and special characters.
- Set up security and privacy settings, such as turning on encryption and capping the amount of data that your devices can share.
- Substitute more secure IoT devices for unsecure ones. To find out which of these devices may have a reasonable baseline of security, look for evaluations that discuss security features and patching support.

5. THE TREND OF CONNECTED DEVICE CHANGES IN THE FUTURE

Trend is a general tendency or direction of a development or change over time. In the coming years, smartphones will face some new rivals. Growth of everyday gadgets like smartphones will decelerate as metaverse tools and wearables like virtual reality (VR) headsets become more widespread. Toward the conclusion, these new technologies as megatrend might start to compete for consumers' attention. It's feasible that during the next five to ten years, augmented reality (AR) and virtual reality (VR) gadgets may overtake smartphones in terms of time spent, even though smartphones may not lose their significance. As more individuals adopt the technology through a variety of mobile apps, the majority of these new users will join via smartphones rather than specialized AR equipment. The ability to access AR through smartphones will also lead to more time being spent using the technology (Caporuscio et al., 2020).

Since the majority (62.6%) of AR users will access that information through social media in 2022, social media will continue to be a significant growth driver for AR and VR. This will increase the amount of time people spend on social media on both smartphones and "other connected devices," which includes wearables.

New uses for these technologies will attract more users as metaverse platforms grow older and more developed.

Industry, commercial, and consumer needs are guiding IoT innovation. As new use cases are made possible by technical advancements, a few main industries are propelling the expansion of connected devices. By 2030, 36% to 40% of the expected unlocked value will be accounted for by factories and human health, for instance, predicts McKinsey. Chips, connection, security, and AI are the four IoT enabling technologies that are enabling cost reduction and improved device quality. Connected gadgets will be able to increasingly infiltrate important areas including consumer appliances, automobiles and transportation, manufacturing and industry, and human health thanks to smaller, more efficient processors and wireless components. Enhanced networks enable more dependable connectivity, enabling previously impractical uses. Demand increases as connected gadgets prove to be valuable. Rob Conant, vice president of software ecosystems at Infineon (MIT, 2023), which offers semiconductor and software solutions to IoT companies, discusses how IoT applications have spread throughout various sectors of the economy, starting with fleet tracking in the 1980s and moving on to industrial manufacturing and the smart grid in the 1990s and 2000s. He observes the spread escalating throughout several businesses: "Connectivity is extending into more and more applications: pool pumps are becoming connected, light bulbs are becoming connected, and even furniture is becoming connected," he claims. As a result of the value propositions they can offer with the IoT, businesses who were not traditionally IT companies are now doing so. That represents a significant change in those businesses (Sangave et al., 2019).

5.1. Next Generation of Connected IoT

The next generation of IoT devices will feature cloud-based software solutions[1], device-based and edge computing[2], new approaches to power management and connectivity, and increased smarts via AI and ML. People now depend on smart, networked devices and sensors to make their lives simpler, more productive, and more efficient whether they are at home, at work, or traveling around the city (Caporuscio et al., 2020).

New IoT application cases are being made possible by technological advancements like lower power chips, improved connection, and advanced AI and ML. Applications in manufacturing, transportation, and healthcare are rapidly expanding. According to a McKinsey research, the value of IoT goods and services would range from $5.5 trillion to $12.6 trillion by 2030. But there are complications with IoT solutions. These can include producing user-focused information or creating sensing devices with safe cloud connectivity. Manufacturers and suppliers are still being impacted by the shortage of semiconductors and supply-chain interruptions brought on by the coronavirus outbreak. Unfortunately, different ecosystems, IP, technologies, and standards have resulted in a fragmented and cumbersome connected device world today. And creating simple, secure products remains difficult. Industry leaders must agree on standards to align manufacturers and device makers in order to fulfill the potential of IoT in the future. Whether they are partners or rivals, IoT product, software, hardware, and chip companies will need to work together to develop new features, products, and innovations and market them more quickly (Kos et al., 2019).

5.2. Connected Devices Create New Opportunities in Field Service

In contemporary service environments, connected devices are more prevalent. However, the market as a whole does not fully utilize their potential for data production, distribution, and applications. The popularity of the IoT is increasing, and according to current Gartner research, it will likely rank among the top strategic technology trends for 2020 (Lee, 2019).

- The use of IoT in field services opens up new possibilities for increasing team productivity and fostering client happiness. According to Forbes, "With this data, organizations can foresee weaknesses, sometimes providing service before parts break down, heading off more expensive or even catastrophic failures.
- There is less time wasted everywhere, as service providers can more efficiently plan, schedule, and complete on-site service, keeping businesses up and running, with a 24/7 view of equipment data."

But without the means of properly organising, storing, and responding to their data, field service teams aren't getting the most out of it. The ability of teams to mine data for insights and plan a multifaceted reaction is a prerequisite for providing the real-time responses that customers are increasingly demanding.

ML, robots, AI, edge computing, and mobile technologies for technicians are current enterprise solutions that support the utilization of IoT data and have the potential to revolutionize how field service teams approach connectivity and data collecting from the field. The extent to which service teams are utilizing these technologies and what use cases might serve as examples of their success are still open questions.

WBR Insights and Field Service will investigate how service firms are integrating their technological environment in this report. We'll learn how far along these trips they are, as well as the use-cases and goals they intend to achieve. We'll assess and project their progress in integrating next-generation technology with connection options, and we'll offer specific actions you can take to implement a coordinated plan for connected devices at your field service company.

5.3. Number of IoT Connected Devices in 2030

The number of IoT devices worldwide is forecast to almost triple from 9.7 billion in 2020 to more than 29 billion IoT devices in 2030. In 2030, the highest number of IoT devices will be found in China with around 5 billion consumer devices. IoT devices are used in all types of industry verticals and consumer markets, with the consumer segment accounting for around 60 percent of all IoT connected devices in 2020. This share is projected to stay at this level over the next ten years (Sangave et al., 2019).

5.4. Major Scenarios of Connected Devices

Electricity, gas, steam, and air conditioning, water supply and waste management, retail and wholesale, transportation and storage, and government are major industry verticals with more than 100 million linked IoT devices at this time. By 2030, there will be more than eight billion IoT devices in use across all industry verticals. Consumer internet and media devices like smartphones, where the number of IoT devices is expected to increase to more than 17 billion by 2030, represent the most significant use case for IoT devices in the consumer market. By 2030, linked (autonomous) vehicles, IT infrastructure, asset tracking & monitoring, and smart grid will all be additional use cases with more than one billion IoT devices (Chouvarda et al., 2019).

Figure 5. The IoT connected devices from 2015 to 2025 (in billions)
Source: https://www.statista.com/

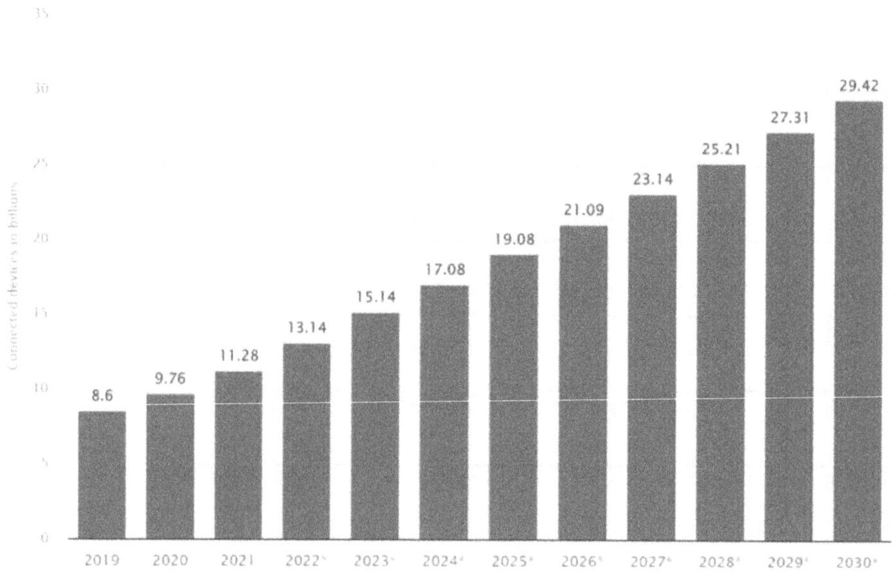

These days, wireless communication and mobility services are relied upon by the entire world. As wireless networking becomes more prevalent, the disadvantage of wireless communication is clearly obvious. The website statistica predicts that by 2020, there will be up to 50 billion smart gadgets worldwide that are interconnected. Up to 2020, approximately 26 billion physical things will be linked to the internet, according to Siemens research (see Figure 1).

It won't be long before billions of physical objects are connected in real time. They can exchange messages, forward information, and process needed data in the cloud. The internet of smart things, however, lacks technical uniformity from a security standpoint. According to a Statistica research, there will be over 75.44 billion linked devices worldwide in 2025. Smart devices, not global population, are the primary cause of this expansion. The use of integrated technologies is essential for connecting physical objects and facilitating information exchange (Goudarzi et al., 2022). In this setting, both humans and machines can communicate with one another through machine-to-machine communication. The IoT is the integration of physical objects, intelligent devices, intelligent buildings, intelligent cars, embedded objects including electronics, programming, sensors, actuators, and network connections for information sharing. The wireless sensor network played a major role in the development of the IoT idea. In 1999, Kevin Ashton introduces the concept of the "internet of things," which uses unique identifiers to locate actual objects on the internet. According fig 6, Three primary parts make up the Internet of Things; Material Things, Sensor Networks and Data Flow.

Figure 6. Three primary parts make up the internet of things

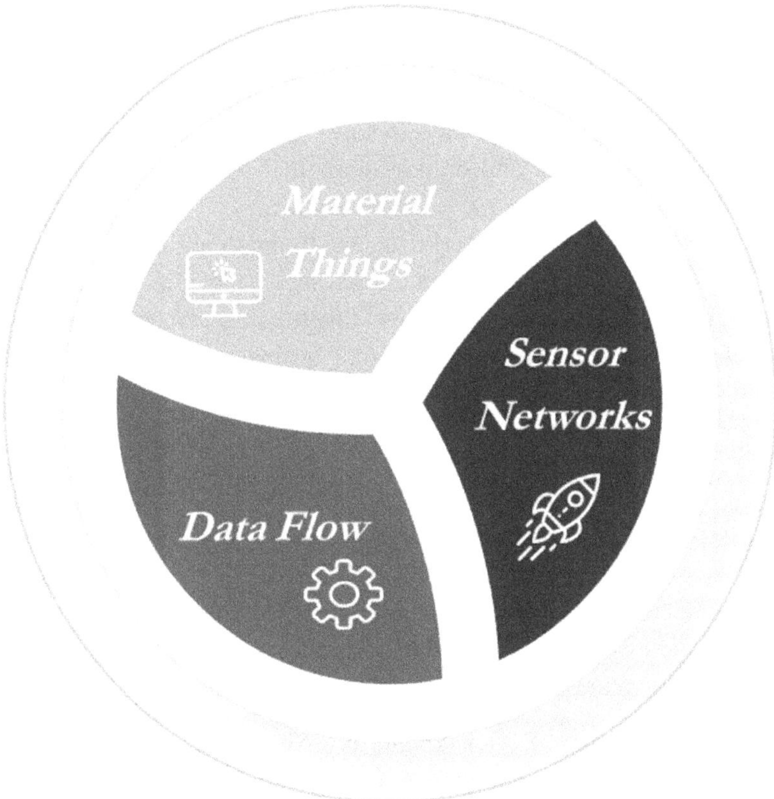

With linked technologies like cloud computing, sensor networks, robotics, and Future Internet technologies, physical things are continuously expanding. The development of the internet of things is experiencing the following challenges (Tawalbeh et L., 2020):

- *Problems with privacy and security.*
- *Problems using uniquely identifying information.*
- *Difficulties in testing at a broad scale using a sophisticated sensor network.*
- *Difficulties in creating a firm that fully utilizes the Internet of Things.*

6. CONCLUSION

Digital businesses have been one of the vital catchphrases among scholastics and specialists since 2015. Adapting to and adjusting to the computerized transformation requires adjusting to unused hones for individuals of an organization and business. In this research, an endeavor has been made to examine the sorts of advanced businesses and the up-and-coming patterns in this field. This great transformation has caused key and deep impacts in businesses and has accelerated processes and all processes. By identifying the needs and challenges of big and small human beings, digital businesses design and build ways to solve these challenges, and over time, they become large companies and organizations that provide more comfort and peace to people.

The topics related to digital businesses and the future trends of this field are very broad and are changing day by day with the advancement of technology. For this reason, in this research, an effort was made to investigate some trends and describe the effects of digital transformations in digital businesses. But what we should keep in mind is the growing and dynamic nature of this type of business, which has affected a large part of our lives and business paths today.

REFERENCES

Bracke, V., Sebrechts, M., Moons, B., Hoebeke, J., De Turck, F., & Volckaert, B. (2021). Design and evaluation of a scalable Internet of Things backend for smart ports. *Software, Practice & Experience*, *51*(7), 1557–1579. doi:10.1002pe.2973

Caporuscio, M., Flammini, F., Khakpour, N., Singh, P., & Thornadtsson, J. (2020). Smart-troubleshooting connected devices: Concept, challenges and opportunities. *Future Generation Computer Systems*, *111*, 681–697. doi:10.1016/j.future.2019.09.004

Chengoden, R., Victor, N., Huynh-The, T., Yenduri, G., Jhaveri, R. H., Alazab, M., Bhattacharya, S., Hegde, P., Maddikunta, P. K. R., & Gadekallu, T. R. (2023). Metaverse for healthcare: A survey on potential applications, challenges and future directions. *IEEE Access : Practical Innovations, Open Solutions*, *11*, 12765–12795. doi:10.1109/ACCESS.2023.3241628

Choi, H. W., Shin, D. W., Yang, J., Lee, S., Figueiredo, C., Sinopoli, S., Ullrich, K., Jovančić, P., Marrani, A., Momentè, R., Gomes, J., Branquinho, R., Emanuele, U., Lee, H., Bang, S. Y., Jung, S.-M., Han, S. D., Zhan, S., Harden-Chaters, W., ... Kim, J. M. (2022). Smart textile lighting/display system with multifunctional fibre devices for large scale smart home and IoT applications. *Nature Communications*, *13*(1), 814. doi:10.103841467-022-28459-6 PMID:35145096

Chouvarda, I., Mountford, N., Trajkovik, V., Loncar-Turukalo, T., & Cusack, T. (2019). Leveraging interdisciplinary education toward securing the future of connected health research in Europe: Qualitative study. *Journal of Medical Internet Research*, *21*(11), e14020. doi:10.2196/14020 PMID:31719026

Cooke, A. D., & Zubcsek, P. P. (2017). The connected consumer: Connected devices and the evolution of customer intelligence. *Journal of the Association for Consumer Research*, *2*(2), 164–178. doi:10.1086/690941

Coutinho, R. W., & Boukerche, A. (2019). Modeling and analysis of a shared edge caching system for connected cars and industrial IoT-based applications. *IEEE Transactions on Industrial Informatics*, *16*(3), 2003–2012. doi:10.1109/TII.2019.2938529

Duraipandian, M., & Vinothkanna, R. (2019). Cloud based Internet of Things for smart connected objects. *Journal of ISMAC*, *1*(02), 111–119.

Goudarzi, A., Ghayoor, F., Waseem, M., Fahad, S., & Traore, I. (2022). A Survey on IoT-Enabled Smart Grids: Emerging, Applications, Challenges, and Outlook. *Energies*, *15*(19), 6984. doi:10.3390/en15196984

Hammi, B., Zeadally, S., Khatoun, R., & Nebhen, J. (2022). Survey on smart homes: Vulnerabilities, risks, and countermeasures. *Computers & Security*, *117*, 102677. doi:10.1016/j.cose.2022.102677

Haque, A. B., Bhushan, B., & Dhiman, G. (2022). Conceptualizing smart city applications: Requirements, architecture, security issues, and emerging trends. *Expert Systems: International Journal of Knowledge Engineering and Neural Networks*, *39*(5), e12753. doi:10.1111/exsy.12753

Holko, M., Litwin, T. R., Munoz, F., Theisz, K. I., Salgin, L., Jenks, N. P., Holmes, B. W., Watson-McGee, P., Winford, E., & Sharma, Y. (2022). Wearable fitness tracker use in federally qualified health center patients: Strategies to improve the health of all of us using digital health devices. *NPJ Digital Medicine*, *5*(1), 53. doi:10.103841746-022-00593-x PMID:35469045

Khan, M. A., Sajjad, I. A., Tahir, M., & Haseeb, A. (2022). IOT Application for Energy Management in Smart Homes. *Engineering Proceedings, 20*(1), 43.

Kos, A., Milutinović, V., & Umek, A. (2019). Challenges in wireless communication for connected sensors and wearable devices used in sport biofeedback applications. *Future Generation Computer Systems, 92*, 582–592. doi:10.1016/j.future.2018.03.032

Lan, L., Shi, R., Wang, B., & Zhang, L. (2019). An IoT unified access platform for heterogeneity sensing devices based on edge computing. *IEEE Access, 7*, 44199-44211.

Lee, I. (2019). The Internet of Things for enterprises: An ecosystem, architecture, and IoT service business model. *Internet of Things : Engineering Cyber Physical Human Systems, 7*, 100078. doi:10.1016/j.iot.2019.100078

Ogudo, K. A., Muwawa Jean Nestor, D., Ibrahim Khalaf, O., & Daei Kasmaei, H. (2019). A device performance and data analytics concept for smartphones' IoT services and machine-type communication in cellular networks. *Symmetry, 11*(4), 593. doi:10.3390ym11040593

Petit, A., & Cambon, L. (2016). Exploratory study of the implications of research on the use of smart connected devices for prevention: A scoping review. *BMC Public Health, 16*(1), 1–13. doi:10.118612889-016-3225-4 PMID:27401769

Rafique, W., Qi, L., Yaqoob, I., Imran, M., Rasool, R. U., & Dou, W. (2020). Complementing IoT services through software defined networking and edge computing: A comprehensive survey. *IEEE Communications Surveys and Tutorials, 22*(3), 1761–1804. doi:10.1109/COMST.2020.2997475

Rath, C. K., Mandal, A. K., & Sarkar, A. (2022). An Event-B based Device Description Model in IoT with the Support of Multimodal System. *Advanced Computing and Systems for Security, 13*, 3–19. doi:10.1007/978-981-16-4287-6_1

Sangave, N. A., Aungst, T. D., & Patel, D. K. (2019). Smart connected insulin pens, caps, and attachments: A review of the future of diabetes technology. *Diabetes Spectrum, 32*(4), 378–384. doi:10.2337/ds18-0069 PMID:31798296

Seydoux, N., Drira, K., Hernandez, N., & Monteil, T. (2016). IoT-O, a core-domain IoT ontology to represent connected devices networks. *Knowledge Engineering and Knowledge Management: 20th International Conference, EKAW 2016, Bologna, Italy, November 19-23, 2016 Proceedings, 20*, 561–576.

Sobin, C. C. (2020). A survey on architecture, protocols and challenges in IoT. *Wireless Personal Communications, 112*(3), 1383–1429. doi:10.100711277-020-07108-5

Steenwinckel, B., De Brouwer, M., Stojchevska, M., Van Der Donckt, J., Nelis, J., Ruyssinck, J., . . . Ongenae, F. (2022). Data analytics for health and connected care: Ontology, knowledge graph and applications. *EAI PervasiveHealth, the 16th EAI International Conference on Pervasive Computing Technologies for Healthcare.*

Tawalbeh, L. A., Muheidat, F., Tawalbeh, M., & Quwaider, M. (2020). IoT Privacy and security: Challenges and solutions. *Applied Sciences (Basel, Switzerland), 10*(12), 4102. doi:10.3390/app10124102

Vijayan, V., Connolly, J. P., Condell, J., McKelvey, N., & Gardiner, P. (2021). Review of wearable devices and data collection considerations for connected health. *Sensors (Basel), 21*(16), 5589. doi:10.339021165589 PMID:34451032

Williams, P. A., & McCauley, V. (2016, December). Always connected: The security challenges of the healthcare Internet of Things. In *2016 IEEE 3rd World Forum on Internet of Things (WF-IoT)* (pp. 30-35). IEEE.

ENDNOTES

1 Cloud-based software simply refers to any software program or application that's stored, managed, and available through the cloud. To access such services or software programs, users must have an internet connection. It is generally stored on shared computing resources; such as cloud servers.

2 Edge computing devices defines as pieces of physical hardware connected to an edge computing platform that serve to collect and transmit data. They are used to accomplish a variety of tasks depending on the software they've been provisioned with.

Chapter 3
Investigating the Role of Transformative Technologies and Smart Processes on Sustainable Business

Masoud Vaseei
https://orcid.org/0000-0002-9221-2128
Department of Industrial Engineering, Islamic Azad University, Lahijan, Iran

Milad Abolghasemian
https://orcid.org/0000-0002-1341-7855
Department of Industrial Engineering, Islamic Azad University, Lahijan, Iran

Mohammadreza Nasiri Jan Agha
https://orcid.org/0009-0009-0322-7212
Department of Industrial Engineering, Islamic Azad University, Lahijan, Iran

Adel Pourghader Chobar
Department of Industrial Engineering, Islamic Azad University, Qazvin, Iran

ABSTRACT

The concept of sustainable development was at first inferred from the biological system. With the advance of related trends, sustainable advancement continuously become a comprehensive concept, counting economy, society, and environment. Sustainable development implies improvement that meets the desires of the present era without compromising the desires of the long-standing age. Rapid changes in digital technologies have transformed the landscape for pursuing the Sustainable Development Goals. At their best, these technologies have contributed to vast

DOI: 10.4018/979-8-3693-0210-1.ch003

improvements in access to public services and economic opportunity for millions of people. The growth of smart businesses based on transformative technologies and the development of smart processes in smart societies is significant as a strategic capacity and driver of development in technology and economy. Considering the importance of the topic in this chapter, the role of these technologies in the sustainable development of smart businesses is examined.

1. INTRODUCTION

Moving towards sustainable development can be considered a particular position for developing countries. Sustainable transportation, sustainable agriculture, sustainable cities, industries, organizations, businesses, etc., are some dimensions of sustainable development. Sustainable development requires actions in its three dimensions through policies that pursue economic growth, greater social equality, and reduced adverse environmental effects. Sustainable development could be a multidimensional concept emphasizing integrating and powerfully adjusting a region's financial, social, and biological angles to ensure intergenerational value. Although diverse analysts defined economic advancement slightly differently, it may be a typical drift that sustainable development incorporates the three measurements of economy, society, and environment. Sustainable development points to arranging financial, social, and natural advancement to adjust intergenerational well-being and maximize all generations' well-being (Qi et al., 2023).

Linking technologies and sustainability, we understand that smart businesses apply digital and communication technologies to process-level activities to improve efficiency, manage complexity, and increase the quality of activities. It leads to stable working operations. Today's ubiquitous communication technologies increasingly provide innovative solutions for complex logistics and make transportation smarter and more efficient. For simplicity of concept, this is called an intelligent supply chain based on increased visibility resulting from real-time data collection and sharing (nozari et al., (a),2023). These features make the process flexible, expandable, and intelligent. Therefore, technologies are increasingly opening their way to the space of smart businesses and changing conventional supply chain communication. It requires investigating how smart processes equipped with technology can increase the sustainability of smart businesses (Zhang et al., 2023).

In addition, smart businesses shaped based on an organization of information and communication technologies assist the city's social and urban development and open unused market openings for entrepreneurs. With the nonstop integration of computerized innovations in items, administrations, and forms, digital innovation and advanced upgrades have pulled analysts and experts into consideration. As automatic creation hypothetically empowers companies to make strides to prepare proficiency and better oversee assets, it should encourage financially and ecologically feasible execution (Trevisan et al., 2023).

Within the literature, studies expect a positive relationship between innovation, digital space, and maintainable commerce. The existing views on the effect of market turbulence on execution are assorted and incorporate both positive and negative results. One of the most critical objectives of digital change is to utilize digital innovations to precisely anticipate changes in client inclinations and give way to better items and administrations. Hence, the current investigation explores the relationship between transformational innovations and new-age businesses for computerized advancement.

2. DIGITAL TRANSFORMATIONS

Nowadays, in developing nations, businesses are known as the spine of the economy since they play a critical part in business, economic development, and the mobilization of innovation and creativity. In any case, most of these companies, particularly within the early stages of their life cycle, have small use and confront a quickly changing world (Son et al., 2023).

The expanding utilization of digital technologies and dependence on them has brought critical changes in business and society. There has been a crucial center on organizational data systems for a long time. This extraordinary consideration comes from better coordinating unused innovations (equipment and programs) with business forms (Su et al., 2023). Commerce forms depend on innovation more than anything else since innovation straightforwardly influences trade forms and changes how they work. Digital innovation is recognized as a primary factor in competition to execute a vital arrangement and bolster center competencies. In this manner, directors have essentially expanded their investment in digital innovation over time Since digital innovations quicken trade show advancement by making esteem, retaining and utilizing resources, and altering the standards of the financial cycle within the industry(Nozari et al., (b), 2023).

The utilization of modern advances can ensure the survival of businesses. With innovations in generation and communication, changes have been made in businesses' appearance, dispersion, and organizational structure strategies. Growing and sending innovation-based innovations, forms, and models constitute imaginative entrepreneurial companies' spine. Digital innovations empower companies to make strides in asset stream, esteem creation, and gathering pledges in real-world situations, empowering trade show advancement. In expansion, digital innovations enable companies to enhance their communication with providers and clients.

The first step is to form a digital transformation strategy to move on the digital path. Every organization needs a specific method for digital transformation, and only by designing a suitable system can the organization achieve incredible results by aligning its resources with digital innovations (Nozari et al., (c),2023). The digital transformation strategy affects all the organization's processes (products and services, marketing, human resources, information technology, and finance). It makes the organization ready for transformation and the creation of distinctive value. With a comprehensive approach, the digital transformation strategy pursues different goals, and a business-oriented company focuses on transforming products and services, processes, and everything that is affected by technologies in the organization. It should be noted that the digital transformation strategy is an alternative. None of the organization's other methods will be aligned with each of them (Pan & Nishant, 2023). The most important benefits of implementing digital transformations in businesses are shown in Figure 1.

Figure 1. The most important benefits of implementing digital transformations in businesses

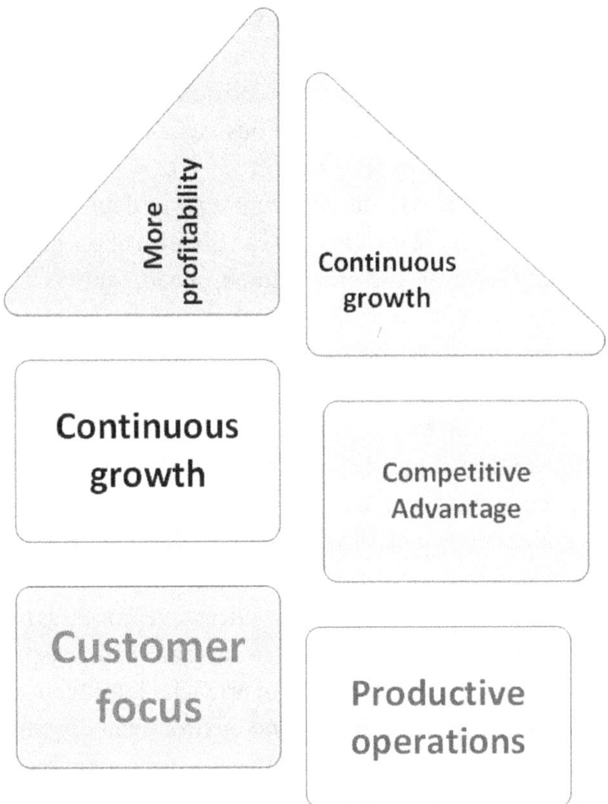

2.1. Artificial Intelligence and Sustainable Smart Business

Artificial intelligence (AI) is basic for digital change since advanced change depends on data. Data is the backbone of any advanced business(Nozari et al., 2022). Each interaction your business has with customers and markets produces information. Artificial intelligence has the potential to convert numerous angles of business operations. This technology can be utilized in different areas, such as information investigation and request estimating, moving forward coordinations and transportation courses, and identifying inefficient focuses within the supply chain. It eventually leads to progressed responsiveness to request changes, diminished conveyance times, and lower costs. AI can be an intelligent assistant for businesses(Gupta et al., 2023). These intelligent assistants constantly learn and improve their performance using machine learning algorithms. One of the main advantages of using artificial intelligence as a smart assistant is its ability to provide support. And immediate assistance to customers. Virtual assistants can simultaneously handle many inquiries, ensuring no request goes unanswered. It reduces response time and provides consistent and accurate information. As a result, it will bring customer satisfaction. It is one of the parameters of sustainable development. Another advantage of using artificial intelligence as an intelligent assistant is its scalability. As businesses grow and customer demands increase, customer support or other processes become challenging and costly. In this case, virtual assistants can handle many tasks and questions simultaneously without additional costs. This scalability ensures that businesses can improve the quality of their support as demand increases (Popkova et al., 2023).

In today's digital age, businesses face vast amounts of data. This data, commonly known as big data, holds valuable insights that can drive business growth and increase customer satisfaction. However, the vast volume, speed, and variety of these data make it impossible for humans to analyze them manually. This is where artificial intelligence comes into play. AI-based analytics tools use advanced algorithms and machine learning techniques to extract meaningful patterns and insights from customer big data (Leal Filho et al., 2023).

Artificial intelligence transforms businesses by increasing efficiency, minimizing environmental impacts, improving safety, and enabling smarter decision-making. As the world faces unprecedented sustainability challenges, artificial intelligence is emerging as a powerful tool for achieving sustainable and resilient infrastructure. Embracing artificial intelligence in business practices and processes is a technological advancement and a commitment to a more sustainable and prosperous future for future generations. By using the capabilities of artificial intelligence, entrepreneurs are ready to create a safer, more efficient, and environmentally responsible world (AlZayani et al., 2023). The analytical framework for smart business based on artificial intelligence is shown in Figure 2.

Figure 2. Analytical framework for smart business based on artificial intelligence (Garrel & Jahn, 2022)

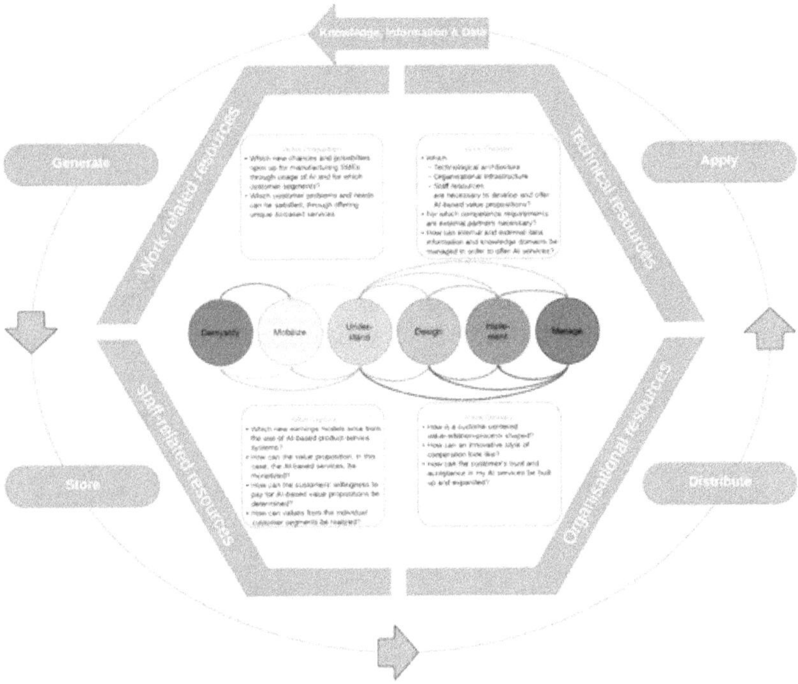

2.2. IoT and Sustainable Smart Business

Considering that every economic, social, and political activity leaves related and mutual effects, without new technology, these activities and their coordination in an integrated and aligned system, the work of sustainable development cannot be carried forward. It requires comprehensive and systematic development (Nozari et al., 2019). As a networked pattern of connected smart objects, Internet of Things technology has provided connection and communication between objects at any time and place. Modern Internet of Things technology is one of the indicators of economic development and growth in countries. Therefore, this emerging technology causes change and is a response to change towards sustainable societal development.

The Internet of Things collects real-time data and uses them to achieve traffic patterns and facility availability, reducing gas consumption and greenhouse gases. So, in general, it can be said that sustainable development improves the quality of a process, including environmental, institutional, and economic sectors, without exerting any pressure on future generations or the pressure that is applied due to the reduction of natural and local resources. In this regard, the optimal management of waste is of particular importance, especially from the environmental and health point of view, due to the high volume of their daily production in all countries. Using Internet of Things solutions in businesses opens new opportunities to develop products and services in new markets. It also reduces current costs, increases productivity, generates income, and creates employment in the field of social sustainability (Karthick et al., 2023).

The Internet of Things creates the ability to unify digital and physical structures. It provides an entirely new surface class of big data applications and services that must be used concerning environmental sustainability. In the scope of sustainable smart businesses, the increase in the volume of data production is beyond imagination. A large amount of information currently available from various areas of business processes is so valuable that it can be used with the cooperation of planners and specialists in information and communication technology to advance environmental sustainability (Nagy et al., 2023). The sustainable IoT framework is shown in Figure 3.

Figure 3. Sustainable IoT framework (Anand et al., 2020)

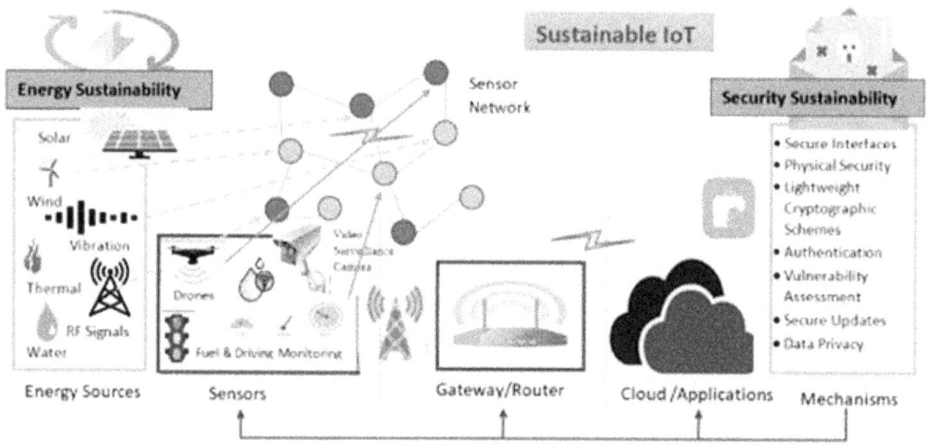

3. THE ROLE OF TRANSFORMATIVE TECHNOLOGIES IN THE SUSTAINABLE DEVELOPMENT OF SMART BUSINESSES

With the impact of climate change and environmental degradation, the involvement of businesses in sustainable initiatives has become vital. Transformational technologies such as artificial intelligence, the Internet of Things, big data, blockchain, social networks, etc., have emerged as powerful tools for businesses, allowing them to act powerfully on environmental issues. It will contribute to a sustainable future (El Archi et al., 2023).

The ability of transformative technologies to analyze large volumes of data and identify patterns and predictions has facilitated industries and enabled people to find innovative solutions to environmental challenges. For example, artificial intelligence uses predictive algorithms to optimize renewable energy and increase the efficiency of solar panels and wind turbines. Also, this tool helps produce smart grids that balance energy supply and demand and help improve energy efficiency.

Skills based on transformative technologies are essential for several reasons. They enable businesses to collect, analyze, and understand environmental data. This data-driven approach helps them create better sustainability programs and interventions that make a difference. People with creative thinking in planning systems in smart businesses can use skills based on transformative technologies to develop innovative solutions such as smart energy grids and advanced waste management systems and increase focus on sustainable performance. By using intelligent algorithms, the use of resources is optimized, waste is reduced, and sustainable consumption is promoted. It leads to improved efficiency, reduced environmental impact, and protection of valuable natural resources. Transformative technologies also provide the ability to develop early warning systems for disasters and adverse weather events, leading to life-saving and resilience measures (Nozari et al., 2021).

Investing in the capabilities of these emerging technologies and accepting their capacity to create a sustainable world for future generations is very important. In addition to promoting sustainability, transformative technologies are vital in improving business supply chain performance. One of the main challenges in supply chain management is the lack of transparency. It is often difficult for companies to trace the origin of their raw materials and ensure that they are sourced transparently and financially. For this reason, technology like blockchain helps in this area. Blockchain technology, supported by artificial intelligence, can create a digital ledger of every transaction in the supply chain. This ledger is transparent and immutable, ensuring that any stakeholder can verify the authenticity and ethicality of the products. The following presents some of the most critical applications of transformative technologies in developing smart businesses (Choi et al., 2023).

- **Using transformative technologies in planning**

Arranging, particularly within the supply chain (as the center of basic processes), is one of the foremost fundamental exercises within the supply chain administration procedure, and it is essential to have dependable and proficient devices to create compelling plans. Executing advances like machine learning in a business can lead to the optimization of the supply chain decision-making forms. Also, you'll adjust the request and supply by analyzing big data and applying intelligent algorithms while optimizing the conveyance forms.

Workforce arranging is fundamental for any present-day organization. It incorporates enlistment, maintenance, representative advancement, redeployment, execution administration, etc. Machine learning and counterfeit insights arrangements can rearrange the forms and make your workforce arranging methodology more compelling. Eventually, much appreciated by this innovation, you may have a more joyful group. A cheerful group is fundamental because employees are more fascinated by their organization and more profitable. As a result, with such a group, your commerce will be more effective (Dong et al., 2023).

- **Analysis of the route and warehouse**

Computer vision (CV) may be a department that looks to create different procedures that assist computers in seeing and getting pictures and recordings. It is precisely the device that can give you distribution center computerization and embrace numerous assignments. For example, computer vision frameworks can mechanize the standardized tag perusing preparation and speed up and disentangle this preparation. In addition, these frameworks can screen the distribution center environment, track representatives, analyze data, and avoid robbery and infringement of security laws. Much appreciated to facial acknowledgment innovation, a computer vision framework will also be able to distinguish individuals entering and taking off the warehouse.

- **Demand forecasting**

To improve the efficiency of manufacturing businesses, you can use transformative technologies to forecast demand or improve demand forecasting. Using these technologies, you can get a detailed analysis of all the factors that may affect the market based on past experiences and make the right decisions for your business. These technologies are much more effective than traditional demand forecasting methods. The point is, maybe you use those methods for factors that have less impact on demand. Therefore, such predictions cannot be as reliable as those made with the help of advanced technology (Bencsik et al., 2023).

- **Route optimization**

Innovations like artificial intelligence can create decisions to diminish transportation costs and speed up its forms, almost choosing the most excellent courses. It is particularly critical to possess an expansive e-commerce company with numerous clients. Since they continuously feel cheerful and satisfied that they get their orders as long as conceivable and without delay. So artificial intelligence is what you wish to analyze the existing courses and optimize the system. In this way, you'll accomplish way better results and more benefits (Olawumi et al., 2023).

Of course, there are many other practical functions for transformative technologies for the sustainable growth of smart businesses. However, companies are under pressure to execute these innovations to progress operational efficiency and streamline commerce choices through forward-looking frameworks. Progressed innovations can also offer assistance to logistics businesses to make the capacity to optimize generation, logistics, warehousing, and last conveyance at numerous levels (Kusiak, 2023).

Embracing these emerging technologies in businesses improves the customer experience. Therefore, using solutions based on machine learning, your products will be delivered in excellent condition and on time. In addition, your business will gain more time and business insights that will help your management team make successful decisions and ensure the growth of your business (Broccardo et al., 2023). Figure 4 shows the alignment of transformative technologies with intelligent companies in the path of sustainable development.

Figure 4. Alignment of transformative technologies with smart businesses in the path of sustainable growth

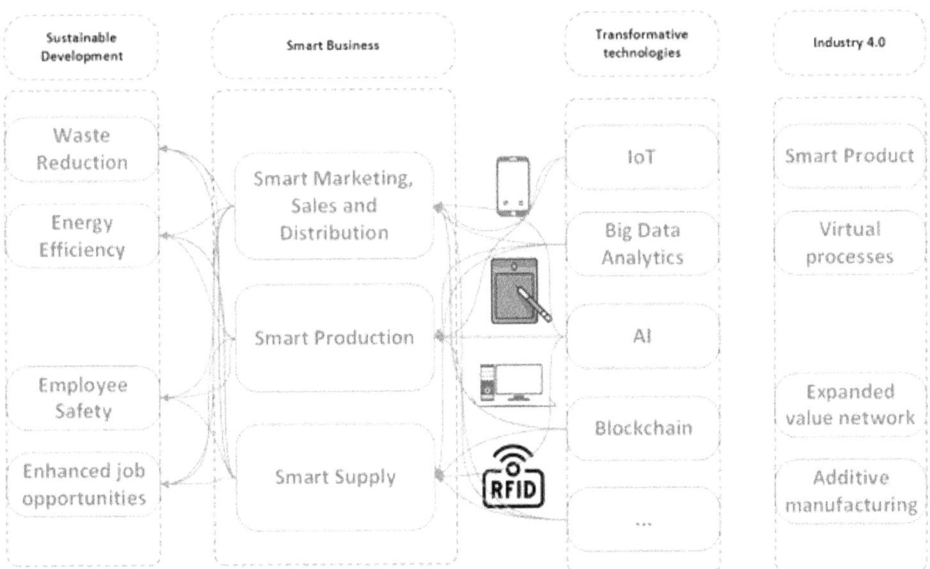

4. CONCLUSION

This study aims to clarify the validity of the impact of digital technologies and smart processes on sustainable business. Digital transformation means creating extensive business processes and operations changes using digital technologies. Instead of fearing or resisting this transformation, smart businesses use digital tools and technologies to improve their performance and efficiency. Overall, digital transformation provides opportunities for businesses to advance and grow smarter. Therefore, a smart business benefits from digital transformation and sees it as an opportunity to experience improvement and progress.

Due to the modern business world, organizations must inevitably adapt to various developments and changes. These changes have penetrated the processes' structure and behavior, representing the changes in the work and business management system. Despite the variety of transformative technologies, the business management system has made many changes compared to two decades ago, which has caused business processes to move towards becoming more intelligent. Smart business process management as an organizational transformation guides organizations to achieve their strategic goals.

Intelligent business processes support activity monitoring, business rule analysis, and decision management, providing the best mechanism for integrated and intelligent cooperation of organizational systems. This system bridges the gap between business operations and IT infrastructure, and by aligning business and IT, it creates reusable assets and supports the necessary changes to improve processes. Slow All these supports help the sustainability of business systems in different regions. The presence of technologies such as the Internet of Things as one of the most significant sources of big data production helps to understand all activities correctly. Accompanying these data with technologies such as artificial intelligence and machine learning gives high analytical power to the processes and reduces costs and sustainable development. In this research, it was tried to identify the factors affecting the development of sustainable smart businesses. A correct understanding of these factors can effectively guide the implementation of these smart, environmentally friendly, and sustainable businesses.

REFERENCES

AlZayani, F., Mohammed, A., & Shoaib, H. M. (2023). The impact of smart technologies on SMEs' sustainability: The mediation effect of sustainability strategy. *Competitiveness Review*. Advance online publication. doi:10.1108/CR-09-2022-0136

Anand, P., Singh, Y., Selwal, A., Alazab, M., Tanwar, S., & Kumar, N. (2020). IoT vulnerability assessment for sustainable computing: Threats, current solutions, and open challenges. *IEEE Access : Practical Innovations, Open Solutions*, *8*, 168825–168853. doi:10.1109/ACCESS.2020.3022842

Bencsik, B., Palmié, M., Parida, V., Wincent, J., & Gassmann, O. (2023). Business models for digital sustainability: Framework, microfoundations of value capture, and empirical evidence from 130 smart city services. *Journal of Business Research*, *160*, 113757. doi:10.1016/j.jbusres.2023.113757

Broccardo, L., Zicari, A., Jabeen, F., & Bhatti, Z. A. (2023). How digitalization supports a sustainable business model: A literature review. *Technological Forecasting and Social Change*, *187*, 122146. doi:10.1016/j.techfore.2022.122146

Choi, K. H., & Kwon, G. H. (2023). Strategies for sensing innovation opportunities in smart grids: In the perspective of interactive relationships between science, technology, and business. *Technological Forecasting and Social Change*, *187*, 122210. doi:10.1016/j.techfore.2022.122210

Dong, L., Ren, M., Xiang, Z., Zheng, P., Cong, J., & Chen, C. H. (2023). A novel smart product-service system configuration method for mass personalization based on knowledge graph. *Journal of Cleaner Production*, *382*, 135270. doi:10.1016/j.jclepro.2022.135270

El Archi, Y., Benbba, B., Nizamatdinova, Z., Issakov, Y., Vargáné, G. I., & Dávid, L. D. (2023). Systematic Literature Review Analysing Smart Tourism Destinations in Context of Sustainable Development: Current Applications and Future Directions. *Sustainability (Basel)*, *15*(6), 5086. doi:10.3390u15065086

Gupta, B. B., Gaurav, A., Panigrahi, P. K., & Arya, V. (2023). Analysis of artificial intelligence-based technologies and approaches on sustainable entrepreneurship. *Technological Forecasting and Social Change*, *186*, 122152. doi:10.1016/j.techfore.2022.122152

Karthick, A. V., & Gopalsamy, S. (2023, January). Role of IoT in Business Sustainability. In *International Conference on Economics, Business and Sustainability* (pp. 9-15). Singapore: Springer Nature Singapore.

Kusiak, A. (2023). Smart manufacturing. In *Springer Handbook of Automation* (pp. 973–985). Springer International Publishing. doi:10.1007/978-3-030-96729-1_45

Leal Filho, W., Yang, P., Eustachio, J. H. P. P., Azul, A. M., Gellers, J. C., Gielczyk, A., Dinis, M. A. P., & Kozlova, V. (2023). Deploying digitalisation and artificial intelligence in sustainable development research. *Environment, Development and Sustainability*, *25*(6), 4957–4988. doi:10.100710668-022-02252-3 PMID:35313685

Nagy, S. G., & Stukovszky, T. (Eds.). (2023). *Smart Business and Digital Transformation: An Industry 4.0 Perspective*. Taylor & Francis. doi:10.4324/9781003390312

Nozari, H., Fallah, M., Kazemipoor, H., & Najafi, S. E. (2021). Big data analysis of IoT-based supply chain management considering FMCG industries. *Бизнес-информатика*, *15*(1), 78–96. doi:10.17323/2587-814X.2021.1.78.96

Nozari, H., Ghahremani-Nahr, J., & Najafi, E. (2023). The Role of Internet of Things and Blockchain in the Development of Agile and Sustainable Supply Chains. In Digital Supply Chain, Disruptive Environments, and the Impact on Retailers (pp. 271-282). IGI Global.

Nozari, H., Ghahremani-Nahr, J., & Szmelter-Jarosz, A. (2023). A multi-stage stochastic inventory management model for transport companies including several different transport modes. *International Journal of Management Science and Engineering Management*, *18*(2), 134–144. doi:10.1080/17509653.2022.2042747

Nozari, H., Ghahremani-Nahr, J., & Szmelter-Jarosz, A. (2023). AI and machine learning for real-world problems. *Advances In Computers*.

Nozari, H., Najafi, E., Fallah, M., & Hosseinzadeh Lotfi, F. (2019). Quantitative analysis of key performance indicators of green supply chain in FMCG industries using non-linear fuzzy method. *Mathematics*, *7*(11), 1020. doi:10.3390/math7111020

Nozari, H., Szmelter-Jarosz, A., & Ghahremani-Nahr, J. (2022). Analysis of the challenges of artificial intelligence of things (AIoT) for the smart supply chain (case study: FMCG industries). *Sensors (Basel)*, *22*(8), 2931. doi:10.339022082931 PMID:35458916

Olawumi, T. O., Chan, D. W., Saka, A. B., Ekundayo, D., & Odeh, A. O. (2023). Are there any gains in green-tech adoption? Unearthing the beneficial outcomes of smart-sustainable practices in Nigeria and Hong Kong built environment. *Journal of Cleaner Production*, *410*, 137280. doi:10.1016/j.jclepro.2023.137280

Pan, S. L., & Nishant, R. (2023). Artificial intelligence for digital sustainability: An insight into domain-specific research and future directions. *International Journal of Information Management*, *72*, 102668. doi:10.1016/j.ijinfomgt.2023.102668

Popkova, E. G., Sergi, B. S., & Bogoviz, A. V. (2023). Evolution of environmental economics and management in the age of artificial intelligence for sustainable development. *Frontiers in Environmental Science*, *11*, 545. doi:10.3389/fenvs.2023.1176612

Qi, B., Shen, Y., & Xu, T. (2023). An artificial-intelligence-enabled sustainable supply chain model for B2C E-commerce business in the international trade. *Technological Forecasting and Social Change*, *191*, 122491. doi:10.1016/j.techfore.2023.122491

Son, T. H., Weedon, Z., Yigitcanlar, T., Sanchez, T., Corchado, J. M., & Mehmood, R. (2023). Algorithmic urban planning for smart and sustainable development: Systematic review of the literature. *Sustainable Cities and Society*, *94*, 104562. doi:10.1016/j.scs.2023.104562

Su, J., Wei, Y., Wang, S., & Liu, Q. (2023). The impact of digital transformation on the total factor productivity of heavily polluting enterprises. *Scientific Reports*, *13*(1), 6386. doi:10.103841598-023-33553-w PMID:37076699

Trevisan, L. V., Eustachio, J. H. P. P., Dias, B. G., Filho, W. L., & Pedrozo, E. Á. (2023). Digital transformation towards sustainability in higher education: State-of-the-art and future research insights. *Environment, Development and Sustainability*, 1–22. doi:10.100710668-022-02874-7 PMID:36624732

von Garrel, J., & Jahn, C. (2022). Design Framework for the Implementation of AI-based (Service) Business Models for Small and Medium-sized Manufacturing Enterprises. *Journal of the Knowledge Economy*, 1–19.

Zhang, X., Nutakor, F., Minlah, M. K., & Li, J. (2023). Can Digital Transformation Drive Green Transformation in Manufacturing Companies?—Based on Socio-Technical Systems Theory Perspective. *Sustainability (Basel)*, *15*(3), 2840. doi:10.3390u15032840

Chapter 4
Emerging Trends for Blockchain Technology in Smart Supply Chain Management

Melisa Ozbiltekin-Pala
Yaşar University, Turkey

ABSTRACT

Smart supply chain management aims to transact more efficiently, quickly, and flexibly by integrating artificial intelligence, big data analytics, machine learning, and other digital technologies into traditional supply chain management processes. With globalization and digitalization reaching significant dimensions, integrating digital technologies in business models is extremely important. In this way, blockchain technology offers a reliable and tamper-proof structure. With the rapid development of technology, the potential of blockchain in smart supply chain management is increasing. Businesses have to integrate blockchain technology into smart supply chain management. For this reason, it is necessary to know the emerging trends for blockchain technology in smart supply chain management. Therefore, the present study focuses on the blockchain technology on smart supply chain management. Accordingly, the aim is to identify emerging trends for blockchain technology on smart supply chain management by using Vosviewer from systematic literature review perspective.

DOI: 10.4018/979-8-3693-0210-1.ch004

1. INTRODUCTION

Smart supply chain management aims to transact more efficiently, quickly and flexibly by integrating artificial intelligence, big data analytics, machine learning and other digital technologies into traditional supply chain management processes (Zhang et al., 2023). With globalization and digitalization reaching significant dimensions, integrating digital technologies into business models is extremely important (Dallasega et al., 2018). Blockchain (BC) technology is an important tool in smart supply chain management (Jum'a, 2023). BC is a decentralized and transparent database technology in which digital data is held in chain-linked blocks (Jain and Chugh, 2021). In this way, BC technology offers a reliable and tamper-proof structure (Choi, 2020). With the rapid development of technology and finding suitable solutions, the potential of BC in smart supply chain management is increasing (Han & Fang, 2023). Businesses are now compelled to undergo a digital transformation and seamlessly integrate BC technology into their smart supply chain management strategies (Jayashri et al., 2023; Ghazanfari et al., 2019). Recognizing and analyzing opportunities in this context is imperative for organizations seeking to stay competitive. Consequently, a comprehensive understanding of the emerging trends for BC technology in smart supply chain management becomes essential. Despite the existing limited studies, acknowledging and actively adapting to these emerging trends is crucial for businesses looking to strengthen their position in the rapidly evolving landscape of smart supply chain management.

To fill the gap of knowledge and to contribute to the literature, this study aims to answer the following questions:

- **Research Question 1:** What are the main issues addressed with BC technology in smart supply chain management?
- **Research Question 2:** What are the emerging trends for BC technology in smart supply chain management?

To find an answer to these research questions, the present study focuses on BC technology in smart supply chain management. Accordingly, the main aim is to identify emerging trends for BC technology on smart supply chain management using Vos Viewer from a systematic literature review perspective. The main contribution of this study is presenting the importance of BC technology in smart supply chain management, thereby expanding theoretical and practical knowledge. Furthermore, the revealed knowledge gap can give future researchers an idea to focus on this field. The results are expected to benefit the business management field and contribute to future research. The following section explains BC technology on smart supply chain management in detail.

2. THEORETICAL BACKGROUND

2.1. BC Technology

The globalizing world order, increasingly complex business processes and supply chain structures cause the adoption of new technologies and the implementation of new applications (Rajasekaran et al., 2022). Originally conceived for Bitcoin, BC technology represents a revolutionary approach to decentralized transaction and data management. It empowers individuals and businesses by securely storing and exchanging value without relying on conventional intermediaries (Wenhua et al., 2023). At its core, BC is a pioneering data management solution that offers key benefits such as data immutability, transparency, traceability, and security (Hefny et al., 2023). This cutting-edge concept allows for the storage of databases in a decentralized and immutable fashion, revolutionizing how we think about data management (Salih & Mhlanga, 2023).

In simpler terms, blockchain (BC) serves as an incorruptible digital information exchange network, going beyond merely recording the history of financial transactions, as seen in the case of Bitcoin, to encompass the storage of any valuable information (Hefny et al., 2023). Originally conceived to facilitate transactions in the realm of Bitcoin, a decentralized digital cryptocurrency operating independently of a central bank (Lai and Lo, 2023), blockchain technology has evolved into a versatile and secure platform for a wide array of applications beyond financial transactions. Its inherent ability to ensure transparency, immutability, and decentralized control makes it a valuable tool for various industries seeking reliable and tamper-proof record-keeping systems.

BC is a distributed ledger designed to establish an enduring repository and monitoring system for transactional data. A distributed ledger represents a distinctive database form collaboratively shared, duplicated, synchronized, and upheld by participants within a decentralized network (Trivedi, 2023). This technology ensures that any authorized entity can scrutinize the data residing on the blockchain, offering transparency and accountability. Furthermore, data stored within the blockchain cannot be subject to deletion or modification. Any updates require stringent validation through network consensus algorithms, as Vaigandla et al. (2023) stipulated. BC technology is a fully distributed system for cryptographically archiving a consistent, immutable and linear log of event transactions between actors in the same network (Singla & Rana,2023).

BC technology has potential uses in many different industries and applications. These areas are briefly listed;

- **Cryptocurrencies:** Cryptocurrencies (e.g., Bitcoin and Ethereum) are one of the most prominent applications of BC (Ghosh et al., 2020). These digital currencies are traded in a decentralized manner and are secured using BC.
- **Smart Contracts**: BC is used to run smart contracts and works as codes that automatically execute transactions when certain conditions are met (Turjo et al., 2021).
- **Decentralized Finance (DeFi):** DeFi means recreating traditional financial instruments and services on the BC. Many services, such as lending, borrowing, liquidity, and other financial transactions, are offered on DeFi platforms.
- **Non-Fungible Token (NFT):** NFTs are BC-based tokens uniquely representing digital assets (Valeonti et al., 2021). Artworks, music, gaming items, digital collectibles, and many more can be represented as NFTs.
- **Registration and Authentication:** BC can be used for reliable and transparent record-keeping in areas such as identity verification, diploma verification, medical records management and real estate registration (Jum'a, 2023).
- **Logistics and Supply Chain Management:** BC facilitates the tracking of products and supply chain elements and makes supply chain data transparent (Jum'a, 2023). This is useful for fraud prevention, product traceability and inventory management (Tijan et al., 2019).
- **Voting Systems:** BC provides a secure and transparent framework for voting systems (Khan et al., 2018). BC-based voting systems are being developed for use in elections and referendums.
- **Health Services:** BC can store medical records and securely share health data (Gökalp et al., 2018). This allows patients to control their medical history and healthcare professionals to access accurate information.
- **Energy Sector:** BC records and shares data regarding energy consumption and production. This can increase energy efficiency and help use energy resources more effectively (Wang and Su, 2020).
- **Education:** BC prevents diploma fraud and reliably verifies academic achievements (Bhaskar et al., 2021).

In recent years, especially with the changes in supply chains, the use of BC technologies has become important. With changes in business models, multi-stakeholder supply chains and the complexity of operations, the concept of a smart supply chain has come to the fore (Mirdad et al., 2023; Rasi & Dolat-Abadi, 2022). Therefore, before discussing the use of BC technology in smart supply chains, it is extremely important to understand it in detail.

Smart supply chains are a modern business model offering a more efficient, flexible and technology-oriented approach than traditional ones (Akyuz and Gursoy, 2020).

These supply chains optimize their operations by actively using data and technology in all processes, from the supply of products or services to their production, from storage to distribution (Mondol, 2021; Doalt-Abadi, 2021). Certainly, the adoption of smart supply chains has witnessed a notable increase in recent years, propelled by the rapid pace of technological advancements (Gohil and Thakker, 2021). Major corporations are actively embracing this innovative approach as a strategic move to secure a competitive edge in the market. By doing so, these companies aim to enhance their ability to deliver products and services with greater speed, efficiency, and sustainability. The integration of smart technologies into supply chain management not only streamlines operations but also enables organizations to adapt to changing market dynamics and consumer demands, reinforcing their position as industry leaders committed to delivering value through cutting-edge and sustainable practices. In considering literature, "smart supply chain" and "digital supply chain" terms are used interchangeably (Bentaher & Rajaa, 2022). Therefore, digital transformation in smart supply chains refers to the widespread adoption of digital technologies to make traditional supply chains more efficient, flexible and competitive (Korpela et al., 2017). One of these technologies is BC technology. BC technology provides secure and traceable data sharing in smart supply chains, building trust among all supply chain stakeholders (Rana et al., 2021). BC is used to verify the origin, supply chain history and quality of products, thus preventing counterfeiting and increasing the security of products. In addition, thanks to the BC, supply chain processes can be managed more transparently and efficiently, helping to reduce logistics problems and errors (Treiblmaier et al., 2022). BC technology has become an extremely important issue in smart supply chains for these purposes. The following section describes BC technology on smart supply chain management.

2.2. BC Technology on Smart Supply Chain Management

Smart supply chain refers to a more efficient, effective and technology-oriented approach beyond traditional supply chain management approaches (Khan & Keramati, 2023). This approach aims to make supply chain processes smarter and data-driven (Prieto et al., 2023). With the globalizing world and the advancement of technologies, the concept of a smart supply chain has become more prominent. The relationship between the global world and the smart supply chain can be explained in a context where technological advances in supply chain management are becoming increasingly important, starting with the complexity and size of global trade (Han & Fang, 2023). In the global world, while products and services are traded worldwide, supply chain stakeholders in different geographies cooperate to transport and trade materials, components and products. This causes supply chain processes to take on a complex and more vulnerable structure (Prieto et al., 2023).

A smart supply chain is an approach developed to manage this complexity, increase efficiency and make the supply chain more competitive (Han & Fang, 2023). This approach aims to optimize supply chain processes using big data analytics, artificial intelligence, IoT (Internet of Things) devices, BC technology and other digital tools (Kashem et al., 2023). Data analytics, for example, helps manage global supply chains more effectively by collecting supply chain data, extracting valuable insights from that data, and making better decisions. In other words, the smart supply chain includes a set of technological tools and strategies used to improve supply chain management and reduce complexity in the global world (Jayashri et al., 2023), and this enables organizations to better meet the demands and challenges of global trade by creating more efficient, transparent and faster supply chains.

As mentioned before, smart supply chains are a modern approach developed using technologies that enable supply chains to be managed in a more efficient, reliable and transparent manner (Zhang et al., 2023). Many technological developments are involved in this approach, including BC technology (Jain and Chugh, 2021). BC operates under the governance of a peer-to-peer network, where participants collaborate in real time to tackle intricate mathematical challenges, a process essential for validating new blocks (Gupta 2018). Data recorded within a block enjoys an inherent quality of immutability; it cannot be altered retroactively without necessitating modifications to all subsequent blocks. This requires obtaining consensus from most network participants (Kizza, 2020). This can be shown as the main reason why BC technology is secure. Some sources state this issue as "a BC is a diary that is almost impossible to counterfeit." (Leeming et al., 2019).

Moreover, BC technology in smart supply chain management is an essential digital innovation tool that allows supply chains to be managed more quickly, transparently and effectively (Jum'a, 2023). Ensuring that data is stored reliably and transparently allows supply chain processes to be managed more efficiently and securely (Liu et al., 2023). As smart supply chains become more complex, involve various stakeholders and rely primarily on several external intermediaries, BC exists as a critical technology to solve all data/document/communication exchanges occurring in the supply chain ecosystem (Choi, 2020). Therefore, it is of great importance to make smart supply chains more competitive and reliable. The benefits of BC technology in smart supply chain management can be summarized in Figure 1.

Figure 1. Benefits of BC technology in smart supply chain management

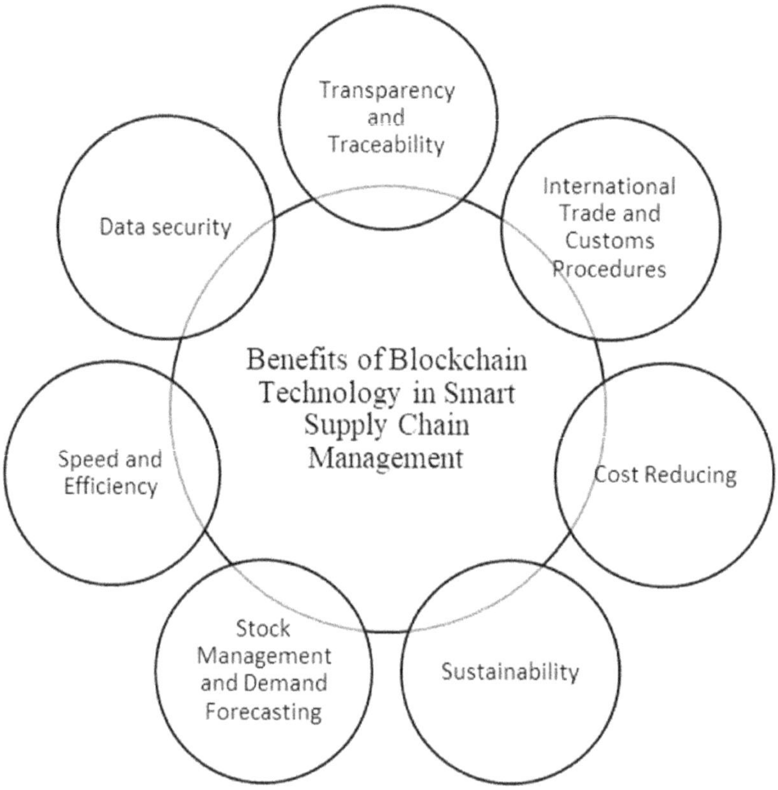

By considering these benefits, they can be explained briefly:

- **Transparency and Traceability:** BC technology allows transparency recording and monitoring of all smart supply chain processes. This makes it possible to reliably track all steps from material sources to the final product.
- **International Trade and Custom Procedures:** BC technology has the potential to revolutionize international trade and customs procedures by increasing transparency, reducing fraud, increasing efficiency and increasing trust between participants.
- **Cost Reducing:** BC automates supply chain transactions and reduces intermediaries. This reduces transaction costs. It can reduce costs during currency conversion and payment transactions, especially in international trade.

- **Sustainability:** BC enables raw materials to be traced back to their source. This enables sustainability and environmental impacts to be monitored and traced.
- **Stock Management and Demand Forecasting:** BC monitoring of every stage of stock, inventory and demand can be achieved with BC technology. This helps better plan supply chain processes and reduce unnecessary stocks.
- **Speed and Efficiency:** This technology automates processes and enables faster and more efficient operations.
- **Data Security:** BC increases data security by using strong cryptography. This makes supply chain processes less sensitive to data leaks and more resilient to attacks.

These benefits of BC technology to smart supply chains enable supply chain management to become more effective, efficient and reliable. However, since the implementation process is complex and costly, it must be planned and implemented carefully.

Although studies on the subject have increased in recent years, the study of BC technology in smart supply chains is a relatively new situation. For example, Zhang et al. (2023) focused on a literature review of smart supply chain management in Industry 4.0. According to Viriyasitavat et al. (2022), they were focused on how BC technology can be applied to smart supply chains in an operational sense from a different perspective. Moreover, Turjo et al. (2021) focused on the benefits of BC and smart contracts in the smart supply chain. By considering the literature review as a research gap, although BC technology is a topic that has existed in the past, supply chains have become a popular topic in the last few years, especially in terms of smart supply chains. The beginning of detailed studies on the use of BC technology in smart supply chains dates back to recent times. In this context, there is a need for detailed studies on the subject.

3. METHODOLOGY

Bibliometric analysis is a research methodology that evaluates the quantitative and qualitative characteristics of scientific research, publications and research fields by examining scientific publications and their citations (Donthu et al., 2021). Bibliometric analyses are used to understand the evolution of scientific research, scientific impact, the evolution of research fields and the structure of scientific communities (Zhang et al., 2023). These analyses provide important information to researchers in decision-making processes, determining research strategies, and identifying gaps in the literature.

VOS viewer is software used to visualize bibliometric data, and this software presents the relationships of scientific articles, authors, words and topics with each other in visual forms such as network maps, line graphs and word clouds (Ullah et al., 2023). VOS viewer provides a better understanding of the structures and trends of scientific communities and is frequently used to analyze scientific publications and identify important keywords in the literature (Oladinrin et al., 2023). In other words, VOS viewer is a powerful tool for visualizing bibliometric analyses and is useful for understanding relationships between research areas, authors, and topics (Sharma et al., 2023). In this study, bibliometric analysis is performed with Vos Viewer in order to determine emerging trends for BC technology in smart supply chain management and to understand current trends.

To sum up, first of all, in this study, a detailed literature review will be carried out with blockchain technology on smart supply chains. This literature review will be completed with data obtained from WOS and SCOPUS databases. Afterwards, bibliometric analysis will be performed with Vos Viewer.

4. IMPLEMENTATION AND RESULTS OF THE CURRENT RESEARCH TRENDS

In implementing this study, firstly, a literature review is conducted in WoS and SCOPUS databases, and the studies between the years 2020-2023 are examined. In this study, WoS and SCOPUS databases are scanned. In terms of research area, critical keywords, which are "smart supply chain" OR "digital supply chain" AND "blockchain" OR "blockchain technology" OR "blockchain" are selected. As mentioned before, "smart supply chain" and "digital supply chain" terms are used interchangeably (Bentaher & Rajaa, 2022). Therefore, to ignore the study in terms of literature review, there is also a "digital supply chain" in the keywords. Vos viewer software is used to determine emerging trends for BC technology in smart supply chain management in line with the results and keywords. Before moving the results of the analysis, the conceptual model of the research process is given in Figure 2.

Figure 2. Conceptual model of research process

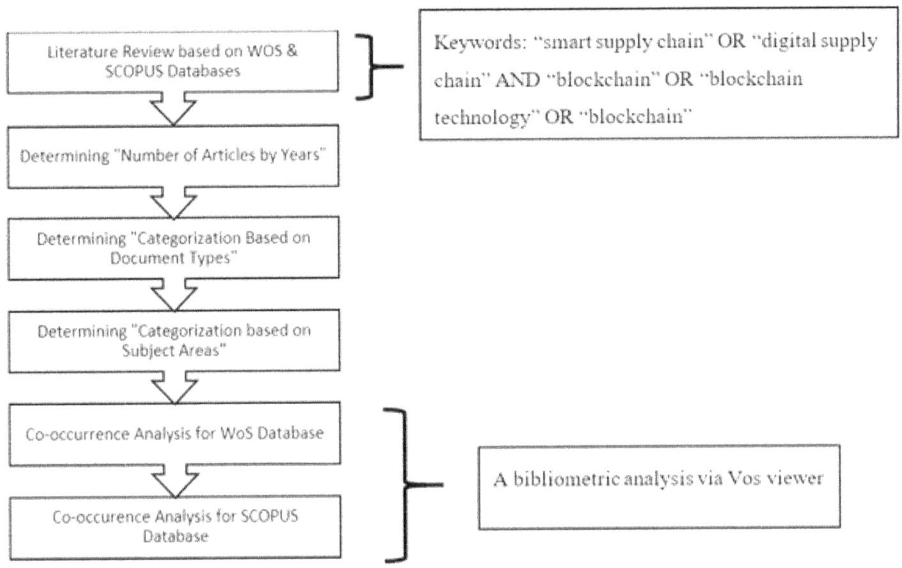

As a result of the literature review, 97 studies are found in the WoS database between 2020-2023. Afterward, 113 studies were identified as a result of the search made for the same years with the exact keywords in the SCOPUS database. It is revealed that 48 studies are in these two databases. Therefore, the total number of articles is determined as 162 between the years of 2020-2023. The distribution of the studies by years is shown in Figure 3.

Figure 3. Number of articles by years

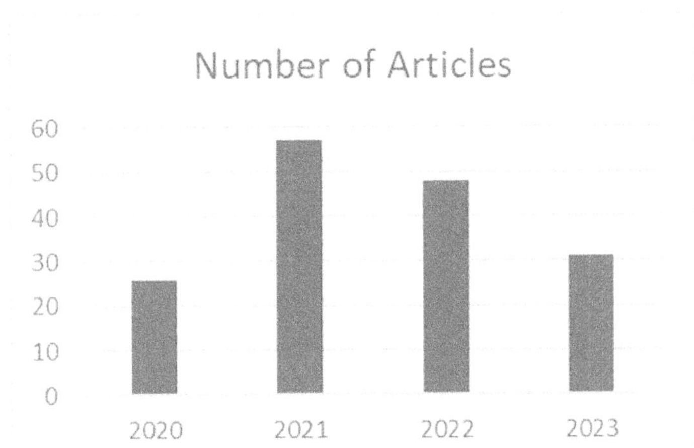

Moreover, as shown in Figure 4, more than half of the studies were prepared as articles. In addition, there are conference papers, proceeding papers, and review types. This situation shows various studies on the subject, but it still needs to be developed theoretically.

Figure 4. Categorization based on document types

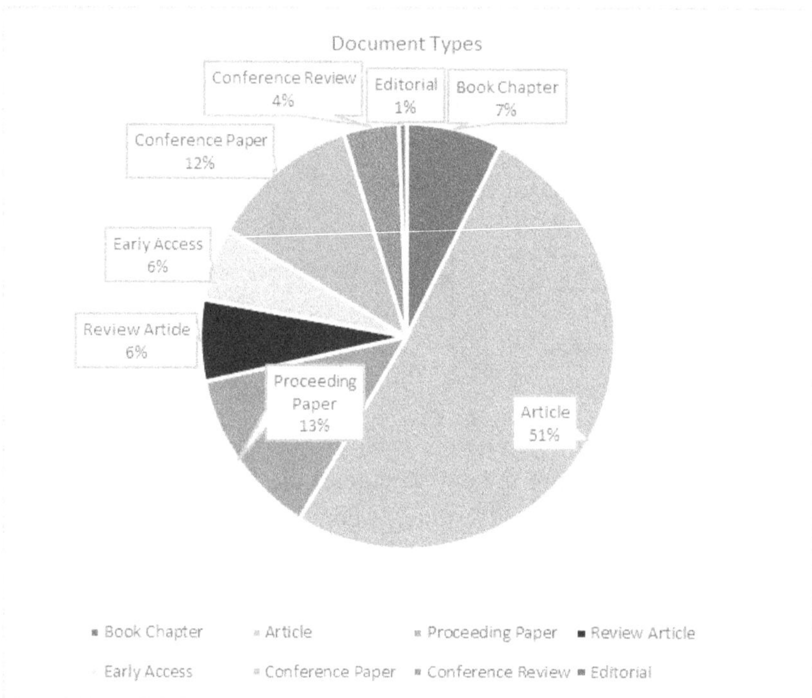

According to the results of the WoS and SCOPUS databases, the subject areas of the studies on the subject vary. Most studies on the subject were obtained in the fields of computer science (26%) and engineering (21%). Decision sciences (19%), business, management and accounting (16%), social sciences (6%) and environmental sciences (6%) follow these two fields, respectively.

Figure 5. Categorization based on subject areas

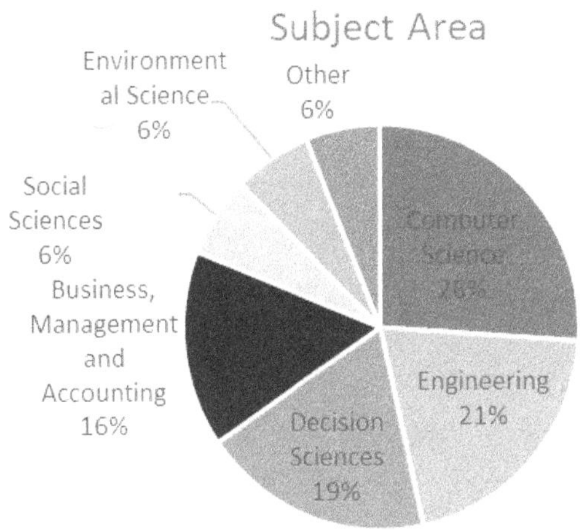

A bibliometric analysis is conducted via Vos viewer after a literature review via WoS and SCOPUS databases. With the Vos viewer program, network maps of individual keywords for WOS and SCOPUS databases were prepared with a focus on the co-occurrence of keywords, and the network maps are shown in Figure 6 and Figure 7, respectively. For the WoS database, words with at least three common links were selected, and an image consisting of 23 keywords was created using 333 keywords (Figure 6.) Similarly, words with at least three common links are chosen for the SCOPUS database using 174 keywords. A visual consisting of keywords was created (Figure 7).

In these maps, the keywords are given as circles, and the relations of the keywords with each other are distributed according to the color codes. The item's size represents the keyword's weight, while the lines between the items represent the relationships between them. The closeness of items or clusters indicates the strength of the relationship between them. Figures 6 and 7 show that the keywords are divided into 4 clusters: yellow, blue, green and red.

Figure 6. Co-occurrence analysis for WoS database

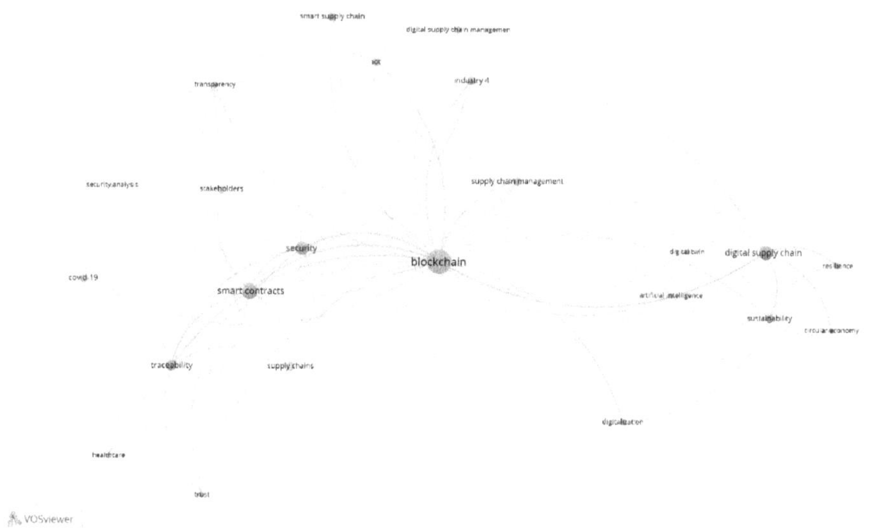

From the WoS database point of view, according to Figure 6, the yellow cluster is the weakest cluster, with only four items. The blue cluster has five items. Moreover, the red and green cluster is the strongest with seven items. Based on each cluster, the yellow cluster covers "security analysis", "Covıd-19" "stakeholders," and "supply chain" items. These items relate to other clusters and, due to the structure of these items, form the theoretical infrastructure for smart supply chain and BC issues.

Moreover, the blue cluster covers the benefits of BC issues such as "traceability, "smart contract", "security", "trust," and "healthcare". Moreover, their strong relationship with each other means that these items are covered in studies together.

In addition, the green cluster covers the digitalization process "Industry 4.0", "transparency", "smart supply chain", "digital supply chain management", "IoT", "supply chain management," and "BC" items. All of these items have a relation with each other.

The red cluster consists of "digital supply chain", "digital twin", "artificial intelligence", "sustainability", "resilience", "circular economy," and "digitalization" items. This cluster includes more digitalization and specific concepts. Sustainability, resilience and circular economy concepts are extremely critical these days.

Figure 7. Co-occurrence analysis for SCOPUS database

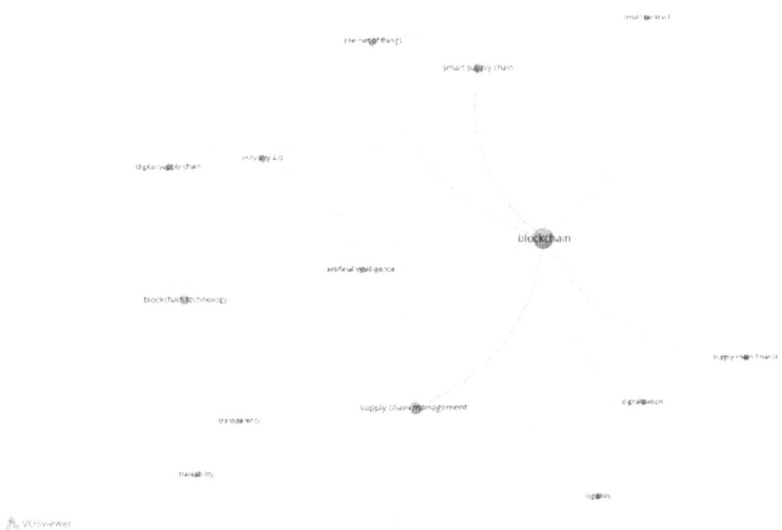

According to Figure 7, the yellow cluster is the weakest, with only two items. The blue cluster has three items, and the green cluster has four items. Moreover, the red cluster is the strongest cluster with five items. Based on each cluster, the yellow cluster has "transparency" and "traceability" items, which benefit this subject area. "Traceability" and "transparency" item has a direct relation with "blockchain". Moreover, the "transparency" item has a direct relation with the "smart supply chain" item. This means that "transparency", "traceability", and "smart supply chains" are discussed in common in studies in this area.

Moreover, the blue cluster covers digital transformation items such as the "internet of things", "smart contract," and "smart supply chain". "Internet of things", "smart contract," and "smart supply chain" have a direct relation with "blockchain" items. This means that these items are covered in studies related to blockchain.

In addition, for the green cluster, some technologies and digitalization processes are covered with "Industry 4.0", "digitalization", "blockchain technology", "digital supply chain," and "artificial intelligence" items. All of these items have a relation with each other and also have a direct relation with "blockchain" items.

A bibliometric analysis of co-authorship in WoS and SCOPUS databases was also performed to map which authors collaborated in emerging trends for BC technology in smart supply chain management research. Still, due to limited studies, only seven authors were associated with each other in the WoS database, while no authors were found in the SCOPUS database. It could not be obtained. The findings show that collaboration between authors from different studies is currently weak in this area. In the following section, managerial insights are given.

5. MANAGERIAL INSIGHTS

As a result of the research, it becomes clear that some managerial perspectives should be taken into account in terms of the scarcity of academic studies and the gaps in sectoral practices. Beginning with trust and transparency issues as managerial insights, since blockchain technology increases trust and transparency in supply chain management, managers must be able to adapt to this process fully. Thus, they can make the supply chain more transparent and perform reliable monitoring by accessing real-time data at every stage of smart supply chain processes.

Additionally, blockchain enables more effective collaboration between supply chain stakeholders. However, this collaboration involves the interaction of many stakeholders, so managers must establish appropriate mechanisms to coordinate the system among all stakeholders effectively. Moreover, blockchain ensures data security using strong cryptography. However, to manage access control to data and protect privacy, administrators must implement effective security policies and technical measures.

Another managerial insight is; is the integration of blockchain technology into smart supply chain systems. This integration should be planned carefully, and training programs should be organized so that employees can use this technology effectively. Furthermore, the costs and potential savings of blockchain applications should be analyzed. Managers should take a strategic approach to implementing this technology by making an accurate cost-benefit analysis. Additionally, it is important to understand the industry-specific regulations and compliance requirements where blockchain applications are located. Managers must have a constantly updated knowledge base and manage supply chain applications within this framework. By paying attention to these recommendations, it is possible to integrate blockchain technology in smart supply chains successfully. However, since the needs of every organization are different, it is important to develop strategies taking into account specific situations. In the following section, discussions and conclusions are given.

6. DISCUSSIONS AND CONCLUSIONS

Smart supply chain is a concept created by integrating digital technologies and data analytics into traditional supply chain management processes. The need for BC technology for smart supply chain management has become evident today as the complexity of supply chains has increased, and reliability has become even more important. BC technology is changing smart supply chain management in an extremely important way. It helps increase trust among smart supply chain stakeholders and reduce fraud by allowing data to be recorded securely, immutable and transparently. In addition, it makes smart supply chain processes faster, more efficient and more reliable, with advantages such as traceability, data security and automation. It also provides the advantage of automating transactions using smart contracts. Sustainability monitoring is also important in facilitating international trade and financing opportunities.

Although BC technology in smart supply chains is a subject that has increased rapidly in recent years, it has been seen that there is a need for more detailed and academic studies as a result of the literature review. The Keywords obtained from bibliometric analysis remained limited even though two databases were examined. The limited number of keywords reveals the need for in-depth research in the field.

As seen from the relations of the keywords, although the "blockchain" and "supply chain management" issues are discussed, the necessity of increasing the "resilience", "circular economy," and "sustainability" links of these issues come to the fore. Furthermore, although "traceability", "trust", and "transparency" issues are directly linked with blockchain, they should be handled under the security issue and studied from a practical perspective.

Based on the results of this study, for future research, the fact that "stakeholders" are among the important keywords also shows that industry collaboration platforms should be increased in a practical sense. Issues such as the spread of smart contracts, traceability and reliability problems, and sustainability monitoring should be detailed theoretically.

Moreover, the fact that the relationship between the authors is limited according to the co-author data obtained from the Vos viewer reveals the necessity of making international collaborations and increasing the number of studies on this subject. In this way, it will be possible to enrich the literature with the geographical distribution of the theoretical infrastructure and practical applications.

This study aims to reveal the gaps related to the subject by considering BC technology in smart supply chains and sharing information for the issues that need to be focused on. In future studies, keywords can be handled more specifically, focusing on different areas within the framework of the same subject.

REFERENCES

Akyuz, G. A., & Gursoy, G. (2020). Transformation of supply chain activities in blockchain environment. *Digital Business Strategies in Blockchain Ecosystems: Transformational Design and Future of Global Business*, 153-175.

Bentaher, C., & Rajaa, M. (2022). Supply Chain Management 4.0: A Literature Review and Research Framework. *European Journal of Business and Management Research, 7*(1), 117–127. doi:10.24018/ejbmr.2022.7.1.1246

Bhaskar, P., Tiwari, C. K., & Joshi, A. (2021). Blockchain in education management: Present and future applications. *Interactive Technology and Smart Education, 18*(1), 1–17. doi:10.1108/ITSE-07-2020-0102

Dallasega, P., Rauch, E., & Linder, C. (2018). Industry 4.0 as an enabler of proximity for construction supply chains: A systematic literature review. *Computers in Industry, 99*, 205–225. doi:10.1016/j.compind.2018.03.039

Dolat-Abadi, H. M. (2021). Optimizing decisions of fresh-product members in daily and bourse markets considering the quantity and quality deterioration: A waste-reduction approach. *Journal of Cleaner Production, 283*, 124647. doi:10.1016/j.jclepro.2020.124647

Donthu, N., Kumar, S., Mukherjee, D., Pandey, N., & Lim, W. M. (2021). How to conduct a bibliometric analysis: An overview and guidelines. *Journal of Business Research, 133*, 285–296. doi:10.1016/j.jbusres.2021.04.070

Ghazanfari, M., Mohammadi, H., Pishvaee, M. S., & Teimoury, E. (2019). Fresh-product trade management under government-backed incentives: A case study of the fresh flower market. *IEEE Transactions on Engineering Management, 66*(4), 774–787. doi:10.1109/TEM.2018.2888982

Ghosh, A., Gupta, S., Dua, A., & Kumar, N. (2020). Security of Cryptocurrencies in blockchain technology: State-of-art, challenges and future prospects. *Journal of Network and Computer Applications, 163*, 102635. doi:10.1016/j.jnca.2020.102635

Gohil, D., & Thakker, S. V. (2021). Blockchain-integrated technologies for solving supply chain challenges. *Modern Supply Chain Research and Applications, 3*(2), 78–97. doi:10.1108/MSCRA-10-2020-0028

Gökalp, E., Gökalp, M. O., Çoban, S., & Eren, P. E. (2018). Analyzing opportunities and challenges of integrated blockchain technologies in healthcare. *Information Systems: Research, Development, Applications, Education: 11th SIGSAND/PLAIS EuroSymposium 2018, Gdansk, Poland, September 20, 2018. Proceedings, 11*, 174–183.

Han, Y., & Fang, X. (2023). Systematic review of adopting blockchain in supply chain management: Bibliometric analysis and theme discussion. *International Journal of Production Research*, 1–26. doi:10.1080/00207543.2023.2236241

Hefny, M. H. M., Helmy, Y., & Abdelsalam, M. (2023). Open Banking API Framework to Improve the Online Transaction between Local Banks in Egypt Using Blockchain Technology. *Journal of Advances in Information Technology, 14*(4), 729–740. doi:10.12720/jait.14.4.729-740

Jayashri, N., Rampur, V., Gangodkar, D., Abirami, M., Balarengadurai, C., & Kumar, A. (2023). Improved block chain system for high secured IoT integrated supply chain. *Measurement. Sensors, 25*, 100633. doi:10.1016/j.measen.2022.100633

Jum'a, L. (2023). The role of blockchain-enabled supply chain applications in improving supply chain performance: The case of Jordanian manufacturing sector. *Management Research Review, 46*(10), 1315–1333. doi:10.1108/MRR-04-2022-0298

Kashem, M. A., Shamsuddoha, M., Nasir, T., & Chowdhury, A. A. (2023). Supply Chain Disruption versus Optimization: A Review on Artificial Intelligence and Blockchain. *Knowledge (Beverly Hills, Calif.), 3*(1), 80–96.

Khan, K., & Keramati, A. (2023). A Framework for Smart Supply Chain Risk Assessment: An Empirical Study. *International Journal of Information Systems and Supply Chain Management, 16*(1), 1–17. doi:10.4018/IJISSCM.316167

Khan, K. M., Arshad, J., & Khan, M. M. (2018). Secure digital voting system based on blockchain technology. *International Journal of Electronic Government Research, 14*(1), 53–62. doi:10.4018/IJEGR.2018010103

Korpela, K., Hallikas, J., & Dahlberg, T. (2017). *Digital supply chain transformation toward blockchain integration*. Academic Press.

Lai, Z., & Lo, E. (2023). Blockchains for Business–Permissioned Blockchains. *Blockchains: Empowering Technologies and Industrial Applications*.

Liu, R., Ran, W., & Liu, S. (2023). Blockchain Technology Applied to Supply Chain Management: A Systems' Analysis. *Mobile Information Systems, 2023*, 2023. doi:10.1155/2023/6046503

Mirdad, A., Hussain, F. K., & Hussain, O. K. (2023). A systematic literature review on pharmaceutical supply chain: Research gaps and future opportunities. *International Journal of Web and Grid Services, 19*(2), 233–258. doi:10.1504/IJWGS.2023.131243

Mondol, E. P. (2021). The impact of block chain and smart inventory system on supply chain performance at retail industry. *International Journal of Computations, Information and Manufacturing, 1*(1).

Oladinrin, O. T., Arif, M., Rana, M. Q., & Gyoh, L. (2023). Interrelations between construction ethics and innovation: A bibliometric analysis using VOSviewer. *Construction Innovation, 23*(3), 505–523. doi:10.1108/CI-07-2021-0130

Prieto, N. P., & Martín-Peña, M. L. (2023). The smart supply chain: A conceptual cyclic framework. *Journal of Industrial Engineering and Management, 16*(1), 54–77. doi:10.3926/jiem.4018

Rajasekaran, A. S., Azees, M., & Al-Turjman, F. (2022). A comprehensive survey on blockchain technology. *Sustainable Energy Technologies and Assessments, 52*, 102039. doi:10.1016/j.seta.2022.102039

Rana, S. K., Kim, H. C., Pani, S. K., Rana, S. K., Joo, M. I., Rana, A. K., & Aich, S. (2021). Blockchain-based model to improve the performance of the next-generation digital supply chain. *Sustainability (Basel), 13*(18), 10008. doi:10.3390u131810008

Rasi, M., & Mohammadi Dolat-Abadi, H. (2022). Proposing a framework for identifying the competitive advantage of small and medium-sized manufacturing organizations under uncertainty conditions. *Journal of Decisions and Operations Research, 7*(4), 515-529.

Salih, S., & Mhlanga, D. (2023). Blockchain for Food Supply Chain: Trust, Traceability, and Transparency Enhancement, How Can Africa Benefit? *The Fourth Industrial Revolution in Africa: Exploring the Development Implications of Smart Technologies in Africa*, 311-325.

Sharma, A., Sharma, A., Bhatia, T., & Singh, R. K. (2023). Blockchain enabled food supply chain management: A systematic literature review and bibliometric analysis. *Operations Management Research*, 1-25.

Singla, D., & Rana, S. (2023). Blockchain-Based Platform for Smart Tracking and Tracing the Pharmaceutical Drug Supply Chain. In *Examining Multimedia Forensics and Content Integrity* (pp. 144–172). IGI Global. doi:10.4018/978-1-6684-6864-7.ch006

Taherdoost, H. (2023). Smart Contracts in Blockchain Technology: A Critical Review. *Information (Basel)*, *14*(2), 117. doi:10.3390/info14020117

Tijan, E., Aksentijević, S., Ivanić, K., & Jardas, M. (2019). Blockchain technology implementation in logistics. *Sustainability (Basel)*, *11*(4), 1185. doi:10.3390u11041185

Treiblmaier, H., Rejeb, A., & Ahmed, W. A. (2022). Blockchain technologies in the digital supply chain. *The Digital Supply Chain*, 127-144.

Trivedi, S. (2023). An Umbrella Review of the Literature on Blockchain and Distributed Ledger Technology and Their Roles in Future Banking. *Perspectives on Blockchain Technology and Responsible Investing*, 29-57.

Turjo, M. D., Khan, M. M., Kaur, M., & Zaguia, A. (2021). Smart supply chain management using the blockchain and smart contract. *Scientific Programming*, *2021*, 1–12. doi:10.1155/2021/6092792

Ullah, F., Shen, L., & Shah, S. H. H. (2023). Value co-creation in business-to-business context: A bibliometric analysis using HistCite and VOS viewer. *Frontiers in Psychology*, *13*, 1027775. doi:10.3389/fpsyg.2022.1027775 PMID:36710832

Vaigandla, K. K., Karne, R., Siluveru, M., & Kesoju, M. (2023). Review on Blockchain Technology: Architecture, Characteristics, Benefits, Algorithms, Challenges and Applications. *Mesopotamian Journal of CyberSecurity*, *2023*, 73–85.

Valeonti, F., Bikakis, A., Terras, M., Speed, C., Hudson-Smith, A., & Chalkias, K. (2021). Crypto collectibles, museum funding and OpenGLAM: Challenges, opportunities and the potential of Non-Fungible Tokens (NFTs). *Applied Sciences (Basel, Switzerland)*, *11*(21), 9931. doi:10.3390/app11219931

Viriyasitavat, W., Bi, Z., & Hoonsopon, D. (2022). Blockchain technologies for interoperation of business processes in smart supply chains. *Journal of Industrial Information Integration*, *26*, 100326. doi:10.1016/j.jii.2022.100326

Wang, Q., & Su, M. (2020). Integrating blockchain technology into the energy sector—From theory of blockchain to research and application of energy blockchain. *Computer Science Review*, *37*, 100275. doi:10.1016/j.cosrev.2020.100275

Wenhua, Z., Qamar, F., Abdali, T. A. N., Hassan, R., Jafri, S. T. A., & Nguyen, Q. N. (2023). Blockchain technology: Security issues, healthcare applications, challenges and future trends. *Electronics (Basel)*, *12*(3), 546. doi:10.3390/electronics12030546

Zhang, A., Duong, L., Seuring, S., & Hartley, J. L. (2023). Circular supply chain management: A bibliometric analysis-based literature review. *International Journal of Logistics Management*, *34*(3), 847–872. doi:10.1108/IJLM-04-2022-0199

Zhang, G., Yang, Y., & Yang, G. (2023). Smart supply chain management in Industry 4.0: The review, research agenda and strategies in North America. *Annals of Operations Research*, *322*(2), 1075–1117. doi:10.100710479-022-04689-1 PMID:35531562

Chapter 5 The Impact of IoT on Intelligent Businesses

Hesamoddin Motevalli
Faculty of Engineering, University of Eyvanekey, Semnan, Iran

ABSTRACT

IoT is about improving trade forms and arrangements using sensors, gadgets, doors, and stages. Utilizing the IoT by collecting all data in one put, producers can make intelligent decisions in their business and design more efficient and optimal processes. Therefore, the IoT can be useful for companies by reducing costs, increasing efficiency, progressing client involvement and fulfillment, and expanding dynamism and adaptability. As a result, by utilizing the IoT in businesses, they have lower upkeep costs and superior disappointment administration. In an inventive trade, an observing framework based on the IoT predicts issues and permits ideal time planning for exercises. By utilizing the IoT, companies can robotize forms and decrease labor costs. It also moves forward benefit conveyance and gives transparency in exchanges to the client. In this respect, this chapter bargains with the essential definition of the IoT, the sorts of IoT gadgets, how to utilize them in businesses, the reason for clever companies, and when it is considered intelligent.

1. INTRODUCTION

IoT is difficult to define for two reasons. First, there are a variety of uses for IoT, like lighting homes, halting trains, and monitoring supply chains. Since IoT technologies have diverse applications, it can be challenging to identify the precise characteristics that link them. Second, technology is frequently mentioned as a triangle component at the heart of the Fourth Industrial Revolution (4IR), along with Artificial Intelligence

DOI: 10.4018/979-8-3693-0210-1.ch005

(AI) and Big Data. This classification makes sense because IoT is a source of the Big Data required to develop AI algorithms, but because of this linkage, we know very little about IoT itself. So, with numerous viewpoints on the technology, the definitions of IoT have evolved throughout the years (Chadli et al., 2022).

IoT can be defined as a network of networked devices that can share data through the Internet in its most basic form. IoT gadgets, including sensors, smart refrigerators, smart home systems, cameras, and fitness trackers, are called "Things" in this context. The term "thing" refers to any item that can connect to the Internet and is used in IoT networks. The potential for exploiting data makes it very clear how much IoT will influence business growth. Businesses may be able to make decisions more quickly because of the direct connection between sensors and real-time data transmission (Kolisnyk et al., 2022).

IoT can change the corporate and customer scene by interfacing with the physical and digital worlds. Any industry that depends on making, transporting, or offering things that weren't already associated with the Internet will benefit. The precise advantages IoT can offer a company will depend on how the technology is applied. For instance, sensors can optimize lighting or heating based on occupancy levels or decrease product spoiling in transit by keeping an eye on temperatures (Lang et al., 2021). IoT may also enhance production and bring in money. For example, acoustic offshore oilfield sensors can analyze pipeline activity to maximize output and find new resource sources. It's helpful to think about the five primary IoT capabilities, connecting, collecting, monitoring, monetizing, and optimizing, to assist in developing an understanding of the possibilities for IoT in any particular firm (Nozari & Ghahremani-Nahr, 2023).

Figure 1. Types of IoT devices

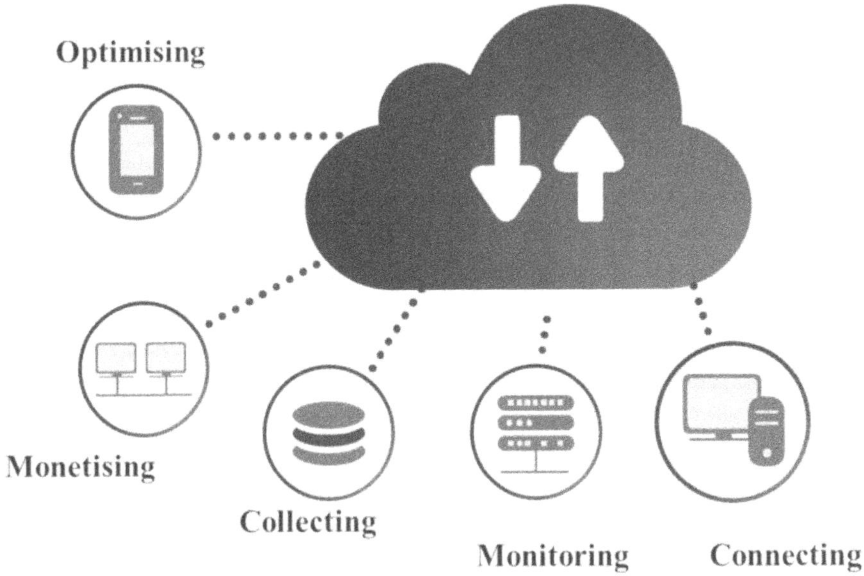

Connecting: The IoT empowers a wide run of gadgets to coordinate and interface, evacuating them from their separate silos and bridging the gap between the digital and physical or "real" worlds. The global communication system gets more stable and adaptable as devices' digital footprints grow.

Gathering: An essential element of IoT technology is the sensor. They gather information from the surface of the thing they are attached to, which can be used to inform further operations. The information collected is also valuable. Data can be gathered, anonymized, and sold to interested parties by businesses.

Monitoring: In its capacity as an aggregator, IoT makes it possible to conduct remote monitoring, offering a rich, in-depth view of the state of the world in real-time. Through preventative and predictive IoT applications, existing compliance and monitoring of processes and assets may be automated and made more effective.

Making money: IoT enables businesses and industries to become data-rich in data collection and analysis, sometimes from unexpected or difficult-to-reach places. With the addition of new functionality that may be marketed to consumers and through aggregation, anonymization, or other means, these new data streams present huge prospects for new revenue streams.

Optimizing: IoT data collection can be used to reach new levels of efficiency, potentially resulting in cost, energy, or time savings in a range of industries, from healthcare to energy.

2. USES OF IOT IN BUSINESSES

The foremost well-known uses of IoT technologies drop into the taking-after categories. Those IoT associations span the globe and over businesses, penetrating people's homes, workplaces, and cars. Automobiles that are linked are one of the foremost eminent applications of IoT. To legitimately travel streets in different activity and climate conditions, self-driving cars and trucks require an assortment of associated contraptions (Lee, 2017). Artificial intelligence (AI)-enabled cameras, movement sensors, and onboard computers are a few innovations utilized. Over the past ten years, Activity administration and roadway framework have become more interconnected. Cameras, sensors, activity light controllers, stopping meters, and even smartphone activity apps presently transmit data to assist in dodging activity blockage, anticipate mischances and guarantee smooth travel. For occasion, cameras can screen activity streams and bolster data to centralized administration groups, who can assess the information to choose whether, how, and when to execute moderation measures. The brightness of activity signals can be balanced by sensors on the developments in reaction to changes in skylight, guaranteeing that they are always evident to cars. Open stopping spaces employ associated gadgets, sending the data to applications or booths to inform drivers. Bridge screens accumulate and transmit data for essential health appraisals, caution specialists of upkeep prerequisites and time for any breakdown or issue (Remondes & Afonso, 2019).

Utilities also utilize IoT to form their energy frameworks more productive and versatile,. Energy is used to move along the lattice in a single heading from the point of creation to the customer. But as two-way communication is conceivable along the total vitality supply chain, from era to dissemination to utilization, utilities can superior transport and manage the energy. Utilities can utilize real-time data from associated gadgets to gather, evaluate, and react to vitality requests and stack changes, recognize blackouts, and reroute dissemination. Whereas this is often happening, smart meters introduced in individual homes and businesses allow customers and utility data approximately current and chronicled utilization patterns that can be analyzed to discover strategies to extend proficiency (Aliahmadi et al., 2022). IoT data that depicts the state and quality of the discuss, water, soil, fisheries, woodlands, and other typical situations can be assembled by associated gadgets. They can also collect data on the climate and the environment.

As a result, IoT makes it possible for various companies across multiple industries to use that data to gain valuable insights. It also makes obtaining substantially more real-time data about the environment at any time and place possible. Such data can aid governmental organizations in better managing and safeguarding land and wildlife populations and improved monitoring and even forecasting of natural disasters like tornadoes. Businesses can utilize this information to reduce their carbon footprint more effectively, demonstrate compliance with environmental laws, and schedule their operations to take advantage of favorable weather conditions. Building owners are utilizing IoT to make all kinds of structures smarter, making them more pleasant, convenient, healthy, and potentially safer (Samadi-Parviznejad & Soltani, 2022).

An IoT ecosystem in a commerce building might screen the HVAC framework, which consistently filters and adjusts the temperature for the most excellent conceivable energy proficiency and comfort using real-time data and automation innovation. In the meantime, AI-powered cameras may offer assistance with crowd control at occasions like sold-out concerts to preserve open security. Consumers can introduce smart domestic apparatuses, entryway locks, indoor regulators, and smoke locators, which help them with everyday needs by synchronizing temperature controls to the owners' routines. Intelligent cities are consolidating ioT establishments, traversing various aspects to give them a comprehensive understanding of what is happening in their zones. As a result, intelligent cities regularly have smart buildings and organized activity administration frameworks. They might also incorporate secretly possessed clever structures. Smart cities may also connect to smart frameworks and utilize natural observing to construct a broader IoT biological system that offers real-time sees of the distinctive variables affecting life in their districts. The objective of savvy cities, like smaller, more obliged IoT arrangements, is to assemble real-time information for an investigation that yields bits of knowledge that civil authorities can utilize for way better decision-making and automated controls to create more productive, successful, versatile, and secure communities. As an outline, the Danish capital of Copenhagen is utilizing IoT innovations to meet its objective of becoming a carbon-neutral city by 2025 (Whig et al., 2022).

On the other hand, low-power sensors, GPS, and other advances that recognize resources as they move through a supply chain have made a difference in modernizing supply chain administration. Directors can more certainly console partners of the area of things being sent or gotten and arrange their techniques more successfully utilizing this data. Although that permeability is invaluable, it speaks to the starting of the esteem IoT conveys to this field. IoT innovations can, moreover, keep track of and oversee conveyance prerequisites. For occasion, they can degree and keep up a specific temperature amid shipment to guarantee quality and security. Also, supply chain improvements like speedier shipment times or more viable courses can be found utilizing IoT-generated data and back-end analytics capabilities.

After all, IoT has numerous employments in commerce and mechanical situations, empowering everything from innovative horticulture to way better office security to prescient support. These differing utilize cases make use of a broad run of IoT innovations. A producer might use machine-to-machine-associated gadgets more accurately to outline workloads as part of a mechanical IoT sending. A producer might track how rapidly gear wears out to arrange preventive support. Bosses can oversee and control physical access to their premises utilizing staff ID identifications or wearable contraptions with RFID chips. Furthermore, agriculturists might select locational innovation coupled with natural sensors and their field hardware to automate and maximize their seed allotments.

3. BENEFITS TO BUSINESSES

Although some IoT use cases are industry-specific, most connected technology installations are similar across various enterprises and traverse all verticals. The advantages of those deployments also cut across industries. The following is a typical ROI:

- *Reduced operational expenses, greater output*
- *Higher security*
- *Improved safety*
- *Improved quality control*
- *Increased comprehension and visibility of real-world actions*

3.1. The Impact of IoT in the Business Sector

The Internet changed communication and disposed of crevices caused by removal between individuals. The approach of the IoT, be that as it may, changed the capacities of contraptions by making it conceivable for them to be associated with the Internet. Envision having a voice-activated caution clock that's online and associated with the Internet. One of the biggest concerns within the tech world is the impact of IoT on the corporate division. More than 14 billion IoT gadgets are as of now online across the globe. IoT gadgets that are associated collectively might sum to 26 billion by 2030. Nearly $750 billion was spent on IoT solutions in 2020, and $1 trillion was spent on these solutions in 2022. According to estimates made by experts, global IoT investment will reach $1.1 trillion in 2023. IoT has been used extensively in connected cars, payment terminals, and consumer media devices (Burby & Atchison, 2007).

The impact of IoT on the corporate sector has also recently gained attention. Businesses seek innovative digital transformation methods and trustworthy technologies to accomplish their goals. How will companies utilize IoT? Which IoT-related business risks and benefits are most notable? How will various business sectors use IoT? In the following guide on the effects of IoT in the business area, let's look for the answers to these questions.

3.2. IoT's Effects on Business

Answers to "What does IoT mean for businesses?" would highlight how IoT is revolutionizing business. You might be able to grasp the responses better if you have a clear picture of how the IoT has transformed many parts of corporate operations. Here are a few significant examples of how IoT has impacted corporate culture.

- **Smart Answers**

Integrating intelligent solutions is the first entry among the advantages of IoT in business. IoT facilitates the development of new intelligent products that enable improved iterations of current technical solutions. First and foremost, smart products and services can assist in gathering precise data regarding the in-use status of equipment. Businesses can then identify the best prospects for modifying their offerings to meet client needs better. IoT can also assist manufacturers in adding new features that provide customers with more excellent value than standard solutions. Smart robot vacuum cleaners and weighing scales exemplify how IoT may transform traditional products into cutting-edge technology (Hussain, 2017).

- **Streamlined Automation**

The automation process's simplicity is the following significant IoT effect on business. The IoT system allows for remote control of devices and changes to their configuration and state. On the other hand, the gadgets might send users messages with notifications and alarms. Automation procedures would be more straightforward, with the ability for two-way communication between IoT devices and users. Additionally, the potential for merging IoT with RPA could assist firms in preparing for the following stage of automation. Drones and IoT technologies can help the various supply chain management stages, such as retail stores or warehouses, to profit from automation.

- **Reduced Downtime**

How IoT devices may reduce downtime is a crucial topic of debate when discussing IoT's impact and problems on enterprises. With IoT sensors monitoring the health of various device components, the IoT has brought conceivable advancements in preventive maintenance methods. With the help of IoT technology, proactive maintenance may be ensured by providing real-time information on asset health, utilization, and failure risks. Therefore, with IoT-based monitoring systems providing optimum schedules for maintenance, organizations are less likely to incur the costs of downtime and repairs. The benefits of predictive maintenance may make it easier to produce high-value equipment quickly (Nozari et al., 2022).

- **Sustainability in the Environment**

IoT's impact on business would open up opportunities for increased environmental sustainability. Enterprises that deploy IoT-based monitoring systems have achieved yearly energy usage reductions of 5% to 15%. IoT's impact on the business world through smart devices may assist in preventing resource leaks. IoT could simultaneously assist in finding practical solutions for improving the efficiency of machinery. According to some predictions, IoT will significantly impact energy use, saving over 1.8 PWh of electricity by 2030. Smart electrical grids may be the next frontier in power distribution and effective power use. With new potential for efficient waste management, the commercial difficulties associated with IoT can be solved. Potential IoT applications are required by the requirement for enterprises to prioritize sustainability.

- **Cloud Development**

The proliferation of IoT would fuel the development of cloud technology. IoT solutions rely on cloud technology to provide the infrastructure to handle and store enormous amounts of data. IoT architecture is not complete without cloud technologies, and as IoT becomes more and more widespread, there is an increased need for cloud technology development. Most importantly, IoT applications encourage the expansion of analytics in parallel, highlighting the necessity of sufficient computational capacity for data management, storage, and analysis within the IoT ecosystem.

- **Better Asset Tracking**

IoT advantages for businesses could increase automation efficiency and better user experiences. What unique benefits does IoT hold for businesses? Real-time asset tracking is one of the most insightful responses to such queries. Companies may track their assets with IoT sensors like RFID or radio frequency identification tags. Businesses will have a clear understanding of the location of their assets, whether it be a computer utilized in the office or a product moving through the supply chain. The intelligent asset monitoring made possible by IoT technology is highlighted by the influence of IoT on business. RFID tags, for instance, might incorporate smart labels with thorough product details.

The impact of IoT on businesses demonstrates how IoT could give firms advantages based on value. When asked, "What does IoT mean for businesses?" the responses would highlight how it lowers operating expenses and boosts productivity. For instance, IoT-enabled real-time asset tracking and intelligent monitoring capabilities can simplify automated workflows and increase corporate productivity.

The ability for organizations to track, monitor, find, and analyze customer data at rapid rates is the most crucial benefit of IoT solutions. As a result, businesses may use IoT to modify their goods and services to meet changing client needs and behavioral trends.

On the other hand, a close look at the statistics on the IoT market proves why business use cases of the IoT should be considered. The answer to this question is explained under the title "What is the biggest impact of the IoT in business?" In this section, we look at how the IoT impacts operations in many different industries and businesses with unique use cases.

- **Healthcare**

Healthcare is the first sector listed among those with the best IoT use cases. The IoT can provide the building blocks for several use cases, including drug management and on-site patient experience management. To cut down on wait times, IoT can assist in monitoring the current workload of emergency departments and general practice clinics. In chronic disorders, healthcare facilities can deploy IoT for patient monitoring. For instance, fitness trackers and other wearables could provide real-time patient health monitoring (Nagy & Stukovszky, 2023).

The examples of IoT applications in healthcare also highlight the need for drug management to limit patients' access to pharmaceuticals. IoT has the potential to enhance operational effectiveness in addition to adding new dimensions to patient care. Applications for the IoT, such as smart beds and remote medical equipment monitoring, could help healthcare facilities run more efficiently. Additionally, IoT applications in healthcare can potentially increase staff operations' efficiency.

- **Manufacturing**

Manufacturing is another sector that has been aggressively implementing IoT. Asset or fleet tracking inside the supply chain is the prime example of IoT applications in manufacturing. Real-time tracking of all supply chain elements, including raw materials, finished items, and containers, might be made possible by manufacturing facilities. IoT instances in the industry have successfully ensured inventory management while reducing risks. The manufacturing sector has also implemented IoT use cases for preventative maintenance by tracking manufacturing equipment and other devices out in the field. To reduce the costs of repair and replacement, predictive maintenance assists in determining the best periods for maintenance.

Automating production workflow is a significant value-based benefit of IoT use cases for manufacturing. The top IoT use cases in manufacturing highlight digital twins, which is the most important. Before deploying machinery, problems can be identified using digital twins to evaluate real-time equipment performance.

- **Logistics**

IoT applications in logistics may be able to support IoT use cases in manufacturing. The most well-known IoT use case is fleet management features in logistics. IoT can enable real-time data regarding vehicle fleets, enabling effective monitoring of truck loads, driver behavior, and performance. In response to the question, intelligent inventory management and supply chain management would also be mentioned as the top uses of IoT in logistics. Storage space optimization might benefit from having access to real-time information about the warehouse, production, and distribution locations. Optimizing stock levels can aid in the efficient management of constrained storage space. IoT may also facilitate effective supply chain management by authenticating and tracking goods and assets (Nayyar & Kumar, 2020).

- **Transportation**

IoT can be used in the transportation sector due to the effectiveness of its applications in logistics. The best IoT use cases in the industry are those that ensure efficient fleet management of cars, trucks, bikes, buses, and other vehicles. IoT may present fresh opportunities for effective operations as demand for car rental services like Uber keeps rising. The IoT facilitates thorough vehicle position monitoring and other information like tire pressure. The IoT case studies in transportation could give a convincing idea of using the IoT in fleet maintenance. At the same time, a thorough understanding of driver performance and behavior provides valuable inputs for business choices. By determining the best route to take in various traffic scenarios, transportation companies might potentially leverage IoT for efficient navigation.

- **Utility and Energy**

IoT use cases in the energy and utilities industries would also be highlighted in the list of popular IoT applications. Solar or wind monitoring and aiding solar or wind control are notable instances of IoT uses in energy and utility monitoring. IoT can help with infrastructure monitoring for solar and wind energy generation to provide the best possible energy efficiency and quick identification of failure. The IoT may support applications in water monitoring that enable effective measurement of water pressure, salinity, turbidity, and other variables. IoT applications for the energy industry also include connected circuit breakers and meters. Through automated invoicing and issue detection, connected meters could aid in monitoring and optimizing the energy infrastructure. On the other hand, coupled circuit breakers might facilitate effective power usage metering and analysis. Real-time monitoring of power poles for preventive maintenance is another prospective application of IoT in the energy sector (Samadi-Parviznejad, 2022).

- **Private Sector**

IoT application cases in the public sector have become the most notable and well-liked. IoT used points with examples of smart cities can be found in the public sector. The IoT can help with both traffic and road management and public space surveillance. IoT devices could optimize the utilization of public places using data collected from security or CCTV camera feeds. IoT technologies could potentially direct changes in how traffic systems are set up to ensure a smoother traffic flow. The most valuable IoT use cases in smart cities include disaster avoidance and monitoring management of public transit. Most importantly, IoT use cases could create opportunities for effective waste management by monitoring trash cans.

- **Agriculture**

IoT applications in agriculture would also be clarified by the responses to the question, "Which are the biggest uses of IoT?" Environmental sensors could provide farmers with up-to-the-minute information on the weather and climate. Farmers may be able to make better judgments if they have quick access to information on soil conditions and humidity, for instance. The application of IoT in agriculture may also help to protect farms against unauthorized incursions. IoT could, therefore, contribute to optimistic increases in agricultural productivity. Smart irrigation for kiwifruit cultivation in Italy is one of the well-known instances of IoT applications in agriculture. Wireless sensor networks were developed by the Italian business FAMOSA, which specializes in technology-based agricultural support services for creating precise irrigation plans (Ghahremani-Nahr et al., 2022).

- **Retail**

The applications of the IoT in the retail industry are included in talks on the finest IoT use cases. The benefits of automated checkout using mobile POS terminals may be facilitated by IoT. IoT technologies like connected cameras, shelf sensors, AI, and smart store sensors may enhance the shopper experience. Additionally, understanding how customers behave in the business could help designers create more orderly layouts. The IoT examples in the retail sector, including automated packaging services and inventory monitoring, may offer practical strategies for improving storage management. Additionally, the retail industry could benefit from IoT's advantages for supply chain optimization and inventory management. You can also use IoT's use cases for predictive maintenance to ensure effective and optimal retail operations.

- **Actual Estate**

IoT applications in real estate lay out the foundations for creating smart houses. Applications for the IoT in real estate include waste management, predictive maintenance, and air quality monitoring. Effective air quality monitoring could increase tenant safety, and predictive maintenance enables ongoing monitoring of building components. Remote lighting control, which can increase energy efficiency, is a fascinating example of an IoT use case in real estate. Similar to that, IoT-based remote temperature management systems could enhance the lives of home dwellers. In addition to enhancing lifestyle and quality of life, smart devices may also play a significant part in lowering costs. Smart security tools like connected locks and video surveillance are among the top IoT use cases in real estate. Additionally, IoT can provide real-time monitoring of occupancy density and utility usage (Vervest, 2009).

- **Hospitality**

IoT use cases may complement the facility of cutting-edge solutions in the hospitality industry in real estate. Owners of hospitality businesses could use IoT to reduce operating expenses and enhance energy efficiency. Most importantly, IoT applications in the hospitality industry may also offer significant benefits for patron experiences. Applications for smartphones that enable users to manage the lights and other amenities in hotel rooms are examples of IoT applications. Additionally, the delivery of virtual concierge services and information services are also highlighted by the usage of IoT in the hospitality sector. IoT usage and the technological prowess of hospitality firms can increase customer confidence. Enhanced maintenance services provided by IoT apps can also benefit organizations in the hospitality industry.

4. BUSINESSES' IOT CHALLENGES

A critical factor in guiding the potential of IoT for organizations is the business difficulties in IoT. For a fair view of IoT business use cases, it is essential to have a general understanding of the implementation problems for IoT in enterprises. Here are a few significant difficulties encountered when using IoT for organizations.

4.1. Data Privacy and Security

IoT networks contain a wealth of private user information, making them an attractive target for hackers. The overview of IoT implications and data security and privacy challenges highlights the constraints of storing and exchanging data across IoT devices. With protections against hardware-based assaults, physical tampering, network-based attacks, and internet attacks, cybersecurity is a top responsibility for IoT networks. Additionally, corporations may incur significant costs due to integrating encryption and security mechanisms across a vast network of IoT devices. Businesses must simultaneously handle the requirement for compliance with data privacy laws. IoT adoption will face considerable obstacles if patient privacy rules are used effectively in healthcare and finance.

4.2. Price of Early Setup and Integration

Integrating IoT with current company systems and the upfront costs associated with setting up the IoT network are the two most prominent business hurdles in IoT. IoT protocols and standards are not widely accepted, making integrating devices difficult. For instance, each device can require a separate configuration and set of hardware connectors. Device deployment requires more time due to the technical difficulty of implementing IoT devices for businesses and thorough network assessments. The problems that IoT poses for business further highlight the expense associated with early setup. Deploying IoT devices requires significant time and financial investment from companies. Businesses would need to make a sizable upfront investment to realize the benefits of cost-effective operations, from the purchase to the setup and deployment of numerous IoT devices (Nahr et al., 2021).

5. FUTURE OF IOT AND SMART BUSINESS

The global IoT and AI market is anticipated to reach $26.79 billion by 2025, expanding at a CAGR of 29.7% from 2020 to 2025, according to a report by ResearchAndMarkets. IoT is also being utilized increasingly in agriculture to monitor crops and increase yield in addition to healthcare. The market for internet-connected things is anticipated to reach US$33.74 billion by 2027, with a startling CAGR of 11.49 between 2022 and 2027. The majority of enterprise IoT installations are in waste management, water supply, electricity, gas, and steam-retail and wholesale industries.

IoT has the potential to have an infinite future. Increased network agility, integrated artificial intelligence (AI), and the ability to install, automate, coordinate, and protect a variety of use cases at hyperscale will expedite the development of the industrial Internet. Because it will allow for a more effective use of resources, the IoT will be successful in the years to come. For instance, self-driving cars can plan their routes to avoid traffic jams, and smart appliances can automatically order replacement parts when they malfunction. With the proliferation of IoT devices, the world is about to become much more connected. This provides businesses with more chances to improve their operations and boost profits. They must also be ready for the initial investment in IoT technology and the amount of work involved in managing the brand-new, cutting-edge infrastructure. This might entail bringing on board fresh, knowledgeable personnel while shifting existing staff to new hotspots. The next great technological boom has already started, and businesses need to be ready if they want to remain competitive in the new environment.

6. CONCLUSION

The IoT's ability to alter the future is demonstrated by the thorough description of its use cases in several industries. Businesses must eventually realize that they must modify their current models to the IoT. Applications of IoT in security, predictive maintenance, and real-time asset monitoring are key factors in promoting IoT adoption. IoT can be used to introduce innovation in addition to changing current business paradigms. Additionally, the potential for combining IoT with other technologies like blockchain and AI opens up new possibilities. Utilize dependable learning materials immediately to learn more about the IoT and how it supports the development of new business models.

REFERENCES

Aliahmadi, A., Nozari, H., & Ghahremani-Nahr, J. (2022). AIoT-based sustainable smart supply chain framework. *International Journal of Innovation in Management, Economics and Social Sciences, 2*(2), 28-38.

Burby, J., & Atchison, S. (2007). *Actionable web analytics: using data to make smart business decisions*. John Wiley & Sons.

Chadli, N., Elhoseny, M., Kabbaj, M. I., & Bakkoury, Z. (2022). Smart business process modeling: Toward an IoT to detect the data flow anomalies in ad hoc mesh network. *Distributed Sensing and Intelligent Systems Proceedings of ICDSIS, 2020*, 13–27.

Ghahremani-Nahr, J., Aliahmadi, A., & Nozari, H. (2022). An IoT-based sustainable supply chain framework and blockchain. *International Journal of Innovation in Engineering*, *2*(1), 12–21. doi:10.59615/ijie.2.1.12

Hussain, F. (2017). Internet of things: Building blocks and business models (No. 978-3, pp. 319-55404). Berlin, Germany: Springer International Publishing.

Kolisnyk, M., Kharchenko, V., & Piskachova, I. (2022). Investigation of the smart business center for IoT systems availability considering attacks on the router. In *Dependable IoT for Human and Industry* (pp. 169–195). River Publishers. doi:10.1201/9781003337843-11

Lang, K. R., Xu, J., Zhu, B., Liu, X., Shaw, M. J., Zhang, H., & Fan, M. (Eds.). (2021). *Smart Business: Technology and Data Enabled Innovative Business Models and Practices: 18th Workshop on E-Business, WeB 2019, Munich, Germany, December 14, 2019, Revised Selected Papers* (Vol. 403). Springer Nature.

Lee, I. (Ed.). (2017). *The Internet of Things in the Modern Business Environment*. IGI Global. doi:10.4018/978-1-5225-2104-4

Nagy, S. G., & Stukovszky, T. (Eds.). (2023). *Smart Business and Digital Transformation: An Industry 4.0 Perspective*. Taylor & Francis. doi:10.4324/9781003390312

Nahr, J. G., Nozari, H., & Sadeghi, M. E. (2021). Green supply chain based on artificial intelligence of things (AIoT). International Journal of Innovation in Management. *Economics and Social Sciences*, *1*(2), 56–63.

Nayyar, A., & Kumar, A. (Eds.). (2020). *A roadmap to industry 4.0: smart production, sharp business and sustainable development* (pp. 1–21). Springer. doi:10.1007/978-3-030-14544-6

Nozari, H., Ghahremani-Nahr, J., & Najafi, E. (2023). The Role of Internet of Things and Blockchain in the Development of Agile and Sustainable Supply Chains. In Digital Supply Chain, Disruptive Environments, and the Impact on Retailers (pp. 271-282). IGI Global. doi:10.4018/978-1-6684-7298-9.ch015

Nozari, H., Ghahremani-Nahr, J., & Szmelter-Jarosz, A. (2023). AI and machine learning for real-world problems. *Advances In Computers*.

Samadi-Parviznejad, P. (2022). The role of big data in digital transformation. *Journal of Data Analytics, 1*(1), 42–47. doi:10.59615/jda.1.1.42

Samadi-Parviznejad, P., & Soltani, Z. (2022). Identifying and evaluating smart city marketing parameters (Case study: Tabriz). *International Journal of Innovation in Marketing Elements, 2*(1), 35-50.

Vervest, P. H., Van Liere, D. W., Zheng, L., Vervest, P. H., & Zheng, L. (2009). *The network experience—New value from smart business networks*. Springer Berlin Heidelberg. doi:10.1007/978-3-540-85582-8

Whig, P., Velu, A., & Nadikattu, R. R. (2022). Blockchain Platform to Resolve Security Issues in IoT and Smart Networks. In AI-Enabled Agile Internet of Things for Sustainable FinTech Ecosystems (pp. 46-65). IGI Global. doi:10.4018/978-1-6684-4176-3.ch003

Chapter 6
IoT-Based Supply Chain for Energy Saving

Esmael Najafi
Department of Industrial Engineering, Islamic Azad University of Science and Research Branch, Tehran, Iran

Iman Atighi
Department of Industrial Engineering, Islamic Azad University, Kish, Iran

ABSTRACT

The conventional supply chain framework included smart objects to upgrade intelligence, mechanization capabilities, and intelligent decision-making. Internet of things (IoT) advances give uncommon openings to extend productivity, diminish supply chain framework costs, and optimize energy consumption. Optimizing energy utilization with the IoT makes moving forward operational productivity in any industry conceivable. The applications of IoT within the energy segment have pulled in the extraordinary consideration of customers, businesses, and indeed, governments. For case, joining sun-oriented energy into control checking systems is one of the benefits of IoT within the supply chain, which changes a supply chain administration framework into a green and energy-saving plan. Utilizing daylight as an energy source empowers commerce to spare costs while giving a nonstop control supply to guarantee gadgets work without battery substitutions. Using renewable vitality, an intelligent framework prepared with the IoT transmits less nursery gases than conventional vitality sources.

DOI: 10.4018/979-8-3693-0210-1.ch006

1. INTRODUCTION

The IoT transforms supply chains' operations by connecting devices, sensors, and machines to enable real-time data exchange and analysis. This technology can potentially revolutionize the energy industry by providing new energy savings and optimization opportunities. By connecting devices and systems across the supply chain, IoT can help companies monitor energy usage, identify areas of inefficiency, and implement strategies for reducing energy consumption (Xie & Chen, 2022).

The IoT allows for the integration various systems and devices, such as smart meters, sensors, and energy management systems, to provide real-time data on energy consumption and usage patterns. This data can be analyzed to identify areas of inefficiency and waste, allowing companies to implement targeted strategies to reduce energy consumption and costs. For illustration, IoT-enabled sensors can monitor temperature and humidity levels in distribution and dissemination centers, permitting companies to optimize their HVAC frameworks and diminish energy utilization. Intelligent lighting frameworks can moreover be utilized to alter lighting levels based on inhabitance naturally, decreasing pointless energy utilization (Shambayati et al., 2022; Ra et al., 2023).

In addition to energy savings, IoT can help companies improve supply chain visibility and efficiency. By connecting devices across the supply chain, companies can track inventory levels, monitor shipping and delivery times, and optimize routes and transportation methods to reduce fuel consumption and emissions. However, there are also several challenges that companies may face when implementing IoT in their supply chains. These include concerns about data privacy and security and the need for significant investment in new technologies and infrastructure (İncekara, 2023). Despite these challenges, the potential benefits of IoT for energy saving in supply chains are substantial. By leveraging real-time data and analytics, companies can identify areas of inefficiency and waste and implement targeted strategies to reduce energy consumption and costs while improving overall supply chain efficiency.

This chapter will explore the potential of IoT for energy saving in supply chains and discuss some of the critical challenges and opportunities that companies may face when implementing this technology.

2. IOT WITHIN THE SUPPLY CHAIN OF THE ENERGY SEGMENT

The energy sector is a complex industry that involves multiple processes and stakeholders, from extraction and production to transportation and distribution. IoT advances can offer assistance to optimize these forms by giving real-time information and experiences, empowering way better decision-making and moving forward generally productivity (Oudani et al., 2023). Figure (1) shows the most crucial roles of the IoT in the energy sector.

Figure 1. The most critical roles of the IoT within the energy segment

Prescient upkeep is one of the key benefits of IoT within the energy supply chain. By utilizing sensors to screen hardware, companies can recognize potential issues that sometimes happen, diminishing downtime and upkeep costs. It not only improves efficiency but also ensures the safety of workers and the environment. Another area where IoT can be beneficial is energy usage optimization. IoT devices can monitor energy consumption in real time, identifying areas for improvement and reducing waste. It can lead to significant cost savings and help companies meet sustainability goals (Bhargava et al., 2022).

Real-time tracking is another important application of IoT in the energy supply chain. By using sensors to track shipments, companies can improve visibility and reduce the risk of lost or delayed shipments. It can help ensure the timely delivery of critical supplies and equipment, which is especially important in the case of emergencies. Remote monitoring is also an important application of IoT in the energy sector. By using sensors to monitor remote sites such as oil rigs or wind farms, companies can reduce the need for on-site inspections, improving safety and reducing costs. Finally, asset tracking is another critical use case for IoT in the energy supply chain. Using sensors to track the location and status of assets, such as vehicles and equipment, companies can improve asset utilization and reduce the risk of theft or loss (Ben-Daya et al., 2019).

Generally, utilizing IoT within the energy supply chain can revolutionize the industry by progressing proficiency, decreasing costs, and moving forward security. In any case, tending to information security and interoperability challenges is fundamental for effective execution.

3. OPTIMIZE ENERGY CONSUMPTION IN THE SUPPLY CHAIN

As mentioned, one of the roles of the IoT in the supply chain is to optimize energy consumption. IoT technologies can be critical in optimizing energy consumption by providing real-time data and insights on energy usage. By using sensors and connected devices, companies can monitor energy consumption in real time, identify areas for improvement, and reduce waste.

For case, IoT gadgets can screen vitality utilization in buildings and recognize regions where vitality is being squandered, such as lights or HVAC frameworks cleared out when not required. This information can be used to adjust and optimize energy usage, leading to significant cost savings and reducing environmental impact. IoT can also be used to optimize energy usage in industrial settings. By monitoring equipment and forms in real time, companies can distinguish wasteful aspects and alter them to decrease energy utilization. It diminishes costs and makes a difference in companies meeting maintainability objectives. In addition, IoT can be used to optimize energy usage in transportation. By using sensors to track fuel consumption and driver behavior, companies can identify areas for improvement and reduce fuel consumption. It not only reduces costs but also helps reduce emissions and improve sustainability.

To better explain the role of IoT in a supply chain, consider Figure (2) as a general supply chain.

Figure 2. The general supply chain

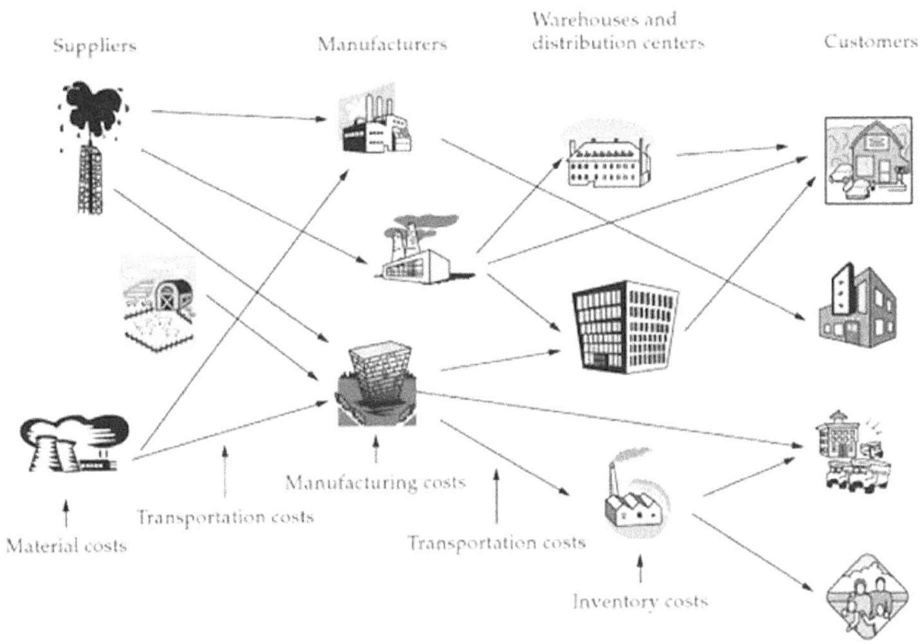

In the given definition, the supply chain may be an organization of all individuals, assets, exercises, and innovations included in making and offering an item. A supply chain incorporates everything from crude materials from the provider to the producer to the ultimate item conveyance to the conclusion client (Ghahremani-Nahr et al., 2022). The supply chain area in any organization will be related to conveying the top item from the maker to the customer as a dissemination thing. The supply chain coordination with the IoT has created a modern concept called the smart supply chain (wu et al., 2016; Azizi et al., 2021).

An intelligent supply chain includes using different rising innovations, big data, IoT, blockchain, and RPA to streamline numerous operations inside the supply chain. These innovations permit supply chain companies to decrease costs, abbreviate item conveyance times, diminish negative natural impacts and accomplish exceptional levels of computerization (Xia& liu, 2021).

A basic point approximately the association between the IoT and the supply chain that gives rise to the smart supply chain is that such a supply chain may be a self-improving and completely adaptable framework that can perform well in an unusual environment. A smart supply chain will also incorporate consistent data sharing and persistent optimization of workflows based on real-time data. To better understand a smart supply chain, you should know that such a system can process many things, including sales history, weather conditions, and the types of data it receives from its sensors, thus providing much better performance in logistics and supply chain. Smart supply chains are built on IoT platforms and can automatically control and analyze large amounts of data (Abdel-Basset et al., 2018).

Whereas within the traditional mode, filtering things and entering data were frequently done manually. This capacity to gather data at the proper time makes a difference businesses react to occasions and demands within the shortest conceivable time and correctly distinguish an event's why, how, and when. However, using these devices in the IoT creates an expansive sum of information, which needs broad audit and investigation. Enormous data investigation apparatuses can oversee comprehensive volumes of data IoT gadgets produce. IoT totals information collected from different sensors, and big data analytics apparatuses can utilize this data to store and make bits of knowledge (Hossein Motlagh et al., 2020).

As clarified, IoT innovation is exceedingly subordinate to big data investigation due to producing expansive volumes of crude data. Big data investigation involves handling complex information and recognizing and foreseeing patterns. Different encounters and proof show that enormous information investigation can fathom numerous business problems. For case, anticipating the precise conveyance time of a product or benefit is one of the foremost essential issues of the supply chain. It is conceivable with the assistance of enormous information examination, considering climate conditions, vehicle characteristics, etc. (Manavalan & Jayakrishna, 2019).

Determining requests more precisely, recognizing the customer's buy handle cycle, and overseeing stockroom stock are among the foremost imperative benefits of big data analysis. For example, with the assistance of this innovation, Amazon has managed to recognize the information of more than 150 million clients based on their buy history, investigation, and client buy behavior designs. On the other hand, big data investigation makes a difference producers and retail companies react to vacillations in request by distinguishing advertise patterns. Determining request, moving forward client benefit, diminishing capacity costs, optimizing the determination of transportation courses, optimizing energy utilization, and generally progressing the commerce circumstance are a few of the foremost critical results of big data investigation. Although these innovations can make essential business openings, combining these two advances appears to lead to a major change within the supply chain.

On the one hand, IoT innovation, with the assistance of gadgets and sensors, increases the speed of accepting real-time data from the state of the supply chain. On the other hand, by handling this massive volume of created data, big data examination brings design identification and drift expectations. However, these two technologies are not yet widespread among all industries and businesses. However, projections appear that the potential of the IoT and big data investigation can bring the supply chain and the logistics industry in a modern heading. A few machine learning algorithms utilize designs and patterns watched from big data and offer assistance in creating prescient analytics with data-driven learning. In collaboration with big data analytics, IoT is making a difference in businesses transform from receptive to proactive. The concurrent utilization of these two innovations leads to an increment within the proficiency of the supply chain and, in this way, the fascination of client fulfillment. Businesses combining these two technologies will become information-based businesses that can make decisions based on accurate and timely data and generally increase business productivity. Reduce energy consumption (Aliahmadi et al., 2022a; Aliahmadi et al., 2022b). An example of a smart supply chain is presented in Figure (3).

Figure 3. The smart supply chain

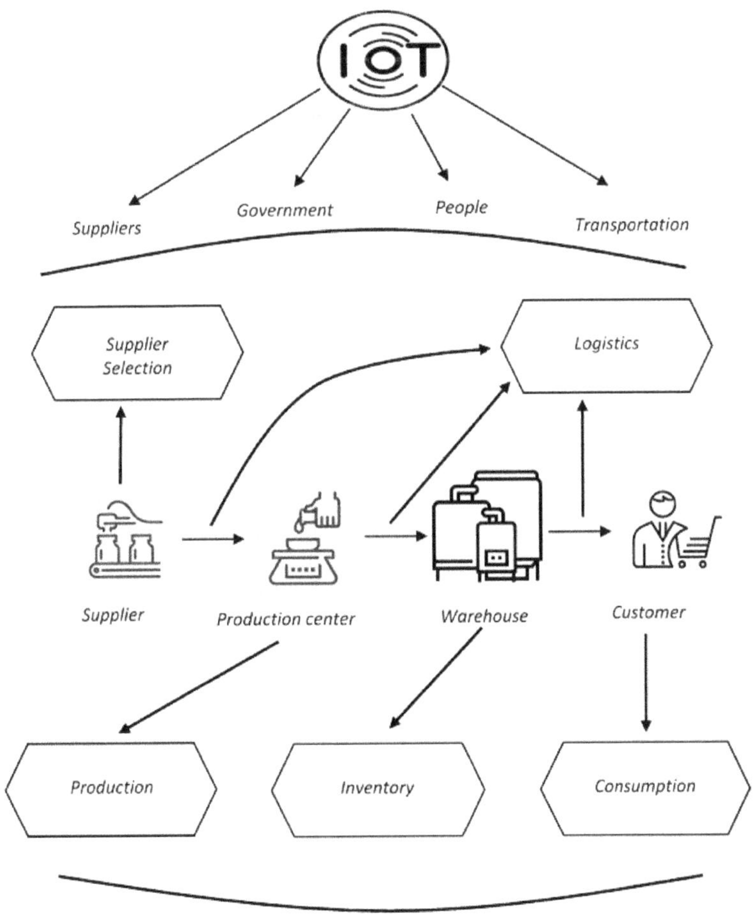

In the following, the most critical applications of the IoT in the optimization of the smart supply chain have been discussed.

- *Control and tracking of product shipment and delivery to the customer*

Control and following of item shipment and conveyance to the client The forms related to the transportation of crude materials and items are one of the foremost critical divisions that are unequivocally influenced by IoT innovation. Transportation has continuously been an eccentric handle that requires control. IoT innovation has allowed vehicles to be prepared with cameras and sensors to assess and analyze the driver's physical and mental condition. This data is sent in real-time to the responsible people to oversee the shipping forms better. In expansion, cargo security is additionally guaranteed in this way more dependably.

With the help of IoT, the product's geographical location, the cargo's arrival time, the stopping time, the weather conditions of the transportation route, and the distance traveled can be tracked with great accuracy. Another advantage of the IoT is the ability to follow the process of providing goods from the warehouse to the delivery time to the customer, which often leads to an increase in the speed of service delivery, customer satisfaction, and reduced energy consumption. With these interpretations, increasing productivity, saving costs, and preventing theft or loss of cargo during the transportation process can be considered as one of the benefits of using IoT solutions to improve supply chain management.

- *Control and tracking of product shipment and delivery to the customer*

Using IoT technology, it is possible to track the product's geographical location, the arrival time of the cargo, the stopping time, the weather conditions of the transportation route, and the distance traveled accurately. This tracking, using the IoT, helps to quickly transfer new information to the driver in case of accidents and routing problems and to perform new routing based on reducing time and energy consumption. Warehouse inventory management Sensors and automatic identification equipment such as RFID and barcode readers are among the IoT devices that make the supply chain brighter. These tools will help you accurately forecast product demand, access essential data from warehouse information, automate the inventory transfer process from warehouse to customer, and calculate inventory costs (ordering, shipping, stock shortages) (Nozari et al., 2023).

Most supply chain forms depend on getting real-time data from the distribution center stock. This issue is fundamental in expansive businesses. In these companies, the scarcest delay may lead to unsalvageable misfortunes. In this respect, utilizing innovations such as the IoT and big data examination makes a difference in knowing the stock status of the distribution center in genuine time without the need to use laborers in entirely different parts of the warehouse. Lineage Logistics is one of the largest wholesale companies that warehouses and delivers millions of products to over 3,000 stores, restaurants, and cafes. This company has developed various intelligent algorithms to predict the amount of product orders to optimize the warehouse stock. Lineage has claimed that with the help of this intelligent algorithm, the efficiency of the warehouse has increased by more than 20%. Amazon company is also one of the biggest retailers that manages the warehouse stock automatically with the help of these two technologies.

- *Demand forecasting*

To explain this possibility, let's look at a practical example. The supply chain of fast food chain Domino's depends significantly on big data analysis. By analyzing the data and identifying existing trends, this company predicts, for example, in a 5-minute period, which types of pizza will be ordered and how many will be ordered. Then, based on this information, the pizza is placed in the oven before the customer orders. Domino's has significantly reduced the order preparation time with this method. On the other hand, identifying trends has helped Domino's identify times of lower demand and implement different marketing campaigns. Encourage customers to place more orders, such as offering discounts (Nozari & Ghahremani-Nahr, 2022).

4. CRITICAL CHALLENGES OF IOT-BASED SUPPLY CHAIN FOR ENERGY SAVING

Some potential key challenges of supply chain based on the IoT things for energy saving are shown in Figure (4) (Lee & Lee, 2015):

Figure 4. Key challenges of IoT-based supply chain

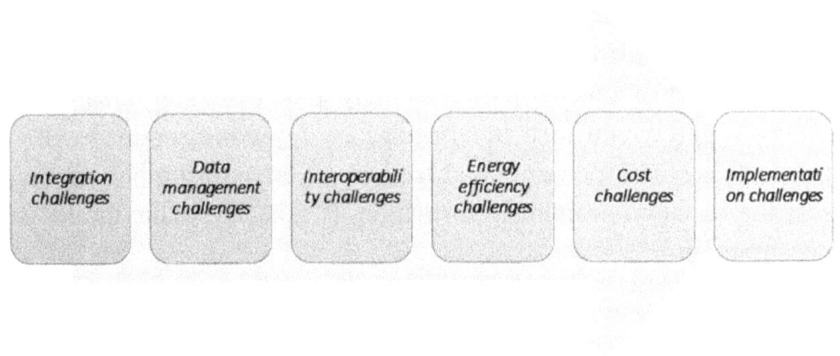

Integration challenges: Integrating IoT devices into existing supply chain systems can be complex and require significant investment in infrastructure and technology. It can be challenging for companies already invested in legacy systems and may not have the resources to upgrade them.

Data management challenges: IoT gadgets create tremendous data, and overseeing this data can be challenging. Guaranteeing data protection and security can also be a concern, as companies must ensure that touchy data is not compromised.

Interoperability challenges: Ensuring that different IoT devices and systems can communicate with each other seamlessly is essential for effective supply chain management. However, achieving interoperability can be challenging due to differences in protocols and standards.

Energy efficiency challenges: IoT devices can help optimize energy usage in the supply chain but also require energy to function. Therefore, ensuring that the energy consumed by IoT devices is offset by energy savings elsewhere in the supply chain can be a challenge.

Cost challenges: Implementing IoT devices in the supply chain can be expensive, and the return on investment may not be immediately apparent. Therefore, finding cost-effective solutions that deliver measurable benefits is essential.

Implementation challenges: Finally, implementing IoT-based solutions in the supply chain requires significant stakeholder planning and coordination. Ensuring everyone is on board and committed to the project can be challenging, as different stakeholders may have other priorities and goals.

5. TEN ADVANTAGES OF IOT FOR MANAGING ENERGY CONSUMPTION

As mentioned, the digitization of life in today's era has brought various benefits to humanity. By summarizing the presented content, ten benefits of IoT for managing energy consumption can be explained as follows (Majeed & Rupasinghe, 2017):

One. IoT reduces energy consumption.

One of the most essential advantages of the IoT is that it can reduce energy consumption. In fact, this technology is important to the government because of the economic impact of using IoT. Interestingly, this technology helps all people in the energy supply chain to better manage energy consumption with various techniques such as smart metering, real-time electricity consumption monitoring, and forecasting based on available information. In this way, using the IoT reduces energy consumption.

Two. IoT will reduce the maximum carbon emissions.

Another thing that humanity has always been looking for in the field of energy production is to reduce the emission of carbon to nature. It is possible to use the IoT. This feature responded to one of humanity's needs for many years in energy production. Different companies and industries are daily improving their use of IoT to prevent carbon emissions to nature.

Three. IoT is more compatible with the rules.

One of the exciting actions companies take in using IoT is the daily review of this technology and its effectiveness following the laws. IoT has provided companies and factories with several capabilities to consider environmental conditions while producing energy.

Four. IoT integrates non-renewable energies with green energies.

All experts and experts in energy production know that moving towards green energy is inevitable. We must accept that the world is moving towards using renewable energy. Therefore, we must look for a way to integrate these two types of energy. The IoT has allowed industries to incorporate non-renewable energy with green energy using energy monitoring sensors and more.

Five. IoT optimizes the maintenance process of machinery

IoT's benefits to humanity are beyond what you can imagine. These benefits are not only limited to the optimization of energy production. For example, besides the fact that sensors and data analysis can be used to reduce energy consumption, they can also be used to optimize the maintenance process of objects.

Six. IoT automates processes.

Different companies in the field of energy production are looking for the latest technologies in the world so that they can do more than manage energy consumption. Another advantage of using the IoT is that the production process is automated and reduces labor costs as much as possible.

Seven. IoT reduces overhead costs as much as possible.

Because IoT in different companies makes the processes go automatically, the additional costs of the companies are reduced as much as possible. For example, it has been assessed that utilizing the progressed expository program can diminish the time and exertion spent on data examination by 90%.

Eight. IoT makes accurate predictions, so you can trust the app.

One of the most excellent benefits of the IoT is the ability to induce precise data and predict the longer-term well for information-based arranging. This feature helps companies to reduce their error percentage in future planning. Also, based on detailed planning, they know how to use their time and labor.

Nine. IoT predicts potential faults.

Another reason companies are so interested in using the IoT is because they can anticipate bugs. In this way, you can avoid significant failures as much as possible by preventing a series of failures.

Ten. IoT tells you the reason for the outage and failure and from which part

Failure and problems in the production process are natural events in companies and factories. Usually, when such issues occur, it takes a long time to find and fix the problem. But if you use the IoT, you can easily find the cause of failure and the desired part. In this way, you can quickly return to the production process.

6. CONCLUSION

One of the most vital and principal parts of the overall management of an organization is the supply chain management. The division is responsible for planning all units from the introductory stages, such as the supply of materials, to the final steps, such as conveyance and after-sales benefits. The presence of comprehensive and reliable data platforms is one of the necessities of overseeing a supply chain. Hence, accurately utilizing coordinates data gadgets such as IoT innovation is essential in organizational administration. Covering this data precisely and at the minute encourages things and makes the advancement of the forms more straightforward. To make strides in this handle, cloud computing is utilized as an arrangement. In expansion, other cloud computing capabilities can be used, such as facilitating the communication of objects, creating integration in checking gadgets and IoT within the capacity, data analysis, and virtual space stage to supply to the client in supply chain administration. For this reason, a show that indicates the relationship between IoT innovation, cloud computing, and supply chain management is required.

In this chapter, the role of IoT in the supply chain to optimize energy consumption was investigated. IoT technology solves the problems of supply chain and logistics management of organizations, such as distribution network regulation, distribution strategy, information circulation, inventory management, and cash flow through a cloud-based vision. Cloud-based technologies facilitate collaboration with partners and customers by sharing information resources, leading to improved productivity and increased innovation. The execution of Internet technology of objects based on data clouds, utilizing exact and real-time data scope, encourages determining and arranging, acquiring and supplying assets, coordinations, bolstering, administration of administrations and saving parts, and numerous sub-processes of the supply chain. These innovations permit organizations to contribute in generation and operational forms rather than paying colossal costs within the program division, resulting in a more cash stream.

REFERENCES

Abdel-Basset, M., Manogaran, G., & Mohamed, M. (2018). Internet of Things (IoT) and its impact on supply chain: A framework for building smart, secure and efficient systems. *Future Generation Computer Systems*, *86*(9), 614–628. doi:10.1016/j.future.2018.04.051

Aliahmadi, A., Nozari, H., & Ghahremani-Nahr, J. (2022a). AIoT-based sustainable smart supply chain framework. *International Journal of Innovation in Management, Economics and Social sciences,* *2*(2), 28-38.

Aliahmadi, A., Nozari, H., & Ghahremani-Nahr, J. (2022b). Big Data IoT-based agile-lean logistic in pharmaceutical industries. International Journal of Innovation in Management. *Economics and Social Sciences*, *2*(3), 70–81.

Azizi, N., Malekzadeh, H., Akhavan, P., Haass, O., Saremi, S., & Mirjalili, S. (2021). IoT–blockchain: Harnessing the power of internet of thing and blockchain for smart supply chain. *Sensors (Basel)*, *21*(18), 6048. doi:10.339021186048 PMID:34577261

Ben-Daya, M., Hassini, E., & Bahroun, Z. (2019). Internet of things and supply chain management: A literature review. *International Journal of Production Research*, *57*(15-16), 4719–4742. doi:10.1080/00207543.2017.1402140

Bhargava, A., Bhargava, D., Kumar, P. N., Sajja, G. S., & Ray, S. (2022). Industrial IoT and AI implementation in vehicular logistics and supply chain management for vehicle mediated transportation systems. *International Journal of System Assurance Engineering and Management*, *13*(S1), 673–680. doi:10.100713198-021-01581-2

Ghahremani-Nahr, J., Aliahmadi, A., & Nozari, H. (2022). An IoT-based sustainable supply chain framework and blockchain. *International Journal of Innovation in Engineering*, *2*(1), 12–21. doi:10.59615/ijie.2.1.12

Ghanbari, M. (2023). Presenting the smart-sustainable supply chain model based on artificial intelligence. *International Journal of Innovation in Management, Economics and Social Sciences*.

Hossein Motlagh, N., Mohammadrezaei, M., Hunt, J., & Zakeri, B. (2020). Internet of Things (IoT) and the energy sector. *Energies*, *13*(2), 494. doi:10.3390/en13020494

İncekara, Ç. Ö. (2023). Industrial internet of things (IIoT) in energy sector. *Advanced Engineering Science*, *3*, 21–30.

Lee, I., & Lee, K. (2015). The Internet of Things (IoT): Applications, investments, and challenges for enterprises. *Business Horizons*, *58*(4), 431–440. doi:10.1016/j.bushor.2015.03.008

Majeed, A. A., & Rupasinghe, T. D. (2017). Internet of things (IoT) embedded future supply chains for industry 4.0: An assessment from an ERP-based fashion apparel and footwear industry. *International Journal of Supply Chain Management*, *6*(1), 25–40.

Manavalan, E., & Jayakrishna, K. (2019). A review of Internet of Things (IoT) embedded sustainable supply chain for industry 4.0 requirements. *Computers & Industrial Engineering*, *127*, 925–953. doi:10.1016/j.cie.2018.11.030

Nozari, H., & Ghahremani-Nahr, J. (2022). Assessing Key performance indicators in Blockchain-Based Supply Chain Financing: Case Study of Chain Stores. *International Journal of Innovation in Engineering*, *2*(3), 42–58. doi:10.59615/ijie.2.3.42

Nozari, H., Ghahremani-Nahr, J., & Szmelter-Jarosz, A. (2023). AI and machine learning for real-world problems. *Advances In Computers*.

Oudani, M., Sebbar, A., Zkik, K., El Harraki, I., & Belhadi, A. (2023). Green Blockchain based IoT for secured supply chain of hazardous materials. *Computers & Industrial Engineering*, *175*, 108814. doi:10.1016/j.cie.2022.108814

Ra, N., Ghosh, A., & Bhattacharjee, A. (2023). IoT-based smart energy management for solar vanadium redox flow battery powered switchable building glazing satisfying the HVAC system of EV charging stations. *Energy Conversion and Management*, *281*, 116851. doi:10.1016/j.enconman.2023.116851

Shambayati, H., Shafiei Nikabadi, M., Khatami Firouzabadi, S. M. A., Rahmanimanesh, M., & Saberi, S. (2022). Optimization of virtual closed-loop supply chain under uncertainty: Application of IoT. *Kybernetes*.

Wu, L., Yue, X., Jin, A., & Yen, D. C. (2016). Smart supply chain management: A review and implications for future research. *International Journal of Logistics Management*, *27*(2), 395–417. doi:10.1108/IJLM-02-2014-0035

Xia, L., & Liu, S. (2021). Intelligent IoT-based cross-border e-commerce supply chain performance optimization. *Wireless Communications and Mobile Computing*, *2021*, 1–13. doi:10.1155/2021/9961925

Xie, J., & Chen, C. (2022). Supply chain and logistics optimization management for international trading enterprises using IoT-based economic logistics model. *Operations Management Research : Advancing Practice Through Research*, *15*(3-4), 711–724. doi:10.100712063-022-00254-y

Chapter 7
Collaboration Analysis in Supply Chain 4.0 for Smart Businesses

Alireza Aliahmadi
Iran University of Science and Technology, Tehran, Iran

Aminmasoud Bakhshi Movahed
Iran University of Science and Technology, Tehran, Iran

Hamed Nozari
https://orcid.org/0000-0002-6500-6708
Azad University of the Emirates, Dubai, UAE

ABSTRACT

This study aims to review collaboration in Supply Chain 4.0. For this objective, dimensions and outcomes of collaboration are analyzed based on businesses. An overview of the different dimensions and outcomes of collaboration was created in Industry 4.0 platform. Research data was obtained from literature review and then refined according to SC experts. The findings show that collaboration in Supply Chain 4.0, with the activation of dimensions including information and communication management, resource planning in the production and logistics process, collaborative decisions for business goals, technology and business development, motivational alignment, performance evaluation in integrated processes, marketing and customer orientation can lead to sustainable performance. In this study, a comprehensive approach is made to accessing collaboration concept among business partners in Industry 4.0 by creating a new conceptual framework to achieve economic, social, and environmental performance.

DOI: 10.4018/979-8-3693-0210-1.ch007

1. INTRODUCTION

The main purpose of this section is identify and analyze the most important actors of Supply Chain Collaboration (SCC) that are effective on businesses in Industry 4.0 conditions. Industry 4.0 technologies changes supply chain management (SCM) from a linear situation to supply chain 4.0. Transforming traditional SCs (Tjahjono et al., 2017) and its developing is an opportunity that SC 4.0 has given to businesses (Frederico et al., 2019). These opportunities based on innovative technologies such as artificial intelligence, Internet of Things, blockchain, machine learning, etc., lead to the growth of capacities in order to develop businesses (Yildiz Ozenc et al., 2023). These technologies make proportions with current world situation in the SCM and defined as Industry Revolution 4.0 that is specify with empower business systems (Awan et al., 2021). Industry 4.0 has influenced business models, and this service & manufacturing paradigm entails a way of new communication management along SCs (Glova et al., 2014).

Understand of Industry 4.0 benefits and applications by companies for using it, needs to create a collaborative partnership among SC members. SCC considered as an essential and fundamental factor to businesses adaptation duo to the trend changes, penetration of technologies and problems caused by companies' non-compliance with current conditions. Commercial organizations and their SCs face increasing challenges due to industry 4.0 conditions. This great challenge has restricted the flow of SC processes, adding uncertainties to the environment of companies. Controlling of these unprecedented changes for SC managers in market is so necessary duo to neutralization of disrupting the actions and stability of SC. Therefore, SCC became a factor for the survival of all SC members (Al-Omoush et al., 2023). Therefore, a thorough inspection needed to uncover collaboration performance under the industry 4.0 technologies to use of businesses for now about a collaborative approach among companies. For this reason, it is important to know the dimensions and outcomes of collaboration in order to make a platform for SCC 4.0.

The latest technological progresses in businesses force SC digitization (Ali, 2022). Industry 4.0 transforms SCC through strategic changes (Veile et al., 2022). The severity of the competitive conditions and the change of customer expectations have led to essential changes in companies. SC partners can respond quickly to dynamic changes in the commercial environment with implementing collaborative activities (Misbauddin et al., 2023). Management applications of SCC 4.0 are also significant. Business partners throughout the SC don't collaborate with other actors in order to jointly develop projects. Collaboration results show coordination at a low level of implementation. It means that there is no close relation among partners to outsource activities that are not part of the company's core business. Therefore, a conceptual framework that businesses players can understand and use it, regardless of their position, leads to development of collaborative relationships and improving business conditions. For example, cloud computing is recognized as a technology with the greatest impact on SCC 4.0. Connection of suppliers and retailers, quality improvement in inventory management, communication and delivery have made with applications of such technologies (Azevedo, 2022).

Collaboration through industry 4.0 let firms to overcome resource constraints, achieve sustainable performance in competitive market (Masoomi et al., 2023). For example, information integration and improving data processing are the most important actions of Internet of Things in improving business collaborative activities (Cui et al., 2022). Lack of SCC is one of the powerful reasons for firm's weakness. So, organizations in today's innovative situation have started to collaborate through new roles in the SC (Akhavan & Philsoophian, 2022). Collaboration is a key emerging dimension of sustainable SCM (Cui et al., 2022). SCC impacts risk management to promote competitive advantage. Firms' collaboration has influenced on competitive advantage due to the technological turbulence with specific strategies (LI et al., 2023). Therefore, collaborative dimensions maintain the business dynamics by SC departments. For example, redesign of SCC network with Industry 4.0 leads to changes in people's lifestyles, transportation, healthcare and increasing the quality of using natural energy (Abbasi et al., 2023). SCC 4.0 by establishing joint and long-term commitments can develop the application of advanced technologies to achieve business goals (Agrawal et al., 2023).

2. LITERATURE REVIEW

Nowadays, challenges consequences due to spread of epidemics such as Covid-19 and wars like the Russian war on Ukraine restricted commercial activities in SC flow. Uncertainties has prompted companies to reflect of a suitable solution and also, Globalization has made SCs more vulnerable to disruption (Bouchenine & Abdel-Aal, 2023). In this situation, SCC as an interaction-oriented factor can lead to accelerating the synchronization of companies with current issues. In the following, the main concepts are explained.

2.1 Supply Chain 4.0

SC 4.0 emphasizes the relationships between Industry 4.0 and SC for facilitate the clarification of the applicability of Industry 4.0 in the context of SC (Frederico et al., 2019). SC 4.0 is integration and synchronization of the companies' value chain with smart technologies to build an interconnected system with real-time communication.

This SC manage flows and leading to an adaptive, autonomous and dynamic network that can meets customers' requirements (Frazzon et al., 2019).

2.2 Supply Chain Collaboration

SCC is described as the organization's capability of utilizing business applications to support knowledge, information and data exchange, coordinate activities with chain members (Al-Omoush et al., 2023). SCC provides ranging from increased knowledge sharing to access to products and expertise (Jraisat et al., 2023). In the next section, the most important components of collaboration affecting on businesses are explained. These factors are categorized in two sections including dimensions and outcomes.

2.3. Dimensions of SCC 4.0 Based on Business Growth

By identifying collaboration dimensions, business partners will able to measure collaboration value and seek improvement in relationships that was positively associated with operational performance (Simatupang & Sridharan, 2005). The dimensions of collaboration are classified in 7 main sections. Dimensions includes different parts that are defined below:

2.3.1. Information and Communication Management

It includes *Information sharing*, *Information management* and *Clear and collaborative communication among business partners*. Business partners interest in making members in SC to communicate with information network. Information management system support managers in better decision making (Sundram et al., 2018). The growing complexity of SCs and risk increasing has made changes in communication between SC actors. Communication management based on industry 4.0 technologies can contribute to the reduction of businesses risks surrounding the activities (El Ouarrak & Hmioui, 2023).

- **Information sharing**

The influence of information sharing in SCM for collaboration development is gradually increasing due to improving the business performance (Şahin & Topal, 2019). Suppliers with information provided (Haque & Islam, 2018), Transparency in exchanging sales information openly with other business partners (Ramanathan, 2012) and Real-time information exchange including sales data and social media data (Ralston et al., 2017) has been defined as information sharing.

- **Information management**

Using collaborative SC software systems (Fernando et al., 2023), information quality, access to information, accuracy of information, information readiness (Afshan et al., 2018), creating shared knowledge, Knowledge and competence (Ho et al., 2020) and formal information assessment structure (Bout, 2011) have formed the meaning of Information management.

- **Clear and collaborative communication among business partners**

A Collaborative communication, communicational capital (Ho et al., 2020), long-term stable relationships with suppliers (Ocicka et al., 2022), compatible communication and information system for business members (Haque & Islam,. 2018), communication orientation based on collaboration (Chakraborty et al., 2014), transparency of communication, satisfaction in collaborative relationships (Uddin & Akhter, 2022), structural capital and The governance of supplier relations (Wu & Chiu, 2018) are the repeatable concept of this component.

2.3.2. Resource Planning in the Production and Logistics Process

It include *Production management*, *Delivery and logistics management* and *Resource planning*. New technologies with industry 4.0 have been made available to companies in order to trace processes through digital resource planning systems. Control systems and manufacturing information are processed so that a detailed database helpful for the monitoring logistics process of the production plant can be built (Ferrari et al., 2021).

- **Production management**

Among the main contents related to important of production in commercial relationship, the value of communication in production plans, long-term capacity plans (Asree et al., 2016), inventory management system through JIT (Haque & Islam, 2018), sharing production plans, co-production and collaborative capacity sharing (Chen et al., 2017) have been reported.

- **Delivery and logistics management**

Investing in concepts such as procurement and logistics issues, sharing delivery schedules and on-time delivery (Ramanathan, 2017), Delivery plans, supplier selection based on time/lead/quality and reliability, logistics integration, Technology integration (Chen et al., 2017) in Delivery and logistics part can help the growth and development of SC's business performance.

- **Resource planning**

Resources sharing, resources integration (Cao & Zhang, 2011; Ramanathan, 2012; Liu, 2018; Ho et al., 2020), joint planning management, supply and demand in real time (Ramanathan, 2017; Hanafiah & Widjaja; 2022; Crum et al., 2011; Richey et al., 2012) and human resources (Gumboh & Gichira, 2015; Simatupang & Sridharan, 2018) are SC Resources.

2.3.3. Collaborative Decisions for Business Goals

It includes *Sharing and coordination in decision making* and *Business goals fit*. Inter-firm collaboration explores the main capabilities that make a business chain open to collaborative activities. This process improves collaboration partnership through SC 4.0 with considering the role of firm and relationship capabilities (Della Corte et al., 2021).

- **Share and coordination in decision making**

Decision making in new conditions has changed and it needs to decision coordination (Cao & Zhang, 2011; Jeng, 2015; Hendayani & Alviyan, 2019; Ho et al, 2020; Ma et al., 2020), joint decision making, pre-decision consultation, collaborative working group with implementation of programs with the participation of other SC partners (Ramanathan, 2012), participation of business partners in forecasting to improve accuracy (Jaturat et al., 2022), participation in planning, collaborative forecasting with partners (Srivastava et al., 2015), strategic planning with integrated decision making (Chen et al., 2017), innovation based on joint ideas and joint decision-making (Pradabwong et al., 2017; Solaimani & van der Veen, 2022; Al-Omoush et al., 2023) for business partners coordination.

- **Business goals fit**

Permissible operational goals (Ramesh et al., 2010; Chauhan et al., 2022) and sharing common goals (Pradabwong et al., 2017) are explained business goals and this is an essential factor in SC 4.0 framework. Also, it is important that business goal needs to be derived out of the human goal and human program. Synchronization of business goals fit with human goals lead to real value for society, individuals and the nature (Talan & Sharma 2020).

2.3.4. Technology and Business Development

It includes *Investment in technology* and *Change and development of business based on new projects*. Commercial organizations are adopting Industry 4.0 technologies to automate operational tasks and optimize decision making. It leads to stable employment and enriched duties, and optimized production process (Margherita & Braccini, 2021).

- **Investment in technology**

One of the fundamental factors in SCC 4.0 implement is technological investment. Appropriate investments for technological development in SC activities (Hague & Islam, 2018), investing in resource development, investing in technology and other resources to support collaboration (Ho et al., 2020) have suggested to build commercial relationship for businesses chain.

- **Change and development of businesses based on new projects**

Schedule changes by SC partners, creating and achieving a new project with SC partners, Expansion or diversification of business with the help of current SCC (Ramanathan & Gunasekaran, 2014) are the solutions to businesses changing that can be implemented with focusing on collaboration.

2.3.5. Motivational Alignment

The motivation for collaboration among SC members in new world stems from the potential profit from match supply with demand of customers based on marketing conditions; because the main determinant of SC 4.0 revenue is the size of the customer at industry 4.0 situation (Simatupang & Sridharan, 2018). Level of motivation redesign, and punishment and motivation (Cao & Zhang, 2011; Chakraborty et al., 2014; Chen et al., 2017; Pradabwong et al., 2017; Um & Kim, 2019; Kittipanya-ngam & Kumar, 2019) are related to motivational alignment in order to improve SCC.

2.3.6. Performance Evaluation in Integrated Processes

It includes *Performance evaluation system* and Business integrated processes. SC performance evaluation is significant because it's the core mechanism for effective SCM. It's an appropriate way to improve SC governance at Industry 4.0 platform by making it more conscious, timely, and valuable decisions by business partners (Oubrahim et al., 2022).

- **Performance evaluation system**

Performance metrics are an essential aspect of managing diverse SCs that improves commercial performance by providing transparent communication between stakeholders of organizations (Kamble & Gunasekaran, 2020). Functional system level of collaboration (Simatupang & Sridharan, 2018), collaborative functional system (Ma et al., 2020), supplier performance evaluation, integration of activities across supply chains (Haque & Islam, 2018), performance measurement (Crum et al., 2011; Ho et al., 2020), partner development through enhanced performance measurement (Srivastava et al., 2015), product design control (Ramanathan & Gunasekaran, 2014), functional coordination, supplier supervision (Chen et al., 2017) have been recognized as evaluation system metrics for SCC.

- **Business process integration**

It is concerned with the coordination of business processes and overall activities across different units with internal process integration, and effective integration of task execution (Narayanan et al., 2011). Internal SC integration, changing in common processes (Richey et al.,2012), integrated cross-task processes with business partners (Srivastava et al., 2015), process and system integration, management of SC processes and activities (Bratucu & Ciofoaia, 2022), supplier integrity, integrated SCM practices (Chen et al., 2017), integrated SC processes (Ma et al., 2020) can improve integration in business process.

2.3.7. Marketing and Customer Orientation

It includes *Marketing mix* and *Customer Orientation*. Customer orientation with technological capability have positive effects on product innovation and marketing with inter-functional coordination between business partners can leads to developed SCC 4.0 (Aydin, 2021).

- **Marketing mix**

SCC 4.0 influenced by technology marketing situation that includes promotion with planning promotional sales, pricing with proper price by suppliers (Ramanathan & Gunasekaran, 2014), product quality (Pradabwong et al., 2017) and sharing responsibility for product improvement (Chen et al., 2023).

- **Customer orientation**

Quality issues (Teng et al., 2022), customer feedback/relationships/processes/ customer related products and services, systematic processes for handling customer complaints, reducing setup time and response time throughout the SC (Haque & Islam, 2018), collaboration and coordination with the customer, monitoring by the customer, integration and alliance with the customer (Chen et al., 2017) are define customer orientation in SCC.

2.4. SCC 4.0 Outcomes Based on Business Achievements

Outcomes refer to the positive results that are obtained for business partners, beneficiaries and non-beneficiaries after collaborative activities. The outcomes of collaboration are classified in 3 main sections that are defined below:

2.4.1. Economic Performance

It includes *Production and Operation*, *Customers*, *Financial*, *Cost*, *Market*, *Knowledge and Innovation* and *Capabilities and Competencies*. Economic performance is one of the effective results of sustainable performance that can be achieved by implementing SCC among business partners. Meanwhile, Industry 4.0 technologies as an enabler can increase the growth rate of economic performance in the industrial and commercial environment.

- **Production and operation**

Reducing inventory costs, time, inventory levels and related costs, faster Inventory turnover, inventory transparency (Jeenanunta & Visanvetchakij, 2013), economies of scale in production, improved forecasting, matching supply and demand (Heaver, 2015), reducing uncertainty, coping with the uncertain external environment (Narayanan et al., 2015), time-related items such as lower delays, reducing lead time and dealing with its risks, reducing SC cycle time and joint product development (Chen et al., 2017), flexibility and agility in SC operations (Lynch, 2019), achieving goals faster (Ho et al., 2020), continuous replenishment in SC (Afshan et al., 2018), better selection of suppliers (Aggarwal & Srivastava, 2016), creating faster cycles for R&D and ordering sustainable development (Al-Doori, 2019) are related to production and operation.

- **Customers**

Timely response, fast response (Al-Doori, 2019), improving quality and product accessibility (Jeenanunta & Visanvetchakij, 2013), increasing customer service, improving customer service, improving value for customers, responding to customer demand with minimal cost (Lynch, 2019) can define customer component in SCC.

- **Financial**

Profit sharing, increase revenue through resource synergy (Narayanan et al., 2015), improving financial performance through profitability (Panahifar et al., 2017), increase Rate of return, improve risk management (Heaver, 2015), better pricing and price stability (Lynch, 2019) are related to financial performance.

- **Cost**

Reducing costs by business partners (Ho et al., 2020), reducing the cost of transactions in commercial relations (Ho et al., 2019), cost saving (Lynch, 2019), cost competitiveness with SC partners (Jeenanunta & Visanvetchakij, 2013; Panahifar et al., 2017) are concepts that can change the result form of collaboration implementing.

- **Market**

Globalization (Salam, 2017), more intense competition, creating a competitive advantage, promotion of competitive advantage (Ho et al., 2020),creating a strategic advantage against market competitors, improving competitiveness (Pradabwong et al., 2017), improving performance and market position through access to markets (Heaver, 2015), improving market intelligence, effective response to market changes, market share growth, sales rate growth (Aggarwal & Srivastava, 2016) are market factors of SCC.

- **Knowledge and innovation**

Increasing the knowledge level of Partners in SC, development of tacit knowledge (Lynch, 2019), increasing innovative methods resulting from the sharing of knowledge and experience among business partners (Panahifar et al., 2017), knowledge transfer beyond company boundaries (Afshan et al., 2018), promotion of innovative capabilities (Heaver, 2015) with digital technologies are sources of innovation in the SC 4.0 (Hopkins, 2021).

- **Capabilities and competencies**

Improving capabilities, competence development and continuous improvement (Aggarwal & Srivastava, 2016), focusing on key activities, capabilities, and competencies of organization (Narayanan et al., 2015), better access to resources, better use of resources (Salam, 2017), access to additional features, using the expertise of commercial partner to achieving a win-win solution (Afshan et al., 2018) through the collaboration can improve the performance of the companies and the SC.

2.4.2. Social Performance

Few firms have taken responsibility of social issues in SCs and it seems unlikely for profit-oriented firms to develop beyond an instrumental view on social sustainable SCM (Hohn & Durach, 2023). Few firms have taken responsibility of social issues in SCs and it seems unlikely for profit-oriented firms to develop beyond an instrumental view on social sustainable SCM (Hohn & Durach, 2023). For this reason, the creation of effective social performance in the direction of sustainable development will be considered, which has been reported as one of the most important results of collaboration in SC. Social stability (Ramanathan, 2014), benefits for people (Aggarwal & Srivastava, 2016), improving sustainability and social performance through the optimal use of raw materials (Chen et al., 2017) are reported for social collaboration outcomes in SC.

2.4.3. Environmental Performance

The environmental impacts in a typical SC should arise beyond the focal firm boundaries. Environmental metrics focus on natural resources, energy and emissions to air. The visibility of environmental aspects are limited and the assessment of environmental impacts does not span beyond the business partners of the focal firms (Tuni et al., 2018). So, recognizing collaboration effect on SC 4.0 can help to businesses for environmental performance improvement. Environmental sustainability (Aggarwal & Srivastava, 2016), increasing green purchases, improving biodiversity (Chen et al., 2017), reducing harmful environmental effects and promoting sustainability, and waste reduction (Chin et al., 2015) are considered as environmental performance.

3. CONCEPTUAL FRAMEWORK

As result, it seems successful implementation of the operational process with commercial company's competitors, mutual benefits be achieved. In order to better understanding of the most important functions of SCC 4.0 in businesses, a conceptual model of 10 main factors is shown in Figure 1.

Figure 1. Conceptual model of SCC 4.0

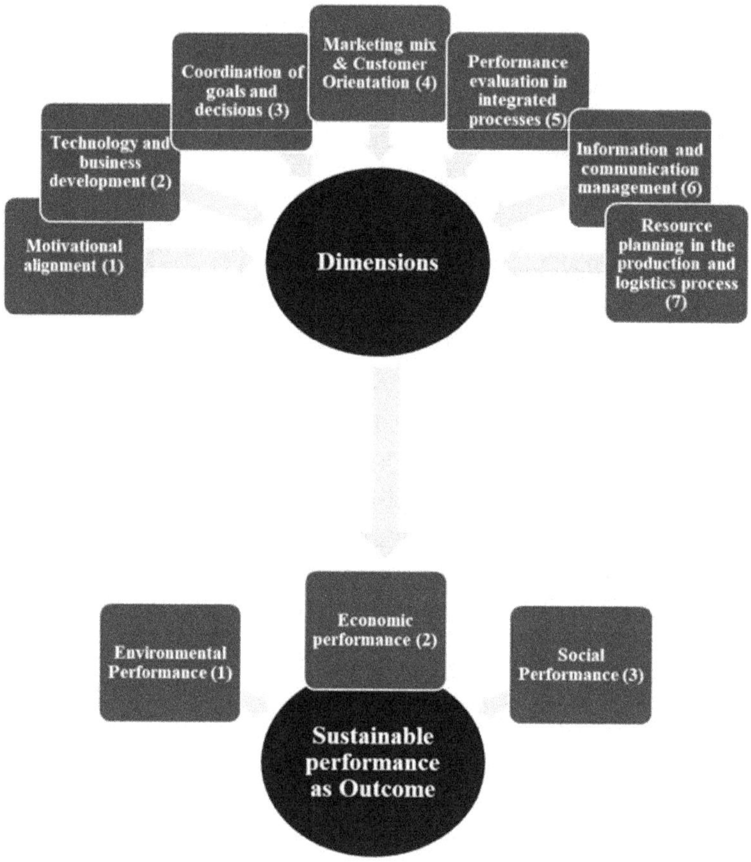

4. CONCLUSION

SCC defined as a long-term partnership process that SC partners aim to increase the mutual benefits. This chapter develops the existing collaboration literature and convinces scientific community to explore the power of collaboration with the impact of Industry 4.0 for SC sustainability. So, it is important to know the main dimensions in order to build a collaboration platform in SC 4.0. Also, recognizing collaboration dimensions can lead to make an overall understanding into result of SCC 4.0 by business partners. The necessity of collaboration in SC 4.0 leads to redesign of common structural processes, long-term commitments related to the sharing of up-to-date technology, and development of goals of business partners and (Raman et al., 2022).

The collaboration conceptual model in this chapter start with dimensions and ends with the formation of collaboration outcomes. Dimensions in seven components included Information and communication management, Resource planning in the production and logistics process, Collaborative decisions for business goals, Technology and business development, Motivational alignment, Performance evaluation in integrated processes, Marketing and Customer Orientation. Economic performance in the seven main sections included production and operation, customers, financial, cost, market, knowledge and innovation, and capabilities and competencies as the most frequent result of the collaboration of SC partners was mentioned by the studies. Social performance and environmental performance is another result of implementing collaboration in the SC. Sustainable performance is measurement of mutual and integrated relationships between commercial, organizational, social, economic and environmental sections. Sustainable performance is a process that supply chain managers can ensure the effectiveness and efficiency of resources obtained to achieve goals. Such performance requires a management framework that connects the main strategies of the supply chain with competitive and commercial policies and integrates economic, environmental and social information with other information (Di Vaio & Varriale.2020).

The activation of dimensions as indicators of collaboration in the SC can be implemented with Industry 4.0 technologies. There are significant relationships between Industry 4.0 technologies and SCC in economic, social and environmental performance (Billah et al, 2023). A combination of collaborative outcomes leads to the sustainable performance for the business partners. Using industry 4.0 technologies for production and operation, involvement of the commercial players within the SC with increasing human interactions, can be caused high sustainable performance.

REFERENCES

Abbasi, S., & Choukolaei, H. A. (2023). A systematic review of green supply chain network design literature focusing on carbon policy. *Decision Analytics Journal*, 100189.

Afshan, N., Chatterjee, S., & Chhetri, P. (2018). Impact of information technology and relational aspect on supply chain collaboration leading to financial performance. *Benchmarking*, *25*(7), 2496–2511. doi:10.1108/BIJ-09-2016-0142

Aggarwal, S., & Srivastava, M. K. (2016). Towards a grounded view of collaboration in Indian agrifood supply chains: A qualitative investigation. *British Food Journal*, *118*(5), 1085–1106. doi:10.1108/BFJ-08-2015-0274

Agrawal, T. K., Angelis, J., Khilji, W. A., Kalaiarasan, R., & Wiktorsson, M. (2023). Demonstration of a blockchain-based framework using smart contracts for supply chain collaboration. *International Journal of Production Research, 61*(5), 1497–1516. doi:10.1080/00207543.2022.2039413

Akhavan, P., & Philsoophian, M. (2022). Improving of supply chain collaboration and performance by using block chain technology as a mediating role and resilience as a moderating variable. *Journal of the Knowledge Economy*, 1–22. doi:10.100713132-022-01085-9

Al-Doori, J. A. (2019). The impact of supply chain collaboration on performance in automotive industry: Empirical evidence. *Journal of Industrial Engineering and Management, 12*(2), 241–253. doi:10.3926/jiem.2835

Al-Omoush, K. S., de Lucas, A., & del Val, M. T. (2023). The role of e-supply chain collaboration in collaborative innovation and value-co creation. *Journal of Business Research, 158*, 113647. doi:10.1016/j.jbusres.2023.113647

Ali, N., Ghazal, T. M., Ahmed, A., Abbas, S., Khan, M. A., Alzoubi, H. M., ... Khan, M. A. (2022). Fusion-based supply chain collaboration using machine learning techniques. *Intelligent Automation & Soft Computing, 31*(3), 1671–1687. doi:10.32604/iasc.2022.019892

Asree, S., Gopalan, S., & Zain, M. (2016). The impact of cultural intelligence on supply chain collaboration. *International Journal of Integrated Supply Management, 10*(3-4), 246–263. doi:10.1504/IJISM.2016.081265

Awan, U., Sroufe, R., & Shahbaz, M. (2021). Industry 4.0 and the circular economy: A literature review and recommendations for future research. *Business Strategy and the Environment, 30*(4), 2038–2060. doi:10.1002/bse.2731

Azevedo, S. G., Pimentel, C. O., & Matias, J. C. (2022, January). The role of supply chain 4.0 on supply chain collaboration-an exploratory case study in the automotive industry. In *2022 The 3rd International Conference on Industrial Engineering and Industrial Management* (pp. 1-8). Academic Press.

Billah, M. M., Alam, S. S., Masukujjaman, M., Ali, M. H., Makhbul, Z. K. M., & Salleh, M. F. M. (2023). Effects of Internet of Things, supply chain collaboration and ethical sensitivity on sustainable performance: Moderating effect of supply chain dynamism. *Journal of Enterprise Information Management, 36*(5), 1270–1295. doi:10.1108/JEIM-06-2022-0213

Bout, A. (2011). *Supply Chain Collaboration – barriers and enablers- a dyadic study of buyer-supplier relationships*. Academic Press.

Bratucu, R., & Ciofoaia, R. A. (2022). *Artificial Intelligence Mediated Supply Chain Collaboration: A Study on how Artificial Intelligence Technologies Influence Collaboration Processes in the Chain*. Academic Press.

Cao, M., & Zhang, Q. (2011). Supply chain collaboration: Impact on collaborative advantage and firm performance. *Journal of Operations Management, 29*(3), 163–180. doi:10.1016/j.jom.2010.12.008

Chakraborty, S., Bhattacharya, S., & Dobrzykowski, D. D. (2014). Impact of supply chain collaboration on value co-creation and firm performance: A healthcare service sector perspective. *Procedia Economics and Finance, 11*, 676–694. doi:10.1016/S2212-5671(14)00233-0

Chauhan, C., Kaur, P., Arrawatia, R., Ractham, P., & Dhir, A. (2022). Supply chain collaboration and sustainable development goals (SDGs). Teamwork makes achieving SDGs dream work. *Journal of Business Research, 147*, 290–307. doi:10.1016/j.jbusres.2022.03.044

Chen, L., Fu, Y., Liu, Y., & Wang, C. (2023). The Impact of Logistics Corporate Social Responsibility on Supply Chain Performance: Using Supply Chain Collaboration as an Intermediary Variable. *Sustainability (Basel), 15*(12), 9613. doi:10.3390u15129613

Chen, L., Zhao, X., Tang, O., Price, L., Zhang, S., & Zhu, W. (2017). Supply chain collaboration for sustainability: A literature review and future research agenda. *International Journal of Production Economics, 194*, 73–87. doi:10.1016/j.ijpe.2017.04.005

Chin, T. A., Tat, H. H., & Sulaiman, Z. (2015). Green supply chain management, environmental collaboration and sustainability performance. *Procedia CIRP, 26*, 695–699. doi:10.1016/j.procir.2014.07.035

Crum, M., Poist, R., & Daugherty, P. J. (2011). Review of logistics and supply chain relationship literature and suggested research agenda. *International Journal of Physical Distribution & Logistics Management, 41*(1), 16–31. doi:10.1108/09600031111101402

Cui, L., Gao, M., Dai, J., & Mou, J. (2022). Improving supply chain collaboration through operational excellence approaches: An IoT perspective. *Industrial Management & Data Systems, 122*(3), 565–591. doi:10.1108/IMDS-01-2020-0016

Della Corte, V., Aria, M., Del Gaudio, G., Barney, J. B., Cobanoglu, C., & Sepe, F. (2021). The relevance of relational capabilities in collaborative decisions. *International Journal of Contemporary Hospitality Management, 33*(12), 4391–4417. doi:10.1108/IJCHM-01-2021-0037

El Ouarrak, Y., & Hmioui, A. (2023, February). Communication between Supply Chain Actors: A Risk Reduction Factor in Supply Chains. In *International Congress on Information and Communication Technology* (pp. 695-703). Singapore: Springer Nature Singapore.

Fernando, Y., Tseng, M. L., Wahyuni-Td, I. S., de Sousa Jabbour, A. B. L., Chiappetta Jabbour, C. J., & Foropon, C. (2023). Cyber supply chain risk management and performance in industry 4.0 era: Information system security practices in Malaysia. *Journal of Industrial and Production Engineering*, *40*(2), 102–116. doi:10.1080/21681015.2022.2116495

Ferrari, A. M., Volpi, L., Settembre-Blundo, D., & García-Muiña, F. E. (2021). Dynamic life cycle assessment (LCA) integrating life cycle inventory (LCI) and Enterprise resource planning (ERP) in an industry 4.0 environment. *Journal of Cleaner Production*, *286*, 125314. doi:10.1016/j.jclepro.2020.125314

Frazzon, E. M., Rodriguez, C. M. T., Pereira, M. M., Pires, M. C., & Uhlmann, I. (2019). Towards supply chain management 4.0. *Brazilian Journal of Operations & Production Management*, *16*(2), 180–191. doi:10.14488/BJOPM.2019.v16.n2.a2

Frederico, G. F., Garza-Reyes, J. A., Anosike, A., & Kumar, V. (2019). Supply Chain 4.0: Concepts, maturity and research agenda. *Supply Chain Management*, *25*(2), 262–282. doi:10.1108/SCM-09-2018-0339

Glova, J., Sabol, T., & Vajda, V. (2014). Business Models for the Internet of Things Environment. *Procedia Economics and Finance*, *15*, 1122–1129. doi:10.1016/S2212-5671(14)00566-8

Gumboh, J., & Gichira, R. (2015). Supply chain collaboration among SMEs in Kenya: A review of collaboration barriers. *International Journal of Humanities and Social Science*, *5*(9), 2–5.

Hanafiah, H., & Widjaja, A. W. (2022). The influence of resource complementary, technology competence and supply chain risk criteria on supply chain collaboration (case study of export import activities in Indonesia). In *Proceeding of the International Conference on Family Business and Entrepreneurship* (*Vol. 3*, No. 1). Academic Press.

Haque, M. & Islam, R. (2018). Impact of supply chain collaboration and knowledge sharing on organizational outcomes in pharmaceutical industry of Bangladesh. *Journal of Global Operations and Strategic Sourcing*.

Heaver, T. D. (2015). Increased collaborative relationships in international logistics: Canadian and other national and corporate examples. *Maritime Policy & Management*, *42*(3), 278–292. doi:10.1080/03088839.2013.873547

Hendayani, R., & Alviyan, B. (2019). The Relationship between Supply Chain Collaboration of Value Innovation in Small Medium Enterprises and Supply Chain Capability as Mediator to Achieve Competitive Advantages. In *1st International Conference on Economics, Business, Entrepreneurship, and Finance*. Atlantis Press. 10.2991/icebef-18.2019.133

Ho, T., Kumar, A., & Shiwakoti, N. (2020). Supply chain collaboration and performance: An empirical study of maturity model. *SN Applied Sciences*, *2*(4), 1–16. doi:10.100742452-020-2468-y

Hohn, M. M., & Durach, C. F. (2023). Taking a different view: Theorizing on firms' development toward an integrative view on socially sustainable supply chain management. *International Journal of Physical Distribution & Logistics Management*, *53*(1), 13–34. doi:10.1108/IJPDLM-09-2021-0410

Hopkins, J. L. (2021). An investigation into emerging industry 4.0 technologies as drivers of supply chain innovation in Australia. *Computers in Industry*, *125*, 103323. doi:10.1016/j.compind.2020.103323

Jaturat, N., Jaturat, M., Tonsakun-Aree, C., & Deelert, J. (2022). *Effect of Enterprise Resource Planning on Supply Chain Forecasting Capability through Collaboration: An Empirical Study of Frozen Foods Industry in Thailand*. Academic Press.

Jeenanunta, C., Ueki, Y., & Visanvetchakij, T. (2013). Supply chain collaboration and firm performance in Thai automotive and electronics industries. *Global Business Perspectives*, *1*(4), 418–432. doi:10.100740196-013-0031-6

Jeng, D. J. F. (2015). Generating a causal model of supply chain collaboration using the fuzzy DEMATEL technique. *Computers & Industrial Engineering*, *87*, 283–295. doi:10.1016/j.cie.2015.05.007

Jraisat, L., Upadhyay, A., Ghalia, T., Jresseit, M., Kumar, V., & Sarpong, D. (2023). Triads in sustainable supply-chain perspective: Why is a collaboration mechanism needed? *International Journal of Production Research*, *61*(14), 4725–4741. doi:1 0.1080/00207543.2021.1936263

Kamble, S. S., & Gunasekaran, A. (2020). Big data-driven supply chain performance measurement system: A review and framework for implementation. *International Journal of Production Research*, *58*(1), 65–86. doi:10.1080/00207543.2019.1630770

Li, S., Xu, T., Park, K. C., & Kang, M. (2023). The effect of supply chain collaboration on firms' risk management under technology turbulence. *Production Planning and Control*, 1–16. doi:10.1080/09537287.2023.2225474

Liu, X. (2018). *LRN 2016 SPECIAL–the antecedents and consequences of reduction within a supply chain collaboration orientation of CO2 emissions: evidence from China*. Academic Press.

Lynch, J. (2019). Effective Supply Chain Collaboration. In Contemporary Operations and Logistics (pp. 193-218). Palgrave Macmillan. doi:10.1007/978-3-030-14493-7_11

Ma, H. L., Wang, Z. X., & Chan, F. T. (2020). How important are supply chain collaborative factors in supply chain finance? A view of financial service providers in China. *International Journal of Production Economics*, *219*, 341–346. doi:10.1016/j.ijpe.2019.07.002

Margherita, E. G., & Braccini, A. M. (2021). Managing industry 4.0 automation for fair ethical business development: A single case study. *Technological Forecasting and Social Change*, *172*, 121048. doi:10.1016/j.techfore.2021.121048

Masoomi, L., Taran-Lala, O., Smith, C. V., & Trollman, H. (2023). Leveraging Industry 4.0 for Supply Chain Collaboration: Creating Competitive Advantage for Small Farms in the United Kingdom and Ukraine. *Engineering Proceedings*, *40*(1), 21.

Misbauddin, S. M., Alam, M. J., Karmaker, C. L., Nabi, M. N. U., & Hasan, M. M. (2023). Exploring the antecedents of supply chain viability in a pandemic context: An empirical study on the commercial flower supply chain of an emerging economy. *Sustainability (Basel)*, *15*(3), 2146. doi:10.3390u15032146

Narayanan, S., Jayaraman, V., Luo, Y., & Swaminathan, J. M. (2011). The antecedents of process integration in business process outsourcing and its effect on firm performance. *Journal of Operations Management*, *29*(1-2), 3–16. doi:10.1016/j.jom.2010.05.001

Ocicka, B., Baraniecka, A., & Jefmański, B. (2022). Exploring supply chain collaboration for green innovations: Evidence from the high-tech industry in Poland. *Energies*, *15*(5), 1750. doi:10.3390/en15051750

Oubrahim, I., Sefiani, N., & Happonen, A. (2022). Supply Chain Performance Evaluation Models: A Literature Review. *Acta logistica*, *9*(2), 207-221.

Pradabwong, J., Braziotis, C., Tannock, J. D., & Pawar, K. S. (2017). Business process management and supply chain collaboration: Effects on performance and competitiveness. *Supply Chain Management*, *22*(2), 107–121. doi:10.1108/SCM-01-2017-0008

Ralston, P. M., Richey, R. G., & Grawe, S. J. (2017). The past and future of supply chain collaboration: A literature synthesis and call for research. *International Journal of Logistics Management*. Advance online publication. doi:10.1108/IJLM-09-2015-0175

Ramanathan, U. (2012). Supply chain collaboration for improved forecast accuracy of promotional sales. *International Journal of Operations & Production Management*, *32*(6), 676–695. doi:10.1108/01443571211230925

Ramanathan, U. (2017). How Smart Operations Help Better Planning and Replenishment? Empirical Study–Supply Chain Collaboration for Smart Operations. In Supply Chain Management in the Big Data Era (pp. 25-49). IGI Global.

Ramanathan, U., & Gunasekaran, A. (2014). Supply chain collaboration: Impact of success in long-term partnerships. *International Journal of Production Economics*, *147*, 252–259. doi:10.1016/j.ijpe.2012.06.002

Ramesh, A., Banwet, D. K., & Shankar, R. (2010). Modeling the barriers of supply chain collaboration. *Journal of Modelling in Management*, *5*(2), 176–193. doi:10.1108/17465661011061014

Richey, R. G., Adams, F. G., & Dalela, V. (2012). Technology and flexibility: Enablers of collaboration and time-based logistics quality. *Journal of Business Logistics*, *33*(1), 34–49. doi:10.1111/j.0000-0000.2011.01036.x

Şahin, H., & Topal, B. (2019). Examination of effect of information sharing on businesses performance in the supply chain process. *International Journal of Production Research*, *57*(3), 815–828. doi:10.1080/00207543.2018.1484954

Salam, M. A. (2017). The mediating role of supply chain collaboration on the relationship between technology, trust and operational performance. *Benchmarking*, *24*(2), 298–317. doi:10.1108/BIJ-07-2015-0075

Simatupang, T. M., & Sridharan, R. (2005). The collaboration index: A measure for supply chain collaboration. *International Journal of Physical Distribution & Logistics Management*, *35*(1), 44–62. doi:10.1108/09600030510577421

Simatupang, T. M. & Sridharan, R. (2018). Complementarities in supply chain collaboration. *Industrial Engineering and Management Systems, 17*(1), 30-42.

Solaimani, S., & van der Veen, J. (2022). Open supply chain innovation: An extended view on supply chain collaboration. *Supply Chain Management*, *27*(5), 597–610. doi:10.1108/SCM-09-2020-0433

Srivastava, P., Srinivasan, M., & Iyer, K. N. (2015). Relational resource antecedents and operational outcome of supply chain collaboration: The role of environmental turbulence. *Transportation Journal*, *54*(2), 240–274. doi:10.5325/transportationj.54.2.0240

Sundram, V. P. K., Bahrin, A. S., Abdul Munir, Z. B., & Zolait, A. H. (2018). The effect of supply chain information management and information system infrastructure: The mediating role of supply chain integration towards manufacturing performance in Malaysia. *Journal of Enterprise Information Management*, *31*(5), 751–770. doi:10.1108/JEIM-06-2017-0084

Talan, G., & Sharma, G. D. (2020). From business goals to societal goals via sustainable investment: An integrative review and research agenda. *World Review of Entrepreneurship, Management and Sustainable Development*, *16*(1), 108–124. doi:10.1504/WREMSD.2020.105530

Teng, T., Tsinopoulos, C., & Tse, Y. K. (2022). IS capabilities, supply chain collaboration and quality performance in services: The moderating effect of environmental dynamism. *Industrial Management & Data Systems*, *122*(7), 1592–1619. doi:10.1108/IMDS-08-2021-0496

Tuni, A., Rentizelas, A., & Duffy, A. (2018). Environmental performance measurement for green supply chains: A systematic analysis and review of quantitative methods. *International Journal of Physical Distribution & Logistics Management*, *48*(8), 765–793. doi:10.1108/IJPDLM-02-2017-0062

Uddin, M. B., & Akhter, B. (2022). Investigating the relationship between top management commitment, supply chain collaboration, and sustainable firm performance in the agro-processing supply chain. *Operations Management Research : Advancing Practice Through Research*, *15*(3-4), 1399–1417. doi:10.100712063-022-00257-9

Veile, J. W., Schmidt, M. C., Müller, J. M., & Voigt, K. I. (2022). The transformation of supply chain collaboration and design through Industry 4.0. *International Journal of Logistics Research and Applications,* 1-29.

Wu, L., & Chiu, M. L. (2018). Examining supply chain collaboration with determinants and performance impact: Social capital, justice, and technology use perspectives. *International Journal of Information Management*, *39*, 5–19. doi:10.1016/j.ijinfomgt.2017.11.004

Yildiz Ozenc, S. C., Er, M., & Firat, S. U. (2023). Risks in Supply Chain 4.0: A Literature Review Study. In *Global Joint Conference on Industrial Engineering and Its Application Areas* (pp. 163-177). Springer. 10.1007/978-3-031-08782-0_13

Chapter 8
Smart Contracts as a Third Party Coordinator:
Tools for Implementing Agreements in E-Business Management

Hossein Mohammadi Dolat-abadi
https://orcid.org/0000-0002-0526-0157
College of Farabi, Department of Industrial Engineering, University of Tehran, Iran

Mahsima Rasi
College of Engineering, Department of Industrial Engineering, University of Tehran, Iran

Seyed Amirsadra Sadat
https://orcid.org/0009-0005-5056-9742
College of Farabi, Department of Industrial Engineering, University of Tehran, Iran

ABSTRACT

One of the important issues in the field of contract implementation is the security and speed of contract implementation in a way that can gain the trust of the contracting parties. In response to this challenge, one of these tools are smart contracts, which compared to other types of electronic contracts have features such as high speed and security and low cost in forming the contract. Smart contracts are currently used in various fields such as finance, law, banking, stock exchange, blockchain, government, industry, charity, etc. These contracts have many advantages, such as

DOI: 10.4018/979-8-3693-0210-1.ch008

reducing costs, increasing speed, improving security, eliminating intermediaries, and preventing fraud. In simpler terms, smart contracts have taken over the task of making transactions with tools, the most important of which is the blockchain platform. Hence, in this research, the framework of using smart contracts in the field of e-commerce is discussed and the advantages, disadvantages, how to apply, successful experiences, and perspectives for the future of these contracts are presented.

1. INTRODUCTION

The contemporary shift towards digitalization within businesses and supply chains, facilitated by the integration of Industry 4.0 technologies, gives rise to significant strategic concerns and economic consequences. The adoption of these technologies has gained popularity in recent years, owing to the perceived advantages they offer and their pivotal role in the realm of digital technology (Ivanov and Dolgui, 2019) .Nevertheless, it is imperative to conduct a more in-depth examination of businesses and supply chains to gain a comprehensive understanding of these swift and escalating developments. This analysis should focus on discerning whether Industry 4.0 technologies indeed offer tangible operational benefits and genuine market prospects (Liu and De Giovanni, 2019). Additionally, it is of utmost importance to scrutinize whether their adoption is merely a contemporary trend influenced by ongoing technological advancements and stimulated by government development initiatives, rather than a substantive integration resulting in tangible advantages. In any event, it is evident that firms and supply chains necessitate a thorough examination of the strategic shifts in behavior that are essential for the appropriate selection and utilization of Industry 4.0 technologies. Furthermore, it is crucial to make precise evaluations of the economic ramifications of such technology integration and to prudently assess the broader implications it holds for the entire supply chain.

Blockchain, as a decentralized ledger technology, serves as a robust means for securely, persistently, and verifiably recording value exchanges among parties. It constitutes the foundational technology for cryptocurrencies like Bitcoin and Ethereum. While blockchain's initial utilization was predominantly in financial transactions, its scope has since expanded, encompassing diverse industries. Supply chain management represents one of the notable domains where blockchain finds practical application. Supply chains, given their intricate nature with multiple stakeholders and diverse business transactions, encounter various challenges, including issues related to transparency, traceability, risk management, disruptions, trust-building, and reputation development. Blockchain technology introduces the prospect of addressing these challenges via the incorporation of smart contracts. Smart contracts represent digital agreements, composed in computer code and deployed on the blockchain, which autonomously execute when predefined conditions are satisfied. Their application streamlines supply chain operations by automating the verification and execution of the numerous business transactions inherent to the process. The presence of a decentralized, Immutable record guarantees equitable access to information for all parties involved and contributes to trust-building within the supply chain(Dolat-Abadi, 2021). Smart contracts play a pivotal role in enhancing transparency, traceability, and overall efficiency, consequently fostering increased agility and reinforcing relationships among supply chain stakeholders.

Several additional challenges are encountered within the supply chain's coordination phase. The participation of multiple entities across various stages of the supply chain leads to complexities in management due to the presence of multiple decision-makers, resulting in information asymmetry. The deficiency in information sharing and traceability within the supply chain can impede progress tracking and the ability to detect and respond to disruptive events, adversely influencing collaboration among the involved parties(Mohammadi et al., 2019). This issue is closely intertwined with the risk management challenge, necessitating organizations to maintain adaptability in an ever-more volatile global landscape, enabling them to effectively address abrupt shifts like natural disasters or production disruptions. To do so, there is a need for greater transparency throughout the supply chain. With consumers exhibiting heightened discernment, there is a growing inclination towards seeking information regarding the origin and history of a product prior to making a purchase. The fundamental thread running through all these challenges is the imperative of establishing trust and cultivating robust relationships among supply chain partners. Such initiatives are essential in sustaining the dependability and effectiveness of the supply chain. Organizations persist in contending with these Issues, and while advancements have been achieved via enhanced technology and management practices, there remains ample scope for enhancement. One prospective avenue for mitigating these coordination hurdles lies in the application of blockchain technology.

2. BLOCKCHAIN TECHNOLOGY

Blockchain technology is "an open, decentralized ledger capable of efficiently recording transactions between two parties in a verifiable and immutable manner". While still in its early stages, the most prominent utilization of this technology has been witnessed in the form of cryptocurrencies, most notably Bitcoin (Yli-Huumo et al., 2016). Three primary advantages underpin the blockchain concept: First, it operates on a global network of computers, eliminating the vulnerability associated with a central database. Second, its openness and public accessibility facilitate continuous scrutiny. Third, robust encryption ensures data security. These attributes collectively serve to reduce two pivotal costs: the verification cost and the networking cost. Given that all transactions are cryptographically validated via consensus and permanently archived on the blockchain, the need for supplementary expenses to confirm trustworthiness is obviated. Furthermore, it simplifies the audit trail review in the event of future issues. Additionally, by integrating blockchain technology with a cryptocurrency such as Bitcoin, the prospect of establishing a decentralized marketplace, free from costly intermediaries, becomes conceivable.

2.1. Blockchain Definition and Principles

Fundamentally, blockchain constitutes a decentralized ledger technology that capitalizes on the resources of a vast peer-to-peer network to validate and authorize transactions. These transactions are methodically cataloged in chronological order within blocks, and these blocks are interconnected through cryptographic means, thus becoming indelibly preserved on the blockchain, forming an unalterable chain. It's noteworthy that there exists no singular copy of the blockchain; instead, duplicates are distributed globally among participants within the network, and these copies are updated in unison. This mechanism guarantees that the ledger remains impervious to manipulation by any single entity, necessitating consensus from the network's majority for any alterations. Additionally, the data encapsulated within the transactions is highly versatile, rendering blockchain technology exceptionally adaptable to diverse applications(Zeng et al., 2020).

2.2. How Blockchain Works

In accordance with its nomenclature, a blockchain comprises a sequential relationship of blocks. Each of these blocks encompasses the transaction data and the accompanying information pertinent to each individual transaction(Singhal et al., 2018). Every transaction, and each block, carries a timestamp signifying the moment at which it was incorporated into the blockchain. Successive blocks need the inclusion of the identifier or hash of the preceding block, forming the essential linkage and relationship that binds all the blocks together in a coherent chain (Figure 1).

Figure 1. Schematically how blockchain works

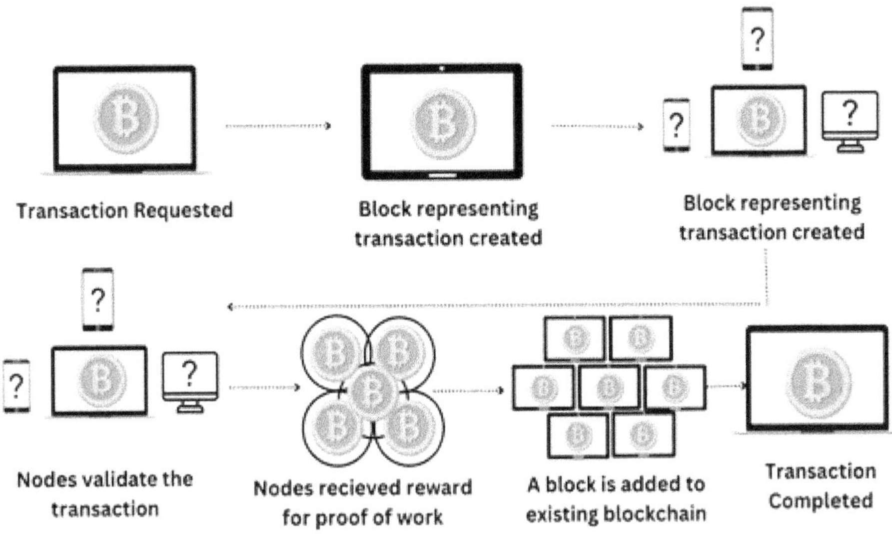

To append new blocks to the blockchain, a process known as 'mining' is imperative. A prevalent method for achieving this is through a proof-of-work framework, in which miners engage in computationally intensive tasks, effectively entering a lottery to earn the privilege of appending the subsequent block to the chain, as elucidated in reference(Sarmah and Engineering, 2018). Miners engage in a competitive endeavor to unravel a complex problem, with the successful miner subsequently disseminating its proof of work to other miners for authentication. A state of consensus is established once a marginal majority, typically at 51%, concurs, signifying the readiness for the inclusion of the new block (Figure 2).

Figure 2. Blockchain process adopted by Elommal et al. (2021)

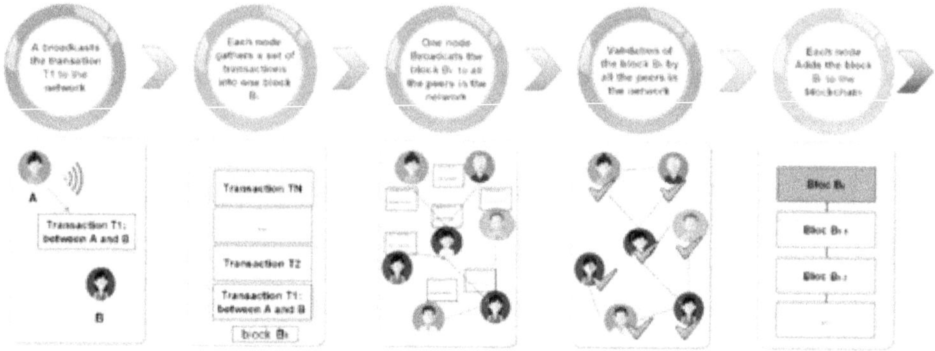

Upon the successful integration of a block, it is diffused across all nodes within the network, ensuring their synchronization with the most recent Version of the blockchain. Furthermore, as a remuneration for their efforts, miners receive rewards typically in the form of cryptocurrency tokens associated with the blockchain(e.g. Bitcoin or Ether). Consequently, transactions executed on the blockchain entail a cost, serving as an incentive for miners to dedicate computational resources to solve the intricate problems. As the blockchain extends in length and garners increased computational backing, any attempts to tamper with a prior transaction become progressively challenging. This is attributed to the necessity of modifying all subsequent blocks and achieving consensus, a task demanding an excessive allocation of resources, as outlined in reference.

2.3. Advantages of Blockchain

In summary, the advantages of blockchain implementing are as follows:

- Immutability. Signifying that once data is recorded, it becomes impervious to deletion or substitution. As a result, blockchain serves as a robust defense against data tampering within the network.
- Transparency. It operates in a decentralized fashion. This decentralization empowers any participant in the network to independently verify data entries on the blockchain, fostering trust among the general public in the integrity of the network.
- Censorship. It operates devoid of single-party control. Consequently, no singular entity, inclusive of governmental authorities, holds the capacity to disrupt the network's functionality. In contrast, conventional databases are

characterized by central authorities overseeing network operations, affording them the ability to engage in censorship. For example, in traditional systems like banking, authorities possess the capacity to suspend user accounts.

- Traceability. This stands as a prominent feature of blockchain technology, as is able to generate an unalterable audit trial, facilitating the effortless tracking of modifications within the network. Conversely, traditional databases lack the transparency and immutability necessary to ensure the existence of a lasting audit trail.

2.4. Limitations of Blockchain

In summary, the limitations of blockchain implementing are as follows:

- **Private keys**

Blockchain security heavily relies on private keys, which assume a pivotal role in authenticating blockchain addresses. When a crypto currency wallet is established, it entails the provision of a private key, essentially functioning as a password, enabling the wallet owner to execute fund withdrawals. A crucial consideration is that the misplacement of this key renders the funds inaccessible. Therefore, imperatively there should be multiple copies maintained of the private key as a precaution against potential loss. It is crucial to underscore that if unauthorized access is obtained to any of these copies, the integrity of the crypto currency wallet is compromised. Additionally, in contrast to the alterable nature of passwords linked to social media or email accounts, any attempt to modify a generated private key is an unattainable endeavor.

- **Possibility of disruption of network security**

Blockchain technology is known worldwide for its top-notch security. However, there is a major drawback. The validation process in a blockchain is done through miners maintaining massive computing power. If a miner with enough computing power to control more than 50% of a blockchain's mining hash rate, a 51% attack can be launched. Therefore, preventing transactions from gaining confirmations and even pausing payments between users becomes plausible. Moreover, reversing the completed transactions leading to double spending on the cryptocurrency is another menacing drawback. Such attack is unlikely on bigger blockchains like Bitcoin or Ethereum. However, new blockchains or forked crypto can suffer huge damage from this activity. Furthermore, there are also instances of fraud in various cryptocurrencies.

- **High costs of implementation**

The integration of blockchain technology within an enterprise necessitates a significant financial commitment. The capital-intensive nature of this investment often acts as a deterrent for many companies considering its adoption. For business owners interested in implementing blockchain, the initial steps involve the recruitment of essential personnel, including core blockchain developers and blockchain software developers, entailing a substantial financial outlay. Subsequently, the development of blockchain-based applications and the procurement of requisite hardware further contribute to the overall cost.

- **Inefficient mining process**

In the realm of blockchain, each block undergoes a mining procedure known as Proof-of-Work. Successful participation in this mining process needs the use of high-performance computing equipment by each miner. The fierce competitiveness among multiple miners to mine a single block results in a sole recipient of the block rewards. Therefore, this competitive mining activity leads to a substantial expenditure of energy and resources, engendering inefficiency in the process.

- **Environmental impacts**

The operations of mining, minting, and transaction validation demand the continuous operation of high-performance systems. Beyond substantial financial investments, these activities are power-intensive, which can result in significant adverse environmental effects. The environmental implications of such power consumption have prompted notable actions, including the ban on blockchain mining in China's Inner Mongolia region, driven by concerns over the disproportionate ecological impact.

- **Storage problems**

Within the blockchain infrastructure, data is disseminated across various network nodes, fostering a decentralized data-sharing model. In this context, the entire data associated with a specific blockchain resides within the storage capacity of a miner's system. As the user base expands, the data volume similarly increases, necessitating periodic enhancements in hard disk capacity. Over time, there may arise a scenario where the cumulative data of a blockchain surpasses the limitations of available hard disk sizes.

- **Anonymity**

Anonymity serves as the pertinent attraction of blockchain technology. While it safeguards one's true identity, it is crucial to consider the implications, particularly concerning potential money laundering activities. An individual with an anonymous identity can initiate fund transfers globally, leaving no discernible trace of these transactions beyond the involved wallet addresses. Investigations have frequently revealed instances of cybercriminals exploiting blockchain technology as a platform for money laundering endeavors.

- **Immutability**

Upon inputting data into a blockchain, it acquires an immutable quality, rendering any subsequent alterations or updates unfeasible. While this unalterable attribute bestows an advantage, safeguarding data integrity from tampering, it's essential to recognize the dual facets of this characteristic.

- **Scalability**

Every block within a blockchain exhibits a predefined data storage capacity, which consequently contributes to the Inert and laborious nature of transaction validation. Regrettably, there exists no provision for expanding the block size on a blockchain. Although networks such as Polygon have introduced mechanisms to enhance the transaction processing speed of Ethereum, renowned for its sluggish network, these measures may serve as temporary solutions, leaving the core issue unresolved.

- **Hard forks**

Hard forks transpire when the majority of blockchain participants seek to introduce novel regulations or, alternatively, when a substantial cohort within the blockchain endeavors to establish a fresh cryptocurrency. In such instances, the pre-existing and the freshly created cryptocurrencies coexist as distinct entities. A common challenge for users arises when the newly minted coin is not promptly accessible on exchange platforms upon its inception.

- **Legal formalities and regulations**

The blockchain sector continues to grapple with regulatory hurdles across different global jurisdictions. Additionally, legal frameworks in various nations and localities impose restrictions on the utilization and adoption of blockchain technology.

While blockchain unquestionably represents the future, it is vital to acknowledge its associated shortcomings if one intends to invest in or deploy it. The technology remains in an evolving phase and undergoes continuous development.

3. SMART CONTRACTS

A smart contract stands as an autonomous computer program that carries out the stipulations of a contract devoid of external intermediaries(Nozari et al., 2023). Smart contract execution encompasses a wide spectrum of activities, including financial transactions, service delivery, the unlocking of digitally rights-managed content, and data manipulation like altering the name on a land title. Furthermore, smart contracts exhibit the capacity to enforce privacy protection by enabling the controlled disclosure of privacy-protected data, thus accommodating specific requests.

Diverse architectural approaches run the development, distribution, management, and maintenance of the software supporting smart contracts. These programs can be stored within blockchain or other distributed ledger technologies, seamlessly integrated into an array of payment systems and digital exchanges, encompassing cryptocurrencies like Bitcoin. It is crucial to note that despite their nomenclature, smart contracts do not inherently possess legal binding force(Wang et al., 2018). Their primary role centers on the automated execution of predefined business logic, enabling a wide array of tasks, processes, or transactions based on programmed responses to specific conditions. Establishing legal links to binding agreements between parties necessitates separate legal procedures.

3.1. How Smart Contracts Work

A brief summary of how smart contracts work in a blockchain is shown in Figure 3. To gain insight into the operational mechanics of smart contracts, it is imperative to grasp the underlying functioning of the Ethereum platform and the role played by smart contracts within this framework. In the case of Ethereum, the fundamental unit of operation is the account, and the blockchain meticulously monitors the status of each account. Every instance involving the transfer of value or data between accounts triggers state transitions recorded on the blockchain. Two distinct categories of accounts exist: Externally Owned Accounts (EOAs), overseen by private keys designated for human users, and Contract Accounts, controlled by their internal code and can solely be activated by an EOA (Guo et al., 2019). Notably, smart contracts find their residence within Contract Accounts situated within the blockchain.

The creation of a smart contract dictates an initial collaborative effort by the concerned parties, who must first identify an opportunity for cooperation and mutually agree upon their respective desired outcomes. These outcomes may lead to various forms of value exchange, such as goods or services. Subsequently, the terms and conditions that run the exchange process are established, delineating conditions triggered by the parties themselves, external conditions, or specific milestones. All the prerequisites and contractual provisions are then meticulously translated into a programmatic form, employing computer logic and code (Giancaspro and review, 2017).

The smart contract, once comprehensively defined, is deployed onto the blockchain, where it stands poised to self-execute upon fulfillment of the predefined conditions. To initiate a smart contract, users begin a transaction with a Contract Account using an Externally Owned Account (EOA), which is then encrypted with the initiator's private key and broadcasted to other nodes within the blockchain. Other users may validate the transaction's legitimacy by employing the generated public key, thereby confirming the initiator's role in the transaction(Hu et al., 2020).

Upon securing consensus from the majority of network nodes, the transaction is permanently appended to the blockchain, thereby effectuating the successful execution of the smart contract and recording its outcomes. Consequently, as the blockchain's state evolves, these changes propagate across all network nodes, ensuring the unchangeable nature of the outcomes (https://www.geeksforgeeks.org/smart-contracts-in-blockchain/).

Figure 3. smart contract under blockchain adopted by Karamitsos et al. (2018)

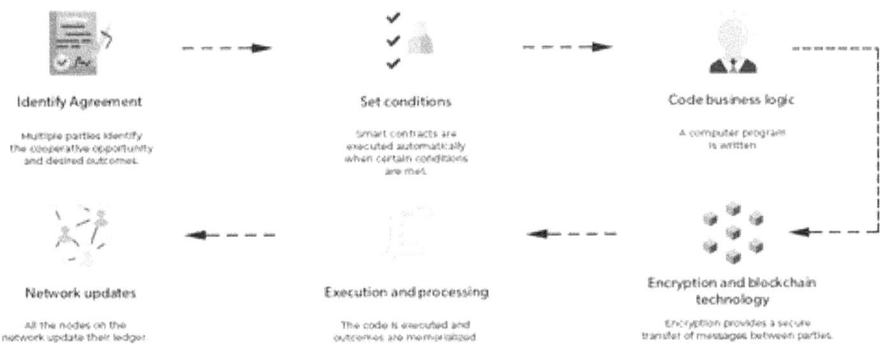

3.2. Smart Contract Use Cases

Blockchain smart contract use cases permeate various industries and domains, including to FinTech & banking, healthcare, supply chain, insurance, real estate, digital identity, IP protection, gaming, retail & and e-commerce, and human resource management, but is not necessarily restricted to any of these (Mohanta et al., 2018).

Figure 4. Smart contracts cases

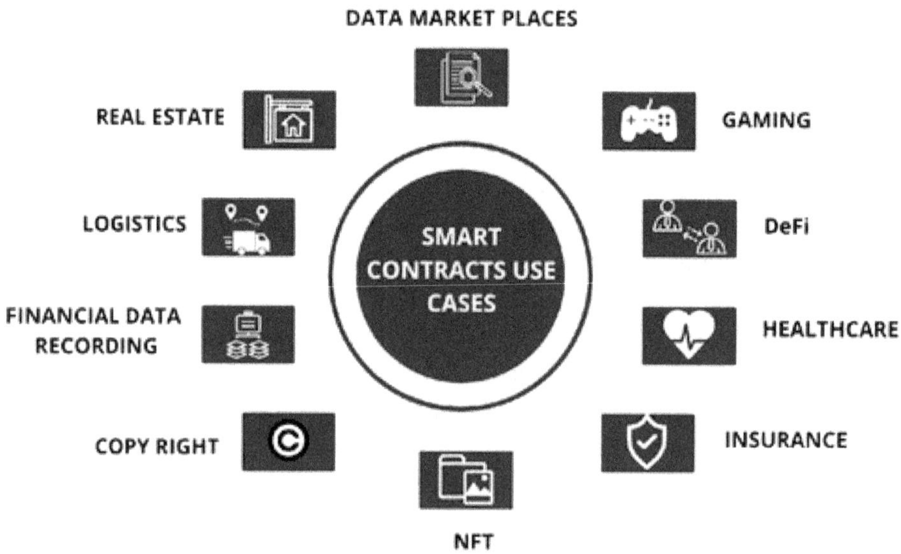

3.3. Challenges Facing Smart Contracts

Blockchain and smart contracts represent emerging technologies with the latent potential to revolutionize procurement processes, leading to improvements in transparency, efficacy, and security. However, the implementation of these innovations is not free of crucial challenges and associated risks, demanding comprehensive evaluation. This article tends to delve into the primary concerns that necessitate consideration before commencing the adoption of blockchain and smart contracts for procurement applications (Khan et al., 2021).

- **Technical complexity**

Blockchain and smart contracts dependence upon complex algorithms and protocols, necessitating a robust degree of technical proficiency and infrastructure for their operation and maintenance. It is imperative to ascertain the availability of essential skills, resources, and support for the formulation, creation, and deployment of these solutions, as well as for addressing any potential issues that might happen.

Additionally, compatibility and Inter-operation ability between the solutions and the existing systems and processes, as well as those of the suppliers and collaborators, must be fastidiously ensured.

- **Legal uncertainty**

Blockchain and smart contracts, being relatively original concepts, remain largely unregulated in numerous law-Related fields, giving rise to legal ambiguity and the potential for disputes. It is necessary to maintain a thorough understanding of the relevant laws and regulations that govern the procurement endeavors, encompassing areas such as contract law, data protection, taxation, and dispute resolution. Moreover, the establishment of precise and applicable terms and conditions for blockchain and smart contract transactions is vital, alongside the adoption of mechanisms for addressing and modifying conflicts or errors that may arise.

- **Cultural resistance**

Blockchain and smart contracts represent factious technologies that check conventional business practices, demanding a shift in mindset and corporate culture. Overcoming potential resistance and skepticism from stakeholders, including employees, suppliers, customers, and regulators, is urgently necessary. Effective communication of the benefits and risks associated with these technologies, as well as the modifications and expectations they bring, is essential. Furthermore, the provision of thorough training and education is vital to enable and nurture the adoption and integration of these technologies.

- **Security threats**

Blockchain and smart contracts, while powered to provide security and resistance to distortion, are not impenetrable to cyberattacks and vicious individuals Protecting the users' data, assets, and transactions against unauthorized access, alteration, or deletion is an essentiality not to be overlooked. The establishment of rigorous security protocols, inclusive of encryption, authentication, authorization, and backup mechanisms prove to be in dire need of implementation. Additionally, continuous monitoring and auditing of blockchain and smart contract operations, engaged with swift and efficient responses to any incidents or breaches of contracts, are indispensable components of a augmented security strategy.

- **Ethical implications**

Blockchain and smart contracts administer considerable influence and can exert both positive and negative effects on society and the environment. Ethical considerations must be at the frontline of the procurement decision-making, surrounding aspects like the sourcing, manufacturing, distribution, and consumption of goods and services. It is mandatory to attain congruence the blockchain and smart contract solutions with the defined values, principles, and standards, as well as those of your stakeholders. Furthermore, the solutions should be scrupulously designed to meet principles of fairness, inclusivity, and responsibility.

4. E-BUSINESS MANAGEMENT

The conventional notion of business organizations has been profoundly reformed by the capabilities of the Internet and web technology. The contemporary understanding of an enterprise embraces a broader spectrum that now encompasses multiple company locations, collaborative business partners, customers, and vendors. The traditional constraints of geographical boundaries have dissipated, as operations can be expanded wherever Internet connectivity is available. This transformation is primarily attributable to the transition from traditional paper-based organizations to information-centric, Internet-enabled E-business enterprises (Aliahmadi et al., 2023).

E-business enterprises exhibit a remarkable characteristic by operating around the clock, remaining accessible 24 hours a day. This independence from temporal constraints allows managers, vendors, and customers to engage in business transactions at their convenience, unhindered by geographical limitations, anytime and from anywhere.

The capabilities of the Internet have handed the E-business enterprises a substantial competitive edge, significantly reinforcing their business value. This technological advancement has inaugurated fresh avenues for commerce, enabling the buying and selling of goods and services via the Internet. The communication capabilities facilitated by the Internet empower businesses to reach new markets globally, transcending geographical restrains. This empowerment extends to both customers and vendors/suppliers, affording them secure access to information and enabling prompt action whenever required. Furthermore the adoption of Internet technologies has led to a decrease, in expenses for businesses in unstable conditions(Combe, 2012). This decrease is mainly due, to the elimination of paper based operations accelerated communication and the creation of environments. Consequently businesses are able to operate with efficiency and cost effectiveness in the realm. The effect of these radical changes is the reduction in administrative and management overheads, reduction in inventory, and faster delivery of goods and services to customers.

The business processes are conducted through enterprise software like ERP, SCM, and CRM supported by data warehouse, decision support, and knowledge management systems. The Firms using e-commerce approaches to enrich faraway locations to deliver products and services. e-commerce approaches such as SCM, ERP, and CRM run on the Internet and Wide Area Network (Lindsay et al., 2003). Indeed, business processes both within the organization and in interactions with external entities are conducted on an E-technology platform. Consequently, modern business firms are commonly referred to as E-enterprises or Digital firms, reflecting the pervasive integration of digital technology into their operations, both internally and externally. This nomenclature demonstrates the transformative effect of technology on contemporary business paradigms.

4.1. Challenges in E-Business Management

E-commerce has long been the most profitable business model for entrepreneurs looking for a good entrepreneurial opportunity. However, this sector is one of the most dynamic and demanding sectors for work. Today, we look at some of the many challenges that come with running an e-commerce business.

- **Finding a unique selling proposition**

Starting an e-commerce requires a sellable product. That's why a unique selling proposition (USP), or messaging angle, is crucial. Apple's USP is privacy. On the other hand, Android's USP is affordability. When seeking a Unique Selling proposition (USP), it is advisable to commence with an area of personal passion. If, for instance, one sells phone covers for a business, it's desired to interpolate the reasons behind the owner's, himself, choice when selecting one design over another. For instance, if one feels a proclivity towards purchasing products inspired by "Doctor Whom," it's likely that numerous number of other individuals have this interest in common. In such a scenario, the USP might revolve around being the ultimate destination for all things related to "Doctor Whom." This would serve as a distinctive selling point, setting the businesses apart in the market and making it eminent.

To look at the market shares and competitors is next plan. Looking at the competitor's product reviews would provide valuable insights on finding the unique angles on which the company should capitalize. Reviews will also illustrate what customers are already gaining from the product and what else they are willing to achieve.

- **Constant lead generation**

One of the most successful ways to get competitive advantage is to run ads on Google search result pages and Facebook. However, if budget balancing is not implemented constantly, these commercial advertisements can lead to huge expenses. Exploring other channels and alternative ways to promote the product is considered beneficent. Consider the option of launching a blog that effectively communicates the value of your product and brand. Broaden content repertoire to encompass educational materials pertaining to your industry and even complementary products that your customer base should consider exploring. Constructing a substantial content library is a long-term endeavor that offers multiple benefits. Not only does it facilitate organic lead generation, but it also consistently delivers value in the long run. However, it is crucial to invest the requisite time and effort into generating high-quality blog posts that cater to the interests and needs of your potential audience.

Based on the product and the target audience, alternative content creation options such as vlogs, podcasts, newsletters, Twitter chats, Clubhouse chat rooms, Facebook groups, and YouTube posts are always being regarded as effective ways of promotion. Publishing content on channels promoting the business, such as a traditional blog or newsletter should be highly advocated. This concept is referred to as "owned media," and its value transcends the dimensions of the cited business. Owned media furnishes the company with communication channels to engage the audience, ensuring that the company and brand can maintain contact even in instances where access to popular social media platforms might be restricted or blocked.

An additional method to guarantee a steady stream of leads is to initiate the construction of email lists. This can be accomplished through the company's blog or within social media communities. As long as the company possesses a pool of individuals who are genuinely interested in hearing from the business, fostering returning customers who may also refer their friends and family to the business becomes more tangible. This approach is instrumental in cultivating customer loyalty and generating referrals.

- **Optimizing the brand's website**

Provide regular usability audits of the website to ensure that visitors are navigating the online store as intended. Enlist the assistance of website testers, friends, and family who can provide feedback on how to enhance the utility of the company's website. This process aids in identifying and rectifying subtle communication gaps that might exist. For instance, consider selling a jacket that has hidden pockets. If this feature is not transparently conveyed in the product description, website visitors may remain unaware of what they are purchasing. It is a must to review the content on every product page, making sure that it inclusively covers all features and functionalities, maintains grammatical and factual accuracy, and includes attractive images that provide a thorough understanding to the buyer. Reducing friction in the customer's online purchasing journey amplifies the likelihood of completing the transaction.

The integration of payment gateways can be a twisted due to the involvement of multiple external vendors and their payment systems. Organizing this aspect to align with audience's preferences might require some time and effort. It is crucial to ensure that each vendor's payment gateway is user-friendly and straightforward to navigate. This proactive approach not only enhances the user experience but also dwindles the likelihood of customer support inquiries stemming from issues with the payment gateway. Considering the following guidance on creating an effective e-commerce website, can prove helpful.

- **Customer nurturing and up-selling**

What E-commerce requires is so much more than setting up the perfect online store. Follow-up Emails, discount codes, weekly special reminders, and Cell-phone push notifications are all indispensable elements reinforcing your brand and products in the customer's mind. Focus on building a customer-nurturing strategy for the business. If a business entails the sale of a solitary product, the approach to customer nurturing remains uniform. However, in cases where multiple products are offered, it becomes prudent to adopt distinctive and tailored follow-up and nurturing strategies for each product. Furthermore, the incorporation of up-selling initiatives within the nurturing framework is a valuable component to consider. If someone bought a book by Margret Atwood, they'll probably be interested in other books by the same author. As Amazon does, displaying these recommendations on the checkout page for instant up-sell opportunities is likely to augment the sails. However, using a customer's purchase data to design customized follow-up email campaigns is a smart alternative.

The ultimate goal of these email campaigns and nurturing efforts is an enhanced customer experience. The customer's satisfaction following a purchase should be considered the sacred objective, in addition to the fact that the company (brand) should depict a recalling picture in customer's mind. To accomplish this objective, company has to establish a reputation for being exceptionally helpful to the extent that customers instinctively turn to your brand. This is the stage at which the inclusion of product support materials, instructional videos, and the redirection of customers to your social media communities becomes relevant. By ensuring that the content is both informative and relevant, customer loyalty and recurrent engagement with the brand becomes expectable.

- **Internal product integration**

In interactions with potential customers, frequently, the presence of isolated or disconnected systems has proven to be a common challenge amongst businesses. These businesses may be utilizing top-tier products within their respective industries, but a lack of integration with their existing information systems leads to operational disruptions and heightened stress levels. When starting an e-commerce enterprise, a crucial step involves identifying the software solutions for each functional aspect of the business. Subsequently, an evaluation should be conducted to determine whether each chosen product possesses native integration capabilities with the pre-existing systems. It's noteworthy that not all products inherently offer seamless integrations. In the event that a preferred application lacks built-in connections, one may explore alternative solutions, such as employing integration tools like Zapier and Zoho Flow, or leveraging an open API to establish connectivity between various systems.

- **Customer experience and loyalty**

Abundance of choices is the inherent challenge of retaining customers—especially for e-commerce businesses. The fact the sheds light on the significance of a robust customer experience strategy is that Brand loyalties oscillations are highly-dependent to economy. According to a study conducted by PricewaterhouseCoopers (PwC), a significant majority of Australians, precisely 74%, deem a friendly customer experience as a pivotal determinant when confronted with multiple choices or options. Leverage that mindset—investing in people and technology that help the company provide good customer service is crucial. Ensuring a smooth and fine interaction with the brand not only not only valorize the customers but also amplifies the brand. For catching delays, bugs, or typos properly in time, a checkout process should be adopted periodically.

A popular way to keep customers coming back is to commence loyalty initiatives, such as an affiliate program, sending discounts and offers for second-time purchases, and providing special-occasion vouchers. Based on the business and the company's rendition of its customers, the implementation of loyalty initiatives vary. Furthermore, these initiatives being adopted are counted as eminent attraction factors for customers, urging them to come back for further purchase or trades.

The establishment and maintenance of brand identity also lead to significant influence in fostering customer loyalty. Notable examples such as Converse and Nike underscore this phenomenon, as these brands possess sizable followings across various social media platforms. While part of this loyalty is attributed to high-profile media mentions and collaborative ventures, a substantial portion can be ascribed to organic word-of-mouth referrals.

Staying engaged on social media, and establishing a community of individuals who appreciate the brand and products can show promising results. This initiative should be done by finding the platform where the followers are intensely active and prioritizing it. Given the potential for social media to become overwhelming, a good approach involves commencing with a modest presence and gradually expanding it in tandem with the growth of available resources. Investing time and budget on social media advertisements broadens the visibility of the brand. Gradually, followers are expected to become customers, and those who make purchases will become brand advocates, spreading the word about your products.

- **Competitive return and refund policies**

Many e-commerce businesses today offer competitive return and refund policies, yet not all of them deliver a smooth experience. Policies must be revised in a way that facilitates returns for customers to the extreme level. Strategies like offering store credits for refunds and covering return shipping costs can ease the return process. While customers often understand the complexities of e-commerce inventory management, policies that seem demanding and might deter purchases due to return inconveniences should be avoided.

- **Adapting to a dynamic market landscape**

E-commerce represents an undeniably fast-evolving business model well-known for its dynamic nature. Failing to maintain pace with this constant transformation can result in significant costs and missed opportunities. In this digital era, a plethora of online resources provide extensive lists of the latest e-commerce trends, which may impose a sense of urgency on businesses to stay current. Nevertheless, not all of these recommendations will align with a particular business's needs and objectives. To navigate this information overload effectively, businesses should focus on detecting the changes that hold the utmost significance for their customers. One constructive approach to achieve this is through engagement with like-minded individuals. Participation in business and networking groups can offer a valuable platform for connecting with fellow entrepreneurs and managers, enabling the exchange of knowledge and collaborative problem-solving. Online platforms such as Meetup.com, which facilitates gatherings of individuals with similar interests based on geographical proximity, can be especially useful. Furthermore, the constraints imposed by the COVID-19 pandemic have given rise to the proliferation of online communities, notably on popular social media platforms like Facebook, LinkedIn, Twitter, and Clubhouse. These forums provide a space for discussions and insights on crucial aspects of e-commerce, including data privacy and integrity.

- **Data privacy and integrity**

When an e-commerce business involves the collection of sensitive customer information, it is imperative to prioritize data protection. Prior to establishing the online store, it is crucial to conduct comprehensive research into software vendors. Should your business aim to operate on an international scale, it is vital to adhere to the privacy regulations of multiple countries. One such example is the General Data Protection Regulation (GDPR), which mandates that data gathered from European Union citizens must be stored and processed within the EU. Failure to comply with these regulations can result in significant financial repercussions, as many brands have experienced. It is worth noting that if the software vendor breaches privacy laws, even inadvertently, the CEO, as a business owner, will be held accountable for the violation.

In terms of evaluating the potential e-commerce vendors, it would be crucial to inquire about their adherence to global data privacy regulations. Vendors should provide information with transparency regarding their data processing capabilities. To illustrate, Zoho's dedication to privacy is evident through its establishment of data centers in various regions, including Australia, Europe, the United States, and India. If an e-commerce business utilizes Zoho Commerce and collects data from a European Union customer, the information will be securely stored and processed in the EU-based data center, thereby ensuring automatic GDPR compliance for the company, its valued customers.

5. SMART CONTRACTS IN E-BUSINESS MANAGEMENT

5.1 Concept Overview and Discussion

Smart contracts in e-commerce will transform the shopping experience for both businesses and consumers by providing value to sellers, consumers and vendors by strengthening trust and streamlining their processes. E-commerce offers suitable platforms for developing smart contracts that can interact with token ID. Conoscenti et al (2016) argued that in e-commerce, the development of smart contracts ensures that blockchain contracts are only enforceable when users meet the specified requirements of a transaction(Conoscenti et al., 2016). For example, when consumers check out from an e-commerce site, the payment they make can be stored in smart contracts. Subsequently, the merchant proceeds to authorize the change of ownership of the products and links the contract to the shipping entity (Udokwu et al., 2018).

After fulfilling the requirements, a smart contract serves as the mechanism for releasing funds to the sellers. These smart contracts facilitate electronic payments by utilizing cryptographic proof, which involves hashing and time stamping various transactions on a blockchain. Consequently, this enables multiple buyers and sellers to engage in direct transactions, effectively eliminating the need for a trusted third party. The presence of a smart contract minimizes the risk associated with one party failing to meet their contractual obligations, as the smart contract automatically facilitates the payment process. As a result, this approach not only ensures greater efficiency but also leads to time and cost savings for both sellers and buyers, who can confidently fulfill their respective commitments.

These transactions offer the advantages of immutability and immediacy, offering a user experience reminiscent of using physical currency. Smart contracts play a crucial role in establishing mutual trust between buyers and sellers, effectively reducing the need to expose sensitive information to third-party applications beyond the user's control. Smart contracts additionally provide a transparent and uniform approach for facilitating the movement of goods across international borders, since all the entities along the supply chain have access to an identical copy of the ledger that exhibits the source and shipping of products while traveling from the sellers to the buyers. This method significantly reduces inaccuracies in untrustworthy record-keeping. Customers have the capability to monitor and verify the items they've purchased to confirm the order's correct status and location in the delivery process. Transactions on distributed ledgers can be made accessible to the public, allowing consumers to conveniently retrieve and manage their delivery orders (Borgogno et al., 2019).

Numerous online or e-commerce businesses have benefited smart contracts, developed and delivered e-commerce solutions to other businesses. For instance, to develop e-commerce company websites using blockchain smart contracts, Elysian entails a platform offering assistance for businesses intending. Besides, Elysian has conducted multifarious solutions, including virtual reality and augmented intelligence that amplify shopping experiences. Another platform is E-Commerce, a decentralized marketplace in which users are regarded as the proprietors of digital assets, such as brands and stores (Suliman et al., 2018). Subsequently, owners have the ability to sell or transfer their digital assets, given their complete control over the store and assets. For consumers, utilizing an E-Commerce platform results in reduced prices and the assurance of perpetual discounts. Another platform with a P2P focus is OpenBazaar. This platform is freely accessible online or via a downloadable application. OpenBazaar resembles conventional platforms like Amazon and eBay but offers users wider control over their data and permits customers to make payments using 50 various altcoins. Additionally, Eligma presents an ideal platform that leverages blockchain smart contracts to manage online shopping in the realm of e-commerce (Tanja, 2018). Eligma's objective is all about ensuring that shoppers experience a more mollified process and are more comfortable while shopping. Eligma adopts artificial intelligence to help consumers save time while monitoring their online shopping and finding the ideal deals. Furthermore, Eligma provides distributed ledger transaction programs that reward shoppers on the platform with ELI tokens. These tokens can be used for additional purchases, effectively promoting the utilization of blockchain smart contracts within the e-commerce domain (Earle et al., 2022).

5.2. Real-Life Cases

The conducted research has shown the effectiveness of classification methods in e-commerce compared to general customer acquisition strategies(Ballestar et al., 2018). A summary of studies of such systems can be found in (Li, S.S. and Karahanna, E.J.J.o.t.a.f.i.s., 2015), who identified relationships that help identify consumers and positively influence consumers and markets. In the broad data analysis and storage capabilities of blockchain, these market forces have already raised fundamental questions under relevant regulations such as GDPR. Poon and Lau (2009) provide an optimistic view of the digital divide and suggest that e-commerce can serve as a suitable tool to bridge this gap (Poon et al., 2009). However, as pointed out by Dong and Ho (2012), a holistic approach is needed to gain a full understanding of ICT development within and between countries, along with its potential implications (Doong et al., 2012). Since blockchain can also be used to enhance security and privacy in smart homes, tech pioneers will soon start using the technology in their own homes, which may widen the digital divide. Therefore, consumers will be faced with many different applications and in many cases will not even be aware of the underlying technology that applies equally to all blockchain types (Dorri, Ali et al., 2017). Table 1 proposes six-main consumer issues and how they may be affected by changes brought about by blockchain.

Table 1. Consumer issues

E-Commerce Variable	References	Blockchain-Issue	References
Payment systems	(Treiblmaier et al., 2021)	Reduction of transaction costs, removal of intermediaries,, enabling of micropayments	(Stix and ethics, 2021)
Mobile applications	(Xu and Gutiérrez, 2006)	Loyalty, privacy programs, social shopping, incentives for data sharing	(Travizano et al., 2018)
Transparency, traceability of data and payments	(Treiblmaier and Pollach, 2011)	New privacy issues / Increased transaction transparency;	(Pesch and Sillaber, 2017)
Segmentation, personalization, customization	(Li, S. and Karahanna, E., 2015)	Custom-objective blockchains in order to individual application use cases, new legal problems	(Kim and Kim, 2023)
Relationships, customer service, trust	(Xiao and Benbasat, 2011)	Novel antecedents of technology adoption, privacy and security, risk management	(Kiktenko et al., 2018)
Digital divide	(Doong and Ho, 2012)	Low powered devices vs resource-intensive blockchains: blockchain scalability	(Dorri, A. et al., 2017)

5.3 Challenges and Limitations of Blockchain Application in E-Commerce

Participants were asked to share their perspectives on the challenges impacting the implementation of smart contracts in the realm of e-commerce (Treiblmaier and Sillaber, 2021).

1. Implementing smart contracts can pose substantial challenges, particularly concerning technical barriers associated with transitioning from legacy systems to blockchain. Furthermore, there's a need for inclusive employee training to ensure a smooth understanding of smart contract operations. Workforce accustomed to traditional systems may show resistance due to the inertia of adapting to new technologies. Additionally, it is important to remind that smart contracts and blockchain technologies can be financially demanding. To effectively integrate this technology, investments in connoisseur personnel and the technology itself are essential. Convincing management or executives to invest in such technology requires demonstrating its capacity to yield favorable and lucrative outcomes. Explaining the benefits of smart contracts to CEOs can be convoluted, especially when they lack a clear understanding of blockchain technology.

2. While smart contracts continue to excel in optimizing transactions, they also introduce a further potential challenge—necessitating unanimous agreement on well-defined standards among all participants. Modifying rules or terms of engagement can prove to be a cumbersome process, requiring the consensus of all parties involved. Delays may occur, especially in cases involving multiple clients within a single smart contract. Moreover, a significant portion of our employees lack the necessary comprehension of smart contracts, prompting the company to allocate resources to educate them on the complexities of these contracts. Finding proficient trainers for this purpose proves to be a demanding endeavor, accompanied by higher costs compared to training in other technological domains. Consequently, organizations with limited financial resources should approach the adoption of smart contracts with caution, prepared for the potential challenges.
3. One challenge arises from the incompatibility of smart contract systems and applications with existing legacy systems. Integrating blockchain systems with the older systems proves to be a formidable task, given their limited maturity. Moreover, numerous newly developed applications in this domain display various flaws and require a high level of improvement. Another factor influencing the company's decision to adopt smart contracts is their performance in transaction validation and processing, as well as their practicability in fraud detection. Smart contracts tend to depict a certain degree of lethargy when handling a high volume of transactions, potentially compromising data security. This dilemma necessitates a trade-off between transaction speed and data security, posing a significant decision for businesses to make. Moreover, Ambiguities persist concerning the legal enforceability of contracts executed through smart contracts, particularly when engaging in business with underdeveloped nations that do not possess inclusive blockchain regulations. In the event of a disagreement, the exclusive option is to turn to dispute resolution, as the effectiveness of smart contract enforcement varies across nations.
4. Smart contracts are in an evolving stage of development. They face a deficiency in a technology-enabled legal framework for dispute resolution. Although certain courts in the United States and Europe acknowledge the significance of blockchain technology, especially in the context of cryptocurrency, their understanding of the technical complexities involved in the execution of such contracts remains restricted. Nevertheless, there is a growing essentiality for these legal bodies to familiar themselves with the utilization of blockchain-based evidence in the process of adjudicating disputes.
5. Retaining all the advantages of blockchain technology without making compromises or trade-offs is regarded challenging. For example, blockchain contracts promote transparency among the parties, as each party receives a copy

of the original document. However, this transparency can become problematic, especially when the parties do not want their information to be disclosed to ensure privacy.

6. The nature of smart contracts is considered vague and many people have little knowledge since they need to have a hand on programing languages like Java, Solidity, Kotlin or Go. Most developers have not publically released their codes to assist individuals when creating the contracts. Without source codes, the rehearsal of documents and obtaining trails for various transactions is quite challenging and demanding. Also, blockchain contracts have proven to be promising since they generate unpredictable random values and codes. However, such randomness might considered redundant. There had been cases where the control over generation and release was manipulated to work in favor of specific miners running a monopoly. Thus, while smart contracts enhance security, sophisticated hackers can still find loops to bypass the security mechanisms.
7. In case of smart contracts, a legal problem might arise when the products or services advertised do not turn out to be as specified in the commercial advertisement. For instance, in occasions where a promoted house is not specified as in the advertisement, a tenant might feel a tendency to take the down payment back. However, the owner of the property refuses. Moreover, since smart contracts are executed without physical meetings, cases of misrepresentation and fraud can increase. Furthermore, the foremost problematic task is to find a person liable for coding errors or when systems malfunction because of unforeseen challenges.

6. CONCLUSION

Blockchain technology has recently gained substantial attention in both industrial and academic circles due to its ability to enable the decentralization of transactions, allowing for their execution without relying on a trusted intermediary. This study explores the practicality of utilizing smart contracts in the e-commerce sector through data acquisition from various industry experts well-versed in the technology. Initially, the research investigates the use cases of implementing smart contracts in e-commerce, as perceived by the participants involved. The findings suggest that smart contracts are employed to streamline financial transactions, encompassing fund transfers, record-keeping, financial trade facilitation, credit authorization, crowdfunding agreements, and other e-commerce functions like storing receipts, customer data, inventory management, property management, and ownership document exchanges. Additionally, this technology finds application in decentralized intelligence, gaming, and transaction security. Furthermore, the insurance sector extensively utilizes this technology to encode policy terms, ensuring prompt payouts to clients. E-commerce enterprises can utilize smart contracts to manage and secure online product exchanges, shipping, and supply chain tracking processes, thereby reducing the risk of theft and order losses. In the aviation industry, blockchain technology plays a significant role in addressing compensation claims for delayed flights. In the realm of real estate, it enhances property management. Despite the enhanced security offered by blockchain technologies compared to traditional systems, adept hackers still pose threats to businesses, applications, and systems reliant on blockchain technologies. Clearly, while smart contracts offer remarkable solutions for e-commerce, it is increasingly apparent that policymakers, researchers, practitioners, and other stakeholders must devote significant effort and time to further the development of the technology and address existing challenges.

REFERENCES

Aliahmadi, A., Ghahremani-Nahr, J., & Nozari, H. (2023). Pricing decisions in the closed-loop supply chain network, taking into account the queuing system in production centers. *Expert Systems with Applications*, *212*, 118741. doi:10.1016/j.eswa.2022.118741

Ballestar, M.T., Grau-Carles, P., & Sainz, J. (2018). *Customer segmentation in e-commerce: Applications to the cashback business model*. Academic Press.

Borgogno. (2019). Usefulness and dangers of smart contracts in consumer and commercial transactions. Academic Press.

Combe, C. (2012). *Introduction to E-business*. Routledge. doi:10.4324/9780080492780

Conoscenti, M., Vetro, A., & De Martin, J. C. (2016). Blockchain for the Internet of Things: A systematic literature review. *2016 IEEE/ACS 13th International Conference of Computer Systems and Applications (AICCSA)*, 1-6.

Dolat-Abadi, H. M. (2021). Optimizing decisions of fresh-product members in daily and bourse markets considering the quantity and quality deterioration: A waste-reduction approach. *Journal of Cleaner Production*, *283*, 124647. doi:10.1016/j.jclepro.2020.124647

Doong, S. H., & Ho, S.-C. (2012). The impact of ICT development on the global digital divide. *Electronic Commerce Research and Applications*, *11*(5), 518–533. doi:10.1016/j.elerap.2012.02.002

Doong, S.H., & Ho, S.-C. (2012). *The impact of ICT development on the global digital divide*. Academic Press.

Dorri, A., Kanhere, S. S., & Jurdak, R. (2017). Towards an Optimized BlockChain for IoT. *2017 IEEE/ACM Second International Conference on Internet-of-Things Design and Implementation (IoTDI),* 173-178.

Dorri, A., Kanhere, S. S., Jurdak, R., & Gauravaram, P. (2017). *Blockchain for IoT security and privacy: The case study of a smart home. In 2017 IEEE international conference on pervasive computing and communications workshops (PerCom workshops)*. IEEE.

Earle, P.C., Gulker, M., & Stringham, E.P. (2022). *Decentralized Marketplaces with Privately Enforced Contracts: A Case Study of OpenBazaar*. Academic Press.

Elommal, N., & Manita, R. (2021). *How blockchain innovation could affect the audit profession: a qualitative study*. Academic Press.

Giancaspro, M, (2017). *Is a 'smart contract'really a smart idea? Insights from a legal perspective*. Academic Press.

Guo, H., Meamari, E., & Shen, C.-C. (2019). Multi-authority attribute-based access control with smart contract. *Proceedings of the 2019 International Conference on Blockchain Technology*, 6-11. https://www.geeksforgeeks.org/smart-contracts-in-blockchain/

Hu, K., Zhu, J., Ding, Y., Bai, X., & Huang, J. (2020). *Smart contract engineering*. Academic Press.

Ivanov, D., & Dolgui, A. (2019). New disruption risk management perspectives in supply chains: Digital twins, the ripple effect, and resileanness. *IFAC-PapersOnLine*, *52*(13), 337–342. doi:10.1016/j.ifacol.2019.11.138

Karamitsos, I., Papadaki, M., & Al Barghuthi, N.B. (2018). *Design of the blockchain smart contract: A use case for real estate*. Academic Press.

Khan, S.N., Loukil, F., Ghedira-Guegan, C., Benkhelifa, E., & Bani-Hani, A. (2021). *Blockchain smart contracts: Applications, challenges, and future trends*. Academic Press.

Kiktenko, E. O., Pozhar, N. O., Anufriev, M. N., Trushechkin, A. S., Yunusov, R. R., Kurochkin, Y. V., Lvovsky, A. I., & Fedorov, A. K. (2018). Quantum-secured blockchain. *Quantum Science and Technology*, *3*(3), 035004. doi:10.1088/2058-9565/aabc6b

Kim, S., & Kim, D. (2023). *Securing the Cyber Resilience of a Blockchain-Based Railroad Non-Stop Customs Clearance System*. Academic Press.

Li, S., & Karahanna, E. (2015). Online Recommendation Systems in a B2C E-Commerce Context: A Review and Future Directions. *Journal of the Association for Information Systems*, *16*(2), 72–107. doi:10.17705/1jais.00389

Li, S.S., & Karahanna, E. (2015). *Online recommendation systems in a B2C E-commerce context: a review and future directions*. Academic Press.

Lindsay, A., Downs, D., & Lunn, K. (2003). *Business processes—attempts to find a definition*. Academic Press.

Liu, B., & De Giovanni, P. (2019). *Green process innovation through Industry 4.0 technologies and supply chain coordination*. Academic Press.

Mohammadi, H., Ghazanfari, M., Pishvaee, M. S., & Teimoury, E. (2019). Fresh-product supply chain coordination and waste reduction using a revenue-and-preservation-technology-investment-sharing contract: A real-life case study. *Journal of Cleaner Production*, *213*, 262–282. doi:10.1016/j.jclepro.2018.12.120

Mohanta, B. K., Panda, S. S., & Jena, D. (2018). An overview of smart contract and use cases in blockchain technology. *2018 9th international conference on computing, communication and networking technologies (ICCCNT)*, 1-4.

Nozari, H., Ghahremani-Nahr, J., & Szmelter-Jarosz, A. (2023). A multi-stage stochastic inventory management model for transport companies including several different transport modes. *International Journal of Management Science and Engineering Management*, *18*(2), 134–144. doi:10.1080/17509653.2022.2042747

Pesch, P.J., & Sillaber, C. (2017). *Distributed ledger, joint control? Blockchains and the GDPR's transparency requirements*. Academic Press.

Poon, T., Choy, K.L., Chow, H.K., Lau, H.C., Chan, F.T., & Ho, K. (2009). *A RFID case-based logistics resource management system for managing order-picking operations in warehouses*. Academic Press.

Sarmah, S. (2018). *Understanding blockchain technology*. Academic Press.

Singhal, B., Dhameja, G., Panda, P.S., Singhal, B., Dhameja, G., & Panda, P.S. (2018). *How blockchain works*. Academic Press.

Stix, C. (2021). *Actionable principles for artificial intelligence policy: Three pathways*. Academic Press.

Travizano, M., Sarraute, C., Ajzenman, G., & Minnoni, M.. (2018). *Wibson: A decentralized data marketplace*. Academic Press.

Treiblmaier, H., & Pollach, I. (2011). *The influence of privacy concerns on perceptions of web personalisation*. Academic Press.

Treiblmaier, H., & Sillaber, C. (2021). The impact of blockchain on e-commerce: A framework for salient research topics. *Electronic Commerce Research and Applications*, *48*, 101054. doi:10.1016/j.elerap.2021.101054

Treiblmaier, H., & Sillaber, C.. (2021). *The impact of blockchain on e-commerce: a framework for salient research topics*. Academic Press.

Udokwu, C., Kormiltsyn, A., Thangalimodzi, K., & Norta, A. (2018). The state of the art for blockchain-enabled smart-contract applications in the organization. *2018 Ivannikov Ispras Open Conference (ISPRAS)*, 137-144. 10.1109/ISPRAS.2018.00029

Wang, S., Yuan, Y., Wang, X., Li, J., Qin, R., & Wang, F.-Y. (2018). An overview of smart contract: architecture, applications, and future trends. *2018 IEEE Intelligent Vehicles Symposium (IV)*, 108-113. 10.1109/IVS.2018.8500488

Xiao, B., & Benbasat, I. (2011). Product-Related Deception in E-Commerce: A Theoretical Perspective. *Management Information Systems Quarterly*, *35*(1), 169–195. doi:10.2307/23043494

Xu, G., & Gutiérrez, J.A. (2006). *An exploratory study of killer applications and critical success factors in m-commerce*. Academic Press.

Yli-Huumo, J., Ko, D., Choi, S., Park, S., & Smolander, K. (2016). *Where is current research on blockchain technology? A systematic review*. Academic Press.

Zeng, S.-Q., Huo, R., Huang, T., Liu, J., Wang, S., & Feng, W. (2020). *Survey of blockchain: principle, progress and application*. Academic Press.

Chapter 9
Identification of Critical Success Factors in the Implementation of Smart and Sustainable Business

Maryam Rahmaty
Department of Management, Islamic Azad University, Chalous, Iran

ABSTRACT

Smart business is the advances and applications that are utilized to gather, coordinate, analyze, and show commerce within the organization. The smart business may be profound and comprehensive information of components such as customers, competitors, financial environment, operations, and organizational processes, which influence the quality of administration choices within the organization. Smart management enables all of an organization's senior managers to make informed decisions about everything from research and development, marketing, and investment tactics to long-term strategies. Therefore, the success of smart businesses in the new era of success depends on various parameters that should be paid special attention to. For this reason, the most important key indicators of success in smart organizations have been evaluated in this research. In order to analyze the results, a fuzzy decision-making method has been used. The results show that adequate budget and infrastructure growth is the most important critical success factor in developing smart businesses.

DOI: 10.4018/979-8-3693-0210-1.ch009

1. INTRODUCTION

Smart business is a topic employers, business owners, or anyone wanting to start their own business should pay attention to. This issue is essential because many technologies have been created that have significantly increased the quality and speed of doing things, so paying attention to this is especially important. Smart business includes all computer technologies, including application software, business models, and patterns that help organizations or companies (Malburg et al., 2023). These patterns transform scattered data into understandable, exchangeable, sharable, and storable information for subsequent decision-making. In other words, intelligent management is a process that includes the legal and ethical collection of information and the controlled transfer of operational intelligence to decision-makers. Smart business is the intelligent and conscious use of information that has been obtained with difficulty and spending a lot of money and is used for management decisions and quick and accurate control of the organization's situation (Coghlan et al., 2023).

A smart business doesn't just look outward; it also looks at its assets, especially its human resources. Because inappropriate or unfair behavior is certainly not a sign of intelligence. A smart business also knows how to value employees' work and reward them accordingly. A smart business knows how to offer benefits and take advantage of new ways to create flexibility at work. In addition, a smart business knows how to properly train and keep its teams up-to-date and keep its people engaged and enthusiastic about the company's goals (Ullah & Al-Turjman, 2023).

In an era of constant change, companies that don't know how to adapt are at risk of extinction. However, a smart company can recognize and adapt to changes. This company cares about understanding customers' needs and desires and can respond to them better and faster than competitors. At the same time, the company has the ability to adapt its structure and production processes to market demand to perform better and be more efficient. Is your company able to do all these things? Therefore, it can be seen that smart businesses have many advantages for both the economy and people. However, organizations always have challenges due to being involved in technology. For this reason, different aspects should always be examined during the implementation of these businesses to guarantee organizations' success. For this reason, extracting the most important critical factors is always very important (Zhang et al., 2023).

Critical success factors are limited factors that play a vital role in the organization's success; if the organization wants to continue its existence, it must provide them. In other words, every critical success factor is a context that must be done in the best way for the organization to succeed. Critical success factors are important factors that make an organization successful. For this reason, this research has targeted critical success factors in smart businesses based on transformative technologies.

In this research, the most important critical success factors in smart businesses have been extracted using the literature review and experts' opinions and evaluated using the multiple decision-making method. The results of this research can help create a successful smart business (Wu et al., 2023).

2. LITERATURE REVIEW

In the rapidly changing business world, success is no longer just a matter of having great products or services but is based on intelligent planning and management of plans and strategies. Smart business is the key not only to survive sustainably but also to thrive in this competitive environment (Mitra et al., 2023).

Business environments are too complex to be framed under a universally recognized theoretical framework. Therefore, based on previous studies, the concept of business environment is updated by adding emerging information about digital public services, big data-based social credit systems, and intelligent processes. Successful intelligent business management is closely related to our understanding and use of technology throughout the business. This means that the use of technology to strengthen business management in the field of smart businesses can only be increased by studying the interaction between technological innovations and management processes in specific business processes (Nozari et al., 2023).

Numerous companies, particularly within the early stages of their life cycle, have small reasonability and confront a quickly changing world. The expanding utilization of digital technologies and dependence on them has brought noteworthy changes in commerce and society. It ought to be famous that the concept of advanced change was presented in 2000. In later a long time, there has been a critical center on organizational data frameworks. This extraordinary attention stems from the got to way better coordinated modern innovations (both equipment and program) with trade forms. Trade forms depend on innovation more than anything else since innovation straightforwardly influences trade forms and changes the way they are done, in this way affecting how examiners plan computer program frameworks (Zhang et al., 2023).

The deployment and sending of innovation-based advances, forms, and models progressively serve as the spine of imaginative entrepreneurial companies. Computerized innovations empower companies to make strides in asset stream, esteem creation, and gathering pledges in real-world situations, in this way empowering commerce show development. Propels in advanced innovation permit companies to optimize and move forward with their forms. In expansion, computerized advances empower companies to improve the way they communicate with providers and clients. For illustration, this may be done by expanding client information and fabric following. A few analysts categorize computerized innovations based on usefulness into information collection, information integration, and information investigation. Information collection advances incorporate sensors (eg, RFID) and gadgets that interface items and clients to the Web (eg, IoT, the artificial intelligence of things). Integration advances store and organize information and empowers the utilization of information examination innovations that produce and create data (Ullah & Al-Turjman, 2023).

The smart business incorporates the combination of three components: savvy individuals, shrewd innovation, and smart collaboration. In this sense, the level of "intelligence" of commerce is to the degree that it can pull in and mobilize human capital utilizing data and communication innovation. In other words, smart businesses are primarily shaped based on their human, social, and informational capital and utilize data innovation and huge information assets, all of which are exceptionally successful in expanding effectiveness and creating a handle. Data and communication innovation in financial processes moves towards fortifying the economy through technological change and development (Coghlan et al., 2023). It increases the sustainability of the economy through the improvement of modern technologies and advancements. Hence, we will conclude that the part of different technologies within the improvement of smart businesses is crucial to forming a comprehensive environment that's straightforward, computerized, comprehensive, adaptable, secure, adaptable, and effectively reasonable. The concept of "smart business" creates modern horizons for companies to supply their challenging administrations in an educated and competitive environment (Nozari, Ghahremani-Nahr and Najafi, 2023). Hence, they advance the imagination, development, and smart and sustainable solutions that are advanced through benefit platforms. In reality, in smart businesses, expanding financial development and social improvement is sought after through innovative advancements, and with the ceaseless alteration in innovation, smart businesses give ideas for future improvement ways. Hence, in this technology-filled world, businesses must alter the way they make, provide, and retain values from environmental, social, and financial points of view. In this manner, cooperation in sustainable development forms can make strides in commerce execution and make shared esteem concepts. In arrange to move towards a sustainable business show, inventive exercises are fundamental to making economic values (Mitra et al., 2023).

Sustainable business show development can make a modern business show, upgrade an ancient trade model, or design and coordinate different business models. As a result, advancement gives a diverse esteem recommendation to customers and shapes a modern esteem framework that supports the sustainable development of the organization. In this manner, all individuals in the smart business structure are potential benefit engineers and advancement drivers. As a result, smart businesses are innovation centers, human capital centers, and a natural combination of the two (Webb, 2023).

With the development of smart businesses, accentuation has been put on smart innovations counting big data and the Internet of Things that optimize the commerce environment. Subsequently, the business environment is a vital exemplification of a country's or region's financial delicate control and international competitiveness. Making a great trade environment is fundamental to making an advanced economic framework and advancing quality advancement. In other words, the intelligentization approach in sustainable business advancement is unequivocally related to development, innovation, and financial enterprise. As a result, smart business techniques are altogether driven by an entrepreneurial approach to advancement. Joining financial and entrepreneurial techniques and business models with IT administrations, forms and stages can encourage advancement in modern advanced advances. Companies are moreover contributing in keen stages utilizing imaginative innovations. As innovative progressions and societal acknowledgment increment, unused commerce models are quickly fueled by technological advancements. Digitalization of businesses within the setting of shrewd cities as an apparatus for advancement in entrepreneurial biological systems can have a possibly positive effect. These modern trade models are really a decision-making strategy and financial arranging apparatus that can offer assistance in overseeing businesses in complex intelligent decision-making forms (Webb, 2023).

The review of the literature conducted in the field of sustainability of smart business has formed the conceptual framework of the research and shows that for the success of smart businesses, key success indicators should always be examined. Identifying the contribution of each component and item in shaping the sustainability of smart businesses can help market stakeholders, strategists, and researchers in analyzing the conditions and requirements for the development and sustainability of smart markets. Therefore, in this research, the help of 17 active experts in the field of smart business was taken. 12 experts had related work records and were familiar with the concepts of intelligent development, and 5 experts were selected from among university experts with relevant research records. In the first stage, the most important critical success factors were selected using the subject literature and the opinions of the experts. Refinement began. Finally, 8 final factors were selected as shown in Table 1.

Table 1. The most important critical success factors in smart businesses

Amazing vision W1
Adequate budget and infrastructure growth W2
Great administration W3
Focus on the community W4
Clarity W5
Integrity W6
performance indicators W7
Making a sustainable smart business culture W8

- ***Amazing vision***

Smart business advancement isn't an errand that can be sought after with an ad hoc approach. Instep, an all-encompassing vision is required to direct decision-making and direct activity plans toward executing reasonable arrangements that convey substantial comes about that can progress organizational forms (Motia et al., 2023).

- ***Adequate budget and infrastructure growth***

Whereas securing satisfactory subsidizing may be troublesome, ready to overcome this challenge by sending essential innovation rather than promptly conveying high-tech arrangements, which permits for expanded efficiency, viably leveraging your starting capital for more advanced solutions. In expansion, expanding advanced proficiency will be a good thing about being more open to more up-to-date mechanical arrangements (Joo, 2023).

- ***Great administration***

Great administration could be a subject that can connect all variables together. Executing solid top-down administration and straightforward arrangements can crystallize the smart business scene. Great administration can moreover help develop economic financing plans agreeing to the desires of the organization while conveying the desired ability to extend administration workplaces. It too underpins communication campaigns to energize partner buy-in required for effective usage (Ungureanu, 2023).

- ***Focus on the community***

An effective technique could be a methodology that considers and reflects the wants and sees of society, counting being customer-centric, centering on moving forward the quality of life and making a competitive advantage for businesses that pull in positive development (Foronda-Robles et al., 2023).

- ***Clarity***

In spite of the fact that ICT is quickly becoming a basic framework in businesses, a savvy commerce methodology can contrast with other basic foundation methodologies since its activities and benefits may be as "cutting the lace" for an unused bridge, building or street isn't clear. Thus, it is imperative that the methodology incorporates illustrations and comes about that are effectively caught on by all partners (Buhalis et al., 2023).

- ***Integrity***

Integrating technology into the public realm is an emerging trend in most businesses around the world. Incorporating a planning component into a smart business strategy is critical to improving business quality. We've all seen evidence of technology being quickly adopted into our communities without thinking about the impact on customer service or the resident experience. These are often technologies that were not planned for or coordinated with other departments. For some more technically inclined people this may sound "good", for others it can paint a picture of business disorganization. Implementation guidelines should be considered as part of strategy development. One approach is to develop a smart business strategy as an integrated effort in the overall business plan process. This approach ensures that the conversation around technology and the built environment happens at the highest level. The best technology deployments are those that provide business benefits (Toth-Peter et al., 2023).

- ***performance indicators***

Crediting victory variables to smart business technique improvement and usage can be challenging and frequently subjective in nature. Whereas numerous particular activities are quantifiable, anticipated results may be less so, particularly on the off chance that there is restricted current data to a degree. Deciding key execution markers related to any trade is a vital task since over time it gets to be an announcing instrument for inside operations as well as an outside message to the business community. A key consideration is to make KPIs that are significant to the partners within the commerce. Following and detailing these things in an easy-to-understand organized, regularly through a dashboard, is a vital component of a shrewd trade (Salama et al., 2023).

- ***Making a sustainable smart business culture***

One of the reasons that numerous businesses take time to create a savvy trade technique is to optimize and coordinate the usage of data and communication innovation within the organization. The method of creating methodologies is often the beginning point for expelling impediments that will exist. The advancement of open information arrangement is additionally frequently the initiator of this discourse. The inclusion of all important partners within the organization is key to making a buying culture that goes past making a smart commerce methodology. Reliable coordination and sharing of challenges and victories (beginning with early wins) as a portion of smart business administration is key to long-term victory. Whereas huge businesses have possibly more noteworthy tangible benefits from keen business activities, we've found that exceedingly dexterous little to medium-sized businesses are in a solid position to make energy and support a culture of nonstop advancement (Ochoa et al., 2023).

3. RESEARCH METHODOLOGY

This research, with a quantitative approach, looks to explore Critical success factors in implementing smart and sustainable businesses. In this inquiry about, exploring the variables, to begin with by utilizing the foundation of the subject and experts' suppositions, and based on the 5-level Likert range, 5 variables were extricated as the foremost critical components. For this reason, 17 active experts were studied. The reason for choosing these individuals was get to to the creators and the work and research records of specialists within the field of consideration. A fuzzy hierarchical investigation procedure was utilized to prioritize the foremost important Critical success factors in implementing smart and sustainable businesses. In this inquiry about, Cronbach's alpha strategy has been utilized to determine the unwavering quality of related surveys utilizing the SPSS program. The Cronbach's alpha esteem of all surveys was 0.889, which is considered favorable. Due to the truth that 8 components were chosen as the foremost important factors in this investigation, an isolated figure investigation was done for each of the pointers. Within the taking after, the quantitative investigation strategy utilized in this investigation is clarified.

In this research, a fuzzy nonlinear hierarchical analysis method, known as the Mikhailov method (Nozari et al., 2022), has been used to prioritize the most important Critical success factors in implementing smart and sustainable businesses. The steps to use this method are as follows:

- Hierarchical structure drawing: which is shown in table number (1).
- Forming the matrix of fuzzy pairwise comparisons: consensus matrices of fuzzy judgment are formed based on the opinions of experts. For this reason, fuzzy numbers have been used to express the preferences of experts in this research.

In order to prioritize the following steps should be done:

Formulating the model and solving the problem: In this method, it is assumed that the fuzzy pairwise comparisons are in the form of triangular fuzzy numbers. The deterministic weight vector $w = (w_1, w_2, \ldots, w_n)$ is extracted in such a way that the priority rate is almost within the range of the basic fuzzy judgments. In other words, the weights are determined in such a way that the following relationship is maintained.

$$l_{ij} \leq \frac{w_i}{w_j} \leq u_{ij} \tag{1}$$

Any definite weight vector w applies to the inclusions in the above fuzzy inequalities, which can be measured through the linear membership function of the following relation:

$$\mu_{ij}\left(\frac{w_i}{w_j}\right) = \begin{cases} \dfrac{(w_i / w_j) - l_{ij}}{m_{ij} - l_{ij}} & \dfrac{w_i}{w_j} \leq m_{ij} \\[2ex] \dfrac{u_{ij} - (w_i / w_j)}{u_{ij} - m_{ij}} & \dfrac{w_i}{w_j} \geq m_{ij} \end{cases} \tag{2}$$

Considering the specific form of the membership functions, the fuzzy prioritization problem becomes a nonlinear optimization problem as follows.

$$
\begin{aligned}
&\max \lambda \\
&Subject\ to: \\
&(m_{ij} - l_{ij})\lambda w_j - w_i + l_{ij} w_j \leq 0 \\
&(u_{ij} - m_{ij})\lambda w_j + w_j - u_{ij} w_j \leq 0 \\
&i = 1,2,\dots,n-1,\ j = 2,3,\dots,n\ ,\ j > i \\
&\sum_{k=1}^{n} w_k = 1\ ,\ w_k > 0,\ \ k = 1,2,\dots,n
\end{aligned} \tag{3}
$$

Considering the non-linearity of the relationship (3), it is obvious that it is not possible to solve it without using software. Therefore, GAMS software was used to solve the models created in this research. The positive optimal values for the λ index indicate that all weight ratios are fully applied in the initial judgment, but if this index is negative, it can be understood that the fuzzy judgments are strongly inconsistent and the weight ratios are almost applied in these judgments.

4. RESEARCH FINDINGS

The process related to ranking critical success factors in implementing smart and sustainable businesses in order to emphasize and develop all-round innovation in this study is divided into two main parts:

1) Determining the network of pairwise comparisons based on the integration of experts' conclusions.
2) Using scientific modeling to rank and get the weight of the variables within the investigative shows.

In order to prioritize the 8 final factors extracted in this research, fuzzy questionnaires using language variables were sent to 17 experts and university professors. 17 questionnaires were completed and received. These pairwise comparison tables are shown in tables (2). This table were used for calculations using the Mikhailov method.

Table 2. Pairwise comparison matrix for critical success factors in implementing smart and sustainable businesses

	W1	W2	W3	W4	W5	W6	W7	W8
W1	(1.26 2.7 4.58)	(1.67 2.47 4.86)	(1.44 3.79 4.02)	(1.67 2.47 4.86)	(1.34 3.79 4.02)	(1.26 2.7 4.58)	(1.67 2.47 4.86)	(1.44 3.79 4.02)
W2	(1.03 3.95 4.91)	(1.9,3.8 4.19)	(1.28 3.42 4.37)	(1.9,3.8 4.19)	(1.28 3.42 4.37)	(1.03 3.95 4.91)	(1.8,3.8 4.19)	(2.28 3.42 4.37)
W3	(2.02 3.44 3.92)	(1.95 3.8 4.8)	(1.05 3.13 4.84)	(1.95 3.8 4.8)	(1.05 3.13 4.84)	(2.02 3.44 3.92)	(1.95 3.8 4.8)	(1.05 3.13 4.84)
W4	(1.74 2.15 3.54)	(1.55 3.1 4.6)	(1.49 2.83 4.01)	(1.55 3.1 4.6)	(1.49 2.83 4.01)	(1.74 2.15 3.54)	(1.55 3.1 4.6)	(1.49 2.83 4.01)
W5	(1.55 3.55 4.07)	(1.38 3.42 4.45)	(1.42 3.05 4.39)	(1.38 3.42 4.45)	(1.22 3.05 4.39)	(1.55 3.55 5.07)	(1.28 3.42 4.45)	(1.42 3.05 4.39)
W6	(1.64 3.9 4.51)	(1.57 2.18 4.96)	(2.02 2.62 4.11)	(1.57 2.18 4.96)	(2.02 2.62 4.11)	(1.64 3.9 4.51)	(1.57 2.18 4.96)	(2.02 2.62 4.11)
W7	(1.03 2.9, 4.25)	(1.28 3.58 4.97)	(1.47 2.92 4.36)	(1.28 3.58 4.97)	(1.47 2.92 4.36)	(1.03 2.9, 4.25)	(1.28 3.58 4.97)	(2.47 2.92 4.36)
W8	(2.01 2.7, 4.23)	(1.63 2.69 4.72)	(1.17 2.37 4.82)	(1.63 2.69 4.72)	(1.17 2.37 4.82)	(2.01 2.7, 4.23)	(1.63 2.69 4.72)	(1.17 2.37 4.82)

By placing the data obtained from Table (2) in the non-linear model (3) and solving the model using GAMS software, the weight and rank of each critical success factor can be obtained. The calculation results related to solving the nonlinear model are shown in Tables (3).

Table 3. Weight and ranking of critical success factors in implementing smart and sustainable businesses

Category	Code	Weight	Rank	Objective Function (λ)
Amazing vision	W1	0.08824	7	0.5412
Adequate budget and infrastructure growth	W2	0.25145	1	
Great administration	W3	0.12012	3	
Focus on the community	W4	0.11214	4	
Clarity	W5	0.14325	2	
Integrity	W6	0.09871	6	
performance indicators	W7	0.08121	8	
Making a sustainable smart business culture	W8	0.10214	5	

Figure 1. Normal weight of critical success factors in implementing smart and sustainable businesses

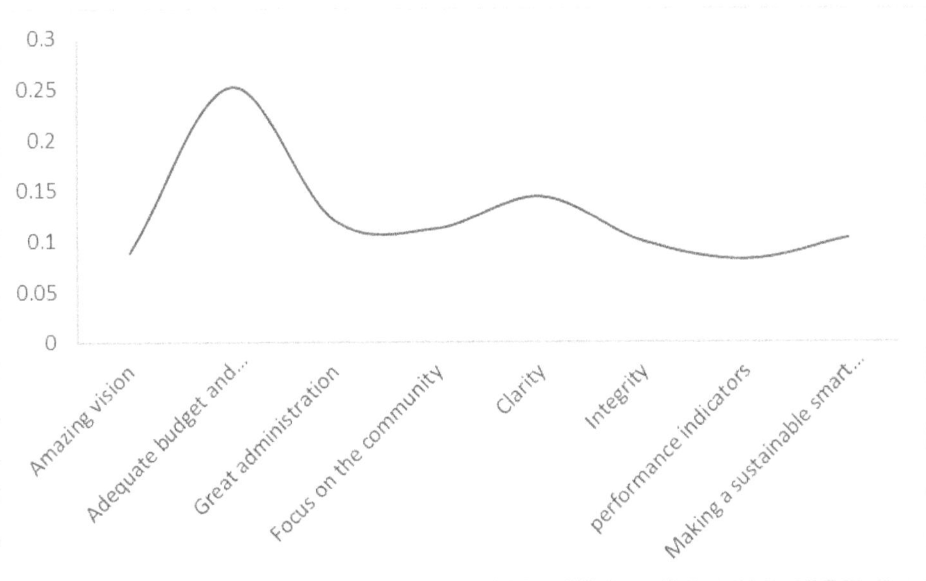

5. CONCLUSION

In today's world where technology is changing rapidly, smart businesses have emerged as a new trend in business. These businesses provide new opportunities for growth and development by using new technologies. By using technology to improve processes, create new products and services, and provide creative solutions, companies can change the competition in the market. In the future, smart businesses are going to play a big role in changing the e-commerce industry. The available statistics provide valid evidence and reasons based on which, smart organizations have been able to reduce the unnecessary costs of deep and more detailed analysis of the intra-organizational state of competitiveness and increase their success rate and achieve a reliable business architecture. Therefore, the importance of these businesses in today's world is very evident and is not hidden from anyone. For this reason, the critical factors of success in this organization should be closely examined and the most important indicators should be emphasized.

Critical success factors (CSF) are a set of factors that are necessary to implement or achieve the operational goals of a project or organization. Undoubtedly, many factors and elements are involved in the implementation of an organizational project. Among these, some factors are very important. The existence of various infrastructures is a basic prerequisite for the implementation of many projects. Therefore, the managers of the organization must identify and evaluate these factors correctly before implementing any project or program. In many organizational projects that require a lot of money and the perceived risk is high. Without these vital factors, the failure of such a project in the organization is certain. Considering this, in this research, the most important critical success factors were analyzed. For this purpose, at first, the most important factors were extracted using the literature review and refined using the opinions of 17 experts. Then, using a fuzzy and non-linear hierarchical decision-making method, these factors were prioritized. The results showed that sufficient budget and Infrastructure development is one of the most important success factors in smart businesses and should be given special attention.

REFERENCES

Buhalis, D., O'Connor, P., & Leung, R. (2023). Smart hospitality: From smart cities and smart tourism towards agile business ecosystems in networked destinations. *International Journal of Contemporary Hospitality Management*, *35*(1), 369–393. doi:10.1108/IJCHM-04-2022-0497

Coghlan, A., Becken, S., & Warren, C. (2023). Modelling a smart tech user journey to decarbonise tourist accommodation. *Journal of Sustainable Tourism*, *31*(3), 840–858. doi:10.1080/09669582.2022.2030344

Foronda-Robles, C., Galindo-Pérez-de-Azpillaga, L., & Fernández-Tabales, A. (2023). Progress and stakes in sustainable tourism: Indicators for smart coastal destinations. *Journal of Sustainable Tourism, 31*(7), 1518–1537. doi:10.1080/09669582.2020.1864386

Joo, Y. M. (2023). Developmentalist smart cities? The cases of Singapore and Seoul. *International Journal of Urban Sciences, 27*(sup1), 164-182.

Malburg, L., Hoffmann, M., & Bergmann, R. (2023). Applying MAPE-K control loops for adaptive workflow management in smart factories. *Journal of Intelligent Information Systems, 61*(1), 1–29. doi:10.100710844-022-00766-w

Mitra, S., Kumar, H., Gupta, M. P., & Bhattacharya, J. (2023). Entrepreneurship in smart cities: Elements of Start-up Ecosystem. *Journal of Science and Technology Policy Management, 14*(3), 592–611. doi:10.1108/JSTPM-06-2021-0078

Motia, K., Kumar, R., & Luthra, S. (2023). Role of cyber-physical system and Industry 4.0 in smart manufacturing industries for business excellence. *International Journal of Business Excellence, 31*(2), 258–271. doi:10.1504/IJBEX.2023.134499

Nozari, H., Ghahremani-Nahr, J., Fallah, M., & Szmelter-Jarosz, A. (2022). Assessment of cyber risks in an IoT-based supply chain using a fuzzy decision-making method. *International Journal of Innovation in Management, Economics and Social Sciences, 2*(1).

Nozari, H., Ghahremani-Nahr, J., & Najafi, E. (2023). The Role of Internet of Things and Blockchain in the Development of Agile and Sustainable Supply Chains. In Digital Supply Chain, Disruptive Environments, and the Impact on Retailers (pp. 271-282). IGI Global. doi:10.4018/978-1-6684-7298-9.ch015

Nozari, H., Ghahremani-Nahr, J., & Szmelter-Jarosz, A. (2023). AI and machine learning for real-world problems. *Advances In Computers*.

Ochoa, W., Larrinaga, F., & Pérez, A. (2023). Architecture for managing AAS-based business processes. *Procedia Computer Science, 217*, 217–226. doi:10.1016/j.procs.2022.12.217

Salama, R., Al-Turjman, F., & Culmone, R. (2023, March). AI-Powered Drone to Address Smart City Security Issues. In *International Conference on Advanced Information Networking and Applications* (pp. 292-300). Cham: Springer International Publishing. 10.1007/978-3-031-28694-0_27

Taherdoost, H. (2023). Smart Contracts in Blockchain Technology: A Critical Review. *Information (Basel), 14*(2), 117. doi:10.3390/info14020117

Toth-Peter, A., de Oliveira, R. T., Mathews, S., Barner, L., & Figueira, S. (2023). Industry 4.0 as an enabler in transitioning to circular business models: A systematic literature review. *Journal of Cleaner Production*, *393*, 136284. doi:10.1016/j.jclepro.2023.136284

Ullah, F., & Al-Turjman, F. (2023). A conceptual framework for blockchain smart contract adoption to manage real estate deals in smart cities. *Neural Computing & Applications*, *35*(7), 5033–5054. doi:10.100700521-021-05800-6

Ungureanu, P. (2023). Putting Space in Place. Multimodal Translation of the Grand Challenge of Regional Smart Specialization from Policy to Cross-sector Partnerships. *Journal of Business Ethics*, *184*(4), 895–915. doi:10.100710551-023-05359-3

Webb, W. (2023). The smart city and COVID-19. In Beyond the Pandemic? Exploring the Impact of COVID-19 on Telecommunications and the Internet (pp. 121-133). Emerald Publishing Limited. doi:10.1108/978-1-80262-049-820231005

Wu, Q., Yan, D., & Umair, M. (2023). Assessing the role of competitive intelligence and practices of dynamic capabilities in business accommodation of SMEs. *Economic Analysis and Policy*, *77*, 1103–1114. doi:10.1016/j.eap.2022.11.024

Zhang, G., Yang, Y., & Yang, G. (2023). Smart supply chain management in Industry 4.0: The review, research agenda and strategies in North America. *Annals of Operations Research*, *322*(2), 1075–1117. doi:10.100710479-022-04689-1 PMID:35531562

Chapter 10
Investigating the Impact of the Internet of Things on the Probability of Entry in Export Market

Saeideh Samadzad
Academic Center for Education, Culture, and Research, Iran

ABSTRACT

The integration of IoT in the export market has brought significant benefits such as improved operational efficiency, cost savings, enhanced security, and better customer satisfaction. As the technology continues to advance, we can expect further innovations and advancements in IoT applications within the export industry. On the other hand, empirical knowledge (export experience) about foreign markets is a driving force in the internationalization of companies. This research investigates the possibility of entering and growing exports, emphasizing the role of export experience for young exporters. The statistical population of the research includes all Iranian food manufacturing companies that have had exports between the years 2019 and 2022. The research data has been extracted from the statistical system of the Islamic Republic of Iran Customs Administration and the Trade Development Organization. STATA econometric software has been used for data analysis.

INTRODUCTION

The Internet of Things (IoT) has the potential to greatly impact the export market by revolutionizing supply chain management, improving efficiency, and enhancing

DOI: 10.4018/979-8-3693-0210-1.ch010

product quality and safety. Here are some key ways IoT can be applied in the export market:

1. Supply Chain Management: IoT devices can provide real-time tracking and monitoring of goods throughout the entire supply chain. This enables exporters to have complete visibility and control over their shipments, reducing the risk of theft, damage, or loss. IoT sensors can also monitor temperature, humidity, and other environmental factors to ensure that goods are transported under optimal conditions.
2. Inventory Management: IoT devices can be used to monitor inventory levels in real-time, automatically triggering reordering or restocking when certain thresholds are reached. This helps exporters avoid stock outs or excess inventory, leading to improved operational efficiency and cost savings.
3. Quality Control: IoT sensors can be integrated into products or packaging to monitor various quality parameters such as temperature, pressure, vibration, or even product usage data. This allows exporters to ensure that products meet quality standards throughout the export process, reducing the risk of product recalls or customer complaints (Omidi et al., 2023)
4. Customs Compliance: IoT devices can assist in automating customs processes by providing accurate and real-time information about shipments. This can help exporters streamline customs clearance procedures and reduce delays or penalties associated with non-compliance.
5. Customer Experience: IoT-enabled devices can provide exporters with valuable data on how customers use their products. This data can be used to improve product design, identify customer preferences, and offer personalized services, ultimately enhancing the overall customer experience.
6. Remote Monitoring and Maintenance: IoT devices can enable exporters to remotely monitor and maintain equipment or machinery located in different export markets. This can help detect and address issues proactively, reducing downtime and maintenance costs.

Overall, the adoption of IoT in the export market can lead to increased efficiency, cost savings, improved product quality, and enhanced customer satisfaction. However, it is important for exporters to consider data security and privacy concerns when implementing IoT solutions.

Increasing dependence of companies on international business and increasing competition makes entering foreign markets one of the most important decisions in international strategy (Liu et al., 2023). Today, the entry of companies into the market is one of the most important mechanisms in the economy (Ahmadi Hajiabadi et al, 2021). In a dynamic economy, the entry and exit of companies is one of the components of competition with the aim of screening unsuccessful companies and creating the ground for emerging companies (Ganotakis et al., 2022). Entry and exit are both essential factors in the market selection process, which leads to restructuring and transformation in the industry. From this point of view, the entry and exit process of companies plays a fundamental role in the transformation and change in the industry. On the other hand, entry and exit are two inevitable aspects of the dynamic competitive process of the market, which leads to the growth of efficient firms and the fall of inefficient firms (Das et al., 2007). In the meantime, the impact of initial entry costs on the company's success in the export market is very important (Lee and Lee, 2015).

On the other hand, to achieve a dynamic economy, the successful flow of exports is a very effective factor (Liu et al., 2023). Every company enters an export market with the aim of developing its activity and creates infrastructure to achieve profitability in that market. In general, the purpose of entering and creating these infrastructures is to operate in a foreign market for several years (He et al., 2023). In addition to the company itself, the benefits of this action extend to the entire economy of the country of origin. For this reason, the development of exports is directly supported by the policy makers of the countries. Examining the business activity of companies shows that although every year many companies enter foreign markets, but in less than a year, they stop their business activities for various reasons. Most of those who remain in the export destination, they do not want to expand their presence and develop their activities in the export destination. Entering the market of a country and exiting it early depends on various factors, one of the most important of which is how to enter the export market (Albornoz et al., 2012). Choosing how to enter the foreign market is a strategic and important decision that determines the organizational structure of the company upon entering the host country market. Also, since the choice of each mode of entry into foreign markets requires the allocation of significant financial and human resources (which are often irreversible), choosing the optimal method is of great importance (Freund and Perola, 2010). Getting to know the methods of entering global markets is one of the important components of companies' success in achieving a greater share of markets. The way to enter an export market is in two general ways: simultaneous entry to several export destinations and gradual (successive) entry to different export markets. The correct selection of each of these two methods according to the conditions governing the company, export objectives and the general state of the economy can lead to the export development of the company and improve its resilience in the matter of exports. It should be noted that in order to enter an export market, companies always incur various fixed and variable costs, including customs fees, establishing a sales office or distribution network, advertising in the destination country, and providing the standards demanded by the destination country. Who expect to use these infrastructures created for several years to sell their products in the destination country and to accelerate and facilitate their return on investment by earning profit and developing the market (Morales et al., 2011).

Therefore, it is important to pay attention to the fact those factors such as export costs, economic conditions and market structure, cultural characteristics, laws and specific standards of the export destination cause uncertainty for the exporting company in the matter of export (Albornoz et al., 2018).

This uncertainty makes it important to understand the export patterns of a company in order to enter different markets. The level of uncertainty in the export market depends on two important factors. One of these factors is the company's export experience in the markets it has sold to in the past. The higher the experience, the lower the uncertainty for operating in the new market. The second important factor is the duration of a company's presence in an export market. The longer a company's activity in a market is, the less uncertainty it has. Therefore, it has been tried to explain the reliable and continuous presence of an economic enterprise in the export destination, and to investigate the effect of export experience and mastery of target market conditions on the success of the active company in exporting. One of the basic assumptions of this research is that the company, while theoretically aware of how to operate in a destination, undoubtedly faces various aspects of uncertainty. This uncertainty cannot be resolved except by physical presence and sales experience in the destination country or a country with a similar cultural structure and behavior pattern. Therefore, this research examines the possibility of entering the export market as well as the growth rate of export in an export destination for start-up companies.

To investigate this effect, it is assumed that the profitability of a company is correlated with the passage of time and duration of presence in a destination and also with profitability in another country. In this regard, the assumptions of the research are as follows:

- In an export market, the possibilities of entry of new exporters are more likely to enter a new export market than experienced exporters.
- In an export market, the rate of growth of the export of a new exporter in the early years of activity is higher than that of an experienced exporter.

The organization of the article is as follows: after presenting the introduction in the first part about impact of IoT on export market, in the second part, the subject literature that includes the theoretical foundations and background of the research is reviewed. In the third part, the methodology and then the estimation and analysis of the research findings are presented. Finally, conclusions and suggestions are discussed.

LITERATURE REVIEW

The Internet of Things (IoT) has the potential to greatly impact the export market by revolutionizing supply chain management, improving efficiency, and enhancing product quality and safety. Here are some key ways IoT can be applied in the export market:

1. Supply Chain Management: IoT devices can provide real-time tracking and monitoring of goods throughout the entire supply chain. This enables exporters to have complete visibility and control over their shipments, reducing the risk of theft, damage, or loss. IoT sensors can also monitor temperature, humidity, and other environmental factors to ensure that goods are transported under optimal conditions.
2. Inventory Management: IoT devices can be used to monitor inventory levels in real-time, automatically triggering reordering or restocking when certain thresholds are reached. This helps exporters avoid stock outs or excess inventory, leading to improved operational efficiency and cost savings.
3. Quality Control: IoT sensors can be integrated into products or packaging to monitor various quality parameters such as temperature, pressure, vibration, or even product usage data. This allows exporters to ensure that products meet quality standards throughout the export process, reducing the risk of product recalls or customer complaints (Omidi et al., 2023).
4. Customs Compliance: IoT devices can assist in automating customs processes by providing accurate and real-time information about shipments. This can help exporters streamline customs clearance procedures and reduce delays or penalties associated with non-compliance.
5. Customer Experience: IoT-enabled devices can provide exporters with valuable data on how customers use their products. This data can be used to improve product design, identify customer preferences, and offer personalized services, ultimately enhancing the overall customer experience.
6. Remote Monitoring and Maintenance: IoT devices can enable exporters to remotely monitor and maintain equipment or machinery located in different export markets. This can help detect and address issues proactively, reducing downtime and maintenance costs.

Overall, the adoption of IoT in the export market can lead to increased efficiency, cost savings, improved product quality, and enhanced customer satisfaction. However, it is important for exporters to consider data security and privacy concerns when implementing IoT solutions (Lee and Lee, 2015).

On the other hand, many studies have studied the effect of initial entry costs on the success of the company in an export target. Nevertheless, the large number of new export companies that enter or leave an export destination every year shows that the cost factor is not the only reason for the success or failure of a company in an export destination. The main premise of this research states that companies initially have very little information about the sustainable profitability of their exports, and over time and based on experience, they become more familiar with its amount and how to obtain it (Arkolakis, 2011). With this assumption, the export profit of a company in the market, although it cannot be calculated for that company at the beginning, but because it is related to the passage of time (continuation of activity in the export destination), operating in a market makes the company familiar with its potential and actual potentials.

This knowledge enables the ability to predict profit for the company (Bernard et al., 2017). In addition, the company will be able to use this experience to start operations and be profitable in other markets. The last statement can lead to a process of "Sequential exports" in which companies use their initial export experience to succeed in their future markets (Aguzzoli et al., 2020).

Another assumption of this research states that the export profitability of a company is related to the passage of time and among different export destinations. Profitability over time depends on factors such as the behavioral experience of the firm, the continuous demand pattern and the discovery of the unknown characteristics of the product offered by the company. For example, the attractiveness of the product may be discovered over time in the target market and cause the product to be in demand (Rasekhi and Sheidaei, 2019).

Also, unknown factors that are stable over time, such as port costs, transportation, distribution of goods, insurance, customs, etc., all of these activities include relatively stable uncertainties that are often unknown to companies until they The company is involved in export. Objective export experience also confirms that in most export markets, especially in developing countries, due to the weakness of data and also the existence of different methods for obtaining the necessary permits, this physical presence and objective experience of the company becomes more important (Albornoz et al., 2023).

However, the similarities in the demand pattern, cost similarities and the manner of export and sales operations in countries with common characteristics make it very effective to use sales experience in one market to enter another market. So that although the possible costs and the way of marketing, selling and exporting are unknown in advance for a company, they are often more or less the same in countries with a cultural, economic structure, common language or colonial relationship, which makes the experience of a company in a market, is effective on its future activities. "Knowledge of internationalization" is the title that Ericsson refers to the knowledge of how to behave, marketing, distribution network design, etc. in the export market, and most importantly, he emphasizes that this knowledge comes from export experience because they have their ability to gain knowledge from institutions and practice exporting in new markets.

The need for new knowledge and skills is associated with uncertainty when entering the market and it also indicates that most of the uncertainty is resolved through export experience (Albornoz et al., 2012).

It is noteworthy that the implicit nature of "self-aware" knowledge has no other convincing alternative and despite the companies' use of export data and theories, a significant part of the information and operational facts are self-aware by the company and in Theoretical studies are neglected. In the following, the structure and mathematical model of the company's decision-making to enter the export market with the knowledge of the export value will be discussed.

Basic Structure

A risk-neutral producer has the option of serving two segmented foreign markets, A and B. Countries A and B are symmetric except for the unit trade costs that the Home firm must pay to export there, denoted by τ^A and τ^B, $\tau^A \leq \tau^B$. To sell in each foreign market, the firm needs to incur in a one-time fixed cost per destination,

F≥0. This corresponds to the costs of establishing distribution channels, of designing a marketing strategy, of learning about exporting procedures, of familiarization with the institutional and policy characteristics of the foreign country, etc. Variable costs comprise two elements: an unknown export unit

cost, c_j, and a unit production cost that is known to the firm. We normalize the latter to zero. In the online appendix we show that allowing for differences in productivity has no qualitative consequence for

our main mechanism. The producer faces the following demand in each market j=A, B:

$$q^j\left(p^j\right) = d^j - p^j \qquad (1)$$

Where q^j denotes the output sold in destination j, p^j denotes the corresponding price, and d^j is an unknown parameter. We therefore allow for uncertainty in both demand and supply parameters. Let

$$\mu^j \equiv d^j - p^j \qquad (2)$$

Be a random variable with a continuous cumulative distribution function G (.) on the support $\left[\mu,\bar{\mu}\right]$. We refer to μ^j as the firm's "export profitability" in market j. $\bar{\mu}$ obtains when the highest possible demand

intercept (d) and the lowest possible export unit cost (c) are realized; μ obtains under the opposite extreme scenario. To ensure that equilibrium prices are always strictly positive, we need that Eμb2dj for all d^j, so

we assume throughout the paper that d > 1/ 2 E_μ.

It is also assumed that profitability is correlated across markets, and this correlation can be in supply or demand parameters or components. To model the decision to enter foreign markets, all expected profits are evaluated, such as the expected profit at t=0, of course, for simplicity, it is assumed that the company does not reduce its future returns. The company's decision to enter the export market is indicated by e_t^j if the company enters the export market j at time t is $e_t^j = 1$ and otherwise $e_t^j = 0$.

The timing is as follows:

t=1: At period 1, the firm decides whether to enter each market. If the firm decides to enter market j, it pays the per-destination fixed entry cost F and chooses how much to sell there in that period, q_1^j. At the end of period 1, export profits in destination j are realized. If the firm has entered and produced $q_1^j \geq \varepsilon$, where ε> 0 is arbitrarily small, it infers μ from its profit.

t = 2: At period 2, if the firm has entered market j at t = 1, it decides whether to keep serving on that market given the realization of export profits. If so, it chooses how much to sell in that market, q_2^j. If the firm has not entered destination j at t = 1, it decides whether to enter that market. If the firm enters, it pays F and chooses q_2^j. At the end of period 2, export profits are realized.

There are three entry strategies for each company, firstly, the firm enters A at t=1 and enters market B at t=2 (sequential entry), secondly, at t=1 the firm enters two or more markets simultaneously. (Simultaneous entry), the third is not to enter any of the markets. The other two possibilities of exporting to B before A and simultaneous entry at t=2 are inside these three possibilities and have a symmetric output (Albornoz et al., 2012). In this research, the two strategies of non-entry and simultaneous entry are not investigated, so they are excluded from the calculations.

Sequential Entry

The company's decision variables are $\left\{q_1^j q_2^j e_1^j e_2^j\right\}$ calculated by reverse inference. It should be noted that due to the research assumption $\tau^A \leq \tau^B$, A will enter the market before B. In each period, after entering each market, the company chooses its export volume by solving the following equation to obtain profit ¼(Albornoz et al., 2012).

j=A, B t=1,2

$$max\left\{\left(\mu-\tau_t^j-q_t^j\right)q_t^j\right\}$$

The result is as follows:

j=A, Bt=1,2

$$q_t^j\left(\tau^j\right)=1_{\{\mu>\tau^j\}}\left(\frac{\mu-\tau^j}{2}\right)$$

$1_{\{\cdot\}}$ The indicator is the index of the equation that shows in this research. Therefore, the profit at t=1 when the company enters country A is obtained by the following equation:

$$v\left(\tau^A\right)=\int_{\tau^A}^{\bar{\pi}}\left(\frac{\pi-\tau^A}{2}\right)^2 dG(\mu)$$

Which $v\left(\tau^A\right)$ is the value of continuing to export after experiencing profitability in foreign markets. If the company cannot make a positive profit, it will exit from it to avoid further losses; otherwise the company will adjust the amount of its product (output) with that market. The company chooses to enter the B market at t=2 if the operating profit is greater than the entry costs for that market:

$$\left(\frac{\mu-\tau^j}{2}\right)^2\geq f$$

Therefore, the company's decision to enter B market at t=2 are equal to:

$$e_2^B\left(\tau^B\right)=1\leftrightarrow\mu\geq 2f^{\frac{1}{2}}+\tau^B$$

If the company enters the B market, it will choose q_2^B as q_1^A and therefore, under the condition of continued export, $e_2^B=1$ and ¼> τ^B. Therefore, the behavior of the company to choose the amount of export is obtained from equation 4 for country B and t=2, according to which the profit of the company can be deduced in the following way:

$$w\left(\tau^{B},f\right)\equiv\int\left[\left(\frac{\mu-\tau^{B}}{2}\right)-f\right]dG(\mu)=\left\{v\left(t^{B}\right)-\int_{\tau^{B}}^{2f^{\frac{1}{2}}-\tau^{B}}\left(\frac{\mu-\tau^{B}}{2}\right)dG(\mu)\right\}-f\left[1-G\left(2f^{\frac{1}{2}}+\tau^{B}\right)\right]$$

The function $w\left(\tau^{B},f\right)$ shows the value of export profits from entering market B after entering market A and gaining experience and learning profitability from the foreign market. The expression inside $\{.\}$ expresses the expected profit from the company's entry into country B at t=2, and the other expression is the product of the fixed cost of entering the market B in the probability of being profitable in this market. Therefore, the output of entering the A market is equal to becoming an "informed exporter" to enter the B market, which avoids repeated costs in the new market (Jovanovic, 1982).

Morales et al. (2011) used a novel moment inequality approach to estimate a trade model for sequential entry into export markets and found that previous export experience in the primary market facilitates entry into other markets for reasons such as geographic similarities or market structure.

Alvarez and Lopez (2014) investigated whether previous export experience has an impact on new exports. The results of their studies, conducted using firm-level data (exported product and destination market), show that previous export experience increases the likelihood of firms exporting their previous exported goods to new markets or exporting different products to their previous export market. Furthermore, the results indicate that as the previous export experience increases, the likelihood of firms engaging in new product exports or new market exports increases because previous export experience reduces entry costs.

Ferve and Beamish (2015) examined the effects of standards on entry into export markets and the competitive advantage of agricultural products. The results of this study showed that compliance with export standards is one of the fundamental and important principles for agricultural product exporters.

Hollaway (2017) demonstrated in a study that sequential entry into distributors allows learning about the quality of their film from market performance. The empirical evidence presented in this article is consistent with new economic models of learning about export profits.

Surdua et al. (2018) conducted a study entitled "organizational learning, organizational quality, and speed of re-entry into foreign markets after initial entry and exit." The results showed that the accumulated experience between initial entry and exit does not lead to previous entries. Instead, the depth of accumulated experience through joint activities and the nature of the experience determined by the exit process have a significant impact on early entry.

Chen et al. (2019) examined a two-stage model to explain the process of exporting companies' re-entry into specific export markets. The results indicate the importance of the exit stage in shaping re-entry decisions, price/quality ratio, and export performance, with time playing a significant role in changing these effects. Albornoz et al. (2019) examined a model of export dynamics under uncertainty for multi-product firms. The results of this study show that most exporters use their initial export experiences and gradually adjust their sales volume, number of products, and destination countries. kasahara and Tang (2019) focused on excessive entry and exit in export markets. The study results showed that on average, 78% of exporters to a country in one year are new exporters. Among these new exporters, on average, 60% stop their exports to the same country the following year. These rates increase if the destination country is a market that Chinese companies are less familiar with.

Aguzzoli et al., (2020) explain Globalization has motivated firms to expand into foreign markets, but internationalization is inherently dynamic. Many firms have exited foreign markets for various reasons, but some later decide to re-enter those same markets. Based on a case study of a Brazilian multinational's activities in Mexico, this study contributes to the literature on re-entry decisions of multinational enterprises and their outcomes, focusing on the roles of institutional voids and the experiences of decision-makers during such processes. The findings suggest that companies learn from their mistakes and reconsider how they approach re-entry and the resources that may need to be mobilized. However, the learning process is not straightforward as it is clouded by international knowledge myopia. This study highlights how multiple actors and considerations influence re-entry events.

Ganotakis et al., (2022) explain how the "time-out period" from exporting affects a) the likelihood of re-starting exporting and b) re-entry export performance. We also explain how foreign collaboration influences these two relationships. We show that the time-out period has an inverted U-shaped relationship with the likelihood of re-starting exporting, and a U-shaped relationship with re-entry export performance. Foreign collaboration enhances managerial confidence and thereby increases the likelihood of re-starting exporting during the earlier phases of the time-out period. It also enhances re-entry export performance by accelerating new knowledge accumulation in the later phases of the time-out period.

Albornoz et al., (2023) explain that Exploiting disaggregated data on French exporters; they show that firms expand their product scope and geographical presence sequentially. This process of internationalization is uneven over time, exhibiting more volatility early than later in the life cycle of exporters. Specifically, young exporters are particularly likely to exit, and if they keep exporting, to expand at the intensive and sub-extensive margins, doing so by widening product scope within a destination before entering new destinations. They also find that firms' core products are particularly resilient despite being used to "test the waters" when entering additional countries. Existing models of firm export dynamics are not designed to explain these empirical regularities. We argue that they can be rationalized by a mechanism where new exporters are uncertain about the profitability of their products in different markets, but learn from their initial export experiences and then adjust their sales, number of products and destination countries accordingly.

In summary, various studies have examined different aspects of the entry and exit of firms into export markets, considering factors such as costs, duration of activity, and export experience. Organizational learning, organizational quality, the impact of standards, and the speed of re-entry into foreign markets after initial entry and exit have also been discussed in previous studies. However, this current research focuses on explaining the role of export experience in the behavior of new firms in two scenarios: the probability of entry and the growth of export, taking into account a wide range of country, firm, and year fixed effects. Lee and Lee (2015) explain The Internet of Things (IoT): Applications, investments, and challenges for enterprises. This article presents five IoT technologies that are essential in the deployment of successful IoT-based products and services and discusses three IoT categories for enterprise applications used to enhance customer value. In addition, it examines the net present value method and the real option approach widely used in the justification of technology projects and illustrates how the real option approach can be applied for IoT investment. Finally, this article discusses five technical and managerial challenges. Dmitriy et al., (2019) explain the implementation of the IoT concept in the post-industrial economy. The purpose of our research is to study the IoT (Internet of Things) acceptance model, its impact on the economy and human capital. Our research is a conceptual framework that links ease of use and utility with social influence and other factors such as cost, trust, IoT knowledge, as well as security and confidentiality of services.

Omidi et al., (2023) explain the use of IoT in export businesses is a new category, therefore, so far, a comprehensive and clear view of the various applications of Internet of Things technology in export businesses has not been presented in a coherent and integrated manner. The results showed that the index of technical infrastructure and the company's environment as background categories, the index of capabilities and costs as categories of causal conditions, the index of decision-making and planning and the facilitation and acceleration of processes as the central phenomenon categories, education indicators.

Methodology

The present study has a practical purpose. The statistical population of the research includes all Iranian food manufacturing companies that have had exports between the years 2014 and 2018. The research data has been extracted from the statistical system of the Islamic Republic of Iran Customs Administration and the Trade Development Organization. STATA econometric software has been used for data analysis. In this study, the Least Squares Dummy Variable (LSDV) method has been used to show the effect of fixed effects variables. This means that when examining the effects of company fixed effects, a dummy variable has been created for each company that assigns values of zero and one at the appropriate time. The same method has also been used to express the effects of country and year fixed effects. The present study has examined the behavior of newly established companies in terms of the likelihood of entry into export destinations, export growth, and the likelihood of exit from export destinations in three sections.

In this study, LSDV method is used to capture the effect of fixed variables. This means that in examining the effects of firm-fixed effects, a dummy variable is created for each firm that assigns values of zero and one at appropriate times. Additionally, the same method is used to represent the fixed effects of country and year. In this study, the behavior of newly established companies in relation to the probability of entering export destination and the probability of exiting export destination are examined in two sectors.

LSDV

The basic assumption of the fixed effects model is that in specifying a regression model, we cannot include appropriate explanatory variables that do not change over time. Therefore, introducing virtual variables is a solution to this neglect and ignorance. The use of panel data with fixed effects is a suitable solution for not distinguishing regression, especially when the specific effects of each unit (individual effects) dominate the time effects (Okoroafor et al., 2020). A common method in formulating mixed data models is based on the assumption that differences between units can be represented as differences in intercepts and therefore, in the following equation, each x_i is an unknown parameter that needs to be estimated.

Assuming that x_i and y_i includes T observations for i[th] and $\sum i$ is a vector except disturbance and has dimensions of T.1, as a result, the relationship will be as follows:

$$y_i = Ia_i + x_i\beta + \varepsilon_i i = 1,\ldots,n$$

$$\begin{pmatrix} Y_1 \\ Y_2 \end{pmatrix} = \begin{pmatrix} I & 0 \\ 0 & I \end{pmatrix} \begin{pmatrix} a_1 \\ a_2 \end{pmatrix} + \begin{pmatrix} X_1 \\ X_2 \end{pmatrix} \beta + \begin{pmatrix} \varepsilon_0 \\ \varepsilon_n \end{pmatrix}$$

Where i is a vector with T.T dimensions and the above model can be written in the following summary form:

$$Y = [d_1, \ldots, d_n x_1, \ldots, x_1] \begin{pmatrix} \alpha \\ \beta \end{pmatrix} + \varepsilon$$

Which is a virtual variable to show i is the cross section. Now, if we define the matrix D as:

$$D = [d_1, \ldots, d_n]$$

Defined by the dimensions $T_{n.n}$, we will have:

$$Y = Da + X\beta + \varepsilon$$

In this regard, it is called Least Squares Dummy Variable (LSDV). The latter model is a classical regression model and no new condition is required for its analysis. The model can be estimated using the OLS method with K repressors in X and n columns in D as a multivariate model with n+k parameters. The intercept in the regression model is different between people because each person or cross-sectional unit has its own characteristics. To consider the intercept, dummy variables can be used. The fixed effects model using dummy variables is called least squares model with LSDV (Park, 2009).

Entry

This section examines the behavior of companies in entering export markets. The research predicts that being a new exporter leads to an increase in entry into new export destinations, which is conditional on the company's survival in exports. To investigate this issue and estimate related data, a binary variable named $entry_{itr}$ is created for each company i to destination s that has exported other than r at time t-1. If company i exports to destination r in time t, this company-country pair leaves the sample in t+1. The sample includes companies that have exported for at least 2 years. Therefore, the following regression is tested:

$$Pr\left(entry_{itr}=1\right)$$

$$=\beta_1 fy_{it-1}+fe+\pi_{irt}$$

Where fy_{it-1} indicates the beginning of the company's export experience in t-1 (in other words, t is the second year that the company exports). A wide range of fixed effects is considered, as shown by . The coefficient β_1 indicates the type of behavior of a new company entering the export market and seeks to answer the question whether Do new exporters enter new export destinations more than experienced exporters or less than them?. Also, by entering the growth rate of the company's export; it is possible to measure the company's attention to the role of productivity and profitability in the matter of exports at the time of entering a new country. For this purpose, the following equation is used to check this issue:

$$Pr\left(entry_{itr}=1\right)=$$

$$\beta_1 fy_{it-1}+\Delta logx_{i-rt}$$

$$+\left(\Delta logx_{i-rt}\times fy_{it-1}\right)+fe+\pi_{irt}$$

DISCUSSION

The statistical analysis of econometric research models for the export data of Iranian food industry companies in three sections: probability of entering the export market and growth of export is as follows:

"Entry": The results with different sets of fixed effects are shown in Table (1).

Table 1. Probability of entering export markets

Output 3	Output 2	Output 1	Variable
0.118 (0.000)	0.265 (0.000)	0.134 (0.000)	fy_{it-1}
-	yes	-	Country - fixed effect
yes	-	-	Firm - fixed effect
-	-	yes	Year - fixed effect

fy_{it-1} Has a positive and significant coefficient in all three characteristics. This coefficient shows the behavior of new companies, which are different from old companies in terms of experience. Although the amounts may seem small at first, it should be considered that the possibility of a specific company entering a specific country among hundreds of export targets in a given year is a very rare event. Therefore, even though these numbers seem small, they are important.

As mentioned, β_1 coefficients seem small, but this itself indicates a significant growth in the possibility of exporting to new destinations in the coming year for companies that have started exporting in the New Year. Therefore, according to the output of the research data and with an average for all three cases, it can be said that if the company is new, the probability of entering the new market increases by almost 17%.

According to the theoretical basis, this increase is also justifiable, and according to the main assumptions of the research, the increase in export experience and the familiarity of the company with the experimental methods of export creates this motivation and courage in the start-up companies to expand their markets. In other words, when companies enter the export business experimentally, they become more motivated by earning profit. Also, by gaining experience and becoming an "internationalized knowledge" company, they also feel the ability and courage to enter a new market. The result of this increase in motivation and courage increases the probability of a new company entering a new market compared to an old company.

Table 2. Probability of entering export markets

Output 2	Output 1	Variable
0.167 (000/0)	0.148 (000/0)	fy_{it-1}
0.005 (0.000)	0.003 (000/0)	$\Delta logX_{i-rt}$
0. 002 (000/0)	0.003 (000/0)	$(\Delta logX_{i-rt} \times fy_{it-1})$
yes	-	Country - fixed effect
-	yes	Firm - fixed effect

As the results of Table 2 show, the FY coefficient remains positive and significant. Therefore, the overall positive effect of being a new exporter to increase the probability of entering a new market still remains. But in this part, it is checked whether being a new exporter is important for entering a newer market among companies that face the growth of export volumes. To investigate the impact of the growth of export volume (which is affected by the increase in productivity and profitability) on the willingness of start-up companies to enter a new market, it is important to pay attention to the coefficient.

CONCLUDING REMARKS

The Internet of Things (IoT) has significantly impacted various industries, including the export market. IoT refers to the network of physical devices, vehicles, appliances, and other objects embedded with sensors, software, and connectivity to exchange data over the internet. In the export market, IoT has revolutionized supply chain management and logistics. Here are some ways IoT is being used in the export market:

- Real-time tracking and monitoring: IoT devices can be attached to shipping containers, vehicles, or products to provide real-time tracking and monitoring throughout the export process. This allows exporters to have visibility into the location, condition, and status of their goods at any given time, enabling better inventory management and reducing the risk of loss or theft.
- Predictive maintenance: IoT sensors can be installed on machinery and equipment used in the export process to monitor their performance and detect any potential issues before they become major problems. This helps prevent

costly breakdowns and downtime, ensuring smooth operations and timely delivery of goods.

- Enhanced security: IoT-enabled surveillance systems can monitor warehouses, ports, and transportation routes, providing enhanced security measures against theft, vandalism, or unauthorized access. These systems can send alerts in case of any suspicious activities, helping exporters protect their valuable assets.
- Optimized fleet management: IoT devices in vehicles used for export transportation can collect data on fuel consumption, driver behavior, and vehicle performance. This data can be analyzed to optimize routes, reduce fuel costs, improve driver safety, and enhance overall fleet management efficiency.
- Quality control and traceability: IoT sensors can be used to monitor and record environmental conditions such as temperature, humidity, or light exposure during the transportation of perishable goods. This ensures that products maintain their quality throughout the export journey. Additionally, IoT technology can enable traceability by providing a detailed record of each stage in the supply chain, allowing exporters to track the origin and movement of their products.
- Demand forecasting and inventory management: IoT devices can collect data on customer preferences, buying patterns, and inventory levels. This data can be analyzed to forecast demand accurately, optimize inventory levels, and ensure that exporters have the right products available at the right time.

This research examines the role of experience in business dynamics. Why are there many entry and exits to export markets every year? Is exporting useful despite high costs and low profits? Is the behavior of a new company in a market different from the old company? In this research, a mathematical model was used to investigate the behavior of partners in the case of entering country A in the first period and gaining experience and understanding the value of continuing to export, and then deciding whether to enter or not enter market B in the second period. The result of this study is to provide a mathematical relationship for the value of continued export in the case of the profitability in each market and to make a decision about continuing to operate in a market. Then, by examining the data related to the export of Iranian food industry companies between 2019 and 2022, the behavior of new entrants in terms of entering the export market, growth of export volume and exit from the export market has been investigated. The output of the data and the analysis of data statistics show that being a new exporter increases the probability of entering a new export market, also by entering the growth rate of export volume to examine the impact of profitability and increase productivity, the behavior of new companies

In increasing the probability of entering new markets, the results indicated the positive effect of being a new exporter on increasing the probability of entering the export market compared to old exporters.. According to the obtained results as well as the statistical analysis of the frequency of data, the following suggestions are recommended in the field of political behavior and future researches:

- Due to the positive impact of the new exporter on the possibility of entering to new markets and increasing the exports due to the role of experience in this matter, it is suggested to start exporting for the first time with a small amount and less operational risk, and in the future markets from The experience gained should be used to expand the number of target markets and the volume of exports.
- Due to the role of experience, physical presence and knowledge of internationalization, the development of new markets should be done for countries with a similar cultural and economic structure to the first market.
- After several years of presence in the target market and the diminution of the role of experience in the growth of commercial activities, it is necessary to pay special attention to the role of credit limits, production capacity, logistics and marketing activities to expand activities.
- Due to the different effect of simultaneous entry or re-entry after the export break, it is recommended to conduct another research to investigate this effect with the data of Iran for the use of industries, active export companies and policymakers.
- Due to the importance of conscious behavior and to clarify the details of entering the export markets as much as possible, it is recommended to conduct another research with the addition of the type of goods along with the variables used in this research. This can lead to the classification of the attractiveness of export destinations based on the type of goods, which will be important in the policy making of companies and responsible institutions.

REFERENCES

Aguzzoli, R., Lengler, J., Sousa, C. M. P., & Benito, G. R. G. (2020). Here We Go Again: A Case Study on Re-entering a Foreign Market. *British Journal of Management*, *32*(2), 416–432. doi:10.1111/1467-8551.12407

Ahmadi Hajiabadia, S., Ul-Haqb, J., & Visasc, H. (2021). Impact of Development Strategy on Economic Growth of Iran: New Structural Economics Perspective. *Iranian Journal of Economic Studies*, *10*(2), 473–487.

Albornoz, F., Calvo Pardo, H. F., Corcos, G., & Ornelas, E. (2012). Sequential exporting. *Journal of International Economics*, *88*(10), 17–31. doi:10.1016/j.jinteco.2012.02.007

Albornoz, F., Calvo Pardo, H. F., Corcos, G., & Ornelas, E. (2018). Sequential Exporting and Third-Country Effects of Trade Policy. *Working Paper*, 1-78.

. Albornoz, F, Calvo Pardo, H.F., Corcos, G. & Ornelas, E. (2023). Sequentially exporting products across countries. *Journal of International Economics*. 142, . *88*(10), 17-31. doi:10.1016/j.jinteco.2023.103735

Alvarez, R., & Lopez, R. (2014). Is Previous Export Experience Important for New Exports? *The Journal of Development Studies*, 1–38.

Arkolakis, C. (2011). *A unified theory of firm selection and growth*. Mimeo. doi:10.3386/w17553

Artopoulos, A., Friel, D., & Hallak, J. C. (2011). Lifting the domestic veil: the challenges of exporting differentiated goods across the development divide. *NBER Working Paper 16947*.

Bernard, A. B., Esther, A. B., Renzo Massari, J. R., & Daria, T. (2017). Exporter Dynamics and Partial-Year Effects. *The American Economic Review*, *107*(10), 3211–3228. doi:10.1257/aer.20141070

Bernard, A. B., Jensen, J. B., Redding, S. J., & Schott, P. K. (2009). The Margins of US Trade. *The American Economic Review*, *99*(2), 487–493. doi:10.1257/aer.99.2.487

Chen, J., Sousa, C. M. P., & He, X. (2019). Export market re-entry: Time-out period and price/quality dynamisms. *Journal of World Business*, *54*(2), 154–168. doi:10.1016/j.jwb.2019.01.001

Das, S., Roberts, M., & Tybout, J. (2007). Market entry costs, producer heterogeneity, and export dynamics. *Econometrica*, *75*(3), 837–873. doi:10.1111/j.1468-0262.2007.00769.x

Dmitriy, N. K., Yulia, S. P., Lyudmila, K. V., & Dilovar, D. (2019). the implementation of the IoT concept in the post-industrial economy. *ESPACIOS*, *40*(38), 28–39.

Ferve, C., & Beamish, P. W. (2015). A Resource-Based Approach to the Study of Export Performance. *Journal of Small Business Management*, *41*, 242–261.

Freund, C., & Pierola, M. (2010). Export entrepreneurs: evidence from Peru. *World Bank Policy Research Working Paper* 5407.

Ganotakis, P., Konara, P., Kafouros, M., & Love, J. H. (2022). Taking a time-out from exporting: Implications for the likelihood of export re-entry and re-entry export performance. *Journal of World Business*, *7*(5), 1–15. doi:10.1016/j.jwb.2022.101349

He, D., Wang, Y., & You, K. (2023). Market entry and the dynamics of export product quality: Evidence from Chinese manufacturing firms. *Economic Analysis and Policy*, *78*, 692–706. doi:10.1016/j.eap.2023.04.001

Hollaway, I. S. (2017). Learning via sequential market entry: Evidence from international releases of U.S. movies. *Journal of International Economics*, *40*, 104–121. doi:10.1016/j.jinteco.2016.10.008

Jovanovic, B. (1982). Selection and the evolution of industry. *Econometrica*, *50*(3), 649–670. doi:10.2307/1912606

Kasahara, H., & Tang, H. (2019). Excessive entry and exit in export markets. *Journal of the Japanese and International Economies*, *53*, 101–131. doi:10.1016/j.jjie.2019.101031

Lee, I., & Lee, K. (2015). The Internet of Things (IoT): Applications, investments, and challenges for enterprises. *Business Horizons*, *15*(4), 1–15. doi:10.1016/j.bushor.2015.03.008

Liu, D., Wang, Q., Wang, A., & Yao, S. (2023). Export profitability and firm R&D: On China's export diversification under trade war. *Structural Change and Economic Dynamics*, *67*, 151–166. doi:10.1016/j.strueco.2023.07.012

Morales, E., Sheu, G., & Zahler, A. (2011). *Gravity and extended gravity: estimating a structural model of export entry.* Mimeo.

Okoroafor, I. B., Okechukwu, C. N., & Anuonye, R. C. & Uka, C. O. (2020). Application of Least Square Dummy Variable (LSDV) In Estimation Of Compensation Of Employée. *European Journal of Statistics and Probability.*, *8*(3), 35–38.

Omidi, F., Hosseini, S.A. and Rekabdar, G. (2023), Designing a Model for the Application of IoT in Export Businesses Using the Grounded Theory (A Case Study of Agricultural Machinery Exporter Companies), *Journal of Business Administration Researches*. doi. doi:10.22034/JBAR.2023.19577.4268

Park, H. M. (2009). *Linear Regression Models for Panel Data Using SAS*. Stata, LIMDEP, and SPSS, University Information Technology Services Center for Statistical and Mathematical Computing Indiana University.

Rasekhi, S., & Sheidaei, Z. (2019). An Empirical Analysis of Strategic Competition and Exchange Rate Pass-through. *Iranian Journal of Economic Studies*, *8*(1), 119–136.

Surdua, I., Mellahi, K., Glaister, K. W., & Nardella, G. (2018). Why wait? Organizational learning, institutional quality and the speed of foreign market re-entry after initial entry and exit. *Journal of World Business*, *53*(6), 911–921. doi:10.1016/j.jwb.2018.07.008

Chapter 11
Viability of Man and Machine as Co-Workers in the Hotel Industry

Sunil Kumar
https://orcid.org/0000-0002-2362-1972
Lovely Professional University, India

Meenakshi Yadav
Lovely Professional University, India

Dinesh Kumar
Lovely Professional University, India

ABSTRACT

This study examines the feasibility of fostering symbiotic relationships between humans and machines in the hotel industry and explores effective strategies for managing their collaboration to maximize benefits. The chapter follows a rigorous methodology, conducting a systematic literature review using scientific databases, analyzing published and unpublished articles and data from various organizations. Key focus areas include the "hospitality industry," "man and machine," and "machine as co-workers." Findings demonstrate that strategic management and implementation of human-machine relationships can enhance organizational performance and yield substantial benefits. Addressing inherent challenges and intricacies is vital for a favorable outcome. The study presents a theoretical framework elucidating the impact of human-machine interaction on organizational outcomes.

DOI: 10.4018/979-8-3693-0210-1.ch011

INTRODUCTION

The hotel and tourism industries are large and rapidly growing sectors crucial in boosting employment rates, attracting foreign investment, and contributing to a country's GDP. In India, the hotel industry contributes 9.4% to the GDP and is among the top 10 industries attracting foreign direct investment. It also provides 80% of employment opportunities, making it vital to create a positive work environment to maximize its economic impact.

To promote employee well-being, it is essential to distribute workloads fairly and address work-related stress in the hotel industry. Taking into account individual capabilities and efficiency when assigning tasks is crucial. The ongoing pandemic has severely affected the tourism industry, leading to job losses and increased pressure on remaining employees, resulting in reduced productivity and job satisfaction.

A new approach has emerged to tackle these challenges involving a collaborative effort between humans and machines. By smartly assigning tasks to human workers and automated systems, employees can experience reduced stress and improved efficiency. Let us explore the origin and principles of this concept.

Industry 5.0, the next phase following Industry 4.0, focuses on collaboration between humans and machines to improve productivity and efficiency (Schwab, 2017). Unlike its predecessor, which heavily leaned on automation, Industry 5.0 fosters cooperation, not competition, between man and machine. Industry 5.0 helps boost efficiency and productivity in the hospitality industry, which is crucial during the ongoing pandemic. The pandemic has hit the hospitality industry hard, resulting in massive job losses and decreased profitability (American Hotel & Lodging Association, 2020; Hao et al., 2020).

Strategies and preventive measures are needed to counter these challenges. A critical factor to consider is the guest's perception of hotel safety and cleanliness, which directly affects profitability and growth. Thus, integrating technology, human expertise, and machinery presents a promising solution (Hao et al., 2020; Jiang & Wen, 2020).

Park et al. (2019) found that hotel guests prioritize hygiene and cleanliness. Due to recent circumstances, guests have become more concerned about personal hygiene and social distancing. Traditional visual inspections by housekeeping staff are insufficient in ensuring hotel cleanliness, as highlighted by Almanza et al. (2015) and Kline et al. (2014).

The hotel industry has adopted technology-driven solutions. Contactless services have become prominent (Gursoy & Chi, 2020; Hao et al., 2020), and hotels are improving safety protocols (Shin & Kang, 2020). Collaborative robots, known as Cobots, serve as contactless waiters (Hao et al., 2020; Jiang & Wen, 2020).

Hospitality 5.0 signifies the hotel industry's symbiotic relationship between humans and machines, embracing Industry 5.0 principles (Schwab, 2017).

LITERATURE REVIEW

The hospitality industry suffers significantly from crises and natural disasters, with the recent coronavirus outbreak particularly devastating (Henderson & Ng, 2004; Hao et al., 2020). This sector has also faced challenges from previous pandemics and epidemics. Currently, hotels prioritize safety, hygiene, and cleanliness, as highlighted by the Hotel Association of Canada (2006), which advocates thorough sanitization of frequently touched areas and proper sanitation of food counters. They also suggest adequate time intervals between shifts for diligent cleaning and sanitation.

Technology plays a vital role in overcoming challenges and managing crises in the hospitality industry (Tew et al., 2008; Lo et al., 2006). Email and video conferencing technologies are recommended for contactless communication with customers, ensuring their safety. Previous research supports using technology and machines to improve situations (Hao et al., 2020; Shin & Kang, 2020). Machines in hotels work in collaboration with human employees to provide service to customers (Gursoy & Chi, 2020; Seyitoglu & Ivanov, 2020), emphasizing the importance of cooperation between humans and machines.

In addition to prioritizing cleanliness, hygiene, contactless service, and safety, machines play a crucial role in effective disaster management within the hospitality industry.

The industrial revolution started in the 18th century with phases that utilized water and steam power, followed by electricity. The fourth industrial revolution saw machines replacing human labour, but the fifth industrial revolution, Industry 5.0, emphasizes human-machine collaboration (Petrillo et al., 2018; Ozdemir & Hekim, 2018).

In Industry 5.0, humans play a significant role, leading to improved cognitive abilities, innovation skills, creativity, and intelligence in the workforce (Longo et al., 2020). Collaborative robots (Cobots) are used in the hospitality industry to offer personalized customer services while ensuring safety (Ozdemir & Hekim, 2018). This synergy between humans and machines mirrors the connected device paradigm of Industry 4.0 (Demir et al., 2019).

Industry 5.0 has the potential to enhance creativity and innovation while reducing workloads, stress, and occupational hazards (Nahavandi, 2019). By fostering collaboration between humans and machines, Industry 5.0 positions humans as collaborative partners in the workforce, leveraging their cognitive capabilities and creativity.

Industry 5.0 brings various benefits to the hospitality industry, including an efficient supply chain, personalized service, smart work environments, agility, customer preference information, cost-effective customization, and improved customer satisfaction (Shamim et al., 2017). Every hotel guest has unique preferences, requiring tailored services (Kuo et al., 2012).

Industry 5.0 is composed of the human-cyber-physical system (HCPS), internet-of-service (IoS), and internet-of-things (IoT), transforming the hospitality industry (Alcacer & Cruz-Machado, 2019). HCPS, with artificial intelligence and human expertise, optimizes customer experiences through high-speed internet connectivity and advanced sensors (Pathak et al., 2019; Hermann et al., 2016). It promotes contactless services, ensuring safety and accurate labeling of products (Iqbal et al., 2017; Li et al., 2020).

The IoT forms a network of interconnected devices, enabling data transfer between humans and computers, supporting contactless operations and enhancing guest safety (Atzori et al., 2010; Mogelonsky, 2020; Nadkarni et al., 2019).

IoS includes internal and cross-organizational services driven by big data and cloud computing, facilitating interconnected guest services and personalized customer experiences (Terzidis et al., 2012; Hurwitz et al., 2009).

Industry 5.0 revolutionizes the hospitality industry, offering optimized supply chains, personalized services, intelligent work environments, agility, customer insights, cost-effective customization, and enhanced satisfaction (Shamim et al., 2017). Hospitality 5.0 embraces technological advancements, shaping the industry's future with virtualization, real-time capabilities, modularity, interoperability, and decentralization.

DISRUPTIVE TECHNOLOGY EXAMPLES IN HOTELS

Robots that prepare meals, clean rooms, and welcome visitors are being tested in some hotels. "A very, thankfully, un-Westworld-like experience from arrival to departure," according to the description of the Henna Hotel in Nagasaki, Japan, which bills itself as the "world's first fully robotic hotel." The robotic arm will store guest luggage in the cloakroom. These are amusing robot moments, which are mechanical yet nevertheless human. The Harlem Aloft Hotel in Manhattan has already adopted a new smartphone key system from Starwood. They offer customers the choice to check in online, which gives them access to an app that lets them use their smartphone as a room key without ever having to interact with anyone in person. Hilton employs a robot concierge named Connie. The robot uses an IBM-developed artificial intelligence platform and can engage with visitors and reply to their inquiries thanks to speech recognition technology. With every encounter, the system adapts and learns, enhancing its responses. When Aloft Hotels debuted A.L.O, or "robotic butler," at its Cupertino location in 2014, it made history as the first hotel chain to employ robot technology. The robot can go around the entire hotel to deliver packages. Its main objective was to deliver packages in rooms as a surprise to guests. The Crowne Plaza in San Jose, Silicon Valley, pioneered robot technology use. Dash, the hotel delivery robot, specializes in bringing guests snacks, toiletries, and other amenities. When summoned, Dash uses a special Wi-Fi connection to navigate the property. The Vijayvada Hotel in India also uses robots to serve food to its patrons.

METHODOLOGY

This conceptual study is based on a literature review utilizing various methodologies. It encompasses various disciplines, including computer science, technological innovation, hospitality operations, the Internet of Things, and cybernetics. The focus is on Industry Revolution 5.0 within the hospitality industry, emphasizing contactless services, cleanliness, hygiene, and safety. Key sources included journal articles, trade journals, statistics, reports, press releases, and conference papers. The main keywords used for the literature search were industrial revolution, industry 5.0, hospitality industry, and man and machine. Only research studies from 2010 onwards were considered to highlight the latest technological advancements.

IMPACT OF HAVING MAN AND MACHINE AS CO-WORKERS

Industry 5.0 emphasizes the collaboration between humans and machines as co-workers, a particularly relevant trend in the hospitality sector. In this industry, technology and machines, including robots, are employed as waiters and manage cleanliness, safety, and hygiene. Online bookings have also become the norm. This study aims to assess the impacts of man and machine working together, considering both positive and negative effects.

The Positive Impacts of Man and Machine as Co-Workers in Hotels

When man and machine collaborate in any organization, they generate numerous opportunities for growth and profitability. Work will be completed more efficiently and in less time, reducing employee stress and workload and providing faster and safer service. Let us consider its positive impact one by one.

- Cost optimization: As hotel co-workers, man and machine took over past improvements, generating more effective and efficient results. Hotel organizations are willing to achieve higher profitability and improve productivity according to Industry Revolution 5.0 because, as per this revolution, man and machine work as co-workers and man and machine work together to make the best financial decisions for a company. (Barber & Scarcelli, J.M., 2010).
- Greener solutions: With the emergence of industry revolution 5.0, many sustainable policies also emerged, and they work to protect the environment. When men and machines work together, they generate minimal waste, and even waste management becomes easy. Not much harm is created to nature. (Galitsky, B., 2019).
- Personalization and creativity: When man and machine work together, it will help in the generation of new and innovative ideas, help in providing better and more effective solutions to any problem, machine help man in becoming more creative, and may get an opportunity to upgrade themselves according to the latest technology and work accordingly. As co-workers in a hotel organization, man and machine will bring innovation and creativity. (Buhalis, & Leung, 2018).
- Trained personnel: The emergence of Industry 5.0, where man and machine start working together, generates employee training and development opportunities. Because employees are now trained according to the latest technology, they can easily adjust to and work with recent technology and upgraded machines (Shin & Kang, 2020).
- The right technology: Nowadays, after the evaluation of Industry 5.0, the most frequently used term is "cobot," which means collaborative robot. The term "Cobots" has been coined concerning Industry 5.0. The main purpose of designing collaborative robots is to interact intuitively with humans. Cobots consider humans and work for the plant's safety and goals (Ivanov & Webster, 2017).
- Create a balance between man and machine: Because of the emergence of Industry Revolution 5.0, man and machine are given equal importance in organizations. Before Industry Revolution 5.0, they were less important than machines, making them feel unjustified and unrelaxed. However, now that men are considered equal to machines, they realize their importance in the organization and feel justified, which increases employee efficiency. (Drexler & Lapr'e, V.B., 2019).
- Productive, economic and commercial consequences: When man and machine collaborate, overall productivity and the economic condition of the

organization improve. It will also aid in the resolution of many commercial issues. (Gilchrist, A., 2016).

- Increasingly powerful: When men and machines collaborate, they create more favourable opportunities for organizations and a strong position and market share. In hotels, when men and machines collaborate, service quality and comfortability for the guest increases, yielding customer satisfaction and aiding in creating a better reputation and goodwill for that particular hotel organization. (Li et al., 2020).

By looking at the various positive impacts of man and machine as co-workers, it can be said that this new industrial revolution will help in overall organizational growth, increase productivity and profitability of the organization, improve employee welfare and personal development, and create a balance between man and machine, all of which will automatically generate positive results for the organization.

The Negative Impact of Man and Machine as Co-Workers

- Task design: When man and machine work together as a team or as co-workers, there is a need to design special tasks and working conditions. Proper evaluation and analysis should be done before putting man and machine together as co-workers on any task. The process and concept of task design have become more complicated (Nahavandi, 2019).
- Increases tanning cost: When working with machines, employees must be well-informed and educated about the machine. Employees have to be trained so that they can work smoothly with machines. Training and development costs will rise (Gurkaynak et al., 2016).
- Increases overall cost: The industry revolution 5.0 promotes equal working of man and machine. They promote man and machine as co-workers. However, when man and machine work together, we must first arrange the latest technology machines, then make the working environment accordingly, arrange all the facilities so that machine can work, and then spend on training and development of employees so that they can work easily and comfortably with machines (Longo et al., 2020).
- It negatively affects the self-esteem of employees: Having man and machine as co-workers in an organization may reduce employee's self-esteem as they feel less important and have a feeling that they are either ignored or considered less efficient; having such a feeling may make them dissatisfied; all this will negatively affect their self-esteem (Demire et al., 2019).
- It induces stress among employees: When employees are required to work with machines as a team member, much pressure is placed on them; they

must work with the latest technology, keep themselves updated, and are also forced to work more efficiently in order to compete with machines (Zhong et al., 2020)

- Increases anger and frustration: When men work with machines, they face many difficulties and challenges; working with machines as a team is not easy, and all the burdens and stress may increase anger and frustration among employees (Atzori et al., 2010).
- It may reduce jobs/ may promote job cuts: When machines begin to work alongside or as a man in an organization, there is a possibility that manpower will be reduced because machines do the same work in less time and more efficiently than men, so it can be said that machines and man as co-workers may result in job cuts. In hotels, hundreds of guests are entertained daily, and men may get tired of doing so, whereas machines such as robots do the same much faster (Mogelonsky, 2020).
- Lack of mutual understanding and team collaboration: Machines are not human, so they cannot understand the feelings and problems of man; man does not create a friendly relationship and environment with machines; machines only work according to the commands provided to them; the lack of mutual understanding and collaboration among employees makes it difficult for a man to work with and adjust to machines (Iqubal et al., 2017).

Without a doubt, having man and machine as co-workers will harm the organization and may result in unfavourable conditions such as decreased productivity and profitability, dissatisfied customers, and decreased employee efficiency. All of these will impact the organization's growth and success rate, as well as its reputation and goodwill.

Measures Should Be Taken While Allowing Man and Machine to Work as Co-Workers

There should be some preventive measures that any organization should follow to avoid all the negative consequences of man and machine as a worker, and these preventive measures are as follow:

- Proper training and development programs should be organized: Employees should provide proper training and development to keep themselves updated, work with the latest technology, and easily adjust to changing environment (Zhong et al., 2020).
- Employees should be well-educated and informed about machines: Machines installed as a co-worker in the organization should be employee-friendly,

and employees should be well-educated and informed about the working and functioning of that machines (Brochado et al., 2016).

- Proper working facilities and arrangements should be made: Before allowing man and machine to work together as co-workers in an organization, all necessary arrangements and facilities must be made to ensure that both work smoothly and efficiently (Bitner et al., 2000).
- Employees should be motivated and encouraged: Employees should be motivated, encouraged, and appreciated for working with machines regularly; by doing so, we can increase employee morale and willingness to work with machines (Shin & Kang, 2020).
- Try to reduce stress and pressure among employees: Always reduce employee stress, anger, pressure, and frustration by making them relaxed and comfortable with machines; they will only work at their best (Pathak et al., 2019).
- Job security should be given to employees: Employees should be provided with job security; if employees' jobs are secure, they will be satisfied with the organization and will work with full dedication (Alcacer'and Cruz-Machado, 2019).
- Employees should be included and realize their importance: A system of inclusion should be in place; employees' importance in the organization should be realized; their participation should be appreciated; and their involvement in decision-making should be encouraged (Neuhofer et al., 2013).
- Work and tasks should be designed by keeping both elements in mind: Work goals, objectives, and tasks should be reliable and easily achievable by both factors; tasks assigned should not be too difficult to achieve or complete (Henderson & Ng, 2004).

By considering all these preventive measures and incorporating them into an organization, it is possible to reduce the negative effect of man and machine as co-workers to a greater extent, and the chance of organizational failure and loss will also be reduced.

Figure 1. Conceptual framework

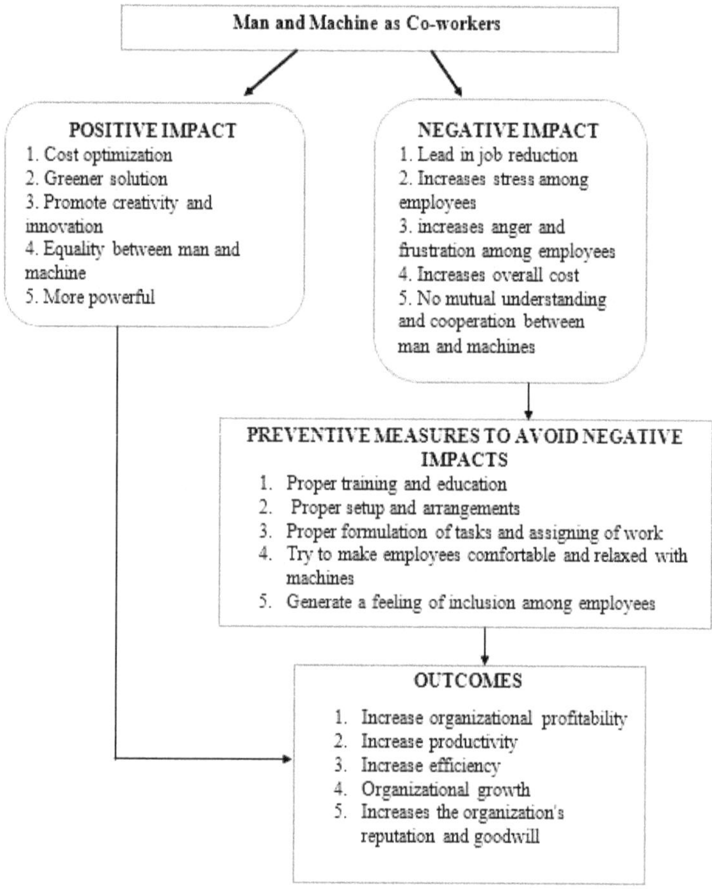

DISCUSSION

This conceptual study explores the effects of human-machine collaboration, a characteristic of Industry Revolution 5.0, particularly in the hospitality industry. The study conducted an extensive literature review from 2010 to 2020 and found the following insights: Industry Revolution 5.0 promotes human-machine co-worker relationships, with the hospitality industry utilizing cooperative robots ("Cobots") as waiters and adopting online bookings and customer service. The study identifies both positive and negative impacts of man and machine working together. The positive outcomes encompass the growth of employees on a personal level, adoption of eco-friendly solutions, fostering innovation, achieving a harmonious balance between human and machine interaction, and optimizing costs, which leads to enhanced productivity, profitability, and overall organizational advancement. Conversely, the negative consequences involve escalated expenses for training and setup, heightened employee stress, reduced job opportunities, and a lack of understanding and cooperation between humans and machines. To alleviate these negative effects, the study proposes various measures, including providing adequate training, educating employees about machine usage, acknowledging their significance, and promoting motivation and appreciation. By implementing these precautions, organizations can harness the benefits of human-machine collaboration and ensure overall growth for the organization.

RESEARCH IMPLICATION

This research investigates the synergistic effects of humans and technology within the hospitality industry, particularly in response to recent developments like the COVID-19 pandemic. It highlights the significant role of technology in elevating customer service and overall industry conditions (Neuhofer et al., 2013). Through the integration of human-machine collaboration, customers can enjoy enriched experiences (Brochado et al., 2016). Technological advancements in hospitality services can confer a competitive edge (Zhong et al., 2020). The study also emphasizes the applicability of Industry 5.0 design principles in the hospitality context, leading to the emergence of Hospitality 5.0 technology. This approach showcases how technology can deliver a high-tech, low-touch experience while upholding hygiene, cleanliness, and safety standards (Bitner et al., 2000). Furthermore, the research examines the impact of contactless technologies on hygiene, cleanliness, and safety in the hospitality sector (Shin & Kang, 2020). Ultimately, the collaboration between humans and machines has the potential to attract more customers and enhance their overall experience.

LIMITATIONS

One limitation of this study is its focus solely on the hospitality industry, specifically hotels and restaurants. Another limitation is its conceptual nature, suggesting the need for further empirical research on the same topic. Artificial intelligence plays a crucial role in the hospitality sector. While the collaboration between humans and machines enhances operational efficiency and adaptability, it also increases costs and expenses. Managing these expenses becomes critical for organizations to avoid potential challenges. Hospitality 5.0 technologies increase hotel organizations' visibility and improve service customization and personalization. However, hotel firms must conduct a cost-benefit analysis and track their return on investment and sunk costs before investing in Hospitality 5.0. Additional research is needed to explore cost management strategies and the financial implications of adopting Hospitality 5.0 (Ivanov & Webster, 2017).

CONCLUSION

This study examines the impact of human-machine collaboration in the hotel industry. As a vital and rapidly growing sector, the hotel industry contributes significantly to income, GDP, and employment opportunities. In line with the emergence of Industry 5.0, which advocates for human-machine collaboration, the hotel industry has also adopted new technologies and practices. For instance, robots are taking over the roles of waiters, and digital platforms are managing orders and reservations. This research investigates the impact of human-machine collaboration in the hotel industry, uncovering both favorable and unfavorable effects. On the upside, it leads to increased productivity, profitability, efficiency, staff growth, stress reduction, environmental sustainability, and task simplification. Conversely, it also presents challenges like heightened employee stress, escalated costs, the need for distinct working conditions, increased training expenditures, implications for employment, and potential lack of teamwork. However, these negative impacts can be mitigated by adopting preventive strategies such as creating an appropriate work environment, providing comprehensive training, utilizing user-friendly machines, and raising employee awareness about machine technology and operations. Enacting these measures can help curb the adverse outcomes of human-machine collaboration.

REFERENCES

Alc'acer, V., & Cruz-Machado, V. (2019). Scanning the industry 4.0: A literature review on technologies for manufacturing systems. *Eng. Sci. Technol. Int. J.* doi:10.1016/j.jestch.2019.01.006

Almanza, B. A., Kirsch, K., Kline, S. F., Sirsat, S., Stroia, O., Choi, J. K., & Neal, J. (2015). How clean are hotel rooms? Part I: Visual observations vs. microbial contamination. *Journal of Environmental Health*, *78*(1), 8–13.

Atzori, L., Iera, A., & Morabito, G. (2010). The Internet of things: A survey. *Computer Networks*, *54*(15), 27–87. doi:10.1016/j.comnet.2010.05.010

Barber, N., & Scarcelli, J. M. (2010). Enhancing the assessment of tangible service quality through the creation of a cleanliness measurement scale. *Managing Service Quality*, *20*(1), 70–88. doi:10.1108/09604521011011630

Bitner, M. J., Brown, S. W., & Meuter, M. L. (2000). Technology infusion in service encounters. *Journal of the Academy of Marketing Science*, *28*(1), 138–149. doi:10.1177/0092070300281013

Brochado, A., Rita, P., & Margarido, A. (2016). High tech meets high touch in upscale hotels. *Journal of Hospitality and Tourism Technology*, *7*(4), 347–365. doi:10.1108/JHTT-07-2016-0038

Buhalis, D., & Leung, R. (2018). Smart hospitality—Interconnectivity and interoperability towards an ecosystem. *International Journal of Hospitality Management*, *71*(January), 41–50. doi:10.1016/j.ijhm.2017.11.011

Demir, K. A., D¨oven, G., & Sezen, B. (2019). Industry 5.0 and human-robot co-working. *Procedia Computer Science*, *158*, 688–695. doi:10.1016/j.procs.2019.09.104

Drexler, N., & Lapr'e, V. B. (2019). For better or for worse: Shaping the hospitality industry through robotics and artificial intelligence. *Res. Hosp. Manag.*, *9*(2), 117–120. doi:10.1080/22243534.2019.1689701

Galitsky, B. (2019). *Developing Enterprise Chatbots. Learning Linguistic Structures*. Springer. doi:10.1007/978-3-030-04299-8

Gilchrist, A., (2016). *Introducing industry 4.0. Industry 4.0.* Apress. . doi:10.1007/978-1-4842-2047-4_13

Gurkaynak, G., Yilmaz, I., Haksever, G., (2016). Stifling artificial intelligence: Human Perils. *Comput. Law Secur. Rep.*, *32*(5), 749–758. https://doi.org/.clsr.2016.05.003 doi:10.1016/j

Gursoy, D., & Chi, C. G. (2020). Effects of COVID-19 pandemic on hospitality industry: Review of the current situations and a research agenda. *Journal of Hospitality Marketing & Management*, *29*(5), 527–529. doi:10.1080/19368623.2020.1788231

Hao, F., Xiao, Q., & Chon, K. (2020). COVID-19 and China's hotel industry: Impacts, a disaster management framework, and post-pandemic agenda. *International Journal of Hospitality Management*, *90*, 102636. doi:10.1016/j.ijhm.2020.102636

Henderson, J. C., & Ng, A. (2004). Responding to crisis: Severe acute respiratory syndrome (SARS) and hotels in Singapore. *International Journal of Tourism Research*, *6*(6), 411–419. doi:10.1002/jtr.505

Hermann, M., Pentek, T., & Otto, B. (2016). Design principles for industry 4.0 scenarios. *49th Hawaii International Conference on System Sciences (HICSS)*, 3928–3937. https://doi.org/10.1109/HICSS.2016.488

Hotel Association of Canada. (2006). *Pandemic Preparedness & Response Plan* (613), 87. Retrieved from. www.hotelassociation.ca

Hurwitz, J., Bloor, R., Kaufman, M., Halper, F., (2009). *Service Oriented Architecture for Dummies®*. IBM Limited Edition.

Iqbal, J., Khan, Z. H., & Khalid, A. (2017). Prospects of robotics in food industry. *Food Science and Technology (Campinas)*, *37*(2), 159–165. doi:10.1590/1678-457x.14616

Ivanov, S., & Webster, C. (2017). Designing robot-friendly hospitality facilities. *Proceedings of the Scientific Conference Tourism. Innovations. Strategies*, 74–81.

Jiang, Y., & Wen, J. (2020). Effects of COVID-19 on hotel marketing and management: A perspective article. *International Journal of Contemporary Hospitality Management*, *32*(8), 2563–2573. doi:10.1108/IJCHM-03-2020-0237

Kline, S., Almanza, B., & Neal, J. (2014). Hotel guest room cleaning: a systematic approach. In B. Almanza, R. Ghiselli, & K. Mahmood (Eds.), *Food Safety: Researching the Hazard in Hazardous Foods* (pp. 303–322). CRC Press Taylor and Francis.

Kuo, C. M., Chen, L. C., & Lu, C. Y. (2012). Factorial validation of hospitality service attitude. *International Journal of Hospitality Management*, *31*(3), 944–951. doi:10.1016/j.ijhm.2011.11.002

Lee, C.K., Song, H.J., Bendle, L.J., Kim, M.J., & Han, H. (2012). The impact of non-pharmaceutical interventions for 2009 H1N1 influenza on travel intentions: A model of goal-directed behavior. *Tour. Manag.*, *33*(1), 89–99. https://doi.org/. tourman.2011.02.006 doi:10.1016/j

Li, X., Wang, B., Liu, C., Freiheit, T., & Epureanu, B. I. (2020). Intelligent manufacturing systems in COVID-19 pandemic and beyond: Framework and impact assessment. *Chinese Journal of Mechanical Engineering*, *33*(1), 58. doi:10.118610033-020-00476-w

Lo, A., Cheung, C., & Law, R. (2006). The survival of hotels during disaster: A case study of Hong Kong in 2003. *Asia Pacific Journal of Tourism Research*, *11*(1), 65–80. doi:10.1080/10941660500500733

Longo, F., Padovano, A., & Umbrello, S. (2020). Value-oriented and ethical technology engineering in industry 5.0: A human-centric perspective for the design of the factory of the future. *Applied Sciences (Basel, Switzerland)*, *10*(12), 1–25. doi:10.3390/app10124182

Mogelonsky, L. (2020). *Why Hoteliers Should Make Guestroom IoT a Top Priority (After COVID Safety Measures)*. https://hoteltechnologynews.com/2020/07/why-hot eliers-should-make-guestroom-iot-a-top-priority-after-covid-safety-measures/

Nadkarni, S., Kriechbaumer, F., Rothenberger, M., & Christodoulidou, N. (2019). The path to the hotel of things: Internet of things and big data converging in hospitality. *Journal of Hospitality and Tourism Technology*, *11*(1), 93–107. doi:10.1108/JHTT-12-2018-0120

Nahavandi, S. (2019). Industry 5.0-a human-centric solution. *Sustainability (Basel)*, *11*(16), 4371. Advance online publication. doi:10.3390u11164371

Neuhofer, B., Buhalis, D., & Ladkin, A. (2013). High tech for high touch experiences: a case study from the hospitality industry. In L. Cantoni & Z. Xiang (Eds.), *Information and Communication Technologies in Tourism 2013*. Springer. doi:10.1007/978-3-642-36309-2_25

Ozdemir, V., & Hekim, N. (2018). Birth of industry 5.0: Making sense of big data with artificial intelligence, "the internet of things" and next-generation technology policy. *Omics A J. Integrative Biology*, *22*(1), 65–76. doi:10.1089/omi.2017.0194

Park, H., Kline, S. F., Kim, J., Almanza, B., & Ma, J. (2019). Does hotel cleanliness correlate with surfaces guests contact? *International Journal of Contemporary Hospitality Management*, *31*(7), 2933–2950. doi:10.1108/IJCHM-02-2018-0105

Pathak, P., Pal, P. R., Shrivastava, M., & Ora, P. (2019). Fifth revolution: Applied AI & human intelligence with cyber physical systems. *International Journal of Engineering and Advanced Technology*, *8*(3), 23–27.

Petrillo, A., Felice, F. D., Cioffi, R., & Zomparelli, F. (2018). *Fourth Industrial Revolution: Current Practices, Challenges, and Opportunities*. https://www.intechopen.com/boo ks/digital-transformation-in-smart-manufacturing/fourth-industrial-revolution-current-practices-challenges-and-opportunities

Seyitoglu, F., & Ivanov, S. (2020). A conceptual framework of the service delivery system design for hospitality firms in the (post-)viral world: The role of service robots. *International Journal of Hospitality Management*, *91*(July), 102661. Advance online publication. doi:10.1016/j.ijhm.2020.102661

Shamim, S., Cang, S., Yu, H., & Li, Y. (2017). Examining the feasibilities of Industry 4.0 for the hospitality sector with the lens of management practice. *Energies*, *10*(4), 499. Advance online publication. doi:10.3390/en10040499

Shin, H., & Kang, J. (2020). Reducing perceived health risk to attract hotel customers in the COVID-19 pandemic era: Focused on technology innovation for social distancing and cleanliness. *International Journal of Hospitality Management*, *91*, 102664. doi:10.1016/j.ijhm.2020.102664

Stroia, O. V., Kirsch, K., Kline, S., Neal, J., Sirsat, S., & Almanza, B. (2012). *Empirical study on the cleanliness of hotels – cleanest and dirtiest spots.* Paper Presented at the 17th Annual Graduate Conference. 5–7 January, Auburn, AL. http://humsci.auburn.edu/hrmt/hospitality/GradConference2012/POSTERpresentations. pdf

Terzidis, O., Oberle, D., Friesen, A., Janiesch, C., & Barros, A. (2012). The Internet of services and USDL. In Handbook of Service Description. Springer. doi:10.1007/978-1-4614-1864-1_1

Tew, P. J., Lu, Z., Tolomiczenko, G., & Gellatly, J. (2008). SARS: Lessons in strategic planning for hoteliers and destination marketers. *International Journal of Contemporary Hospitality Management*, *20*(3), 332–346. doi:10.1108/09596110810866145

Zhong, L., Sun, S., Law, R., & Zhang, X. (2020). Impact of robot hotel service on consumers' purchase intention: A control experiment. *Asia Pacific Journal of Tourism Research*, *25*(7), 780–798. doi:10.1080/10941665.2020.1726421

Chapter 12
Development of Smart Hospitals Based on the Internet of Things and Cloud Computing

Amirhesam Davari
Guilan University of Medical Science, Iran

ABSTRACT

With the expansion of the internet of things (IoT) and its impact on today's life, a significant improvement can be seen in hospital services. The IoT allows patients to take control of their condition. This method can reduce the anxiety of patients to some extent. On the other hand, by collecting the patient's data during the hospital stay, doctors gain clearer views of the patient's body physiology and can provide more specialized and special care plans. With the method provided by the IoT, the interaction between the doctor and the patient increases, and it also helps by monitoring the patient's health remotely and reducing the time spent in the hospital. Storing information from the IoT locally is not only expensive but also brings certain complications for medical centers. For this reason, hospitals are turning to cloud storage of patient information. In this research, in addition to describing the basic features of smart hospitals based on the IoT and cloud computing, a hospital chart based on these technologies is also presented.

DOI: 10.4018/979-8-3693-0210-1.ch012

1. INTRODUCTION

A smart hospital means a hospital that redesigns or optimizes clinical processes, management systems, and even infrastructure. This optimization is done using the digital network infrastructure and the Internet of Things, and its goal is to provide services that are not available in the non-intelligent mode. An important component of smart hospitals is the ability to collect data and provide insights from the information. This is what distinguishes the smart hospital from the digital hospital. In other words, to make the hospital smart, it is not enough to remove paper processes and digitize them. Rather, we must be able to collect the necessary data and go one step beyond digitalization (Nahr et al., 2021).

As the integration of Internet of Things technology into everyday life increases, there is a significant improvement in hospital services. The Internet of Things allows patients to take control of the situation and enables doctors and hospital staff to provide the most effective care possible. By increasing transparency and allowing patients to control environmental conditions, patients can be confident that they are receiving the best medical care. On the other hand, by collecting the patient's data during the stay in the hospital, doctors gain clearer views on the physiology of the patient's body and can provide more specialized and special care plans.

Many patients feel fear or anxiety during hospitalization. In smart hospitals, it is possible for the patient to be aware of his body's vital signs. As the nurse records the patient's vital signs, smart devices send the information to the patient's mobile phone. These devices can enable real-time information with VR and AR technologies so that patients can see and understand their body's activities. Also, this information is considered part of the patient's digital report, collecting this information continuously will benefit the patient and the doctor. Between doctor and nurse visits, patients can control a variety of physical conditions in the room, including temperature, light, and sound, as well as access a complete information system and food selection via their mobile phones. Adding these features to hospital rooms helps patients feel more comfortable (Nozari et al., 2021).

Patients do not need to fill out additional documents to pay their fees. A summary of the report of their time spent in the hospital is sent to them via email, and patients can retrieve this information through their mobile phones. After a stressful hospital stay, it is often difficult to remember discharge instructions from your doctor. With new technologies, patients will have access to recommended activities, prescription reminders, physical therapy treatment, and follow-up appointments. If a patient has a question for their doctor, there's no need to wait for it to be addressed or try to contact a health care system. Instead, the patient can simply send an instant message to the caregiver and enable real-time communication for medical purposes.

Internet of Medical Things (IoMT)is a subset of this very large set and it is natural to say that IoT and IoMT have many similarities. IoMT devices are manufactured for medical purposes. Usually, the use of the Internet of Things in the hospital, especially hospital equipment such as the surgeon robot, etc., is included in the IoMT subcategory (Nozari et al., 2023). Of course, over time and with the expansion of devices' capabilities, the border between the Internet of Things and its subsets will decrease over time. In the rest of this chapter of the book, each of these institutions will be fully explained.

2. SMART HOSPITAL

Digital innovations and systems based on this technology have affected various aspects of our lives. This impact is so great that nowadays there is hardly any field that has not benefited from the influence of digital systems and its innovations. One of the fields that has seen significant progress under the influence of digital technologies is the field of health and treatment (Nozari and fallah, 2021). The use of systems based on digital technologies and systems known as smart tools have played an effective role in improving the process of diagnosis and treatment of various diseases. Therefore, perhaps considering that the medical staff and patients have found the necessary preparation to welcome the technologies; It is time for hospitals to be equipped with digital systems. The presence of digital technologies in future smart hospitals undoubtedly promises to enter a new era in the field of treatment and medicine. The smartening of large medical centers, such as hospitals, as a part of the smart city, is discussed and investigated in three ways, which we will explain below.

❖ ***Intelligent systems for managing hospital facilities***

According to the area, location, and type of the hospital, the intelligent control of the hospital can be managed at different levels. The facilities and systems implemented in smart hospitals are very diverse. The implementation of any type of intelligent hospital control system depends on the designer and the request of the client's team. On the other hand, according to the needs of each employer for whom security, energy, environment, etc. issues are more important, the work method will be different. But among the most important, efficient, and popular smart systems implemented in hospitals, the following can be mentioned:

a) Lighting control and adjustment:
b) Reducing energy consumption:
c) Traffic control systems
d) Peripheral protection systems

e) fire alarm systems
f) Central or local paging systems
g) Helicopter landing assistance navigation systems on the roof of the hospital
h) Intelligent robotic pharmacy system.
i) Hospital parking management system.

❖ ***Intelligent hospital information systems***

Smart hospital notification systems include providing any information related to the patient's profile and status, controlling the presence of doctors and nurses, etc. With the help of this system, all treatment steps and schedules are controlled using a smart and very efficient system. Among the advantages of using intelligent information systems, the following can be mentioned (Thakare et al., 2022).

- Controlling the condition of the bed, lights and lighting, ventilation and heating and cooling systems, curtains, etc.
- Providing necessary tips and medical instructions as well as nursing care.
- Communicating with different departments of the hospital at a specific time to address the patient's condition and prescribe medication.
- Providing necessary general information along with medical advice.
- Clearly saving time and energy consumption and speeding up hospital affairs.
- Announcing patient requests as soon as possible.
- Paging the nurse.
- Reminding nurses and doctors of essential and vital points.
- Intelligent queuing systems.

❖ ***Diagnosis, investigation, and treatment systems in the smart hospital***

Diagnosis of disease, taking pictures, performing diagnostic tests, and even performing surgery depends on the use of computer equipment. All medical information and results of medical examinations are sent to the dedicated tablet of the patient's doctor. Also, by using computer systems, help is given to the treating physician in the field of diagnosing the type of disease and how to treat it. The use of tablets and smartphones enables the virtual presence of doctors in different departments of the hospital at any hour of the day and night, and the doctor can prescribe the desired drugs to the patient through the barcodes that are installed on the drugs. And in short, control all the things that he is responsible for doing. All hospital rooms are equipped with computer communication terminals that are connected through cloud computing systems. Therefore, all information from disease diagnosis to doctor's recommendations to the nurse's station and drug prescription will be recorded electronically (Mukherjee et al., 2022).

❖ ***Use of hospital information system***

The hospital information system is a mechanized system for managing information and documents in a smart hospital. Due to the extensive developments in medical technology and increasing expectations of patients, there is an increasing need to use the hospital information system in the hospital. In the age of technology and the explosion of information in the healthcare field, experts believe that in the 21st century, hospitals that do not have a hospital information system will have nothing to say and will not be able to compete with other hospitals (Ganesh et al., 2023).

The hospital information system is a powerful information tool that can help hospital managers in the process of managing hospitals and making correct decisions and significantly increase the positive performance of hospitals. The ineffectiveness of manual methods, the growth of medical research in the world, the progress of the insurance industry and the change in the reimbursement methods to the contracting parties, the new methods of medical education, the huge development of medical equipment and facilities, the increase in the level of expertise of the staff, the transformation in the way of service and hospital management, the growth of costs, increasing patient expectations, the necessity of communication between medical centers and medical science specialists, etc. are among the most important reasons and necessities of hospital information system automation. Also, the existence of a good management information system is necessary to evaluate the quality of care provided to the patient. Figure 1 shows the solutions of telemedicine (Rejeb et al., 2023).

Figure 1. Telemedicine strategies

In general, the advantages of implementing intelligent hospital systems are:

- Increasing the quality of providing services to patients and improving the quality level of the hospital.
- Reducing the time to provide services to patients.
- Reducing medical errors.
- Storing patient information electronically in the Smart Hospital Data Center in order to maintain patient records and transfer to other hospitals if needed.
- Reducing the costs of hospital services.
- Optimizing the use of hospital resources and equipment.
- Optimizing the use of hospital human resources.
- Increasing the level of hospital safety and security.
- Reducing hospital energy consumption.
- Increasing the useful life of the equipment and reducing the cost of their maintenance and repairs.

A digital dashboard in the hospital rooms provides the necessary information about the health status of the patients. To relieve the patient's anxiety, the exact time of the doctor's or nurse's visit is displayed. When a patient calls a nurse, the nurse's geographic location within the hospital is determined and the nurse's movement is tracked. As doctors provide medical care to the patient, they can take the necessary actions and add relevant information. Once the doctor has completed all of their care, the patient can retrieve their detailed care instructions via a mobile app. A doctor or nurse can activate medication reminders from the hospital room and send them directly to the patient's mobile phone, smartwatch, email, etc. It often happens that the doctor goes on vacation and for any reason cannot go to the hospital in a sensitive situation where the doctor's presence is required. At this time, by using the Internet of Things, the doctor can easily check the condition of his patient remotely and give the necessary patient care instructions to his colleagues in the hospital (Aliahmadi et al., 2016).

3. INTERNET OF THINGS IN HEALTH

The health industry is one of the fastest fields that has been able to adapt to existing and expanding technologies such as the Internet of Things and use these technologies to improve the diagnosis and treatment of body diseases. When talking about the Internet of Things in smart health, several advantages such as improving the efficiency and quality of services with its development in medical devices should be considered. Smart technology is used for health purposes. The Internet of Things in smart health is capable of capturing health data from sensors and data storage, and automatically calculates them and makes personalized recommendations or automated actions obtained from the collected data. The combination of personal health recording and the possibilities of data analysis enables smart health technologies to provide engaging and personalized output (Nozari & Szmelter-Jarosz, 2022).

One of the most popular and clear applications of the Internet of Things in the field of smart hospitals is remote monitoring, which is sometimes known as telehealth. It also improves the patient's quality of life by eliminating the need to travel. If the patient has limited mobility or cannot use the transportation system, this condition can be very useful for him. The use of 24-hour monitoring of vital signs, access to care details and the progress of the disease is possible using tablets and smart mobile phones. It enables the virtual presence of doctors in different departments of the hospital at any hour of the day and night. By accessing the patient's smart electronic file information, the doctor can visit the patient through the web with video exchanges, IP cameras and audio facilities and prescribe the desired drugs for the patient. The main prerequisite for using the facilities of a smart hospital is to create a unique identity for each of the patients, doctors, nurses and other personnel in the hospital, which can be provided by assigning a code to the personnel or checking their fingerprints (Chen et al., 2023). But the solution that exists to identify all people, including clients and hospital staff, is to give an RFID tag to each of the personnel and visiting people who travel in the building and install RFID reader devices in all parts of the building. These tags for patients can be embedded in bracelets that are tied to their hands as soon as they enter the department, and the basic information of these people along with the assigned tag code is registered in the system (Cáceres et al., 2019). The basic information of these people along with the assigned tag code is recorded in the Internet of Things platform and can be traced. Figure 2 shows the architecture of the Internet of Things in health systems.

Figure 2. Internet of things architecture in health systems

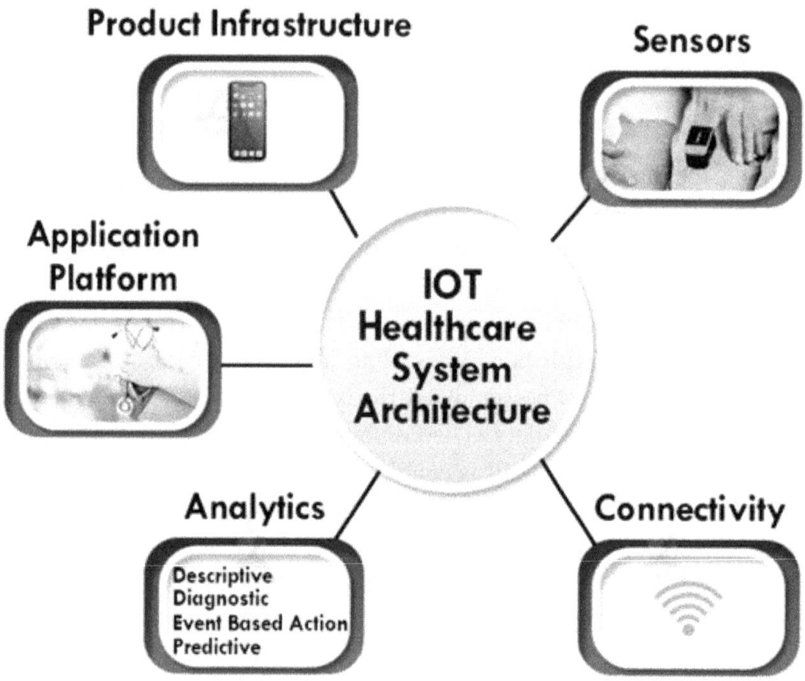

In general, artificial intelligence in healthcare refers to the use of advanced algorithms. These algorithms are designed to perform specific tasks automatically. As doctors, researchers, and scientists feed data into computers, these algorithms can review, intervene, and even make suggestions for solving complex medical problems.

They use their products. Drug discovery and development is a time-consuming and costly process. Artificial intelligence can significantly reduce this process and costs by evaluating newly discovered drug structures in virtual simulators (Zhao et al., 2023). A clinical trial is one type of medical study that is conducted on human populations. An important application of clinical trials is to study the effects of drugs and new treatment methods. The major part of this process is done offline and without an integrated solution, which, for example, eliminates the possibility of tracking progress and collecting data. Artificial intelligence helps to find and select suitable patients for conducting studies. Also, in the better design and management of these clinical studies, artificial intelligence can help a lot (Aliahmadi et al., 2022).

By placing the medical tele sensor chip on the fingertip, it is possible to record several vital parameters and send them. These parameters show body temperature, blood pressure, oxygen level, heart rate, and several other parameters. These types of sensors, which for the first time aim to monitor the vital signs of military soldiers in war zones and send these signs to a recording center. The remote control used is non-invasively attached to different parts of the body like an adhesive and reports the results. It will also be able to wirelessly send physiological data to a smart monitor on another soldier's helmet, in which case if the received data indicates that the physical condition is at one of 5 pre-determined levels of injury, the monitor will alarm. Call for help and help will be provided in the shortest possible time. Wireless monitors that can be installed on the skin can display valuable information about the physiological conditions of patients under special care. Items such as fitbit (smart wristband) and IoT personal monitor systems help people share their disease information with the doctor (Balasundaram et al., 2023).

4. CLOUD COMPUTING TECHNOLOGY IN THE FIELD OF MEDICINE

In recent years, cloud computing has entered the medical field with significant speed. The unlimited resources provided by cloud computing and the inherent flexibility of this technology have led to the use of this technology for the development and provision of medical services. In addition, cloud computing power is also used in medical studies in fields such as genetics and molecular medicine. Among the services that have developed more with the help of cloud computing, we can mention telemedicine. Also, thanks to cloud computing, the possibility of holding video conferences and sharing medical information of patients has become easier than in the past. In the field of clinical research, with the help of cloud computing, it is possible to receive and regularly store patients' information, and researchers can access data stored in the cloud from different places to carry out their research (Zhu et al., 2019).

Storing patient information locally, either in the form of old physical archives or electronically and on internal servers, is not only expensive, but also brings certain complications for medical centers. For this reason, hospitals and medical centers are also turning to cloud storage of patients' information, this issue allows doctors and patients to access the information they need at any time without visiting medical centers. Facilitating group work is also one of the advantages of cloud computing in the medical field. Suppose a critical decision is to be made about a patient's condition. Traditionally, coordinating medical team meetings and sharing patient information among team members is a time-consuming task. Thanks to cloud computing, not only will it be incredibly easy to share patient information, but the need for face-to-face meetings will also be eliminated. Figure 3 shows the framework of IoT-Cloud-based E-healthcare system (Ennafiri et al., 2021).

Figure 3. The framework of IoT-cloud-based e-healthcare system (Du et al., 2018)

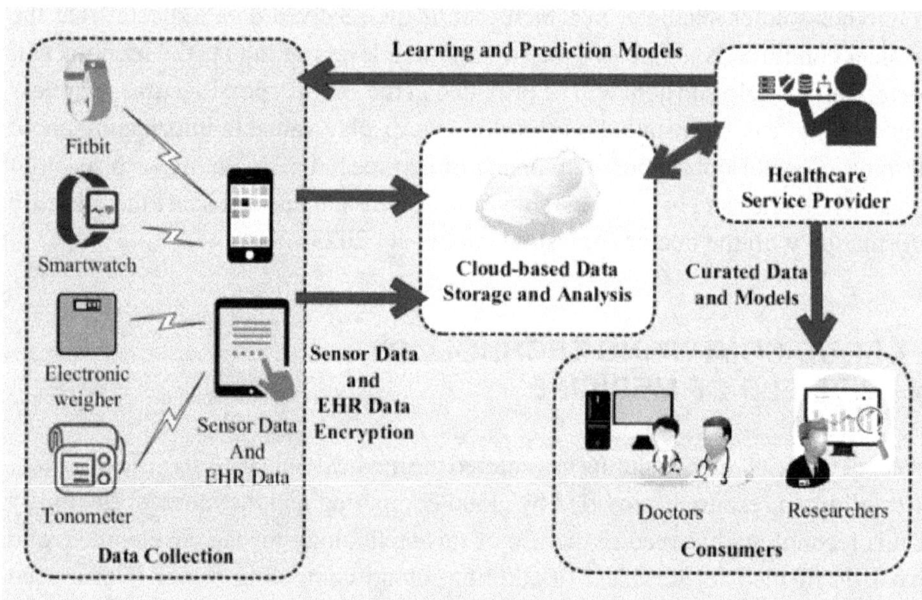

As doctors provide medical care to patients, they can perform necessary actions and add relevant information. Once the doctor has completed all of their care, the patient can retrieve their detailed care instructions via a mobile app. A doctor or nurse can activate medication reminders from the hospital room and send them directly to the patient's mobile phone, smartwatch, email, etc. It often happens that the doctor goes on vacation and for any reason cannot go to the hospital in a sensitive situation where the doctor's presence is required. At this time, by using the Internet of Things, the doctor can easily check the condition of his patient remotely and give the necessary patient care instructions to his colleagues in the hospital. Audio, video, and data integration is done to establish seamless and secure communication between patients and their caregivers, family, staff, and health service providers, and reduce the health risks of patients using the Internet of Things. At this time, you can use the sensors of the Internet of Things and record them in the patient's electronic file. These sensors regularly check the patient's vital signs and send the necessary information to the doctor, who records this information in the patient's smart files (Quasim et al., 2019).

5. CONCLUSION

With the increase in people's interest in the Internet of Things and also the increase of IoMT devices, we can see a bright future for the Medical Internet of Things. Of course, strict rules for data security must be established and followed, so that everyone can enjoy IoMT with peace of mind. The Internet of Things in smart health will engineer and digitize all the information of medical records. Clinical and business processes will be used in such a way that the system flows completely paperless and automated. Whenever possible, information is stored in discrete, structured formats (as opposed to existing systems that scan printed records). So that it is always available for reporting and analysis. A digital dashboard in the hospital rooms provides the necessary information about the health status of the patients. To relieve the patient's anxiety, the exact time of the doctor's or nurse's visit is displayed. When a patient calls a nurse, the geographic location of the nurse is determined inside the hospital and the movement of that nurse is tracked. The Internet of Things in medicine is not without challenges. Devices connected to the Internet of Things will capture huge amounts of data, including sensitive information, and will raise concerns about data security. Of course, the Internet of Things protocol is very new, but it is developing rapidly, and every day it presents its ability to create a modern and intelligent life with new news.

REFERENCES

Aliahmadi, A., Jafari-Eskandari, M., Mozafari, A., & Nozari, H. (2016). Comparing linear regression and artificial neural networks to forecast total productivity growth in Iran. *International Journal of Information, Business and Management, 8*(1), 93.

Aliahmadi, A., Nozari, H., & Ghahremani-Nahr, J. (2022). AIoT-based sustainable smart supply chain framework. *International Journal of Innovation in Management, Economics and Social Sciences, 2*(2), 28-38.

Cáceres, C., Rosário, J. M., & Amaya, D. (2019). Proposal of a smart hospital based on internet of things (IoT) concept. In *Processing and Analysis of Biomedical Information: First International SIPAIM Workshop, SaMBa 2018, Held in Conjunction with MICCAI 2018, Granada, Spain, September 20, 2018, Revised Selected Papers 1* (pp. 93-104). Springer International Publishing.

Chen, X., He, C., Chen, Y., & Xie, Z. (2023). Internet of Things (IoT)—Blockchain-enabled pharmaceutical supply chain resilience in the post-pandemic era. *Frontiers of Engineering Management, 10*(1), 82–95. doi:10.100742524-022-0233-1

Du, J., Jiang, C., Gelenbe, E., Xu, L., Li, J., & Ren, Y. (2018). Distributed data privacy preservation in IoT applications. *IEEE Wireless Communications, 25*(6), 68–76. doi:10.1109/MWC.2017.1800094

Ennafiri, M., & Mazri, T. (2021). Internet of things for smart healthcare: A review on a potential IOT based system and technologies to control COVID-19 pandemic. In *Innovations in Smart Cities Applications Volume 4: The Proceedings of the 5th International Conference on Smart City Applications* (pp. 1256-1269). Springer International Publishing. 10.1007/978-3-030-66840-2_96

Mukherjee, S., Kumar, R., & Banerjee, S. (2022). Smart Healthcare Remote Monitoring System Using Internet of Things. In *Intelligent Systems for Social Good: Theory and Practice* (pp. 99–115). Springer Nature Singapore. doi:10.1007/978-981-19-0770-8_9

Nahr, J. G., Nozari, H., & Sadeghi, M. E. (2021). Green supply chain based on artificial intelligence of things (AIoT). *International Journal of Innovation in Management, Economics and Social Sciences, 1*(2), 56–63.

Nozari, H., Ghahremani-Nahr, J., & Szmelter-Jarosz, A. (2023). AI and machine learning for real-world problems. *Advances In Computers.*

Nozari, H., & Sadeghi, M. E. (2021). Artificial intelligence and Machine Learning for Real-world problems (A survey). *International Journal of Innovation in Engineering, 1*(3), 38–47. doi:10.59615/ijie.1.3.38

Nozari, H., & Szmelter-Jarosz, A. (2022). *IoT-based Supply Chain For Smart Business* (Vol. 1). ISNET.

Nozari, H., Tavakkoli-Moghaddam, R., Ghahremani-Nahr, J., & Najafi, E. (2023). *A conceptual framework for Artificial Intelligence of Medical Things (AIoMT).* Academic Press.

Nozari, H., Fallah, M., Szmelter-Jarosz, A., & Krzemiński, M. (2021). Analysis of security criteria for IoT-based supply chain: a case study of FMCG industries. *Central European Management Journal, 29*(4).

Quasim, M. T., Khan, M. A., Abdullah, M., Meraj, M., Singh, S. P., & Johri, P. (2019, December). Internet of things for smart healthcare: a hardware perspective. In *2019 First International Conference of Intelligent Computing and Engineering (ICOICE)* (pp. 1-5). IEEE. 10.1109/ICOICE48418.2019.9035175

Rejeb, A., Rejeb, K., Treiblmaier, H., Appolloni, A., Alghamdi, S., Alhasawi, Y., & Iranmanesh, M. (2023). The Internet of Things (IoT) in Healthcare: Taking Stock and Moving Forward. *Internet of Things*, 100721.

Thakare, V., Khire, G., & Kumbhar, M. (2022). Artificial Intelligence (AI) And Internet Of Things (IoT) In Healthcare: Opportunities And Challenges. *ECS Transactions, 107*(1), 7941–7951. doi:10.1149/10701.7941ecst

Zhao, Z., Li, X., Luan, B., Jiang, W., Gao, W., & Neelakandan, S. (2023). Secure Internet of Things (IoT) using a Novel Brooks Iyengar Quantum Byzantine Agreement-centered Blockchain Networking (BIQBA-BCN) Model in Smart Healthcare. *Information Sciences, 629*, 440–455. doi:10.1016/j.ins.2023.01.020

Zhu, H., Wu, C. K., Koo, C. H., Tsang, Y. T., Liu, Y., Chi, H. R., & Tsang, K. F. (2019). Smart healthcare in the era of internet-of-things. *IEEE Consumer Electronics Magazine, 8*(5), 26–30. doi:10.1109/MCE.2019.2923929

Chapter 13
The Potential Role of Blockchain in Supply Chain Management in the Automotive Industry

Catarina Teixeira
University of Porto, Portugal

Gabriela Bessa
University of Porto, Portugal

Inês Ricardo
University of Porto, Portugal

Mariana Ferreira
University of Porto, Portugal

Rafaela Martins
University of Porto, Portugal

Belem Barbosa
https://orcid.org/0000-0002-4057-360X
University of Porto, Portugal

ABSTRACT

The complexity of automotive supply chain management presents significant challenges, demanding rigorous coordination of tasks to ensure efficiency in its operations. This chapter examines the potential benefits of adopting blockchain technology in supply chain management. The study employs a case study methodology, focusing on a prominent European automotive company that, compared to its major competitors, appears hesitant to integrate blockchain into its supply chain management practices. The analysis relies on secondary data and utilizes a range of strategic analysis tools to gain deeper insights into the advantages that blockchain technology could offer in supply chain management. Based on the findings, this chapter offers 12 strategic recommendations pertaining to blockchain technology, which can aid the company in addressing various management issues by enhancing security, efficiency, and technological advancements.

DOI: 10.4018/979-8-3693-0210-1.ch013

INTRODUCTION

The rapid development of blockchain technology continues to progress at a fast pace. While initially associated with the financial sector as the foundation of Bitcoin and cryptocurrency solutions, blockchain has swiftly demonstrated its potential across a wide range of industries. As a result, interest in blockchain technology has surged among managers in various sectors. One context that shows great potential for blockchain technology is supply chain management. According to Difrancesco et al. (2022), globalization has led to increasingly complex supply chains. Consequently, firms must proactively adapt to customers' diverse requirements, necessitating fast, agile, and dynamic supply chains. To survive, firms must consider factors such as efficiency, effectiveness, speed, and transparency in their supply chains, as these are crucial in today's business landscape (Difrancesco et al., 2022).

The automotive industry, renowned for its technological sensitivity, has witnessed significant advancements through breakthrough technologies and the industrialization of production processes (Fabbe-Costes & Lechaptois, 2022). Supply chains within the automotive industry are notably intricate, involving multiple layers of suppliers for raw materials, components, and systems. However, this complexity also introduces inefficiencies and vulnerabilities, including the risk of counterfeit parts infiltrating the system Blockchain technology offers effective means of collecting, recording, and sharing data across various levels of supply chain management, thus addressing these issues.

Nevertheless, the full extent of the benefits of blockchain technology in this industry remains underexplored. To help fill this gap, the main objective of this chapter is to investigate the applicability of blockchain technology in supply chain management and provide managers with valuable insights into its implementation, which is crucial for decision-making. The chapter adopts a case study approach, focusing on the Peugeot case, given its apparent reluctance to embrace this technology compared to its competitors. The analysis relies on secondary data obtained from public sources such as scientific articles, industry reports, and the company's website and annual reports. To systematize the collected data, a range of strategic analysis tools commonly employed by managers for strategy planning and monitoring are utilized. Overall, these tools enable a deeper understanding of the advantages that blockchain technology can offer in supply chain management.

The present research is divided into six sections. It begins with a theoretical background, highlighting key contributions from the literature, followed by a presentation of the research methodology. Subsequently, the results are presented, incorporating the analysis conducted using strategic tools. The paper then discusses solutions and recommendations, with a particular emphasis on strategic recommendations for Peugeot. This is followed by suggestions for future research, and finally, a concise conclusion of the study.

BACKGROUND

Treiblmaier (2018) defines the blockchain as "a digital, decentralized, and distributed ledger in which transactions are logged and added in chronological order to create permanent and tamper-proof records". In this context, a blockchain unit represents a single transaction involving one or more entities, such as a payment or information transfer. The term "blockchain" refers to the addition of a valid block to the existing chain of blocks. Blockchains are distinguished by their resistance to data alteration, as the interconnected blocks prevent modifications to transactions. Furthermore, blockchain operates based on smart contracts, which mitigate potential disputes among participants and enable instant payment triggers.

Advantages and Disadvantages of Blockchain

Companies have begun to reassess their business strategies and explore the potential of blockchain technology, recognizing the advantages it can bring to their organizations. The literature acknowledges that blockchain has the potential to benefit various functions within corporations (Gurtu & Johny, 2019), such as distributed storage and listings, transactional validity, persistence, and anonymity. One significant advantage of blockchain technology is the elimination of a central authority for transaction validation, leading to improved efficiency and reduced transaction costs. Additionally, a shared secure ledger facilitates the recording of payment transfers between buyers and sellers. In general, blockchain has the potential to enhance transparency, traceability, responsiveness, and speed while offering versatility (Cole et al., 2019).

However, despite these advantages, blockchain technology also presents risks and limitations. Being a relatively new technology, it often raises skepticism among managers due to the significant investment required (Difrancesco et al., 2022). One major limitation, as highlighted by Difrancesco et al. (2022), is that the effectiveness of adopting blockchain technology relies on the involvement of all partners. If one supplier does not participate, implementing blockchain technology may not be viable. Furthermore, blockchain technology raises concerns related to data protection and privacy. Some countries grant users the right to request the removal of their personal information, which can hinder blockchain implementation since data permanence is a fundamental feature of the technology (Difrancesco et al., 2022).

Relevance of Blockchain for Supply Chain Management

Despite its drawbacks, blockchain technology has gained popularity and is being increasingly applied Beyond the finance sector, blockchain technology has found utility in areas such as supply chain management, electricity, and food/agriculture, primarily due to the suitability of these sectors, which often results in a quick return on investment (Gurtu & Johny, 2019). A study conducted by Markus and Buijs (2022) demonstrated the positive impact of blockchain across various sectors, including food, health, and automotive. Specifically, their research highlighted the benefits of blockchain in the food sector, where it improves dependability through enhanced information access along the supply chain. The literature also emphasizes the advantages of blockchain for consumers, as it enables transparency and helps them understand the quality of food products, thereby enhancing the overall quality of goods (Markus & Buijs, 2022).

In the context of supply chain management, blockchain is considered an emerging enabling technology that offers unique features such as cyber-security, traceability, real-time information sharing, and transparency, collectively improving the efficiency of the supply chain (Cole et al., 2019). Aslam et al. (2021) suggest that blockchain has the capability to enhance supply chain integration and coordination by improving various supply chain functions and practices, including outsourcing, subcontracting, and establishing closer relationships with customers and suppliers. Additionally, blockchain expands the auditability of products, materials, and supply chain management-related information, while accelerating product and transaction transparency (Aslam et al., 2021). The use of blockchain technology abolishes the need for verification and minimizes the number of process steps, saving time and making communication more efficient. This allows for the sharing of inventory information along the entire supply chain without the risk of data breaches (Gurtu & Johny, 2019). Trust-building through blockchain technology reduces uncertainty in decision-making and collaboration among supply chain participants, as trusting partners believe in the reliability of each other (Cole et al., 2019).

However, despite the numerous advantages of blockchain technology, it also presents limitations and risks, with novelty being one of the most intrinsic factors. Managers often hesitate to invest significant amounts of money in a relatively new technology like blockchain (Difrancesco et al., 2022). Furthermore, for blockchain to be effectively adopted, the involvement of all parties is essential, as it would not be beneficial if only one supplier implements the technology while others in the supply chain do not (Difrancesco et al., 2022). Additionally, data protection and privacy are crucial considerations due to current privacy legislation, such as the EU's regulations, which grant users the right to request the deletion of personal data.

However, the permanent nature of data in blockchain, particularly in public systems, makes it challenging to comply with such directives (Difrancesco et al., 2022).

Blockchain to Supply Chain Management in Different Industries

The integration of blockchain technology into supply chain management has been implemented in various industries and sectors, including the food industry as shown by Modak (2023). For instance, in the pharmaceutical industry, blockchain is used to track medications throughout the supply chain, providing a tamper-proof source of truth that eliminates opportunities for malicious actors. Similarly, the diamond industry has embraced blockchain to address inefficiencies in its supply chain by enabling the tracking of individual diamonds and recording detailed information about each stone's condition for customers. The potential benefits of blockchain technology are significant, and its complete implementation across various sectors of the supply chain can greatly benefit a wide range of industries (Modak, 2023).

In the automotive industry, known for its technological advancements, blockchain technology provides a seamless decentralized platform for recording, tracking, and managing information related to insurance, proof of ownership, patents, repairs, maintenance, and tangible and intangible assets (Sharma et al., 2019). Blockchain in the automotive industry can be categorized into record keeping functions, such as static registry, identity, and smart contracts, as well as transactional functions, such as dynamic registry or payments infrastructure (Sharma et al., 2019). A key challenge in current traceability applications in the automotive industry lies in their centralized architecture, which introduces a single point of failure and raises concerns about the trustworthiness of shared information. By integrating blockchain into the automotive supply chain, intermediaries are eliminated, ensuring data integrity and significantly reducing the possibility of tampering. Additionally, blockchains enable supply chain participants to trace the history of a product or service, fostering engagement and enhancing the credibility of the entire system (Alsadi et al., 2023). According to Alsadi et al. (2023), providing real-time data about processes and products within the supply chain facilitates decision-making and helps original equipment manufacturers gain deeper insights.

METHOD

The method employed in this paper involved the utilization of a case study to gain a comprehensive understanding of the selected case (Bryman, 2012). The chosen case for this chapter is Peugeot. According to its website, Peugeot (n.d.-a) was established in 1810 and introduced its first automobile, a steam-powered three-wheeler, in 1889. Following the Second World War, the company launched the first unibody car, the Peugeot 203, in 1948. In early 2021, the PSA Group, the parent company of Peugeot, merged with Fiat Chrysler Automobiles, forming Stellantis, a multinational automotive manufacturing corporation. The merger established one of the largest automotive groups worldwide (Stellantis, n.d.). Peugeot manufactures automobiles and light commercial vehicles, as well as motorbikes, scooters, hydraulic engines, vehicle components, and also provides after-sales services. Presently, Peugeot employs over 200,000 individuals globally. The company operates in most markets, with the exception of the United States, from which it withdrew in 1991 (Archawski & Wolek, 1995).

As elucidated by Yin (2009), a case study is an empirical scientific approach that facilitates a thorough and real-world examination of a contemporary phenomenon. In the context of this study, the phenomenon under investigation pertains to the adoption of blockchain technology for supply chain management. Peugeot, in particular, presents an intriguing case as the company has notably delayed the implementation of blockchain in its supply chain management practices. Thus, exploring this case is significant in order to assess the potential benefits and derive a set of recommendations in this domain.

The data utilized for this study was obtained from reputable and publicly accessible sources, including scientific articles, industry reports and statistics, news outlets, as well as the official websites and annual reports of the company. To organize the gathered information, established frameworks commonly employed by managers to define and assess management strategies were employed. These frameworks encompassed the PESTEL analysis, VRIO analysis, the Five Forces model by Porter, and the Ansoff Matrix. Each framework's application and relevance to the study's findings are contextualized in the results section.

RESULTS

This section encompasses the analysis of the data gathered for the case study. Firstly, frameworks for examining the macro and micro environments are introduced and specifically tailored to the case study. Subsequently, the frameworks facilitating internal analysis are presented in comprehensive detail. The findings of this section are succinctly summarized through the application of a SWOT analysis.

External Analysis

Macro Environment

One essential tool to understand the macro environment surrounding the company is the PESTEL analysis. As explained by Whittington et al. (2022), it combines six external domains (political, economic, social, technological, environmental, and legal) that comprise opportunities and constraints to the company's decision making in terms of strategy and influences its performance and success. While the decision to adopt blockchain technology rests within management's purview, it is important to acknowledge that certain external factors can make this strategy attractive or not, considering the main challenges and opportunities posed. A summary of the factors identified for this study are presented in Table 1.

Table 1. PESTEL analysis

Politics	**Economy**	**Society**
• Government regulation • War in Ukraine • Economic statecraft • EU sustainability directives • Global dependence on the Asian's manufacturing sector	• Pandemic impact • Inflation • Fuel prices • Rising in inequality • Rising in interest rates	• Eco-friendly mentality • Social status • Transition to online businesses
	PESTEL Analysis	
• Internet of things • Blockchain and cryptocurrency • Artificial intelligence and AV • Robots and Automation • Cybersecurity • 3D printing, extended and virtual reality, and quantum computing	• Increased use of renewable energy sources • Recycling • Second-hand products • Circular economy • SDG by UN	• Environmental legislation • Regulations on cryptocurrency platforms • Limitations on the use of artificial intelligence in several fields • Drivers' safety regulations • Digital Nomads
Technology	**Environment**	**Law**

Governments play a crucial role in altering and influencing the dynamics of firms by implementing taxes, fees, regulating markets, and enforcing trade laws. Political conflicts, such as the ongoing war in Europe, is also a relevant fact that conditions management decision. Furthermore, there is a growing trend in global politics that involves the use of economic statecraft, where countries utilize trade and regulatory mechanisms to shape the behavior of others in order to accomplish their geopolitical objectives. By 2023, this trend is particularly evident in areas such as chip supply, climate change initiatives, and energy supply control (Mathieson, 2023). In line with this, some political initiatives to reduce the dependence from China's manufactures main trigger a reconfiguration of global supply chains. Furthermore, over the last decade with increasing concern about sustainability, there have been various support policies for eco-friendly businesses in certain key markets, such as electric vehicles. As a result, several EU directives and regulations are now under review to align with the environmental stated ambitions (International Energy Agency, 2020). Therefore, government regulation can have a direct impact on various types of industries. They are intended to benefit consumers and protect the environment, and non-compliance can lead to substantial fines and penalties for manufacturers (Investopedia, 2021).

Additionally, all industry sectors must closely monitor these economic factors to make informed decisions and mitigate potential risks, including the current trends of rising inflation and interest rates (World Bank, 2023). The ongoing military conflict in Europe, which have characterized the period of analysis, have had significant impacts on prices, particularly fuel prices. This situation is likely to decrease savings, purchasing power, and adversely affect the quality of life, especially for lower-income families. Moreover, this is exacerbated by the fact that economies have not fully recovered from the pandemic period that dominated the early 2020s.

Regarding the social environment, we currently exist in an evolving world driven by sustainability, technology, and shifting consumer preferences (Forbes, 2021a). Consumers are increasingly demanding eco-friendly and technology-driven products, which puts pressure on businesses to invest in sustainable practices and enhance service efficiency. Additionally, a new generation of eco-conscious employees is entering the workforce, potentially challenging traditional manufacturing practices and advocating for sustainable approaches to reduce material consumption and conserve energy (Forbes, 2021b).

The use of existing technology or future developments in this field will affect any business, which makes adaptability an essential skill. One notable technological trend is the Internet of Things (IoT), where embedded computing devices in everyday objects can transmit and receive data over the internet. IoT offers benefits such as cost reduction, increased efficiency, improved customer service, faster decision-making, and competitive advantage (Arora, 2023). Another significant trend is the rise of self-driving or autonomous cars, which will revolutionize daily transportation by eliminating the need for human drivers. This technology expands last-mile deliveries, reduces downtime, and enhances the safety of public transportation. The automotive sector is also experiencing the dominance of electric cars as a future trend. Furthermore, blockchain technology provides enhanced security, transparency, and efficiency through shared and immutable ledgers, enabling instant traceability and automation across business networks, as discussed in the previous sections. Artificial intelligence (AI) plays a vital role in businesses, offering benefits such as the development of new products and services, increased productivity and quality, improved customer service, and energy savings. The European Union recognizes the significance of AI and aims to establish a high-quality digital infrastructure and legal framework respecting privacy and free speech to become a global leader in the data economy (European Parliament, 2021). Robotics also holds great importance, as connected robots, along with AI and digital automation, are transforming manufacturing within a digital ecosystem that includes Cloud Computing, Big Data Analytics, and 5G mobile networks (International Federation of Robotics, 2023). Moreover, technological trends such as mobile applications, communication infrastructure, 3D printing, extended reality, genomics, quantum computing, virtual reality, and augmented reality shape various industries. Given the technological nature of the automotive industry, cybersecurity becomes crucial in safeguarding against threats like hacking, data breaches, and supply-chain attacks (European Parliament, 2023b). Due to the nature of this assignment, it can be concluded that the automotive industry is a highly technological sector, which means technological innovations are extremely relevant to this industry.

Several environmental factors are crucial for understanding the macro environment. Climate change has become a global priority, leading to increased demands for environmental regulations from governments and pressure groups. Embracing a sustainable business model is becoming the norm. Firstly, businesses are adopting renewable energy sources and promoting recycling. There is a growing focus on sustainable transportation options and the use of eco-friendly materials in product manufacturing. Additionally, the trend of purchasing second-hand products is gaining popularity across various industries. Plant-based and alternative foods have also garnered increased interest. Brands are increasingly embracing responsibility and transparency (Mckay, 2023). In fact, the transition to a net-zero economy is expected to create $13 trillion in annual business opportunities (Olynec, 2023). Secondly, the circular economy represents a major trend that not only protects the environment but also harnesses natural resources, promotes new sectors, generates employment, and cultivates talents in a more sustainable manner (UNCTAD, 2022). Furthermore, the United Nations' 17 Sustainable Development Goals (SDGs) are critical in efforts to transform the world, addressing poverty, inequality, environmental protection, and ensuring health, justice, and prosperity for all, with a commitment to leaving no one behind (World Health Organization, n.d.).

Legislation significantly impacts the profitability and operations of companies, particularly in the automotive industry. Firstly, the European Union has implemented legislation mandating zero CO2 emissions from automobiles sold in the EU by 2035, with a 55% reduction in CO2 emissions by 2030. These goals aim to accelerate the decarbonization of new vehicle fleets across Europe, making it more challenging to sell combustion engine vehicles in the EU from 2035 onwards (Abnett, 2023). Secondly, several regulations ensure compliance with UN standards and enhance safety in the sector (UNECE, 2023). In the realm of AI, the EU is establishing rules for its utilization in various sectors such as military, education, culture, and audio-visual industries. As Europe embraces a digital economy, AI is recognized as a tool to benefit both the public and private sectors (European Parliament, 2023a). In the United States, 28 states have implemented legislation regarding blockchain, smart contracts, and verifiable credentials (Morton, n.d.). Furthermore, several European countries have introduced legislation to simplify and enhance transparency for digital nomads and remote workers. Data security is also paramount, leading the European Commission to develop the General Data Protection Regulation (GDPR) that ensures data security and compliance with legislation across all member countries.

In conclusion, the PESTEL factors have significant influence the business environment and are crucial for business success. The factors pointed in this section have direct and indirect effect on the management decisions, including regarding the adoption of blockchain technology.

Micro Environment

One of the most renowned frameworks for analyzing industry dynamics and competition is Porter's Five Forces model (Whittington et al., 2022). This framework was developed by Michael Porter as a tool to assist managers in analyzing the profitability potential of different types of industries and how they can best position their firm to gain and maintain competitive advantages (Rothaermel, 2021). According to this model, competition is more than just creating economic value, as it is also important for firms to capture a substantial share of the economic value they generate in order to avoid losing that value to their competitors, suppliers, or customers (Rothaermel, 2021). Additionally, the five forces model allows managers to take control of their firm's strategy as well as understanding their industry environment (Rothaermel, 2021). Porter's Five Forces Model pinpoints five key competitive forces: the threat of entry, power of suppliers, power of buyers, threat of substitutes, and rivalry among existing competitors. The main factors identified for this case study are highlighted in Table 2.

Table 2. Porter's five forces framework

<table>
<tr><td>• Large-scale production
• Economies of scale
• High-technological level
• Capital-intensive sector
• Brand loyalty</td><td rowspan="4">Rivalry among Competitors
High
• Saturated industry
• Massive innovation
• Heavy investments
• Demand for electric alternatives</td><td>• Differentiation and adaptability to the company
• Large number of suppliers
• High switching costs</td></tr>
<tr><td>Threat of New Entry
Weak</td><td>Power of Suppliers
Strong</td></tr>
<tr><td>• High cost of vehicles
• Bicycles
• Public transportation</td><td>• Large number of consumers and variety
• Low switching costs</td></tr>
<tr><td>Threat of Substitutes
Moderate</td><td>Power of Buyers
Moderate</td></tr>
</table>

Regarding the power of buyers, consumers consider various factors when purchasing a vehicle, such as fuel efficiency and safety. However, they also weigh the balance between price and quality according to their own standards (Armstrong, 2022b). Despite this, the automotive industry involves a large number of consumers, which reduces buyer power. For example, China has surpassed Japan in auto sales, becoming the "third largest auto market in the world" with sales exceeding 4.25 million units (Jain, 2023). Furthermore, the industry caters to diverse consumer segments. On one hand, individual and business consumers are the final buyers, acquiring vehicles for personal or commercial use respectively. On the other hand, intermediary consumers, such as car dealerships and leasing companies, play a role in the industry. Dealerships purchase vehicles from manufacturers to sell them to end customers, while leasing companies acquire vehicles to offer usage periods and eventual purchase options to customers. Unlike end customers, intermediary consumers have negotiating power with manufacturers to select the brands they wish to sell. Additionally, consumers can switch from one manufacturer to another without significant costs, resulting in low switching costs. Considering these factors, buyer power can be considered moderated in the industry.

Several suppliers are involved in the automotive supply chain, which illustrates the complexity of the industry. Since there are over 50.000 suppliers in the automotive industry, there are many manufacturers controlling supply, reducing the negotiating power of suppliers (Volza, 2023). Moreover, the European Association of Automotive Suppliers is investing over €30 billion yearly in research and development of innovative technology and components for safe, smart, and sustainable mobility (CLEPA, s.d.). This could increase the supplier's negotiating power, as manufacturers will be interested in acquiring the latest technologies for their own operations. This is due to the high degree of differentiation in supplies in this industry, which could increase the supplier's power. Companies adapt their processes based on their relationships with suppliers, namely how they incorporate and shape materials into their value chain, which leads to a vehicle with appropriate performance and final price. For example, Peugeot doesn't have the same suppliers as Ferrari due to its low performance and high price expectations. However, there are high switching costs associated with the suppliers, which will decrease competition between companies. Concluding, even if there is a large number of suppliers, the power of suppliers is strong due to their differentiation and adaptability to the company.

Regarding the threat of new entrants, Rothaermel (2021) argues that large-scale production is essential for new entrants to be successful in the automobile industry. This allows them to benefit from economies of scale, employ technology more effectively, specialize labor, and negotiate better terms with suppliers. Additionally, large-scale production enables greater innovation and better customer service. To penetrate the market, new entrants must provide compelling benefits or incentives to lure customers away from established firms, such as superior features, lower prices, exceptional customer service, or other innovative value propositions. However, Rothaermel (2021) notes that the main determinant of the entrant decision depends on the expected return on investment. The automotive industry is a well-established industry with a bundle of resources that new entrants do not have, providing a competitive advantage to incumbent companies. Additionally, in the automotive industry, there are various segments available to capture different target markets, giving established firms more power in the industry, including the ability to engage in price wars (Rothaermel, 2021). Considering these factors, it can be concluded that the threat of entry is relatively weak.

Despite the strong market position of the automotive industry, there are a number of potential substitutes that can pose a threat to it. For instance, carpooling is a growing trend, driven by consumers' environmental concerns (Hartl et al., 2020). Additionally, car ownership entails various expenses such as monthly payments, insurance, fuel, maintenance, fees, and taxes, which may prompt consumers to seek alternatives. Therefore, bicycles, public transportation, and carpooling are viable substitutes for automotive industry products due to their affordability and lower ongoing costs. Cars are still favored for their ability to reach higher speeds and travel longer distances more efficiently. However, they are losing their aspirational nature for consumers in many countries (Armstrong, 2022a), which presents additional challenges for the automotive industry. Consequently, it can be concluded that the threat of substitutes is moderate.

To conclude the Five Forces analysis, the automotive industry is characterized by consolidation among a few large firms, differentiated products, high barriers to entry, and a certain degree of pricing power (Rothaermel, 2021). Therefore, it can be inferred that there is intense rivalry among the existing competitors, as they share the market with major players in the industry. Continuous research and development

(R&D) and innovation are essential for companies to differentiate themselves from their competitors. Additionally, rivalry tends to increase when the market growth is slow, leading companies to adopt more aggressive marketing strategies to maintain their sales volume and challenge their competitors' market share (Rothaermel, 2021). Moreover, exit barriers are high in the automotive industry due to heavy investments in machinery and facilities. In conclusion, the rivalry among existing competitors is high in the automotive industry.

Internal Analysis

VRIO Analysis

The VRIO analysis, based on the resource-based view, helps firms gain and sustain a competitive advantage by evaluating their resources and capabilities and predicting firm-level competitive advantage (Rothaermel, 2021). To achieve sustained competitive advantages, resources and capabilities should meet four criteria: Value, Rarity, Imitability, and Organizational support (Whittington et al., 2022). Valuable resources and capabilities create value for customers, enable the organization to respond to opportunities or threats, and generate profits (Whittington et al., 2022). However, if resources and capabilities are common among competitors, they are unlikely to provide a competitive advantage, as uniqueness is required (Whittington et al., 2022). Inimitable resources and capabilities are difficult for competitors to imitate, obtain, or substitute, thus creating a competitive advantage (Whittington et al., 2022). Lastly, the company needs an organized structure and management that support and facilitate the exploitation of resources and capabilities for them to be fully advantageous (Whittington et al., 2022). Whenever the resources and capabilities are valuable but don't meet at least one of the other VRIO criteria, the competitive advantages could be temporary or corresponding to a competitive parity. Some examples are presented in Table 3 regarding the case study.

Table 3. VRIO analysis

Resources & Capabilities	Valuable	Rare	Inimitable	Supported by the Organization	Competitive Advantage
Strong European presence	**Yes**	**Yes**	**Yes**	**Yes**	**Sustained**
Qualified human capital	**Yes**	**Yes**	*No*		**Temporary**
Customer support system	**Yes**	*No*			**Parity**
Customer service	**Yes**	**Yes**	*No*		**Temporary**
Relationship with financial sector	**Yes**	**Yes**	*No*		**Temporary**
Wide range of models	**Yes**	**Yes**	*No*		**Temporary**
Exploring the electric market	**Yes**	*No*			**Parity**
Innovation and technology	**Yes**	**Yes**	**Yes**	**Yes**	**Sustained**

From this analysis, two capabilities that provide sustained competitive advantage to Peugeot are its strong European presence and its focus on innovation and technology. Peugeot has a reputable position in the automotive industry, exemplified by the Peugeot 208 becoming the best-selling car in Europe in 2022, surpassing the long-standing dominance of the VW Golf (JATO, 2023). Additionally, Peugeot is actively investing in evolving technologies and software to enhance their vehicles and deliver an enhanced driving experience (Peugeot, n.d.-b). In pursuit of high-performance, low-emission vehicles, the company is developing electric and hybrid technology and incorporating driving aids into their cockpit design (Peugeot, n.d.-b).

Moreover, Peugeot benefits from a highly skilled workforce with extensive experience in the automotive industry (Peugeot, n.d.-b). The company also provides personalized customer care support available 24/7, including breakdown and accident assistance, as well as additional services like driver training and pick-and-drop services (Peugeot, n.d.-b). Furthermore, Peugeot has established partnerships with banks and insurance companies, enabling them to offer diverse financial solutions to customers at favorable rates (Peugeot, n.d.-b). In terms of product offerings, Peugeot stands out by providing a wide range of models, from city cars to SUVs, with options for diesel, plug-in hybrids, and electric powertrains, offering more choices compared to competitors. The company has responded to the growing demand for electric vehicles by developing various hybrid and electric cars, earning recognition such as the "Britain's Best Cars Award" for the Peugeot e-208 in 2020. However, these resources and capabilities are either common or easy to imitate, thus unable to provide sustainable competitive advantage to the company.

Value Chain

According to Whittington et al. (2022), value chain is the framework created by Michael Porter that "describes the categories of activities within an organisation which, together, create a product or service" (p. 107). This analysis is crucial for understanding the activities that contribute the most to value creation and attaining a competitive advantage. It encompasses both the primary activities directly related to production and delivery (inbound logistics, operations, outbound logistics, marketing and sales, and services) and the supporting activities (firm infrastructure, human resources management, technology development, and procurement). These activities collectively determine the business margin and explain its profitability. Table 4 presents a summary of the value chain proposed for this case study.

Table 4. Value chain

<table>
<tr><td colspan="5">Firm Infrastructure - Peugeot operates an extensive network of dealerships worldwide to sell their cars, enabling direct contact with customers. Additionally, the company has several production facilities, often referred to as warehouses, located in different countries around the world, facilitating the vehicle assembly process.</td></tr>
<tr><td colspan="5">HR Management - Employee recruitment, hiring, training, retention, and compensation are included in the company's operations. While these activities are similar across different industries, Peugeot, like any other company, has these functions. Currently, the company employs approximately 200,000 employees.</td></tr>
<tr><td colspan="5">Technology Development - As a major player in the automotive industry, Peugeot believes in harnessing technology to enhance the joy of driving. Currently, the company is investing in rechargeable hybrid technology, electric technology, and continuous improvements to various car components.</td></tr>
<tr><td colspan="5">Procurement - These activities encompass supplier assessment and selection, price and term negotiation, ordering, and purchasing. At Peugeot, these activities involve acquiring inputs for its value chain, which may include raw materials, supplies, machinery, laboratory equipment, office equipment, and buildings from various suppliers.</td></tr>
<tr><td>Inbound Logistics</td><td>Operations</td><td>Outbound Logistics</td><td>Marketing & Sales</td><td>Services</td></tr>
<tr><td>Peugeot relies on vendors to supply components such as engines, transmissions, and other parts. As a result, the majority of these components are exclusively manufactured by Japanese suppliers, despite the firm having a large supply base.</td><td>As part of the manufacturing process, various Peugeot car components are produced and assembled, leading to the final vehicle being built and ready for sale. In 2020, Peugeot manufactured nearly one million passenger cars globally.</td><td>This is critical for Peugeot as it ensures that its products are transported to customers in the correct conditions, safely packaged, and delivered on time. Peugeot relies on these activities to distribute the final products to channel partners, including automotive dealerships.</td><td>Besides conventional methods of promoting its brand, such as social media advertisements, television commercials, and outdoors, and a strong sales force, Peugeot maintains a strong presence in rally races worldwide. This serves as a powerful platform for showcasing the quality of its products.</td><td>Customer services before and after sales are essential to the business model, profitability, and customer satisfaction. For instance, Peugeot provides after-sales services such as training, quality assurance, repair, customer service, and maintenance, which are essential for ensuring the successful use of their vehicles.</td></tr>
</table>

The analysis reveals that Peugeot's component suppliers are primarily Japanese, which raises concerns about over-dependency and the susceptibility of the supply chain to disruptions. In the event of disruptions, the implementation of blockchain technology could facilitate the acquisition of additional suppliers by establishing a direct line of communication. Peugeot holds a competitive advantage in sales and marketing due to its presence in motor races. Therefore, this particular activity may require less improvement, allowing Peugeot to allocate its resources to other areas. Despite the rise of technology and increased online transactions, Peugeot maintains a strong brand identity with personalized customer service, preserving a personal connection with its customers. However, there is still room for improvement in Peugeot's technological capabilities. As one of the few automotive companies without blockchain integration in its operations, Peugeot must prioritize investments in technology development to establish a distinct position in the highly competitive automotive industry.

SWOT

To summarize the internal and external analysis, Table 5 uses the SWOT framework to summarize the main strengths and weaknesses identified in this case study, as well as the main positive and negative factors from the company's environment that offer opportunities and threats.

Table 5. SWOT analysis

Strengths	Weaknesses
• Top 10 brand with most patents • Big investment in Innovations and Technologies • Strong European presence • Wide range of models • Customised and differentiated service • Rebranding	• High reliance on few suppliers • Higher inflation and crisis reduced the medium class consumer purchase • High switching cost of suppliers • Few revenue streams
Opportunities	**Threats**
• Variety of potential suppliers • More eco-friendly culture • Business model adapted to electric evolution • Integration of AI and robots in operations • Implementation of blockchain in the supply chain • Develop autonomous vehicles with blockchain support • New concepts of car ownership - shared mobility and improve tracking automotive data	• Possibility of cyberattacks • Strong brand loyalty in the automotive industry • High competition and rivalry • Second-hand car dealers compromise the brand reputation • Economic crisis harnesses customer purchasing power • Ride-sharing platforms offer convenient and unexpensive mobility solutions for consumers

Despite being identified as a significant opportunity in the SWOT analysis, blockchain technology offers more than just benefits to the company. It has the potential to enhance the company's strengths and address its weaknesses. In the following section, a range of solutions and recommendations derived from the analysis will illustrate how blockchain technology can effectively improve the company's performance in the current circumstances.

SOLUTIONS AND RECOMMENDATIONS

In the medium to long term, blockchain is expected to become an integral part of business in general due to its benefits in several aspects. However, in the automotive business, blockchain integration is still in its early phases. Accordingly, Peugeot should apply this technology in supply chain management in the short term to establish a competitive advantage and stay up with the main competitors in the automotive sector. The integration of blockchain into Peugeot's supply chain is advocated in this study in order to boost process efficiency and minimise operating expenses. Secondly, blockchain is utilised to reinforce the technological backdrop and information necessary to achieve near-perfect performance and production, a path pursued by Peugeot. Finally, the article examines blockchain as a security upgrade, namely the software utilised, procedures connected to activities, and information systems.

Applications of Blockchain Technology in the Automotive Industry

Based on the findings presented in the previous sections, this study puts forward twelve recommendations for adopting blockchain technology in supply chain management within the automotive industry, focusing specifically on the case under study. These recommendations address various aspects within the company, including enhancing supply chain efficiency, leveraging the technical advancements brought by blockchain adoption, and improving security from different perspectives, such as production, driver safety, and cybersecurity. The twelve recommendations are as follows:

1. **Track all resources throughout the supply chain:** Due to the complex nature of the automotive supply chain, there can be challenges in resource allocation and information management. To address this issue, the implementation of blockchain technology is highly recommended. By utilizing blockchain, the company can achieve better inventory management through real-time visibility and monitoring of commodities and products. It enables the recording and verification of the origin, production data, and quality certificates of each component. This allows for tracing the activities of each stage, enabling necessary

adjustments and ensuring the utilization of only high-quality components in manufacturing. Consequently, operational planning is facilitated, leading to lower operating costs and improved supply chain efficiency. Furthermore, blockchain implementation promotes transparency and trust among all parties involved in the supply chain.

2. **Employment of Smart contracts in suppliers' relationship:** Peugeot heavily depends on suppliers, most of which are located in Asia and hold significant bargaining power. One solution to address this issue is the utilization of smart contracts. Smart contracts are automated contracts that enforce specific conditions for activities like ownership transfers. By implementing blockchain technology supported by smart contracts, Peugeot can enhance transparency and trust in its interactions with suppliers. This improved communication and increased bargaining power will mitigate risks arising from asymmetrical information. It also facilitates better organization of information, reducing Peugeot's reliance on suppliers and enabling renegotiation of terms.
3. **Modify Vehicle offer according to data records:** Blockchain enables comprehensive tracking of information across the entire supply chain, allowing the company to identify any issues related to vehicles, ranging from engine errors to minor technological flaws. This enhanced visibility not only improves production efficiency and eliminates flaws but also provides Peugeot with a competitive edge. In the event of malfunctions or accidents caused by the vehicle itself, blockchain enables Peugeot to gain a more accurate understanding of the specific problems associated with each vehicle model and production line. This enables the company to present viable solutions, make necessary alterations to vehicle features and components, and provide effective support in cases of breakdown or accidents.
4. **Increase automation and robots in Peugeot's manufacturing operations:** Peugeot can leverage blockchain technology to enhance production speed and automation, resulting in improved efficiency and organization. By implementing automated data verification through blockchain, the company can enhance security and accuracy by detecting forgeries and ensuring the authenticity of incoming documents. Furthermore, blockchain enables data tracking without the need for additional documentation. The use of automated information reduces production errors by identifying potential flaws and predicting malfunctions more accurately, particularly in operational machinery. Additionally, implementing a robotics-based process automation system can further enhance supply chain efficiency and performance. This system improves process precision, reduces the risk of employee injuries, increases productivity, lowers error rates, minimizes inventory check frequency, and optimizes picking, sorting, and storing times.

5. **Implementation of quality control measures through blockchain technology:** Blockchain technology enables real-time quality control measures, monitoring, and safeguarding of the production process. It also stores information about the quality and compliance of individual components or vehicles, creating a transparent and tamper-resistant audit trail. By utilizing blockchain, Peugeot can ensure the safety and quality of its vehicles throughout the entire supply chain. This technology guarantees that components meet stringent specifications and provides alerts in the event of any deviation from the normal production process. As a result, Peugeot can make necessary adjustments to its supply chain, maintaining the highest standards of quality and compliance.
6. **Alignment of production with consumers' preferences:** The usage of consumption information plays an essential role in understanding how to best attract customers. Blockchain technology plays a critical role in capturing and analyzing customer preferences, allowing Peugeot to produce products on a larger scale that align with these preferences and develop future models that closely meet customer interests. The organization can more efficiently assess market information, such as the demand for each model, and base their decisions on this data. For example, Peugeot can determine the categories of automobiles buyers are anticipating and the specific aesthetic characteristics, such as dashboard design and vehicle design, that they are interested in. By leveraging blockchain technology, Peugeot gains valuable insights into customer preferences, enabling them to tailor their offerings and meet customer expectations effectively.
7. **Creation of digital vehicle passport through blockchain:** The implementation of blockchain supports the creation of a digital vehicle passport, providing end-users with a digital platform containing information about the car's specifications, ownership, insurance, maintenance, and more. This information serves various purposes. Firstly, owners can easily keep track of automotive insurance and inspections. They can quickly identify when insurance is due for renewal, when payments need to be made, and when inspections are required. Digital identification enables the tracing of the vehicle's history, including previous transactions and real-time events like maintenance and accidents. This allows car owners to review the complete service history provided by previous owners or other parties, offering assurance when purchasing a durable product, especially when acquiring a second-hand car with existing maintenance records. Furthermore, the digital passport enables insurance companies to offer cost-effective coverage by ensuring that the vehicle has not been stolen, fraudulently modified, or involved in a major accident that would impact the insurance policy. Blockchain technology facilitates the tracking of

all information related to a car's production, providing transparency and easy access to the vehicle's history..

8. **Using Blockchain to develop self-driving cars:** Blockchain can be utilized to develop autonomous vehicles, revolutionizing the automotive industry. By leveraging effective data management, self-driving cars can reduce accidents, identify optimal routes, and minimize travel time through real-time traffic evaluation. Furthermore, blockchain enables secure and cost-effective storage, sharing, and monetization of autonomous vehicle data. In the event of an accident involving self-driving vehicles, blockchain technology simplifies the automatic sharing and verification of incident-related data, including sensor logs and vehicle diagnostics. This ensures greater transparency, facilitates liability determination, and expedites claims settlements. Moreover, blockchain guarantees that only approved, tamper-proof software updates are deployed in autonomous vehicles, enhancing their security—a crucial aspect considering their autonomous nature.
9. **Monitoring and adjusting the ecological footprint of each phase of the supply chain:** There is a growing concern about the environmental impact of manufacturing organizations these days, due to new regulations regarding corporate sustainability. To become more environmentally friendly, the company can monitor the ecological footprint of each stage of the supply chain. This can be accomplished by analyzing key performance indicators related to this issue, such as greenhouse gas emissions, energy consumption, water usage, and supply chain waste, among others. Peugeot can reduce its environmental impact by examining this data and identifying which phases of the supply chain are less sustainable.
10. **Safeguarding against cyber-attacks through blockchain:** Regarding smart contracts, the information contained within them is encrypted, which enhances security and provides better protection against cyber-attacks. In fact, blockchain is considered one of the most secure technologies, offering a high level of safety to companies that implement it. Therefore, it is essential for Peugeot to utilize blockchain technology to secure its confidential information. This technology is based on a decentralized principle, which means that the interconnected blocks of data prevent hacking attempts.
11. **Ensure production safety through blockchain:** Blockchain can also be utilized to enhance employee safety by providing transparency of information. By employing blockchain, Peugeot can ensure that key documents such as safety procedures, training materials, and emergency response plans are easily accessible and kept up to date. Storing these documents on the blockchain enables staff to make well-informed decisions and effectively respond to potential incidents. Additionally, the company can integrate blockchain technology

throughout the supply chain, particularly in the production phase. This helps secure both the quality and safety of the products by mitigating associated risks. Moreover, blockchain ensures compliance with detailed requirements for components, further enhancing production safety.

12. **Ensure driver safety:** Blockchain enables Peugeot to enhance drivers' safety by leveraging customer data and implementing personalized experiences. By securely collecting and analyzing vehicle data, the company can conduct driver performance evaluations and utilize vehicle sensors to detect and address any defects promptly. This leads to improved road safety through the enhancement of car safety features like automated braking systems. Additionally, blockchain technology facilitates efficient communication among various stakeholders such as car manufacturers, insurance companies, regulatory authorities, and law enforcement agencies. This streamlined communication enables faster response times and enhanced incident management, further contributing to drivers' safety.

Strategy Evaluation

The 12 presented strategies solve a specific supply chain problem for Peugeot, leveraging blockchain technology. Whittington et al. (2022) stress that there are three main criteria for evaluating strategic options, suitability, acceptability, and feasibility (SAFe). They define suitability as "assessing which proposed strategies address the key opportunities and threats an organisation faces through an understanding of the strategic position of an organisation" (p. 380). Acceptability concerns with "whether the expected performance outcomes of a proposed strategy meet the expectations of stakeholders" (p.387). And feasibility refers to "whether an organisation has the capacity to deliver a strategy" (p. 399), including but not limited to the financial resources to implement it. As a result, a Suitability-Acceptability-Feasibility (SAFe) analysis was conducted in order to determine which strategies are more viable in this case study. Figure 1 presents a suitability analysis, that considers the intersection of key strategic options resulting from VRIO, PESTEL, and other analyses performed before, and the strategic options proposed in this chapter for applying blockchain technology. The expected impacts of each strategic option enabled initial insights on the priorities suggested for Peugeot.

Moreover, the acceptability analysis presented in Figure 2 evaluates each of the strategic options proposed in this case study in terms of risk, implementation cost, implementation return, cost-benefit balance, and expected reactions from stakeholders.

To complete the SAFe analysis, Table 6 summarizes the expected effort in terms of various resources that each of the proposed strategic option implies for the company.

Figure 1. Suitability analysis

STRATEGIC OPTIONS	Key Strategic Factors: Reduce suppliers' reliance	Buyers' purchasing power	Ensure system security	Customer support system	End user satisfaction	Eco friendly mentality	Increase technological development	Transparency of process and information	Diversity customers segments	RANKING	
Track all resources throughout the supply chain		×		×					×	B	5-3
Employment of Smart contracts in suppliers' relationship				×	×	×			×	C	4-4
Modify vehicle offer according to its records	×		×	×		×				C	5-4
Integration of Automation and Robots in Peugeot's manufacturing operations	×			×	×	×			×	D	4-5
Implementation of quality control measures through blockchain technology	×			×		×			×	C	4-4
Alignment of production with customers' preferences	×		×			×				B	6-3
Creation of digital vehicle passport through blockchain									×	A	7-1
Using blockchain to develop self-driving cars		×				×				A	6-2
Monitoring and adjust ecological footprint of each phase of the supply chain		×	×							A	6-2
Safeguarding Against Cyber Attacks through blockchain	×	×		×		×			×	D	4-5
Ensure Production Safety through blockchain	×	×		×	×	×			×	D	3-6
Ensure driver safety	×	×				×				B	5-3

Figure 2. Acceptability analysis

STRATEGIES	RISK	IMPLEMENTATION COST	IMPLEMENTATION RETURN	COST BENEFIT BALANCE	STAKEHOLDERS' REACTION	RANKING
Track all resources throughout the supply chain	Low	Moderate	Moderate	Positive	Positive (suppliers)	B
Employment of Smart contracts in suppliers' relationship	Low	Moderate	High	Positive	Positive (suppliers)	A
Modify Vehicle offer according to its records	Low	Moderate	Moderate	Positive	Positive (customers)	B
Integration of Automation and Robots in Peugeot's manufacturing operations	Moderate	Moderate	High	Positive	Positive (suppliers, customers & investors)	A
Implementation of quality control measures through blockchain technology	Low	Moderate	Moderate	Positive	Positive (employees & suppliers)	B
Alignment of production with customers' preferences	Low	Moderate	High	Positive	Positive (customers & suppliers)	A
Creation of digital vehicle passport through blockchain	Low	Moderate	Moderate	Positive	Positive (customers & suppliers)	B
Using blockchain to develop self-driving cars	Moderate	Moderate	High	Positive	Positive (suppliers, customers & investors)	A
Monitoring and adjust ecological footprint of each phase of the SC	Low	Moderate	Moderate	Positive	Positive (customers & governments)	B
Safeguarding Against Cyber Attacks through blockchain	Moderate	Moderate	Moderate	Neutral	Positive (customers & suppliers)	C
Ensure Production Safety through blockchain	Low	Moderate	Low	Neutral Negative	Positive (employees & suppliers)	C
Ensure driver safety	Low	Moderate	Low	Neutral Negative	Positive (customers)	C

Table 6. Feasibility analysis

Proposed Strategy	People and Skills	Resources	Financial Feasibility	Rank
1. Track all resources throughout the supply chain	• Competencies in blockchain comprehension • Competencies in stock management, operational planning, and communication	• Technological resources to support blockchain usage • Hardware to allow the application of blockchain in all supply chain phases	• Blockchain technology expenses	A
2. Employment of Smart contracts in suppliers' relationship	• Workers with experience in supplier relationship • Employees responsive for supplier data analysis • Competencies in communication and negotiation	• Technological resources to support blockchain usage • Hardware to allow the application of blockchain in all supply chain phases	• Blockchain technology expenses	A
3. Modify vehicle offer according to its records	• Employees for mechanical data analysis • Competencies: Blockchain comprehension, analysis skills, mechanical engineering knowledge	• Blockchain training time for analysis personnel • Technological resources for blockchain usage • Mechanical resources for vehicle performance improvement	• Blockchain technology expenses	A
4. Increase automation and robots in Peugeot's manufacturing operations	• Employees for automation and robotics implementation • Competencies: Blockchain comprehension and technological/ mechanical knowledge	• Technological resources for blockchain implementation • Financial resources for robots and automation • Equipment and process adaptation for automation	• Blockchain technology expenses • Robot implementation costs	C
5. Implementation of quality control measures through blockchain technology	• Competencies: blockchain comprehension/insights, analysis and critical reflection capabilities, and knowledge in the mechanical engineering field, namely quality control	• Technological resources to support blockchain usage • Quality protocol to assess quality • KPIs to measure vehicle performance and dependability	• Blockchain technology expenses • Expenses with quality control measures	A
6. Alignment of production with consumers' preferences	• Employees in charge of analyzing customer information to help with decision-making • Competences: blockchain; data analysis; market knowledge	• Technological resources to support blockchain usage • Software to analyse consumer's data	• Blockchain technology expenses • Expenses with improvement towards customers' preferences	C
7. Creation of digital vehicle passport through blockchain	• Competencies: blockchain comprehension/insights, analysis and critical reflection capabilities, aggregation of data • Employees able to create platforms to share information necessary to the digital passport	• Technological resources to support blockchain usage • Additional software to aggregate data for digital passport • Creation of platform	• Blockchain Technology expenses • Expenses related to the development and maintenance of a platform/app for use of consumers and other parties	A
8. Using Blockchain to develop self-driving cars	• Employees for mechanical data analysis and technical failures • Competencies: blockchain comprehension, analysis, critical reflection, mechanical engineering knowledge, AI experience	• Technological resources to support blockchain usage • AI instruments • Mechanical parts necessary for self-driving cars, namely sensors, cameras and radars	• Blockchain technology expenses • Mechanical expenses with self-driving cars, namely new software, hardware and parts of vehicle	D
9. Monitoring and adjusting the ecological footprint of each phase of the supply chain	• Competencies: blockchain comprehension, analysis, critical reflection • Employees in sustainability implementing eco-friendly strategies	• Technological resources to support blockchain usage • Monitoring instruments - use of ecological KPIs	• Blockchain technology expenses • Instruments to monitor and decrease the footprint	C
10. Safeguarding against cyber-attacks through blockchain	• Employees with skills in cybersecurity • Competences: blockchain comprehension and data analysis	• Technological resources to support blockchain usage • Cybersecurity instruments	• Blockchain technology expenses	B
11. Ensure production safety through blockchain	• Competences: blockchain comprehension, analysis of data • Knowledge in the production field	• Technological resources to support blockchain usage • Implementation of a safety protocol with blockchain	• Blockchain technology expenses • Expenses with safety control measures	B

Continued on following page

Table 6. Continued

Proposed Strategy	People and Skills	Resources	Financial Feasibility	Rank
12. Ensure driver safety	• Employees for mechanical data analysis and technical failures • Competencies: blockchain comprehension, analysis, critical reflection, mechanical engineering knowledge	• Blockchain training for thorough analysis • Technological resources for blockchain usage • Mechanical resources for improving vehicle safety based on data analysis	• Blockchain technology expenses • Mechanical expenses with improvement of safety	C

To conclude the strategy evaluation analysis, Figure 3 presents a summary of the SAFe analysis, which compares the ranking results for each of its three domains. In light of this analysis, five main strategies were identified as the recommended priority for blockchain integration: tracking all resources throughout the supply chain; employment of Smart contracts in suppliers' relationship; modify Vehicle offer according to its records; alignment of production with customers' preferences; creation of a digital vehicle passport through blockchain.

Figure 3. Summary of SAFe analysis

STRATEGIES	SUITABILITY	ACCEPTABILITY	FEASIBILITY	FINAL RANKING
Track all resources throughout the supply chain	B	B	A	A
Employment of Smart contracts in suppliers' relationship	C	A	A	A
Modify Vehicle offer according to its records	C	B	A	B
Integration of Automation and Robots in Peugeot's manufacturing operations	D	A	C	C
Implementation of quality control measures through blockchain technology	C	B	A	B
Alignment of production with customers' preferences	B	A	C	B
Creation of digital vehicle passport through blockchain	A	B	A	A
Using blockchain to develop self-driving cars	A	A	D	C
Monitoring and adjust ecological footprint of each phase of the SC	A	B	C	B
Safeguarding Against Cyber Attacks through blockchain	D	C	B	C
Ensure Production Safety through blockchain	D	C	B	C
Guarantee drivers safety	B	C	C	C

FUTURE RESEARCH DIRECTIONS

The case study analysis presented in these pages relied solely on publicly accessible information. Two limitations result from this fact. Firstly, the data collected is limited and does not provide complete information on the case study. Furthermore, the findings were not cross-validated with managers and other stakeholders of the company. Consequently, future studies should consider a wider range of information sources to gather data, including more specific information on the management, characteristics, and performance of the supply chain, as well as the views of managers and other stakeholders, for instance through a series of interviews.

This study primarily focuses on the key advantages provided by blockchain technology for supply chain management, while acknowledging that there are further aspects of this technology that can greatly impact a company's strategy. Therefore, there is a need for a more in-depth exploration of blockchain, particularly in terms of its scalability in business operations.

Another avenue for future research is to consider the implementation of change perspective, as organizational change relies on developing proper protocols for transitioning between current protocols to ensure efficient communication among all involved parties in the supply chain. Additional perspectives to consider include the implications of blockchain technology on employees' daily activities. Gaining insights into their perspectives, challenges, and potential benefits of leveraging this technology to improve productivity and reduce workload, thus allowing more time for strategic and analytical tasks, would be particularly valuable.

Naturally, the fact that the study adopted a single case study implies that the generalization of findings should be approached with caution, and future research should replicate this study with different companies to further validate the findings. Future research can also consider studying other companies within the automotive sector and examine a group of suppliers in this industry, as they are essential partners in the adoption of blockchain technology for supply chain management. Comparative studies across different industries would also contribute to a wider understanding of this phenomenon, benefiting both managers and researchers. Considering that various industries can benefit from integrating this technology into their operations, it is crucial that future research considers other industries in their studies to fully understand the potential of blockchain for supply chain management.

CONCLUSION

The automotive supply chain is highly demanding in terms of information, communication, logistics, and personnel, underscoring the importance of embracing technological advancements that can streamline implementation, management, reduce costs, and enhance performance. Therefore, blockchain technology holds great potential for enhancing supply chain processes, improving efficiency, and reducing expenses. Consequently, Peugeot, as one of the few automotive companies yet to adopt blockchain in its supply chain, can leverage this technology to its advantage.

This chapter provides compelling evidence of the significant and positive impact that blockchain can have on the automotive industry's supply chain. As a result, it is recommended that companies resistant to implementing this technology seriously consider its adoption for supply chain management. Drawing from a case study of a company that has not yet implemented blockchain, the authors develop twelve potential strategies for integrating blockchain technology into supply chain management. These strategies focus on improving efficiency, reducing costs, enhancing organizational safety, and leveraging the technological advancements that blockchain offers for operational enhancements. Furthermore, the researchers evaluate the strategies using the SAFe analysis method to ensure alignment with the case's specific needs and financial capabilities. This evaluation yields five strong recommendations for the company's implementation. These strategies effectively demonstrate how blockchain technology can bring about positive improvements throughout the entire supply chain of an automotive firm, as exemplified by the focused case study.

Given the increasing shift toward a more technologically-driven industrial landscape, it is imperative for companies, particularly those in the automotive industry, to stay abreast of these changes and prioritize investments in innovation to maximize business efficiency and security.

REFERENCES

Abnett, K. (2023). *EU countries approve 2035 phaseout of CO2-emitting cars*. https://www.reuters.com/business/autos-transportation/eu-countries-poised-approve-2035-phaseout-co2-emitting-cars-2023-03-28/

Alsadi, M., Arshad, J., Ali, J., Prince, A., & Shishank, S. (2023). TruCert: Blockchain-based trustworthy product certification within autonomous automotive supply chains. *Computers & Electrical Engineering*, *109*, 108738. doi:10.1016/j.compeleceng.2023.108738

Archawski, J.-L., & Wolek, F. W. (1995). The long farewell: Peugeot'departure from the US market. *Business Horizons*, *38*(3), 39–47. doi:10.1016/0007-6813(95)90021-7

Armstrong, M. (2022a). *Are Cars Still Aspirational Purchases?* Statista. https://www.statista.com/chart/28182/share-of-car-non-owners-intending-to-buy-one/

Armstrong, M. (2022b). *Most important factors when buying a car*. Statista. https://www.statista.com/chart/13075/most-important-factors-when-buying-a-car/

Arora, S. (2023). *IoT explained: What it is, how it works, why it matters*. https://www.simplilearn.com/what-is-iot-how-and-why-it-matters-article

Aslam, J., Saleem, A., Khan, N. T., & Kim, Y. B. (2021). Factors influencing blockchain adoption in supply chain management practices: A study based on the oil industry. *Journal of Innovation & Knowledge*, *6*(2), 124–134. doi:10.1016/j.jik.2021.01.002

Bryman, A. (2012). *Social Research Methods* (4th ed.). Oxford University Press.

Cole, R., Stevenson, M., & Aitken, J. (2019). Blockchain technology: Implications for operations and supply chain management. *Supply Chain Management*, *24*(4), 469–483. doi:10.1108/SCM-09-2018-0309

Difrancesco, R. M., Meena, P., & Kumar, G. (2022). How blockchain technology improves sustainable supply chain processes: a practical guide. *Operations Management Research*. doi:10.1007/s12063-022-00343-y

European Parliament. (2021). *What is artificial intelligence and how is it used?* https://www.europarl.europa.eu/news/en/headlines/society/20200827STO85804/what-is-artificial-intelligence-and-how-is-it-used

European Parliament. (2023a). *AI rules: What the European Parliament wants*. https://www.europarl.europa.eu/news/en/headlines/priorities/artificial-intelligence-in-the-eu/20201015STO89417/ai-rules-what-the-european-parliament-wants

European Parliament. (2023b). *Cybersecurity: Main and emerging threats*. https://www.europarl.europa.eu/news/en/headlines/society/20220120STO21428/cybersecurity-main-and-emerging-threats

Fabbe-Costes, N., & Lechaptois, L. (2022). Automotive supply chain digitalization: Lessons and perspectives. In B. L. MacCarthy & D. Ivanov (Eds.), *The Digital Supply Chain* (pp. 289–308). Elsevier. doi:10.1016/B978-0-323-91614-1.00017-4

Forbes. (2021a). *The Future of Automotive and Mobility*. Forbes. https://www.forbes.com/sites/sap/2021/05/05/the-future-of-automotive-and-mobility/

Forbes. (2021b). *How The Automotive Industry Is Driving Toward A Sustainable Future*. Forbes. https://www.forbes.com/sites/sap/2021/12/01/how-the-automotive-industry-is-driving-toward-a-sustainable-future/

Gurtu, A., & Johny, J. (2019). Potential of blockchain technology in supply chain management: A literature review. *International Journal of Physical Distribution & Logistics Management, 49*(9), 881–900. doi:10.1108/IJPDLM-11-2018-0371

Hartl, B., Kamleitner, B., & Holub, S. (2020). Take me on a ride: The role of environmentalist identity for carpooling. *Psychology and Marketing, 37*(5), 663–676. doi:10.1002/mar.21340 PMID:32421017

International Energy Agency. (2020). *Global EV Outlook 2020*. https://www.iea.org/reports/global-ev-outlook-2020

International Federation of Robotics. (2023). *Top 5 robot trends 2023*. https://ifr.org/ifr-press-releases/news/top-5-robot-trends-2023

Investopedia. (2021). *What Regulations Affect the Automotive Sector?* Investopedia. https://www.investopedia.com/ask/answers/042015/how-much-impact-does-government-regulation-have-automotive-sector.asp

Jain, A. (2023). *After China and US, India becomes world's 3rd largest auto market: Report*. Mint. https://www.livemint.com/news/india/india-becomes-world-s-3rd-largest-auto-market-report-11673164107467.html

JATO. (2023). *Peugeot 208 ends Volkswagen Golf's 14 year reign as Europe's best-selling car in 2022*. https://www.jato.com/peugeot-208-ends-volkswagen-golfs-14-year-reign-as-europes-best-selling-car-in-2022/

Markus, S., & Buijs, P. (2022). Beyond the hype: How blockchain affects supply chain performance. *Supply Chain Management, 27*(7), 177–193. doi:10.1108/SCM-03-2022-0109

Mathieson, R. (2023). *These 10 Things Will Shape Politics in 2023*. Bloomberg. https://www.bloomberg.com/news/newsletters/2023-01-03/these-10-things-will-shape-politics-in-2023

Mckay, B. (2023). *Global Sustainability Trends for 2023 - according to 42 experts*. Greenmatch. https://www.greenmatch.co.uk/blog/sustainability-trends

Modak, S. K. S. (2023). Application of Blockchain in Supply Chain Management. *International Journal For Multidisciplinary Research, 5*(2), 1–9. doi:10.36948/ijfmr.2023.v05i02.2216

Morton, H. (n.d.). *Summary blockchain 2022 legislation*. National Conference of State Legislatures. https://www.ncsl.org/financial-services/blockchain-2022-legislation

Olynec, N. (2023). *13 sustainability trends driving business in 2023*. IMD. https://www.imd.org/ibyimd/sustainability/13-sustainability-trends-driving-business-in-2023/

Peugeot. (n.d.-a). *History: an incredible story since 1810*. Peugeot. https://www.peugeot.co.nz/brand/peugeot-universe/history.html

Peugeot. (n.d.-b). *Our competitive advantage and value-added services*. https://www.peugeot.co.ke/about-us/our-competitive-advantage-and-value-added-services.html

Rothaermel, F. T. (2021). *Strategic Management* (4th ed.). McGraw Hill Education.

Sharma, P. K., Kumar, N., & Park, J. H. (2019). Blockchain-based distributed framework for automotive industry in a smart city. *IEEE Transactions on Industrial Informatics*, *15*(7), 4197–4205. doi:10.1109/TII.2018.2887101

Stellantis. (n.d.). *About Us*. Stellantis. https://www.stellantis.com/en/company/about-us

Treiblmaier, H. (2018). The impact of the blockchain on the supply chain: A theory-based research framework and a call for action. *Supply Chain Management*, *23*(6), 545–559. doi:10.1108/SCM-01-2018-0029

UNCTAD. (2022). *Circular economy*. https://unctad.org/topic/trade-and-environment/circular-economy

UNECE. (2023). *UNECE adopts two new regulations to improve the safety of vulnerable road users*. https://unece.org/sustainable-development/press/unece-adopts-two-new-regulations-improve-safety-vulnerable-road-users

Volza. (2023). *Directory of automotive suppliers & manufacturers in the world*. https://www.volza.com/p/automotive/manufacturers/

Whittington, R., Regnér, P., Angwin, D., Johnson, G., & Scholes, K. (2022). *Exploring Strategy* (12th ed.). Pearson.

World Bank. (2023). *Sharp, Long-lasting Slowdown to Hit Developing Countries Hard*. https://www.worldbank.org/en/news/press-release/2023/01/10/global-economic-prospects

World Health Organization. (n.d.). *Sustainable development goals*. https://www.who.int/europe/about-us/our-work/sustainable-development-goals

Yin, R. K. (2009). Case Study Research: Design and Methods. *Sage (Atlanta, Ga.)*.

Chapter 14
Harnessing the Power of Digital Transformation and Sustainability: The Chinese Experience

Mohamad Zreik
https://orcid.org/0000-0002-6812-6529
Sun Yat-sen University, China

ABSTRACT

In this chapter, the author takes a look at the big picture of digital disruption. This chapter analyzes China's remarkable rise to economic leadership by tracing the ways in which the country has combined digital innovation with a commitment to environmental responsibility in its approach to doing business. The impact of the COVID-19 pandemic in hastening the transition from analog to digital business models is highlighted. It reveals more about China's cutting-edge strategy for smart supply chains, which makes use of big data, AI, IoT, and blockchain to improve supply chain management and make it more nimble, robust, and productive. The birth of sustainable smart enterprises thanks to the strategic merging of digital transformation and sustainability is a major achievement. Insights into China's path toward a sustainable digital future are provided, making this an ideal resource for students, academics, and professionals in business and IT management.

DOI: 10.4018/979-8-3693-0210-1.ch014

1. INTRODUCTION

China's economic development over the past few decades has been truly amazing. China's rise to the world's second-largest economy by nominal GDP of $19.373 trillion in 2023, after the United States, is largely attributable to the country's transformation from a centrally planned economy to a more market-oriented one, a process that began with the economic reforms of the late 1970s and was overseen by Deng Xiaoping (Perkins, 2023).

Large-scale investments in infrastructure, urbanization, and industry, as well as a sizable work force, have all contributed to the country's swift economic ascension. The creation of special economic zones (SEZs), which are designed to attract foreign investment and encourage export-oriented companies, has been important to the country's economic development.

China has also made significant progress in reducing poverty. According to the World Bank, China's economic policies have helped more than 800 million people escape poverty over the past four decades (Morrison, 2019).

The Chinese economy has historically been driven by foreign investment and exports, but in recent years it has shifted to emphasize local consumption and services. In light of mounting environmental concerns and an increasingly graying population, this change is in keeping with the government's objective to promote more sustainable and balanced growth.

The tale of China's economic growth is complex, involving a unique interplay of state choices, market reforms, and demographic variables. China was able to bypass more conventional growth patterns and quickly position itself as a frontrunner in the digital economy thanks to the foundation that this expansion provided.

Sustainability and digital transformation are now two of the most important cornerstones of any successful business plan. They propel development and change, adjusting enterprises to shifting demographics, consumer tastes, and society norms.

The term "digital transformation" is used to describe the wholesale adoption of digital technologies across an organization, which results in a dramatic shift in the way that businesses function and provide value to their consumers (Sanchez & Zuntini, 2018). Digital transformation is the process of integrating digital technologies into business, improving operational efficiency by up to 30-40% according to McKinsey & Company. It's not enough to simply digitize operations; instead, businesses must use digital technologies to innovate their internal workings and provide customers with better service. This is especially important now, as developments in artificial intelligence (AI), big data (BD), the internet of things (IoT), and blockchain (Blockchain) are altering the business landscape at breakneck speed.

However, sustainability focuses on the long-term prosperity of a company without negatively impacting the environment or the community. Sustainability is the practice of using resources without depleting them for future generations, aiming to reduce carbon footprint by a quantifiable amount, such as 20% over five years. Businesses are feeling more pressure to support sustainable development as public awareness of environmental and social issues rises. Sustainable businesses work to improve the economic, social, and environmental conditions in their communities. Everything from guaranteeing ethical labor standards and fostering diversity and inclusion to lowering one's carbon footprint can fall under this category (Sodiq et al., 2019).

A powerful synergy can be achieved between digital transformation and sustainability. By facilitating more effective resource utilization, reducing waste, increasing supply chain transparency, and encouraging ethical consumption and production habits, digital technology can aid businesses in meeting their sustainability objectives. In a similar vein, a commitment to sustainability can propel the digital transition by inspiring the creation of technological answers to pressing social and environmental problems. In tandem, digital transformation and sustainability can strengthen businesses, fuel innovation, and benefit all parties involved for the long haul.

In this study the conceptual model starts with independent variables such as the adoption rate of Artificial Intelligence, Big Data, Internet of Things, and Blockchain, along with governmental policies, consumer demands, and global market pressures. These variables impact dependent outcomes like operational efficiency, reduced carbon footprints, economic growth, and competitive advantage. Mediating variables like organizational culture, business strategy, and sustainable supply chain management elucidate how independent variables interact to produce dependent outcomes. The model also incorporates moderating variables such as economic fluctuations and technological advancements that could intensify or mitigate these relationships.

2. THE EVOLUTION OF THE DIGITAL LANDSCAPE IN CHINA

2.1. Transition From Traditional to Digital Business Models

Over the past few decades, China's digital landscape has seen dramatic change. After establishing itself on the backs of conventional business practices, China has recently made a dramatic transition to digital methods and is now widely regarded as a digital innovation frontrunner (Allen, Gu, & Jagtiani, 2022).

Brick-and-mortar shops, physical products, manual processes, and distinct divisions between industries defined China's conventional business methods. However, with the rise of the internet and other digital technologies, these paradigms began to change. The vast potential of digital technologies to boost productivity, stimulate growth, and inspire new ideas was gradually recognized by businesses. Due to the proliferation of online shopping platforms, the retail business was completely transformed by companies like Alibaba and JD.com (Akpan, Udoh, & Adebisi, 2022).

At the same time, digital technologies started to revolutionize other industries as well. Digital payment platforms like Alipay and WeChat Pay have become commonplace, while traditional banking has given way to fintech innovations (Chen et al., 2017). TikTok and iQIYI are just two examples of the platforms that have revolutionized the production and consumption of entertainment material.

The boundaries between industries began to blur as tech firms diversified into new fields. Alibaba, for instance, is not just the largest online retailer, but also a major player in the financial technology, media, and cloud computing industries. This intersectoral cooperation has emerged as a defining characteristic of China's digital landscape, giving rise to a one-of-a-kind ecosystem in which companies capitalize on cross-industry synergies (Shen, 2021).

The use of new technologies was just one facet of this conceptual shift to digital business models. By becoming more customer-focused, data-driven, and agile, Chinese enterprises have adopted a culture of experimentation and quick iteration. The government's policies and activities to encourage digital entrepreneurship and innovation were essential in this shift.

2.2. Impact of the COVID-19 Pandemic on Digital Transformation in China

The COVID-19 pandemic has had a dramatic effect on China's digital transition, functioning as a catalyst that has considerably sped up the process. Already deeply rooted in digital technologies, the country witnessed an acceleration of these tendencies as the pandemic compelled businesses and consumers to adjust to a new normal.

After widespread lockdowns and other forms of social isolation were instituted, it became crucial to rely on digital technologies to keep businesses running and daily life moving forward (Zreik, 2023a). Even though they may have been resistant to change, many offline businesses were hastily moving their operations online. Retailers, for instance, either created their own e-commerce platforms or partnered with preexisting ones to get their wares to customers online. To stay afloat, restaurants started using food delivery apps (Boh et al., 2023).

The demand for online entertainment and remote work tools both increased. Lockdowns saw a rise in the popularity of online video streaming, online gaming, and social media as people looked for ways to pass the time (Zreik & Abunamous, 2021). Concurrently, internet platforms for remote employment and education, such as DingTalk and Tencent Meeting, became critical in allowing people to work and study from the comfort of their own homes (Chen et al., 2021).

Additionally, the pandemic sparked technological advancements in the medical field. Patients' access to doctors was greatly expanded with the advent of telemedicine services. Contacts were tracked, pandemics were predicted, and public health actions were coordinated with the use of AI and big data (Lee & Lee, 2021).

During the pandemic, the Chinese government was instrumental in advancing digital transformation. It fostered digital innovations in government and pushed for the expansion of 5G networks to better serve online enterprises. For instance, in China, some provinces have released "Health Code" apps that use big data to determine an individual's vulnerability to getting COVID-19 and make it easier for them to move around during quarantines (Guo, Chen, & Liu, 2022).

3. DIGITAL TRANSFORMATION IN CHINA'S BUSINESS ENVIRONMENT

3.1. Key Components and Indicators of China's Digital Businesses

Several major factors and indicators have influenced the development and rapid expansion of China's digital companies. The development of new technologies is an important factor in the success of China's digital companies. Investments in R&D by companies like Alibaba, Tencent, and Baidu have led to revolutionary developments in areas like AI, ML, cloud computing, and data analytics (Lundvall & Rikap, 2022). These innovations not only underpin their digital infrastructures, but also open the way for brand new forms of digital media and services.

Digital companies in China care deeply about their customers. They can learn so much about their customers' habits and interests with the help of AI and big data that they can tailor their offerings to each individual. To further increase consumer happiness, they use intuitive interfaces, simple digital payment methods, and helpful support staff (Helbing, 2019). Big data is a large data sets that, when analyzed effectively, can improve decision-making accuracy by up to 33%, according to a report by the Boston Consulting Group.

Many digital companies in China operate outside of their original industries. E-commerce, financial technology, the entertainment industry, logistics, and more are just a few of the fields into which internet behemoths like Alibaba and Tencent have branched out (Shen, 2021). By working together across industries, they are better able to take advantage of synergies, create robust digital ecosystems, and offer unified services to their respective consumer bases.

The expansion of China's digital economy can be directly attributed to the government's proactive measures. The government's financial and regulatory backing, as well as initiatives like the "Internet Plus" plan, which seeks to merge the internet with conventional businesses, have all fostered digital innovation (Pedro, 2023).

China has made substantial investments in its digital infrastructure, which serves as the backbone for the country's thriving digital economy. The proliferation of smartphones, the speed with which 4G and 5G networks are being rolled out, and the development of cloud computing have all contributed to the expansion of online enterprises (Vagadia, 2020).

Market capitalization, user base size, user engagement levels, revenue growth, and innovative capacities are all markers of the success of digital firms in China. Alibaba and Tencent, for instance, are two of the most valuable technology businesses in the world due to their massive user bases and varying sources of revenue. Their dedication to new ideas and expansion is seen in their persistent funding of research and development.

3.2. Case Studies of Successful Digital Transformations

The Alibaba Group, started by Jack Ma in 1999 as a business-to-business marketplace, is a shining example of China's effective adoption of digital technology. The company morphed quickly, taking advantage of the increasing availability of the Internet in China to launch Taobao, a business-to-consumer platform, and Tmall, which focuses on the luxury market (Lee & Low, 2018; Tan, 2011).

Also, by launching Alipay, Alibaba was able to enter the realm of online financial transactions. Alipay, a third-party online payment network, has significantly altered the ways in which Chinese consumers pay for goods and services. It has grown to become a major mobile payment system (Kwak, Zhang, & Yu, 2019).

Alibaba has expanded into many different industries, not just e-commerce and digital payments. Alibaba has expanded into new areas, including cloud computing with Alibaba Cloud, the entertainment industry with the debut of Alibaba Entertainment Group, and smart logistics with the creation of the Cainiao network (Wu & Gereffi, 2018). Thanks to its successful digital diversification, Alibaba is now a multifaceted IT powerhouse that is leading the way in China and beyond.

Tencent, one of China's largest and most valuable technology enterprises, is another impressive case study in the effectiveness of digital transformation. QQ formed the foundation for Tencent's early success, but the release of the multi-purpose super-app WeChat propelled the company into the international spotlight.

WeChat was originally just a messaging app, but its parent company, Tencent, has steadily expanded its functionality to include social networking, mobile payments (WeChat Pay), online shopping, and even ride-hailing. Because of this revolutionary strategy, WeChat now has more than a billion monthly active users in China (Chen, Mao, & Qiu, 2018).

Tencent has also made great strides in the gaming sector, rising to become the most profitable video game firm in the world (Yang & Chan, 2021). Fintech, the entertainment industry, and artificial intelligence are just a few of the other areas it has financed. Tencent's digital services are the most widely used in China because of the company's flexibility, creativity, and integration.

When it comes to the revolutionary power of digital technologies, consumer-centric strategy, and creative diversification, look no farther than Alibaba and Tencent. Case studies like this are invaluable for any company starting out on the road to digital transformation.

4. SMART SUPPLY CHAIN MANAGEMENT IN CHINA

4.1. Role of Big Data and AI in Supply Chain Management

China has made great strides in supply chain management, particularly in the use of big data and artificial intelligence. These innovations are transforming supply chains to be faster, more flexible, and more responsive to market demands. Supply chain management is a system that can increase production efficiency by as much as 25% by streamlining the flow of goods from manufacturer to consumer, according to a study by the University of Tennessee.

The term "big data" is used to describe the massive amounts of data, both organized and unstructured, that companies acquire from a variety of channels, such as sales records, consumer comments, and inventory records (Xie et al., 2016). Utilizing big data's ability to reveal patterns and trends, businesses can better streamline their supply chain operations. By looking at past sales figures, a business may make more precise predictions about future demand and stock up on just the right amount of inventory at just the right moment. Big data can also be used to spot inefficiencies in the supply chain, allowing businesses to fix the underlying problems and boost output (Sanders, 2014).

On the other side, artificial intelligence facilitates supply chain management through its automation and foresight. AI is a technology that can reduce business costs by up to 60% by automating routine tasks, according to Accenture. Decisions may be made in real time with the help of AI algorithms that can process and analyze large amounts of data considerably more rapidly and correctly than humans. In order to save time and effort, AI can be utilized to automate processes like order processing. In addition, AI can foresee supply chain problems like weather-related delays, enabling businesses to prepare in advance.

The "Cainiao Network 菜鸟网络" of Alibaba Group is one of the best instances of intelligent supply chain management in China. Cainiao oversees a logistics information platform that organizes delivery between numerous couriers and fulfillment hubs using big data and AI. Cainiao enables timely and cost-effective delivery by foreseeing the optimum routes and optimizing resource allocation (Chen, 2019).

4.2. Incorporation of IoT and Blockchain in Supply Chains

Supply chains in China are entering a new era of openness, efficiency, and reliability because to the widespread implementation of Internet of Things (IoT) and blockchain technology.

The IoT enables real-time tracking and monitoring, revolutionizing supply chain management. Throughout the supply chain, IoT devices such as GPS trackers and sensors give constant data on the location and condition of products. In the case of perishable items, for instance, temperature sensors can keep tabs on storage conditions and sound an alarm if temperatures rise above predetermined thresholds (Rejeb, Keogh, & Treiblmaier, 2019). With this kind of real-time insight, businesses can see problems and implement fixes quickly, cutting costs and boosting customer happiness. Further, information gathered from the Internet of Things might provide helpful insights for bettering supply chain activities including route planning and inventory management (Nagy et al., 2018). IoT is a network of connected devices that can increase operational efficiency by up to 27% by automating and optimizing systems, according to Gartner.

Meanwhile, blockchain technology provides a trustworthy and transparent ledger for digital currencies like Bitcoin. Blockchain technology can be used to construct a decentralized record of all transactions in supply chain management, from the procurement of raw materials through the shipment of finished goods. Blockchain is a secure digital ledger that can reduce fraud by up to 45% by enhancing transparency and accountability in transactions, according to a report by Deloitte. Every exchange is recorded as a new block on the chain, creating an immutable log that can be accessed by anybody involved in the supply chain (Raja Santhi & Muthuswamy, 2022). This increases openness and trust by making it simpler to check the legitimacy of items and track down their origins should there be any problems.

Walmart China's Blockchain Traceability Platform is a blockchain-based supply chain management solution developed in partnership with VeChain, PwC, and others (Bal & Pawlicka, 2021). This system documents the origin, logistics, and results of inspections for food goods as they move through the supply chain. Scanning a QR code will provide buyers access to this data, which will increase their confidence in the product's reliability.

The Internet of Things and blockchain technology are revolutionizing the supply chains in China. These innovations are boosting supply chain performance in terms of both sustainability and customer trust by increasing transparency, efficiency, and reliability. They are a major development in the history of intelligent supply chain management.

4.3. Case Studies of Innovative Smart Supply Chains

Alibaba's Cainiao Network and JD.com's supply chain system are two examples of cutting-edge smart supply chains in China.

Alibaba's Cainiao Network: Cainiao Network, Alibaba's logistics subsidiary, is a prototypical modern Chinese supply chain. It is a digital hub that coordinates a supply chain across several warehouses and distribution hubs. Cainiao uses big data and AI to determine the optimal delivery routes in real time, taking into account factors like traffic and weather. As a result, it is a logistics system that can reliably and swiftly transport millions of packages every day.

Cainiao's operations would not be possible without the Internet of Things. Packages may be tracked in real time by smart devices, which benefits both customers and companies (Tang & Veelenturf, 2019). Internet of Things sensors track environmental conditions like temperature and humidity in storage facilities and transport vehicles to guarantee product quality. Cainiao has achieved unprecedented levels of supply chain effectiveness and customer happiness thanks to the integration of AI, big data, and the Internet of Things.

JD.com's Supply Chain: When it comes to smart supply chain innovation, JD.com, one of China's leading e-commerce enterprises, has been at the forefront. The company makes use of AI and big data to improve its distribution network, inventory management, and forecasting abilities. Artificial intelligence algorithms developed by JD.com can sift through mountains of data to determine which goods will be in highest demand and where. Customer satisfaction rises as do operational efficiencies as a result of shorter delivery times and reduced storage expenses (Rainer & Prince, 2022; Zreik, 2023b).

When it comes to innovative logistics practices, JD.com is in the forefront. Robots in its automated facilities choose and pack items far more quickly than humans can. Meanwhile, drones have reduced delivery times and eliminated logistical issues for shipping to outlying places. JD.com has also been exploring blockchain technology as a means of making its supply chain more transparent and trackable (Tang & Veelenturf, 2019).

Smart supply chains can be developed through the innovative use of digital technology, as shown by the case studies of Alibaba's Cainiao Network and JD.com. These businesses have paved the way for the future of supply chain management in China and abroad by increasing productivity while decreasing expenses and enhancing customer service.

5. MERGING DIGITAL TRANSFORMATION AND SUSTAINABILITY

5.1. Strategic Merging of Digital and Sustainable Practices in Chinese Businesses

Chinese companies are adopting sustainability in addition to technology integration in this age of digital transformation. They are consciously fusing technology and sustainable practices to develop new kinds of enterprises that are good for both people and the planet.

Examples of digital technologies used to achieve these goals include artificial intelligence (AI), the internet of things (IoT), and blockchain. Artificial intelligence and large data sets can help optimize manufacturing and logistics processes, leading to lower energy usage and fewer emissions. Buildings and factories can save money on their energy bills by using IoT devices to track and manage their energy consumption. Supply chain transparency can be increased through the use of blockchain technology, which allows companies to confirm the ethical origins of their materials (Minoli, Sohraby, & Occhiogrosso, 2017).

Meanwhile, online communities are being used to spread the word about eco-friendly purchasing practices. Online marketplaces like Alibaba and JD.com are educating customers about the environmental benefits of purchasing green items. In addition, they are taking steps to reduce their carbon footprint by developing green packaging initiatives and streamlining delivery routes.

Tech behemoths in China are also putting money into green technologies like solar and wind power. For instance, Tencent has pledged to become carbon neutral and is funding green data centers and alternative energy initiatives. Carbon neutrality is a goal that aims to offset 100% of carbon emissions through various methods such as renewable energy investments or reforestation projects. With the help of AI, Alibaba Cloud is making major strides toward lowering the carbon footprint of its data centers (Tourk & Marsh, 2016).

Digital companies in China are also making a positive impact on the local community. They're using technology to help people in rural and underserved areas get the education, healthcare, and financial services they need. Through the use of digital mediums, they are also generating employment prospects and stimulating business creation.

China's government is actively encouraging businesses to adopt digital and environmentally friendly processes. Through policies and programs like the 14th Five-Year Plan and the "New Infrastructure" project, it is encouraging environmentally friendly growth (Yu, Chang, & Mandizvidza, 2023).

5.2. Examination of Sustainable Smart Business Models

Sustainable smart business models, especially in the Chinese setting, feature an intriguing synthesis of cutting-edge innovation, ecological awareness, and social/economic considerations. Businesses that adopt these approaches are efficient, responsible, and ahead of the curve because they combine digital innovations like AI, IoT, and big data with sustainable practices.

The use of renewable energy sources in operational models is one example. Tech behemoths like Tencent are making substantial bets on renewable energy to power their server farms. Their carbon footprint is diminished, global environmental goals are met, and an expanding consumer base is served by adopting these environmentally responsible policies (Dauvergne, 2020). These businesses may reduce their financial and environmental impacts by optimizing their energy use with the help of AI and machine learning.

The concept of circular economy is another paradigm with the same overarching goals of reducing waste and optimizing resource use. Circular economy is an economic model that aims to reduce waste by up to 50% by reusing and recycling materials, according to the Ellen MacArthur Foundation. For instance, Alibaba has begun a recycling operation to collect, sift, and use previously used packaging. They use AI to automate sorting and big data to predict recycling needs (Kouhizadeh, Zhu, & Sarkis, 2020). Together, sustainability and digital technology are revolutionizing the concept of waste management and making online shopping a more environmentally friendly endeavor.

In addition to boosting efficiency, smart supply chains that utilize the Internet of Things (IoT), artificial intelligence (AI), and blockchain are also increasing traceability and transparency. Companies may now reliably educate customers about where their items were made thanks to blockchain. Customers will have more faith in firms as a result, and accountability will be increased.

Finally, digital platforms also aid in social sustainability by making basic services more accessible to more people. One way that digital technology is being used to expand access to financial services to disadvantaged communities, particularly in rural areas, is through the work of Ant Financial (a subsidiary of Alibaba) (Hua & Huang, 2021).

These examples show the potential for technologically advanced, environmentally conscious enterprises to thrive in the long run. They show how companies may use digital transformation to foster sustainability, benefiting not only the company but also its stakeholders and society at large. This convergence of digital and sustainable practices is opening up new markets and providing a blueprint for the organizations of the future.

5.3. Case Studies of Successful Sustainable Digital Transformations

Alibaba's Hema Supermarket: Alibaba's Hema Supermarket (also known as Freshippo) is an omnichannel platform with a focus on sustainability that was built as part of the company's "New Retail" strategy (Fang, 2020). Omnichannel platform is a sales approach that increases customer engagement rates by as much as 89% by providing an integrated shopping experience across multiple platforms, according to the Harvard Business Review. In order to promote sustainability and deliver a streamlined shopping experience, the stores use AI, big data, and smart logistics. Scannable QR codes on items provide instant access to extensive information, such as ingredients and provenance, and encourage informed purchasing decisions.

Hema also works to address a major barrier to sustainable living: food waste. Small stockpiles are kept and big data is used for accurate demand forecasting, cutting down on both overstocking and waste. In addition, Hema's ready-to-eat meals frequently use unsold fresh products.

Didi Chuxing: Didi Chuxing, China's most popular ride-hailing app, is yet another successful example of digital transformation. Didi uses machine learning and big data to quickly pair up drivers with passengers, cutting down on wait times and increasing efficiency. In addition to being good for business, cutting down on gas usage and pollution is a nice bonus (Wang & Yang, 2019).

Didi has taken major moves toward electrification in response to concerns about the environmental impact of transportation. It has pledged to have one million EVs on its platform and has formed a joint venture to construct charging infrastructure for EVs. Didi's platform has the potential to sway millions of drivers and users, hastening the transition to greener modes of transportation (Teece, 2019).

Alibaba's Hema Supermarket and Didi Chuxing show how a focus on sustainability may be linked with digital transformation. In addition to enhancing productivity and the customer service they provide; they are leveraging digital technologies to solve major problems in environmental sustainability. Their achievements can serve as examples for other companies seeking to implement lasting digital changes.

6. THE FUTURE OF DIGITAL TRANSFORMATION AND SUSTAINABILITY IN CHINA

6.1. Future Prospects for Digital Transformation and Sustainability

Looking ahead, we can see that digital transformation and sustainability in China will remain intrinsically intertwined and crucial to the country's future growth and development.

Businesses in all kinds of industries will speed up their digital transformation efforts as they learn to fully leverage AI, big data, the Internet of Things (IoT), blockchain, and other cutting-edge innovations. We may anticipate a deeper use of digital technologies within conventional sectors, which will revolutionize these businesses' internal workings, boost their productivity, and make them more competitive.

With the help of AI and big data analytics, businesses may better understand customer behavior, make more informed business decisions, and provide more customized goods and services to consumers. Improved analytics, automation, and real-time visibility will lead to even more intelligent supply chains in the future. As time goes on, digital platforms will improve, allowing them to offer an even broader range of services and making even greater contributions to the digital economy.

Considering China's pledge to become carbon neutral by 2060, it is more important than ever for businesses to adopt sustainable practices (Wang, Li, & Yang, 2020). Companies will be encouraged to embrace low-carbon technologies and increase energy efficiency in order to better match with the national green development goals. More businesses will adopt Circular Economy principles, such as reducing waste and conserving resources through more environmentally friendly manufacturing and consumption practices.

Businesses will also need to step up their sustainability efforts to fulfill the rising demands of environmentally conscientious customers. Companies who provide sustainable products and services, as well as those with transparent and traceable supply chains, will gain an advantage in the market.

6.2. Implications for Global Business and IT Management

Businesses and IT managers around the world may learn a lot from China's approach to combining digital transformation and sustainability, as it establishes new benchmarks and opens up new avenues for cooperation.

To begin, companies all across the world can learn from China's digital transformation success stories. Chinese businesses are a good example of how to use digital technologies to boost internal processes, enrich interactions with customers, and launch innovative new lines of business. Notable among these developments is the application of IoT, AI, and blockchain technology to smart supply chains, which in turn has improved efficiency, transparency, and resilience.

However, there is more to this than the technology itself. One distinctive feature of the Chinese model is the purposeful integration of digital and environmentally sound activities (Su, Hsu, & Boostrom, 2020). This synergy can serve as a model for multinational corporations everywhere as they attempt to negotiate the challenges of the digital age while simultaneously meeting the pressing demand for sustainability. The Chinese model can serve as a guide for developing environmentally responsible, socially responsible, and socially responsible firms all over the world.

In terms of IT management, the Chinese example demonstrates how technology can be used not only to improve operational efficiency but also to propel strategic change. It stresses the importance of IT managers seeing technology in a broader context, with its potential to promote business innovation, improve customer experiences, and aid in sustainability all in mind. This necessitates a change from conventional methods of IT management to ones that are more strategic, adaptive, and team-oriented.

In addition, China is becoming a major player in the international technology market because of its continued digital technology innovation (Zreik, 2022). For international corporations and their IT departments, this creates a mixed bag of advantages and difficulties. It provides chances for growth in knowledge, connections, and business. However, it also creates competitive pressures that force companies to stay up with emerging technologies and respond flexibly to shifts in the marketplace.

7. CONCLUSION

As we wrap off this chapter, it's important to think back on China's monumental path toward digital transformation and sustainability, from which it has drawn a roadmap for the future.

A more in-depth investigation into China's transition from analog to digital business models is warranted by the country's phenomenal economic development story. Not only has China's digital transformation and sustainability altered the country's commercial landscape, but they have also established China as a world leader in the digital economy and green growth.

China's digitalization strategy and unique circumstances, like the COVID-19 pandemic, have fueled the country's rapid digital development over the past two decades. China's digital path has been nothing short of inspiring, from the creation of digital platforms to the introduction of intelligent supply chain management, from the incorporation of AI, big data, IoT, and blockchain to the dedication to sustainability.

The chapter explored how Alibaba and JD.com, two Chinese e-commerce giants, have implemented machine learning and AI to optimize their supply chain operations, leading to more efficient manufacturing, shipping, and delivery. The chapter dug deeper into how Chinese companies are integrating digital and green initiatives, looking at examples like Alibaba's Hema Supermarket and Didi Chuxing, which have undergone successful sustainable digital revolutions.

These accounts present a picture of a China that continues to develop and lead in the technology sphere while being conscious of its environmental and social responsibilities, and they provide significant insights into China's digital transformation and sustainability in the future.

Is there anything that international corporations and IT managers can learn from China's experience? First, other countries can learn from this strategy of combining digital revolution and sustainability. The combination of embracing digital technologies and working toward sustainability has shown to be a winning formula for success in the corporate world of the twenty-first century.

China's example also shows how a progressive policy climate may help advance digital and environmentally friendly industries. The adoption of digital technologies and environmentally sustainable practices by enterprises is greatly aided by government laws and efforts.

Finally, the Chinese case studies illustrate how digital transformation may be used by organizations to promote long-term viability. They show how digital technology may boost productivity, cut down on waste, increase traceability, and open the door to more environmentally friendly consumption and production routines.

But we still have a long way to go on this path. As firms continue to pioneer new ideas, new technologies emerge, and sustainability issues become more pressing, the future seems both daunting and thrilling. Keeping aware of these changes, learning from the Chinese experience, and adjusting plans to meet the needs of the digital era and a sustainable future is essential for enterprises and IT managers throughout the world.

REFERENCES

Akpan, I. J., Udoh, E. A. P., & Adebisi, B. (2022). Small business awareness and adoption of state-of-the-art technologies in emerging and developing markets, and lessons from the COVID-19 pandemic. *Journal of Small Business and Entrepreneurship*, *34*(2), 123–140. doi:10.1080/08276331.2020.1820185

Allen, F., Gu, X., & Jagtiani, J. (2022). Fintech, cryptocurrencies, and CBDC: Financial structural transformation in China. *Journal of International Money and Finance*, *124*, 102625. doi:10.1016/j.jimonfin.2022.102625

Bal, M., & Pawlicka, K. (2021). Supply chain finance and challenges of modern supply chains. *LogForum*, *17*(1), 71–82. doi:10.17270/J.LOG.2021.525

Boh, W., Constantinides, P., Padmanabhan, B., & Viswanathan, S. (2023). Building digital resilience against major shocks. *Management Information Systems Quarterly*, *47*(1), 343–360.

Chen, X. (2019). The development trend and practical innovation of smart cities under the integration of new technologies. *Frontiers of Engineering Management*, *6*(4), 485–502. doi:10.100742524-019-0057-9

Chen, X., Chen, S., Wang, X., & Huang, Y. (2021). "I was afraid, but now I enjoy being a streamer!" Understanding the Challenges and Prospects of Using Live Streaming for Online Education. *Proceedings of the ACM on Human-Computer Interaction, 4*(CSCW3), 1-32.

Chen, Y., Mao, Z., & Qiu, J. L. (2018). *Super-sticky WeChat and Chinese society*. Emerald Group Publishing. doi:10.1108/9781787430914

Chen, Z., Li, Y., Wu, Y., & Luo, J. (2017). The transition from traditional banking to mobile internet finance: An organizational innovation perspective-a comparative study of Citibank and ICBC. *Financial Innovation*, *3*(1), 1–16. doi:10.118640854-017-0062-0

Dauvergne, P. (2020). *AI in the Wild: Sustainability in the Age of Artificial Intelligence*. MIT Press. doi:10.7551/mitpress/12350.001.0001

Fang, X. (2020). *Exploring the impact of e-commerce on cities and villages: The case of Amazon and Alibaba* [Doctoral dissertation]. Tufts University.

Guo, Y., Chen, J., & Liu, Z. (2022). Government responsiveness and public acceptance of big-data technology in urban governance: Evidence from China during the COVID-19 pandemic. *Cities (London, England)*, *122*, 103536. doi:10.1016/j.cities.2021.103536 PMID:34903901

Helbing, D. (2019). *Societal, economic, ethical and legal challenges of the digital revolution: from big data to deep learning, artificial intelligence, and manipulative technologies*. Springer International Publishing.

Hua, X., & Huang, Y. (2021). Understanding China's fintech sector: Development, impacts and risks. *European Journal of Finance*, *27*(4-5), 321–333. doi:10.1080/1351847X.2020.1811131

Kouhizadeh, M., Zhu, Q., & Sarkis, J. (2020). Blockchain and the circular economy: Potential tensions and critical reflections from practice. *Production Planning and Control*, *31*(11-12), 950–966. doi:10.1080/09537287.2019.1695925

Kwak, J., Zhang, Y., & Yu, J. (2019). Legitimacy building and e-commerce platform development in China: The experience of Alibaba. *Technological Forecasting and Social Change*, *139*, 115–124. doi:10.1016/j.techfore.2018.06.038 PMID:32287407

Lee, D. K. C., & Low, L. (2018). *Inclusive fintech: blockchain, cryptocurrency and ICO*. World Scientific. doi:10.1142/9789813238640_0007

Lee, S. M., & Lee, D. (2021). Opportunities and challenges for contactless healthcare services in the post-COVID-19 Era. *Technological Forecasting and Social Change*, *167*, 120712. doi:10.1016/j.techfore.2021.120712 PMID:33654330

Lundvall, B. Å., & Rikap, C. (2022). China's catching-up in artificial intelligence seen as a co-evolution of corporate and national innovation systems. *Research Policy*, *51*(1), 104395. doi:10.1016/j.respol.2021.104395

Minoli, D., Sohraby, K., & Occhiogrosso, B. (2017). IoT considerations, requirements, and architectures for smart buildings—Energy optimization and next-generation building management systems. *IEEE Internet of Things Journal*, *4*(1), 269–283. doi:10.1109/JIOT.2017.2647881

Morrison, W. M. (2019). China's economic rise: History, trends, challenges, and implications for the United States. *Current Politics and Economics of Northern and Western Asia*, *28*(2/3), 189–242.

Nagy, J., Oláh, J., Erdei, E., Máté, D., & Popp, J. (2018). The role and impact of Industry 4.0 and the internet of things on the business strategy of the value chain—The case of Hungary. *Sustainability (Basel)*, *10*(10), 3491. doi:10.3390u10103491

Pedro, F. (2023). Foundational Aspects of Smart Cities Leading the Digital Economy-An Review. *Journal of Computing and Natural Science, 3*(1), 35-45.

Perkins, D. H. (2023). Structural challenges to sustained economic growth in China. *China & World Economy*, *31*(1), 22–43. doi:10.1111/cwe.12457

Rainer, R. K., & Prince, B. (2022). *Introduction to information systems: Supporting and transforming business*. John Wiley & Sons.

Raja Santhi, A., & Muthuswamy, P. (2022). Influence of blockchain technology in manufacturing supply chain and logistics. *Logistics*, *6*(1), 15. doi:10.3390/logistics6010015

Rejeb, A., Keogh, J. G., & Treiblmaier, H. (2019). Leveraging the internet of things and blockchain technology in supply chain management. *Future Internet*, *11*(7), 161. doi:10.3390/fi11070161

Sanchez, M. A., & Zuntini, J. I. (2018). Organizational readiness for the digital transformation: A case study research. *Revista Gestão & Tecnologia*, *18*(2), 70–99. doi:10.20397/2177-6652/2018.v18i2.1316

Sanders, N. R. (2014). *Big data driven supply chain management: A framework for implementing analytics and turning information into intelligence*. Pearson Education.

Shen, H. (2021). *Alibaba: Infrastructuring Global China*. Routledge. doi:10.4324/9781003169055

Sodiq, A., Baloch, A. A., Khan, S. A., Sezer, N., Mahmoud, S., Jama, M., & Abdelaal, A. (2019). Towards modern sustainable cities: Review of sustainability principles and trends. *Journal of Cleaner Production*, *227*, 972–1001. doi:10.1016/j.jclepro.2019.04.106

Su, L., Hsu, M. K., & Boostrom, R. E. Jr. (2020). From recreation to responsibility: Increasing environmentally responsible behavior in tourism. *Journal of Business Research*, *109*, 557–573. doi:10.1016/j.jbusres.2018.12.055

Tan, Y. (2011). *Chinnovation: How Chinese innovators are changing the world*. John Wiley and Sons.

Tang, C. S., & Veelenturf, L. P. (2019). The strategic role of logistics in the industry 4.0 era. *Transportation Research Part E, Logistics and Transportation Review*, *129*, 1–11. doi:10.1016/j.tre.2019.06.004

Teece, D. J. (2019). China and the reshaping of the auto industry: A dynamic capabilities perspective. *Management and Organization Review*, *15*(1), 177–199. doi:10.1017/mor.2019.4

Tourk, K., & Marsh, P. (2016). The new industrial revolution and industrial upgrading in China: Achievements and challenges. *Economic and Political Studies*, *4*(2), 187–209. doi:10.1080/20954816.2016.1180769

Vagadia, B. (2020). *Digital Disruption*. Springer Nature. doi:10.1007/978-3-030-54494-2

Wang, G., Li, S., & Yang, L. (2022). Research on the pathway of green financial system to implement the realization of China's carbon neutrality target. *International Journal of Environmental Research and Public Health, 19*(4), 2451. doi:10.3390/ijerph19042451 PMID:35206639

Wang, H., & Yang, H. (2019). Ridesourcing systems: A framework and review. *Transportation Research Part B: Methodological, 129*, 122–155. doi:10.1016/j.trb.2019.07.009

Wu, X., & Gereffi, G. (2018). Amazon and Alibaba: Internet governance, business models, and internationalization strategies. In International business in the information and digital age (Vol. 13, pp. 327-356). Emerald Publishing Limited.

Xie, K., Wu, Y., Xiao, J., & Hu, Q. (2016). Value co-creation between firms and customers: The role of big data-based cooperative assets. *Information & Management, 53*(8), 1034–1048. doi:10.1016/j.im.2016.06.003

Yang, C., & Chan, D. Y. T. (2021). Market Expansion of Domestic Gaming Firms in Shenzhen, China: Dilemma of Globalisation and Regionalisation. *Tijdschrift voor Economische en Sociale Geografie, 112*(3), 256–273. doi:10.1111/tesg.12459

Yu, P., Chang, X., & Mandizvidza, K. (2023). Development of New Energy Vehicles in Entrepreneurial Ecosystem Under the Carbon Neutrality Policy in China. In Corporate Sustainability as a Tool for Improving Economic, Social, and Environmental Performance (pp. 55-84). IGI Global. doi:10.4018/978-1-6684-7422-8.ch004

Zreik, M. (2022). Contemporary geopolitics of Eurasia and the Belt and Road Initiative. *Eurasian Research Journal, 4*(1), 7–26. doi:10.53277/2519-2442-2022.1-01

Zreik, M. (2023a). From Boom to Bust: A Study of China's Economy in the Wake of COVID-19 Outbreak in H1 2020. *BRICS Journal of Economics, 4*(1), 147–171. doi:10.3897/brics-econ.4.e101050

Zreik, M. (2023b). China's Economic Development: Digital Transformation, Energy Efficiency, and Climate Change. In M. Okur Dinçsoy & H. Can (Eds.), *Optimizing Energy Efficiency During a Global Energy Crisis* (pp. 51–64). IGI Global. doi:10.4018/979-8-3693-0400-6.ch004

Zreik, M., & Abunamous, M. O. (2021). Human thinking at the time of Covid-19 and the role of swot analysis: A case study on the Chinese and Palestinian societies. *Psychology Research on Education and Social Sciences, 2*(1), 31–40.

KEY TERMS AND DEFINITIONS

Artificial Intelligence (AI): A field of computer science that simulates human intelligence processes—such as learning, reasoning, and self-correction—by algorithms and software. In businesses, AI can be used for various applications including data analytics, automation, and customer service.

Big Data: Large and complex data sets that traditional data processing software cannot handle. Big data is characterized by high volume, velocity, and variety, and it requires specialized tools for analysis, storage, and processing.

Blockchain: A digital ledger technology that allows multiple parties to have simultaneous access to a constantly updated database that is secure and unchangeable. In business, blockchain can be used for secure transactions, traceability, and enhanced transparency.

Carbon Neutrality: The practice of balancing the amount of emitted greenhouse gases with an equivalent amount of carbon offsets or through carbon capture and storage technologies, thus achieving a zero-carbon footprint.

Circular Economy: An economic model that aims to design out waste and pollution, keep products and materials in use, and regenerate natural systems. This approach contrasts with the traditional linear economy, which follows a "take, make, dispose" model.

Digital Transformation: The integration of digital technologies into various aspects of business, fundamentally changing how organizations operate and deliver value to their customers. This process aims to optimize efficiency, enhance customer engagement, and drive innovation.

Internet of Things (IoT): The network of physical devices, vehicles, buildings, and other objects embedded with sensors, software, and other technologies for the purpose of connecting and exchanging data. IoT applications in businesses range from smart supply chains to automated manufacturing processes.

Omnichannel Platform: A multi-channel approach to sales that provides customers with an integrated shopping experience. These platforms use data analytics and technological solutions to seamlessly connect online and offline retail environments.

Supply Chain Management: The comprehensive oversight of materials, information, and finances as they move from supplier to manufacturer to wholesaler to retailer to consumer. Effective supply chain management leverages digital technologies to improve efficiency and responsiveness.

Sustainability: The practice of utilizing resources in a way that meets the needs of the present without compromising the ability of future generations to meet their own needs. In a business context, this refers to long-term economic, social, and environmental viability.

Compilation of References

. Albornoz, F, Calvo Pardo, H.F., Corcos, G. & Ornelas, E. (2023). Sequentially exporting products across countries. *Journal of International Economics*. 142, . *88*(10), 17-31. doi:10.1016/j.jinteco.2023.103735

Abbasi, S., & Choukolaei, H. A. (2023). A systematic review of green supply chain network design literature focusing on carbon policy. *Decision Analytics Journal*, 100189.

Abdel-Basset, M., Manogaran, G., & Mohamed, M. (2018). Internet of Things (IoT) and its impact on supply chain: A framework for building smart, secure and efficient systems. *Future Generation Computer Systems*, *86*(9), 614–628. doi:10.1016/j.future.2018.04.051

Abnett, K. (2023). *EU countries approve 2035 phaseout of CO2-emitting cars*. https://www.reuters.com/business/autos-transportation/eu-countries-poised-approve-2035-phaseout-co2-emitting-cars-2023-03-28/

Afshan, N., Chatterjee, S., & Chhetri, P. (2018). Impact of information technology and relational aspect on supply chain collaboration leading to financial performance. *Benchmarking*, *25*(7), 2496–2511. doi:10.1108/BIJ-09-2016-0142

Aggarwal, S., & Srivastava, M. K. (2016). Towards a grounded view of collaboration in Indian agrifood supply chains: A qualitative investigation. *British Food Journal*, *118*(5), 1085–1106. doi:10.1108/BFJ-08-2015-0274

Agrawal, T. K., Angelis, J., Khilji, W. A., Kalaiarasan, R., & Wiktorsson, M. (2023). Demonstration of a blockchain-based framework using smart contracts for supply chain collaboration. *International Journal of Production Research*, *61*(5), 1497–1516. doi:10.1080/00207543.2022.2039413

Aguzzoli, R., Lengler, J., Sousa, C. M. P., & Benito, G. R. G. (2020). Here We Go Again: A Case Study on Re-entering a Foreign Market. *British Journal of Management*, *32*(2), 416–432. doi:10.1111/1467-8551.12407

Ahmadi Hajiabadia, S., Ul-Haqb, J., & Visasc, H. (2021). Impact of Development Strategy on Economic Growth of Iran: New Structural Economics Perspective. *Iranian Journal of Economic Studies*, *10*(2), 473–487.

Akhavan, P., & Philsoophian, M. (2022). Improving of supply chain collaboration and performance by using block chain technology as a mediating role and resilience as a moderating variable. *Journal of the Knowledge Economy*, 1–22. doi:10.100713132-022-01085-9

Akpan, I. J., Udoh, E. A. P., & Adebisi, B. (2022). Small business awareness and adoption of state-of-the-art technologies in emerging and developing markets, and lessons from the COVID-19 pandemic. *Journal of Small Business and Entrepreneurship, 34*(2), 123–140. doi:10.1080/08276331.2020.1820185

Akyuz, G. A., & Gursoy, G. (2020). Transformation of supply chain activities in blockchain environment. *Digital Business Strategies in Blockchain Ecosystems: Transformational Design and Future of Global Business*, 153-175.

Albornoz, F., Calvo Pardo, H. F., Corcos, G., & Ornelas, E. (2018). Sequential Exporting and Third-Country Effects of Trade Policy. *Working Paper*, 1-78.

Albornoz, F., Calvo Pardo, H. F., Corcos, G., & Ornelas, E. (2012). Sequential exporting. *Journal of International Economics, 88*(10), 17–31. doi:10.1016/j.jinteco.2012.02.007

Alc'acer, V., & Cruz-Machado, V. (2019). Scanning the industry 4.0: A literature review on technologies for manufacturing systems. *Eng. Sci. Technol. Int. J.* doi:10.1016/j.jestch.2019.01.006

Al-Doori, J. A. (2019). The impact of supply chain collaboration on performance in automotive industry: Empirical evidence. *Journal of Industrial Engineering and Management, 12*(2), 241–253. doi:10.3926/jiem.2835

Aliahmadi, A., Nozari, H., & Ghahremani-Nahr, J. (2022). AIoT-based sustainable smart supply chain framework. *International Journal of Innovation in Management, Economics and Social Sciences, 2*(2), 28-38.

Aliahmadi, A., Nozari, H., & Ghahremani-Nahr, J. (2022a). AIoT-based sustainable smart supply chain framework. *International Journal of Innovation in Management, Economics and Social sciences, 2*(2), 28-38.

Aliahmadi, A., Ghahremani-Nahr, J., & Nozari, H. (2023). Pricing decisions in the closed-loop supply chain network, taking into account the queuing system in production centers. *Expert Systems with Applications, 212*, 118741. doi:10.1016/j.eswa.2022.118741

Aliahmadi, A., Jafari-Eskandari, M., Mozafari, A., & Nozari, H. (2016). Comparing linear regression and artificial neural networks to forecast total productivity growth in Iran. *International Journal of Information, Business and Management, 8*(1), 93.

Aliahmadi, A., & Nozari, H. (2023, January). Evaluation of security metrics in AIoT and blockchain-based supply chain by Neutrosophic decision-making method. *Supply Chain Forum International Journal (Toronto, Ont.), 24*(1), 31–42.

Aliahmadi, A., Nozari, H., & Ghahremani-Nahr, J. (2022b). Big Data IoT-based agile-lean logistic in pharmaceutical industries. International Journal of Innovation in Management. *Economics and Social Sciences, 2*(3), 70–81.

Ali, N., Ghazal, T. M., Ahmed, A., Abbas, S., Khan, M. A., Alzoubi, H. M., ... Khan, M. A. (2022). Fusion-based supply chain collaboration using machine learning techniques. *Intelligent Automation & Soft Computing, 31*(3), 1671–1687. doi:10.32604/iasc.2022.019892

Allen, F., Gu, X., & Jagtiani, J. (2022). Fintech, cryptocurrencies, and CBDC: Financial structural transformation in China. *Journal of International Money and Finance, 124*, 102625. doi:10.1016/j.jimonfin.2022.102625

Almanza, B. A., Kirsch, K., Kline, S. F., Sirsat, S., Stroia, O., Choi, J. K., & Neal, J. (2015). How clean are hotel rooms? Part I: Visual observations vs. microbial contamination. *Journal of Environmental Health, 78*(1), 8–13.

Al-Omoush, K. S., de Lucas, A., & del Val, M. T. (2023). The role of e-supply chain collaboration in collaborative innovation and value-co creation. *Journal of Business Research, 158*, 113647. doi:10.1016/j.jbusres.2023.113647

Alsadi, M., Arshad, J., Ali, J., Prince, A., & Shishank, S. (2023). TruCert: Blockchain-based trustworthy product certification within autonomous automotive supply chains. *Computers & Electrical Engineering, 109*, 108738. doi:10.1016/j.compeleceng.2023.108738

Alvarez, R., & Lopez, R. (2014). Is Previous Export Experience Important for New Exports? *The Journal of Development Studies*, 1–38.

AlZayani, F., Mohammed, A., & Shoaib, H. M. (2023). The impact of smart technologies on SMEs' sustainability: The mediation effect of sustainability strategy. *Competitiveness Review*. Advance online publication. doi:10.1108/CR-09-2022-0136

Anand, P., Singh, Y., Selwal, A., Alazab, M., Tanwar, S., & Kumar, N. (2020). IoT vulnerability assessment for sustainable computing: Threats, current solutions, and open challenges. *IEEE Access : Practical Innovations, Open Solutions, 8*, 168825–168853. doi:10.1109/ACCESS.2020.3022842

Archawski, J.-L., & Wolek, F. W. (1995). The long farewell: Peugeot'departure from the US market. *Business Horizons, 38*(3), 39–47. doi:10.1016/0007-6813(95)90021-7

Arkolakis, C. (2011). *A unified theory of firm selection and growth*. Mimeo. doi:10.3386/w17553

Armstrong, M. (2022a). *Are Cars Still Aspirational Purchases?* Statista. https://www.statista.com/chart/28182/share-of-car-non-owners-intending-to-buy-one/

Armstrong, M. (2022b). *Most important factors when buying a car*. Statista. https://www.statista.com/chart/13075/most-important-factors-when-buying-a-car/

Arora, S. (2023). *IoT explained: What it is, how it works, why it matters*. https://www.simplilearn.com/what-is-iot-how-and-why-it-matters-article

Artopoulos, A., Friel, D., & Hallak, J. C. (2011). Lifting the domestic veil: the challenges of exporting differentiated goods across the development divide. *NBER Working Paper 16947*.

Aslam, J., Saleem, A., Khan, N. T., & Kim, Y. B. (2021). Factors influencing blockchain adoption in supply chain management practices: A study based on the oil industry. *Journal of Innovation & Knowledge*, *6*(2), 124–134. doi:10.1016/j.jik.2021.01.002

Asree, S., Gopalan, S., & Zain, M. (2016). The impact of cultural intelligence on supply chain collaboration. *International Journal of Integrated Supply Management*, *10*(3-4), 246–263. doi:10.1504/IJISM.2016.081265

Atzori, L., Iera, A., & Morabito, G. (2010). The Internet of things: A survey. *Computer Networks*, *54*(15), 27–87. doi:10.1016/j.comnet.2010.05.010

Awan, U., Sroufe, R., & Shahbaz, M. (2021). Industry 4.0 and the circular economy: A literature review and recommendations for future research. *Business Strategy and the Environment*, *30*(4), 2038–2060. doi:10.1002/bse.2731

Azevedo, S. G., Pimentel, C. O., & Matias, J. C. (2022, January). The role of supply chain 4.0 on supply chain collaboration-an exploratory case study in the automotive industry. In *2022 The 3rd International Conference on Industrial Engineering and Industrial Management* (pp. 1-8). Academic Press.

Azizi, N., Malekzadeh, H., Akhavan, P., Haass, O., Saremi, S., & Mirjalili, S. (2021). IoT–blockchain: Harnessing the power of internet of thing and blockchain for smart supply chain. *Sensors (Basel)*, *21*(18), 6048. doi:10.339021186048 PMID:34577261

Ballestar, M.T., Grau-Carles, P., & Sainz, J. (2018). *Customer segmentation in e-commerce: Applications to the cashback business model*. Academic Press.

Bal, M., & Pawlicka, K. (2021). Supply chain finance and challenges of modern supply chains. *LogForum*, *17*(1), 71–82. doi:10.17270/J.LOG.2021.525

Barber, N., & Scarcelli, J. M. (2010). Enhancing the assessment of tangible service quality through the creation of a cleanliness measurement scale. *Managing Service Quality*, *20*(1), 70–88. doi:10.1108/09604521011011630

Bencsik, B., Palmié, M., Parida, V., Wincent, J., & Gassmann, O. (2023). Business models for digital sustainability: Framework, microfoundations of value capture, and empirical evidence from 130 smart city services. *Journal of Business Research*, *160*, 113757. doi:10.1016/j.jbusres.2023.113757

Ben-Daya, M., Hassini, E., & Bahroun, Z. (2019). Internet of things and supply chain management: A literature review. *International Journal of Production Research*, *57*(15-16), 4719–4742. doi:10.1080/00207543.2017.1402140

Bentaher, C., & Rajaa, M. (2022). Supply Chain Management 4.0: A Literature Review and Research Framework. *European Journal of Business and Management Research*, *7*(1), 117–127. doi:10.24018/ejbmr.2022.7.1.1246

Bernard, A. B., Esther, A. B., Renzo Massari, J. R., & Daria, T. (2017). Exporter Dynamics and Partial-Year Effects. *The American Economic Review, 107*(10), 3211–3228. doi:10.1257/aer.20141070

Bernard, A. B., Jensen, J. B., Redding, S. J., & Schott, P. K. (2009). The Margins of US Trade. *The American Economic Review, 99*(2), 487–493. doi:10.1257/aer.99.2.487

Bhargava, A., Bhargava, D., Kumar, P. N., Sajja, G. S., & Ray, S. (2022). Industrial IoT and AI implementation in vehicular logistics and supply chain management for vehicle mediated transportation systems. *International Journal of System Assurance Engineering and Management, 13*(S1), 673–680. doi:10.100713198-021-01581-2

Bhaskar, P., Tiwari, C. K., & Joshi, A. (2021). Blockchain in education management: Present and future applications. *Interactive Technology and Smart Education, 18*(1), 1–17. doi:10.1108/ITSE-07-2020-0102

Billah, M. M., Alam, S. S., Masukujjaman, M., Ali, M. H., Makhbul, Z. K. M., & Salleh, M. F. M. (2023). Effects of Internet of Things, supply chain collaboration and ethical sensitivity on sustainable performance: Moderating effect of supply chain dynamism. *Journal of Enterprise Information Management, 36*(5), 1270–1295. doi:10.1108/JEIM-06-2022-0213

Bitner, M. J., Brown, S. W., & Meuter, M. L. (2000). Technology infusion in service encounters. *Journal of the Academy of Marketing Science, 28*(1), 138–149. doi:10.1177/0092070300281013

Boh, W., Constantinides, P., Padmanabhan, B., & Viswanathan, S. (2023). Building digital resilience against major shocks. *Management Information Systems Quarterly, 47*(1), 343–360.

Borgogno. (2019). Usefulness and dangers of smart contracts in consumer and commercial transactions. Academic Press.

Bout, A. (2011). *Supply Chain Collaboration – barriers and enablers- a dyadic study of buyer-supplier relationships*. Academic Press.

Bracke, V., Sebrechts, M., Moons, B., Hoebeke, J., De Turck, F., & Volckaert, B. (2021). Design and evaluation of a scalable Internet of Things backend for smart ports. *Software, Practice & Experience, 51*(7), 1557–1579. doi:10.1002pe.2973

Bratucu, R., & Ciofoaia, R. A. (2022). *Artificial Intelligence Mediated Supply Chain Collaboration: A Study on how Artificial Intelligence Technologies Influence Collaboration Processes in the Chain*. Academic Press.

Broccardo, L., Zicari, A., Jabeen, F., & Bhatti, Z. A. (2023). How digitalization supports a sustainable business model: A literature review. *Technological Forecasting and Social Change, 187*, 122146. doi:10.1016/j.techfore.2022.122146

Brochado, A., Rita, P., & Margarido, A. (2016). High tech meets high touch in upscale hotels. *Journal of Hospitality and Tourism Technology, 7*(4), 347–365. doi:10.1108/JHTT-07-2016-0038

Bryman, A. (2012). *Social Research Methods* (4th ed.). Oxford University Press.

Buhalis, D., & Leung, R. (2018). Smart hospitality—Interconnectivity and interoperability towards an ecosystem. *International Journal of Hospitality Management*, *71*(January), 41–50. doi:10.1016/j.ijhm.2017.11.011

Buhalis, D., O'Connor, P., & Leung, R. (2023). Smart hospitality: From smart cities and smart tourism towards agile business ecosystems in networked destinations. *International Journal of Contemporary Hospitality Management*, *35*(1), 369–393. doi:10.1108/IJCHM-04-2022-0497

Burby, J., & Atchison, S. (2007). *Actionable web analytics: using data to make smart business decisions*. John Wiley & Sons.

Cáceres, C., Rosário, J. M., & Amaya, D. (2019). Proposal of a smart hospital based on internet of things (IoT) concept. In *Processing and Analysis of Biomedical Information: First International SIPAIM Workshop, SaMBa 2018, Held in Conjunction with MICCAI 2018, Granada, Spain, September 20, 2018, Revised Selected Papers 1* (pp. 93-104). Springer International Publishing.

Cao, M., & Zhang, Q. (2011). Supply chain collaboration: Impact on collaborative advantage and firm performance. *Journal of Operations Management*, *29*(3), 163–180. doi:10.1016/j.jom.2010.12.008

Caporuscio, M., Flammini, F., Khakpour, N., Singh, P., & Thornadtsson, J. (2020). Smart-troubleshooting connected devices: Concept, challenges and opportunities. *Future Generation Computer Systems*, *111*, 681–697. doi:10.1016/j.future.2019.09.004

Chadli, N., Elhoseny, M., Kabbaj, M. I., & Bakkoury, Z. (2022). Smart business process modeling: Toward an IoT to detect the data flow anomalies in ad hoc mesh network. *Distributed Sensing and Intelligent Systems Proceedings of ICDSIS*, *2020*, 13–27.

Chakraborty, S., Bhattacharya, S., & Dobrzykowski, D. D. (2014). Impact of supply chain collaboration on value co-creation and firm performance: A healthcare service sector perspective. *Procedia Economics and Finance*, *11*, 676–694. doi:10.1016/S2212-5671(14)00233-0

Chauhan, C., Kaur, P., Arrawatia, R., Ractham, P., & Dhir, A. (2022). Supply chain collaboration and sustainable development goals (SDGs). Teamwork makes achieving SDGs dream work. *Journal of Business Research*, *147*, 290–307. doi:10.1016/j.jbusres.2022.03.044

Chengoden, R., Victor, N., Huynh-The, T., Yenduri, G., Jhaveri, R. H., Alazab, M., Bhattacharya, S., Hegde, P., Maddikunta, P. K. R., & Gadekallu, T. R. (2023). Metaverse for healthcare: A survey on potential applications, challenges and future directions. *IEEE Access : Practical Innovations, Open Solutions*, *11*, 12765–12795. doi:10.1109/ACCESS.2023.3241628

Chen, J., Sousa, C. M. P., & He, X. (2019). Export market re-entry: Time-out period and price/quality dynamisms. *Journal of World Business*, *54*(2), 154–168. doi:10.1016/j.jwb.2019.01.001

Chen, L., Fu, Y., Liu, Y., & Wang, C. (2023). The Impact of Logistics Corporate Social Responsibility on Supply Chain Performance: Using Supply Chain Collaboration as an Intermediary Variable. *Sustainability (Basel)*, *15*(12), 9613. doi:10.3390u15129613

Chen, L., Zhao, X., Tang, O., Price, L., Zhang, S., & Zhu, W. (2017). Supply chain collaboration for sustainability: A literature review and future research agenda. *International Journal of Production Economics*, *194*, 73–87. doi:10.1016/j.ijpe.2017.04.005

Chen, X. (2019). The development trend and practical innovation of smart cities under the integration of new technologies. *Frontiers of Engineering Management*, *6*(4), 485–502. doi:10.100742524-019-0057-9

Chen, X., Chen, S., Wang, X., & Huang, Y. (2021). "I was afraid, but now I enjoy being a streamer!" Understanding the Challenges and Prospects of Using Live Streaming for Online Education. *Proceedings of the ACM on Human-Computer Interaction, 4*(CSCW3), 1-32.

Chen, X., He, C., Chen, Y., & Xie, Z. (2023). Internet of Things (IoT)—Blockchain-enabled pharmaceutical supply chain resilience in the post-pandemic era. *Frontiers of Engineering Management, 10*(1), 82–95. doi:10.100742524-022-0233-1

Chen, Y., Mao, Z., & Qiu, J. L. (2018). *Super-sticky WeChat and Chinese society*. Emerald Group Publishing. doi:10.1108/9781787430914

Chen, Z., Li, Y., Wu, Y., & Luo, J. (2017). The transition from traditional banking to mobile internet finance: An organizational innovation perspective-a comparative study of Citibank and ICBC. *Financial Innovation*, *3*(1), 1–16. doi:10.118640854-017-0062-0

Chin, T. A., Tat, H. H., & Sulaiman, Z. (2015). Green supply chain management, environmental collaboration and sustainability performance. *Procedia CIRP*, *26*, 695–699. doi:10.1016/j.procir.2014.07.035

Choi, H. W., Shin, D. W., Yang, J., Lee, S., Figueiredo, C., Sinopoli, S., Ullrich, K., Jovančić, P., Marrani, A., Momentè, R., Gomes, J., Branquinho, R., Emanuele, U., Lee, H., Bang, S. Y., Jung, S.-M., Han, S. D., Zhan, S., Harden-Chaters, W., ... Kim, J. M. (2022). Smart textile lighting/display system with multifunctional fibre devices for large scale smart home and IoT applications. *Nature Communications*, *13*(1), 814. doi:10.103841467-022-28459-6 PMID:35145096

Choi, K. H., & Kwon, G. H. (2023). Strategies for sensing innovation opportunities in smart grids: In the perspective of interactive relationships between science, technology, and business. *Technological Forecasting and Social Change*, *187*, 122210. doi:10.1016/j.techfore.2022.122210

Chouvarda, I., Mountford, N., Trajkovik, V., Loncar-Turukalo, T., & Cusack, T. (2019). Leveraging interdisciplinary education toward securing the future of connected health research in Europe: Qualitative study. *Journal of Medical Internet Research*, *21*(11), e14020. doi:10.2196/14020 PMID:31719026

Coghlan, A., Becken, S., & Warren, C. (2023). Modelling a smart tech user journey to decarbonise tourist accommodation. *Journal of Sustainable Tourism*, *31*(3), 840–858. doi:10.1080/09669582.2022.2030344

Cole, R., Stevenson, M., & Aitken, J. (2019). Blockchain technology: Implications for operations and supply chain management. *Supply Chain Management, 24*(4), 469–483. doi:10.1108/SCM-09-2018-0309

Combe, C. (2012). *Introduction to E-business*. Routledge. doi:10.4324/9780080492780

Conoscenti, M., Vetro, A., & De Martin, J. C. (2016). Blockchain for the Internet of Things: A systematic literature review. *2016 IEEE/ACS 13th International Conference of Computer Systems and Applications (AICCSA)*, 1-6.

Cooke, A. D., & Zubcsek, P. P. (2017). The connected consumer: Connected devices and the evolution of customer intelligence. *Journal of the Association for Consumer Research, 2*(2), 164–178. doi:10.1086/690941

Coutinho, R. W., & Boukerche, A. (2019). Modeling and analysis of a shared edge caching system for connected cars and industrial IoT-based applications. *IEEE Transactions on Industrial Informatics, 16*(3), 2003–2012. doi:10.1109/TII.2019.2938529

Crum, M., Poist, R., & Daugherty, P. J. (2011). Review of logistics and supply chain relationship literature and suggested research agenda. *International Journal of Physical Distribution & Logistics Management, 41*(1), 16–31. doi:10.1108/09600031111101402

Cui, L., Gao, M., Dai, J., & Mou, J. (2022). Improving supply chain collaboration through operational excellence approaches: An IoT perspective. *Industrial Management & Data Systems, 122*(3), 565–591. doi:10.1108/IMDS-01-2020-0016

Dallasega, P., Rauch, E., & Linder, C. (2018). Industry 4.0 as an enabler of proximity for construction supply chains: A systematic literature review. *Computers in Industry, 99*, 205–225. doi:10.1016/j.compind.2018.03.039

Das, S., Roberts, M., & Tybout, J. (2007). Market entry costs, producer heterogeneity, and export dynamics. *Econometrica, 75*(3), 837–873. doi:10.1111/j.1468-0262.2007.00769.x

Dauvergne, P. (2020). *AI in the Wild: Sustainability in the Age of Artificial Intelligence*. MIT Press. doi:10.7551/mitpress/12350.001.0001

Della Corte, V., Aria, M., Del Gaudio, G., Barney, J. B., Cobanoglu, C., & Sepe, F. (2021). The relevance of relational capabilities in collaborative decisions. *International Journal of Contemporary Hospitality Management, 33*(12), 4391–4417. doi:10.1108/IJCHM-01-2021-0037

Demir, K. A., D¨oven, G., & Sezen, B. (2019). Industry 5.0 and human-robot co-working. *Procedia Computer Science, 158*, 688–695. doi:10.1016/j.procs.2019.09.104

Difrancesco, R. M., Meena, P., & Kumar, G. (2022). How blockchain technology improves sustainable supply chain processes: a practical guide. *Operations Management Research*. doi:10.1007/s12063-022-00343-y

Dmitriy, N. K., Yulia, S. P., Lyudmila, K. V., & Dilovar, D. (2019). the implementation of the IoT concept in the post-industrial economy. *ESPACIOS, 40*(38), 28–39.

Dolat-Abadi, H. M. (2021). Optimizing decisions of fresh-product members in daily and bourse markets considering the quantity and quality deterioration: A waste-reduction approach. *Journal of Cleaner Production, 283*, 124647. doi:10.1016/j.jclepro.2020.124647

Dong, L., Ren, M., Xiang, Z., Zheng, P., Cong, J., & Chen, C. H. (2023). A novel smart product-service system configuration method for mass personalization based on knowledge graph. *Journal of Cleaner Production, 382*, 135270. doi:10.1016/j.jclepro.2022.135270

Donthu, N., Kumar, S., Mukherjee, D., Pandey, N., & Lim, W. M. (2021). How to conduct a bibliometric analysis: An overview and guidelines. *Journal of Business Research, 133*, 285–296. doi:10.1016/j.jbusres.2021.04.070

Doong, S.H., & Ho, S.-C. (2012). *The impact of ICT development on the global digital divide.* Academic Press.

Doong, S. H., & Ho, S.-C. (2012). The impact of ICT development on the global digital divide. *Electronic Commerce Research and Applications, 11*(5), 518–533. doi:10.1016/j.elerap.2012.02.002

Dorri, A., Kanhere, S. S., & Jurdak, R. (2017). Towards an Optimized BlockChain for IoT. *2017 IEEE/ACM Second International Conference on Internet-of-Things Design and Implementation (IoTDI),* 173-178.

Dorri, A., Kanhere, S. S., Jurdak, R., & Gauravaram, P. (2017). *Blockchain for IoT security and privacy: The case study of a smart home. In 2017 IEEE international conference on pervasive computing and communications workshops (PerCom workshops).* IEEE.

Drexler, N., & Lapr'e, V. B. (2019). For better or for worse: Shaping the hospitality industry through robotics and artificial intelligence. *Res. Hosp. Manag., 9*(2), 117–120. doi:10.1080/22243534.2019.1689701

Du, J., Jiang, C., Gelenbe, E., Xu, L., Li, J., & Ren, Y. (2018). Distributed data privacy preservation in IoT applications. *IEEE Wireless Communications, 25*(6), 68–76. doi:10.1109/MWC.2017.1800094

Duraipandian, M., & Vinothkanna, R. (2019). Cloud based Internet of Things for smart connected objects. *Journal of ISMAC, 1*(02), 111–119.

Earle, P.C., Gulker, M., & Stringham, E.P. (2022). *Decentralized Marketplaces with Privately Enforced Contracts: A Case Study of OpenBazaar*. Academic Press.

El Archi, Y., Benbba, B., Nizamatdinova, Z., Issakov, Y., Vargáné, G. I., & Dávid, L. D. (2023). Systematic Literature Review Analysing Smart Tourism Destinations in Context of Sustainable Development: Current Applications and Future Directions. *Sustainability (Basel), 15*(6), 5086. doi:10.3390u15065086

El Ouarrak, Y., & Hmioui, A. (2023, February). Communication between Supply Chain Actors: A Risk Reduction Factor in Supply Chains. In *International Congress on Information and Communication Technology* (pp. 695-703). Singapore: Springer Nature Singapore.

Elommal, N., & Manita, R. (2021). *How blockchain innovation could affect the audit profession: a qualitative study*. Academic Press.

Ennafiri, M., & Mazri, T. (2021). Internet of things for smart healthcare: A review on a potential IOT based system and technologies to control COVID-19 pandemic. In *Innovations in Smart Cities Applications Volume 4: The Proceedings of the 5th International Conference on Smart City Applications* (pp. 1256-1269). Springer International Publishing. 10.1007/978-3-030-66840-2_96

European Parliament. (2021). *What is artificial intelligence and how is it used?* https://www.europarl.europa.eu/news/en/headlines/society/20200827STO85804/what-is-artificial-intelligence-and-how-is-it-used

European Parliament. (2023a). *AI rules: What the European Parliament wants*. https://www.europarl.europa.eu/news/en/headlines/priorities/artificial-intelligence-in-the-eu/20201015STO89417/ai-rules-what-the-european-parliament-wants

European Parliament. (2023b). *Cybersecurity: Main and emerging threats*. https://www.europarl.europa.eu/news/en/headlines/society/20220120STO21428/cybersecurity-main-and-emerging-threats

Fabbe-Costes, N., & Lechaptois, L. (2022). Automotive supply chain digitalization: Lessons and perspectives. In B. L. MacCarthy & D. Ivanov (Eds.), *The Digital Supply Chain* (pp. 289–308). Elsevier. doi:10.1016/B978-0-323-91614-1.00017-4

Fang, X. (2020). *Exploring the impact of e-commerce on cities and villages: The case of Amazon and Alibaba* [Doctoral dissertation]. Tufts University.

Fernando, Y., Tseng, M. L., Wahyuni-Td, I. S., de Sousa Jabbour, A. B. L., Chiappetta Jabbour, C. J., & Foropon, C. (2023). Cyber supply chain risk management and performance in industry 4.0 era: Information system security practices in Malaysia. *Journal of Industrial and Production Engineering*, *40*(2), 102–116. doi:10.1080/21681015.2022.2116495

Ferrari, A. M., Volpi, L., Settembre-Blundo, D., & García-Muiña, F. E. (2021). Dynamic life cycle assessment (LCA) integrating life cycle inventory (LCI) and Enterprise resource planning (ERP) in an industry 4.0 environment. *Journal of Cleaner Production*, *286*, 125314. doi:10.1016/j.jclepro.2020.125314

Ferve, C., & Beamish, P. W. (2015). A Resource-Based Approach to the Study of Export Performance. *Journal of Small Business Management*, *41*, 242–261.

Forbes. (2021a). *The Future of Automotive and Mobility*. Forbes. https://www.forbes.com/sites/sap/2021/05/05/the-future-of-automotive-and-mobility/

Forbes. (2021b). *How The Automotive Industry Is Driving Toward A Sustainable Future*. Forbes. https://www.forbes.com/sites/sap/2021/12/01/how-the-automotive-industry-is-driving-toward-a-sustainable-future/

Foronda-Robles, C., Galindo-Pérez-de-Azpillaga, L., & Fernández-Tabales, A. (2023). Progress and stakes in sustainable tourism: Indicators for smart coastal destinations. *Journal of Sustainable Tourism*, *31*(7), 1518–1537. doi:10.1080/09669582.2020.1864386

Frazzon, E. M., Rodriguez, C. M. T., Pereira, M. M., Pires, M. C., & Uhlmann, I. (2019). Towards supply chain management 4.0. *Brazilian Journal of Operations & Production Management*, *16*(2), 180–191. doi:10.14488/BJOPM.2019.v16.n2.a2

Frederico, G. F. (2021). From supply chain 4.0 to supply chain 5.0: Findings from a systematic literature review and research directions. *Logistics*, *5*(3), 49. doi:10.3390/logistics5030049

Frederico, G. F., Garza-Reyes, J. A., Anosike, A., & Kumar, V. (2019). Supply Chain 4.0: Concepts, maturity and research agenda. *Supply Chain Management*, *25*(2), 262–282. doi:10.1108/SCM-09-2018-0339

Freund, C., & Pierola, M. (2010). Export entrepreneurs: evidence from Peru. *World Bank Policy Research Working Paper* 5407.

Galitsky, B. (2019). *Developing Enterprise Chatbots. Learning Linguistic Structures*. Springer. doi:10.1007/978-3-030-04299-8

Gamal, A., Abd El-Gawad, A. F., & Abouhawwash, M. (2023). Towards a Responsive Resilient Supply Chain based on Industry 5.0: A Case Study in Healthcare Systems. *Neutrosophic Systems with Applications*, *2*, 8–24. doi:10.61356/j.nswa.2023.7

Ganotakis, P., Konara, P., Kafouros, M., & Love, J. H. (2022). Taking a time-out from exporting: Implications for the likelihood of export re-entry and re-entry export performance. *Journal of World Business*, *7*(5), 1–15. doi:10.1016/j.jwb.2022.101349

Ghahremani-Nahr, J., Aliahmadi, A., & Nozari, H. (2022). An IoT-based sustainable supply chain framework and blockchain. *International Journal of Innovation in Engineering*, *2*(1), 12–21. doi:10.59615/ijie.2.1.12

Ghanbari, M. (2023). Presenting the smart-sustainable supply chain model based on artificial intelligence. *International Journal of Innovation in Management, Economics and Social Sciences*.

Ghazanfari, M., Mohammadi, H., Pishvaee, M. S., & Teimoury, E. (2019). Fresh-product trade management under government-backed incentives: A case study of the fresh flower market. *IEEE Transactions on Engineering Management*, *66*(4), 774–787. doi:10.1109/TEM.2018.2888982

Ghobakhloo, M., Iranmanesh, M., Morales, M. E., Nilashi, M., & Amran, A. (2023). Actions and approaches for enabling Industry 5.0-driven sustainable industrial transformation: A strategy roadmap. *Corporate Social Responsibility and Environmental Management*, *30*(3), 1473–1494. doi:10.1002/csr.2431

Ghosh, A., Gupta, S., Dua, A., & Kumar, N. (2020). Security of Cryptocurrencies in blockchain technology: State-of-art, challenges and future prospects. *Journal of Network and Computer Applications*, *163*, 102635. doi:10.1016/j.jnca.2020.102635

Giancaspro, M, (2017). *Is a 'smart contract' really a smart idea? Insights from a legal perspective*. Academic Press.

Gilchrist, A., (2016). *Introducing industry 4.0. Industry 4.0*. Apress. . doi:10.1007/978-1-4842-2047-4_13

Glova, J., Sabol, T., & Vajda, V. (2014). Business Models for the Internet of Things Environment. *Procedia Economics and Finance*, *15*, 1122–1129. doi:10.1016/S2212-5671(14)00566-8

Gohil, D., & Thakker, S. V. (2021). Blockchain-integrated technologies for solving supply chain challenges. *Modern Supply Chain Research and Applications*, *3*(2), 78–97. doi:10.1108/MSCRA-10-2020-0028

Gökalp, E., Gökalp, M. O., Çoban, S., & Eren, P. E. (2018). Analyzing opportunities and challenges of integrated blockchain technologies in healthcare. *Information Systems: Research, Development, Applications, Education: 11th SIGSAND/PLAIS EuroSymposium 2018, Gdansk, Poland, September 20, 2018. Proceedings*, *11*, 174–183.

Goudarzi, A., Ghayoor, F., Waseem, M., Fahad, S., & Traore, I. (2022). A Survey on IoT-Enabled Smart Grids: Emerging, Applications, Challenges, and Outlook. *Energies*, *15*(19), 6984. doi:10.3390/en15196984

Govindan, K., Salehian, F., Kian, H., Hosseini, S. T., & Mina, H. (2023). A location-inventory-routing problem to design a circular closed-loop supply chain network with carbon tax policy for achieving circular economy: An augmented epsilon-constraint approach. *International Journal of Production Economics*, *257*, 108771. doi:10.1016/j.ijpe.2023.108771

Gumboh, J., & Gichira, R. (2015). Supply chain collaboration among SMEs in Kenya: A review of collaboration barriers. *International Journal of Humanities and Social Science*, *5*(9), 2–5.

Guo, H., Meamari, E., & Shen, C.-C. (2019). Multi-authority attribute-based access control with smart contract. *Proceedings of the 2019 International Conference on Blockchain Technology*, 6-11. https://www.geeksforgeeks.org/smart-contracts-in-blockchain/

Guo, Y., Chen, J., & Liu, Z. (2022). Government responsiveness and public acceptance of big-data technology in urban governance: Evidence from China during the COVID-19 pandemic. *Cities (London, England)*, *122*, 103536. doi:10.1016/j.cities.2021.103536 PMID:34903901

Gupta, B. B., Gaurav, A., Panigrahi, P. K., & Arya, V. (2023). Analysis of artificial intelligence-based technologies and approaches on sustainable entrepreneurship. *Technological Forecasting and Social Change*, *186*, 122152. doi:10.1016/j.techfore.2022.122152

Gurkaynak, G., Yilmaz, I., Haksever, G., (2016). Stifling artificial intelligence: Human Perils. *Comput. Law Secur. Rep.*, *32*(5), 749–758. https://doi.org/.clsr.2016.05.003 doi:10.1016/j

Gursoy, D., & Chi, C. G. (2020). Effects of COVID-19 pandemic on hospitality industry: Review of the current situations and a research agenda. *Journal of Hospitality Marketing & Management*, *29*(5), 527–529. doi:10.1080/19368623.2020.1788231

Gurtu, A., & Johny, J. (2019). Potential of blockchain technology in supply chain management: A literature review. *International Journal of Physical Distribution & Logistics Management*, *49*(9), 881–900. doi:10.1108/IJPDLM-11-2018-0371

Hammi, B., Zeadally, S., Khatoun, R., & Nebhen, J. (2022). Survey on smart homes: Vulnerabilities, risks, and countermeasures. *Computers & Security*, *117*, 102677. doi:10.1016/j.cose.2022.102677

Hanafiah, H., & Widjaja, A. W. (2022). The influence of resource complementary, technology competence and supply chain risk criteria on supply chain collaboration (case study of export import activities in Indonesia). In *Proceeding of the International Conference on Family Business and Entrepreneurship* (*Vol. 3*, No. 1). Academic Press.

Han, Y., & Fang, X. (2023). Systematic review of adopting blockchain in supply chain management: Bibliometric analysis and theme discussion. *International Journal of Production Research*, 1–26. doi:10.1080/00207543.2023.2236241

Hao, F., Xiao, Q., & Chon, K. (2020). COVID-19 and China's hotel industry: Impacts, a disaster management framework, and post-pandemic agenda. *International Journal of Hospitality Management*, *90*, 102636. doi:10.1016/j.ijhm.2020.102636

Haque, M. & Islam, R. (2018). Impact of supply chain collaboration and knowledge sharing on organizational outcomes in pharmaceutical industry of Bangladesh. *Journal of Global Operations and Strategic Sourcing*.

Haque, A. B., Bhushan, B., & Dhiman, G. (2022). Conceptualizing smart city applications: Requirements, architecture, security issues, and emerging trends. *Expert Systems: International Journal of Knowledge Engineering and Neural Networks*, *39*(5), e12753. doi:10.1111/exsy.12753

Hartl, B., Kamleitner, B., & Holub, S. (2020). Take me on a ride: The role of environmentalist identity for carpooling. *Psychology and Marketing*, *37*(5), 663–676. doi:10.1002/mar.21340 PMID:32421017

Heaver, T. D. (2015). Increased collaborative relationships in international logistics: Canadian and other national and corporate examples. *Maritime Policy & Management*, *42*(3), 278–292. doi:10.1080/03088839.2013.873547

He, D., Wang, Y., & You, K. (2023). Market entry and the dynamics of export product quality: Evidence from Chinese manufacturing firms. *Economic Analysis and Policy*, *78*, 692–706. doi:10.1016/j.eap.2023.04.001

Hefny, M. H. M., Helmy, Y., & Abdelsalam, M. (2023). Open Banking API Framework to Improve the Online Transaction between Local Banks in Egypt Using Blockchain Technology. *Journal of Advances in Information Technology*, *14*(4), 729–740. doi:10.12720/jait.14.4.729-740

Helbing, D. (2019). *Societal, economic, ethical and legal challenges of the digital revolution: from big data to deep learning, artificial intelligence, and manipulative technologies*. Springer International Publishing.

Hendayani, R., & Alviyan, B. (2019). The Relationship between Supply Chain Collaboration of Value Innovation in Small Medium Enterprises and Supply Chain Capability as Mediator to Achieve Competitive Advantages. In *1st International Conference on Economics, Business, Entrepreneurship, and Finance.* Atlantis Press. 10.2991/icebef-18.2019.133

Henderson, J. C., & Ng, A. (2004). Responding to crisis: Severe acute respiratory syndrome (SARS) and hotels in Singapore. *International Journal of Tourism Research, 6*(6), 411–419. doi:10.1002/jtr.505

Hermann, M., Pentek, T., & Otto, B. (2016). Design principles for industry 4.0 scenarios. *49th Hawaii International Conference on System Sciences (HICSS)*, 3928–3937. https://doi.org/10.1109/HICSS.2016.488

Hohn, M. M., & Durach, C. F. (2023). Taking a different view: Theorizing on firms' development toward an integrative view on socially sustainable supply chain management. *International Journal of Physical Distribution & Logistics Management, 53*(1), 13–34. doi:10.1108/IJPDLM-09-2021-0410

Holko, M., Litwin, T. R., Munoz, F., Theisz, K. I., Salgin, L., Jenks, N. P., Holmes, B. W., Watson-McGee, P., Winford, E., & Sharma, Y. (2022). Wearable fitness tracker use in federally qualified health center patients: Strategies to improve the health of all of us using digital health devices. *NPJ Digital Medicine, 5*(1), 53. doi:10.103841746-022-00593-x PMID:35469045

Hollaway, I. S. (2017). Learning via sequential market entry: Evidence from international releases of U.S. movies. *Journal of International Economics, 40*, 104–121. doi:10.1016/j.jinteco.2016.10.008

Hopkins, J. L. (2021). An investigation into emerging industry 4.0 technologies as drivers of supply chain innovation in Australia. *Computers in Industry, 125*, 103323. doi:10.1016/j.compind.2020.103323

Hossein Motlagh, N., Mohammadrezaei, M., Hunt, J., & Zakeri, B. (2020). Internet of Things (IoT) and the energy sector. *Energies, 13*(2), 494. doi:10.3390/en13020494

Ho, T., Kumar, A., & Shiwakoti, N. (2020). Supply chain collaboration and performance: An empirical study of maturity model. *SN Applied Sciences, 2*(4), 1–16. doi:10.100742452-020-2468-y

Hotel Association of Canada. (2006). *Pandemic Preparedness & Response Plan* (613), 87. Retrieved from. www.hotelassociation.ca

Hu, K., Zhu, J., Ding, Y., Bai, X., & Huang, J. (2020). *Smart contract engineering*. Academic Press.

Hua, X., & Huang, Y. (2021). Understanding China's fintech sector: Development, impacts and risks. *European Journal of Finance, 27*(4-5), 321–333. doi:10.1080/1351847X.2020.1811131

Hurwitz, J., Bloor, R., Kaufman, M., Halper, F., (2009). *Service Oriented Architecture for Dummies®*. IBM Limited Edition.

Hussain, F. (2017). Internet of things: Building blocks and business models (No. 978-3, pp. 319-55404). Berlin, Germany: Springer International Publishing.

İncekara, Ç. Ö. (2023). Industrial internet of things (IIoT) in energy sector. *Advanced Engineering Science*, *3*, 21–30.

International Energy Agency. (2020). *Global EV Outlook 2020*. https://www.iea.org/reports/global-ev-outlook-2020

International Federation of Robotics. (2023). *Top 5 robot trends 2023*. https://ifr.org/ifr-press-releases/news/top-5-robot-trends-2023

Investopedia. (2021). *What Regulations Affect the Automotive Sector?* Investopedia. https://www.investopedia.com/ask/answers/042015/how-much-impact-does-government-regulation-have-automotive-sector.asp

Iqbal, J., Khan, Z. H., & Khalid, A. (2017). Prospects of robotics in food industry. *Food Science and Technology (Campinas)*, *37*(2), 159–165. doi:10.1590/1678-457x.14616

Ivanov, S., & Webster, C. (2017). Designing robot-friendly hospitality facilities. *Proceedings of the Scientific Conference Tourism. Innovations. Strategies*, 74–81.

Ivanov, D. (2023). The Industry 5.0 framework: Viability-based integration of the resilience, sustainability, and human-centricity perspectives. *International Journal of Production Research*, *61*(5), 1683–1695. doi:10.1080/00207543.2022.2118892

Ivanov, D., & Dolgui, A. (2019). New disruption risk management perspectives in supply chains: Digital twins, the ripple effect, and resileanness. *IFAC-PapersOnLine*, *52*(13), 337–342. doi:10.1016/j.ifacol.2019.11.138

Jain, A. (2023). *After China and US, India becomes world's 3rd largest auto market: Report*. Mint. https://www.livemint.com/news/india/india-becomes-world-s-3rd-largest-auto-market-report-11673164107467.html

JATO. (2023). *Peugeot 208 ends Volkswagen Golf's 14 year reign as Europe's best-selling car in 2022*. https://www.jato.com/peugeot-208-ends-volkswagen-golfs-14-year-reign-as-europes-best-selling-car-in-2022/

Jaturat, N., Jaturat, M., Tonsakun-Aree, C., & Deelert, J. (2022). *Effect of Enterprise Resource Planning on Supply Chain Forecasting Capability through Collaboration: An Empirical Study of Frozen Foods Industry in Thailand*. Academic Press.

Jayashri, N., Rampur, V., Gangodkar, D., Abirami, M., Balarengadurai, C., & Kumar, A. (2023). Improved block chain system for high secured IoT integrated supply chain. *Measurement. Sensors*, *25*, 100633. doi:10.1016/j.measen.2022.100633

Jeenanunta, C., Ueki, Y., & Visanvetchakij, T. (2013). Supply chain collaboration and firm performance in Thai automotive and electronics industries. *Global Business Perspectives*, *1*(4), 418–432. doi:10.100740196-013-0031-6

Jeng, D. J. F. (2015). Generating a causal model of supply chain collaboration using the fuzzy DEMATEL technique. *Computers & Industrial Engineering*, *87*, 283–295. doi:10.1016/j.cie.2015.05.007

Jiang, Y., & Wen, J. (2020). Effects of COVID-19 on hotel marketing and management: A perspective article. *International Journal of Contemporary Hospitality Management*, *32*(8), 2563–2573. doi:10.1108/IJCHM-03-2020-0237

Joo, Y. M. (2023). Developmentalist smart cities? The cases of Singapore and Seoul. *International Journal of Urban Sciences*, *27*(sup1), 164-182.

Jovanovic, B. (1982). Selection and the evolution of industry. *Econometrica*, *50*(3), 649–670. doi:10.2307/1912606

Jraisat, L., Upadhyay, A., Ghalia, T., Jresseit, M., Kumar, V., & Sarpong, D. (2023). Triads in sustainable supply-chain perspective: Why is a collaboration mechanism needed? *International Journal of Production Research*, *61*(14), 4725–4741. doi:10.1080/00207543.2021.1936263

Jum'a, L. (2023). The role of blockchain-enabled supply chain applications in improving supply chain performance: The case of Jordanian manufacturing sector. *Management Research Review*, *46*(10), 1315–1333. doi:10.1108/MRR-04-2022-0298

Kamble, S. S., & Gunasekaran, A. (2020). Big data-driven supply chain performance measurement system: A review and framework for implementation. *International Journal of Production Research*, *58*(1), 65–86. doi:10.1080/00207543.2019.1630770

Kamble, S. S., Gunasekaran, A., Subramanian, N., Ghadge, A., Belhadi, A., & Venkatesh, M. (2023). Blockchain technology's impact on supply chain integration and sustainable supply chain performance: Evidence from the automotive industry. *Annals of Operations Research*, *327*(1), 575–600. doi:10.100710479-021-04129-6

Karamitsos, I., Papadaki, M., & Al Barghuthi, N.B. (2018). *Design of the blockchain smart contract: A use case for real estate*. Academic Press.

Karmaker, C. L., Bari, A. M., Anam, M. Z., Ahmed, T., Ali, S. M., de Jesus Pacheco, D. A., & Moktadir, M. A. (2023). Industry 5.0 challenges for post-pandemic supply chain sustainability in an emerging economy. *International Journal of Production Economics*, *258*, 108806. doi:10.1016/j.ijpe.2023.108806

Karthick, A. V., & Gopalsamy, S. (2023, January). Role of IoT in Business Sustainability. In *International Conference on Economics, Business and Sustainability* (pp. 9-15). Singapore: Springer Nature Singapore.

Kasahara, H., & Tang, H. (2019). Excessive entry and exit in export markets. *Journal of the Japanese and International Economies*, *53*, 101–131. doi:10.1016/j.jjie.2019.101031

Kashem, M. A., Shamsuddoha, M., Nasir, T., & Chowdhury, A. A. (2023). Supply Chain Disruption versus Optimization: A Review on Artificial Intelligence and Blockchain. *Knowledge (Beverly Hills, Calif.)*, *3*(1), 80–96.

Khan, S.N., Loukil, F., Ghedira-Guegan, C., Benkhelifa, E., & Bani-Hani, A. (2021). *Blockchain smart contracts: Applications, challenges, and future trends*. Academic Press.

Khan, K. M., Arshad, J., & Khan, M. M. (2018). Secure digital voting system based on blockchain technology. *International Journal of Electronic Government Research*, *14*(1), 53–62. doi:10.4018/IJEGR.2018010103

Khan, K., & Keramati, A. (2023). A Framework for Smart Supply Chain Risk Assessment: An Empirical Study. *International Journal of Information Systems and Supply Chain Management*, *16*(1), 1–17. doi:10.4018/IJISSCM.316167

Khan, M. A., Sajjad, I. A., Tahir, M., & Haseeb, A. (2022). IOT Application for Energy Management in Smart Homes. *Engineering Proceedings*, *20*(1), 43.

Kiktenko, E. O., Pozhar, N. O., Anufriev, M. N., Trushechkin, A. S., Yunusov, R. R., Kurochkin, Y. V., Lvovsky, A. I., & Fedorov, A. K. (2018). Quantum-secured blockchain. *Quantum Science and Technology*, *3*(3), 035004. doi:10.1088/2058-9565/aabc6b

Kim, S., & Kim, D. (2023). *Securing the Cyber Resilience of a Blockchain-Based Railroad Non-Stop Customs Clearance System*. Academic Press.

Kline, S., Almanza, B., & Neal, J. (2014). Hotel guest room cleaning: a systematic approach. In B. Almanza, R. Ghiselli, & K. Mahmood (Eds.), *Food Safety: Researching the Hazard in Hazardous Foods* (pp. 303–322). CRC Press Taylor and Francis.

Kolisnyk, M., Kharchenko, V., & Piskachova, I. (2022). Investigation of the smart business center for IoT systems availability considering attacks on the router. In *Dependable IoT for Human and Industry* (pp. 169–195). River Publishers. doi:10.1201/9781003337843-11

Korpela, K., Hallikas, J., & Dahlberg, T. (2017). *Digital supply chain transformation toward blockchain integration*. Academic Press.

Kos, A., Milutinović, V., & Umek, A. (2019). Challenges in wireless communication for connected sensors and wearable devices used in sport biofeedback applications. *Future Generation Computer Systems*, *92*, 582–592. doi:10.1016/j.future.2018.03.032

Kouhizadeh, M., Zhu, Q., & Sarkis, J. (2020). Blockchain and the circular economy: Potential tensions and critical reflections from practice. *Production Planning and Control*, *31*(11-12), 950–966. doi:10.1080/09537287.2019.1695925

Kumar, S., & Mallipeddi, R. R. (2022). Impact of cybersecurity on operations and supply chain management: Emerging trends and future research directions. *Production and Operations Management*, *31*(12), 4488–4500. doi:10.1111/poms.13859

Kuo, C. M., Chen, L. C., & Lu, C. Y. (2012). Factorial validation of hospitality service attitude. *International Journal of Hospitality Management*, *31*(3), 944–951. doi:10.1016/j.ijhm.2011.11.002

Kusiak, A. (2023). Smart manufacturing. In *Springer Handbook of Automation* (pp. 973–985). Springer International Publishing. doi:10.1007/978-3-030-96729-1_45

Kwak, J., Zhang, Y., & Yu, J. (2019). Legitimacy building and e-commerce platform development in China: The experience of Alibaba. *Technological Forecasting and Social Change, 139*, 115–124. doi:10.1016/j.techfore.2018.06.038 PMID:32287407

Lai, Z., & Lo, E. (2023). Blockchains for Business–Permissioned Blockchains. *Blockchains: Empowering Technologies and Industrial Applications*.

Lang, K. R., Xu, J., Zhu, B., Liu, X., Shaw, M. J., Zhang, H., & Fan, M. (Eds.). (2021). *Smart Business: Technology and Data Enabled Innovative Business Models and Practices: 18th Workshop on E-Business, WeB 2019, Munich, Germany, December 14, 2019, Revised Selected Papers* (Vol. 403). Springer Nature.

Lan, L., Shi, R., Wang, B., & Zhang, L. (2019). An IoT unified access platform for heterogeneity sensing devices based on edge computing. *IEEE Access, 7*, 44199-44211.

Leal Filho, W., Yang, P., Eustachio, J. H. P. P., Azul, A. M., Gellers, J. C., Gielczyk, A., Dinis, M. A. P., & Kozlova, V. (2023). Deploying digitalisation and artificial intelligence in sustainable development research. *Environment, Development and Sustainability, 25*(6), 4957–4988. doi:10.100710668-022-02252-3 PMID:35313685

Lee, D. K. C., & Low, L. (2018). *Inclusive fintech: blockchain, cryptocurrency and ICO*. World Scientific. doi:10.1142/9789813238640_0007

Lee, I. (2019). The Internet of Things for enterprises: An ecosystem, architecture, and IoT service business model. *Internet of Things : Engineering Cyber Physical Human Systems, 7*, 100078. doi:10.1016/j.iot.2019.100078

Lee, I. (Ed.). (2017). *The Internet of Things in the Modern Business Environment*. IGI Global. doi:10.4018/978-1-5225-2104-4

Lee, I., & Lee, K. (2015). The Internet of Things (IoT): Applications, investments, and challenges for enterprises. *Business Horizons, 58*(4), 431–440. doi:10.1016/j.bushor.2015.03.008

Lee, S. M., & Lee, D. (2021). Opportunities and challenges for contactless healthcare services in the post-COVID-19 Era. *Technological Forecasting and Social Change, 167*, 120712. doi:10.1016/j.techfore.2021.120712 PMID:33654330

Li, S.S., & Karahanna, E. (2015). *Online recommendation systems in a B2C E-commerce context: a review and future directions*. Academic Press.

Lindsay, A., Downs, D., & Lunn, K. (2003). *Business processes—attempts to find a definition*. Academic Press.

Li, S., & Karahanna, E. (2015). Online Recommendation Systems in a B2C E-Commerce Context: A Review and Future Directions. *Journal of the Association for Information Systems, 16*(2), 72–107. doi:10.17705/1jais.00389

Li, S., Xu, T., Park, K. C., & Kang, M. (2023). The effect of supply chain collaboration on firms' risk management under technology turbulence. *Production Planning and Control*, 1–16. doi:10.1080/09537287.2023.2225474

Liu, B., & De Giovanni, P. (2019). *Green process innovation through Industry 4.0 technologies and supply chain coordination*. Academic Press.

Liu, X. (2018). *LRN 2016 SPECIAL–the antecedents and consequences of reduction within a supply chain collaboration orientation of CO2 emissions: evidence from China*. Academic Press.

Liu, D., Wang, Q., Wang, A., & Yao, S. (2023). Export profitability and firm R&D: On China's export diversification under trade war. *Structural Change and Economic Dynamics*, *67*, 151–166. doi:10.1016/j.strueco.2023.07.012

Liu, R., Ran, W., & Liu, S. (2023). Blockchain Technology Applied to Supply Chain Management: A Systems' Analysis. *Mobile Information Systems*, *2023*, 2023. doi:10.1155/2023/6046503

Li, X., Wang, B., Liu, C., Freiheit, T., & Epureanu, B. I. (2020). Intelligent manufacturing systems in COVID-19 pandemic and beyond: Framework and impact assessment. *Chinese Journal of Mechanical Engineering*, *33*(1), 58. doi:10.118610033-020-00476-w

Lo, A., Cheung, C., & Law, R. (2006). The survival of hotels during disaster: A case study of Hong Kong in 2003. *Asia Pacific Journal of Tourism Research*, *11*(1), 65–80. doi:10.1080/10941660500500733

Longo, F., Padovano, A., & Umbrello, S. (2020). Value-oriented and ethical technology engineering in industry 5.0: A human-centric perspective for the design of the factory of the future. *Applied Sciences (Basel, Switzerland)*, *10*(12), 1–25. doi:10.3390/app10124182

Lundvall, B. Å., & Rikap, C. (2022). China's catching-up in artificial intelligence seen as a co-evolution of corporate and national innovation systems. *Research Policy*, *51*(1), 104395. doi:10.1016/j.respol.2021.104395

Lynch, J. (2019). Effective Supply Chain Collaboration. In Contemporary Operations and Logistics (pp. 193-218). Palgrave Macmillan. doi:10.1007/978-3-030-14493-7_11

Maddikunta, P. K. R., Pham, Q. V., Prabadevi, B., Deepa, N., Dev, K., Gadekallu, T. R., ... Liyanage, M. (2022). Industry 5.0: A survey on enabling technologies and potential applications. *Journal of Industrial Information Integration*, *26*, 100257. doi:10.1016/j.jii.2021.100257

Ma, H. L., Wang, Z. X., & Chan, F. T. (2020). How important are supply chain collaborative factors in supply chain finance? A view of financial service providers in China. *International Journal of Production Economics*, *219*, 341–346. doi:10.1016/j.ijpe.2019.07.002

Majeed, A. A., & Rupasinghe, T. D. (2017). Internet of things (IoT) embedded future supply chains for industry 4.0: An assessment from an ERP-based fashion apparel and footwear industry. *International Journal of Supply Chain Management*, *6*(1), 25–40.

Malburg, L., Hoffmann, M., & Bergmann, R. (2023). Applying MAPE-K control loops for adaptive workflow management in smart factories. *Journal of Intelligent Information Systems*, *61*(1), 1–29. doi:10.100710844-022-00766-w

Manavalan, E., & Jayakrishna, K. (2019). A review of Internet of Things (IoT) embedded sustainable supply chain for industry 4.0 requirements. *Computers & Industrial Engineering*, *127*, 925–953. doi:10.1016/j.cie.2018.11.030

Margherita, E. G., & Braccini, A. M. (2021). Managing industry 4.0 automation for fair ethical business development: A single case study. *Technological Forecasting and Social Change*, *172*, 121048. doi:10.1016/j.techfore.2021.121048

Markus, S., & Buijs, P. (2022). Beyond the hype: How blockchain affects supply chain performance. *Supply Chain Management*, *27*(7), 177–193. doi:10.1108/SCM-03-2022-0109

Masoomi, L., Taran-Lala, O., Smith, C. V., & Trollman, H. (2023). Leveraging Industry 4.0 for Supply Chain Collaboration: Creating Competitive Advantage for Small Farms in the United Kingdom and Ukraine. *Engineering Proceedings*, *40*(1), 21.

Mathieson, R. (2023). *These 10 Things Will Shape Politics in 2023*. Bloomberg. https://www.bloomberg.com/news/newsletters/2023-01-03/these-10-things-will-shape-politics-in-2023

Mckay, B. (2023). *Global Sustainability Trends for 2023 - according to 42 experts*. Greenmatch. https://www.greenmatch.co.uk/blog/sustainability-trends

Minoli, D., Sohraby, K., & Occhiogrosso, B. (2017). IoT considerations, requirements, and architectures for smart buildings—Energy optimization and next-generation building management systems. *IEEE Internet of Things Journal*, *4*(1), 269–283. doi:10.1109/JIOT.2017.2647881

Mirdad, A., Hussain, F. K., & Hussain, O. K. (2023). A systematic literature review on pharmaceutical supply chain: Research gaps and future opportunities. *International Journal of Web and Grid Services*, *19*(2), 233–258. doi:10.1504/IJWGS.2023.131243

Misbauddin, S. M., Alam, M. J., Karmaker, C. L., Nabi, M. N. U., & Hasan, M. M. (2023). Exploring the antecedents of supply chain viability in a pandemic context: An empirical study on the commercial flower supply chain of an emerging economy. *Sustainability (Basel)*, *15*(3), 2146. doi:10.3390u15032146

Mitra, S., Kumar, H., Gupta, M. P., & Bhattacharya, J. (2023). Entrepreneurship in smart cities: Elements of Start-up Ecosystem. *Journal of Science and Technology Policy Management*, *14*(3), 592–611. doi:10.1108/JSTPM-06-2021-0078

Modak, S. K. S. (2023). Application of Blockchain in Supply Chain Management. *International Journal For Multidisciplinary Research*, *5*(2), 1–9. doi:10.36948/ijfmr.2023.v05i02.2216

Mogelonsky, L. (2020). *Why Hoteliers Should Make Guestroom IoT a Top Priority (After COVID Safety Measures)*. https://hoteltechnologynews.com/2020/07/why-hot eliers-should-make-guestroom-iot-a-top-priority-after-covid-safety-measures/

Mohammadi, H., Ghazanfari, M., Pishvaee, M. S., & Teimoury, E. (2019). Fresh-product supply chain coordination and waste reduction using a revenue-and-preservation-technology-investment-sharing contract: A real-life case study. *Journal of Cleaner Production*, *213*, 262–282. doi:10.1016/j.jclepro.2018.12.120

Mohanta, B. K., Panda, S. S., & Jena, D. (2018). An overview of smart contract and use cases in blockchain technology. *2018 9th international conference on computing, communication and networking technologies (ICCCNT)*, 1-4.

Mondol, E. P. (2021). The impact of block chain and smart inventory system on supply chain performance at retail industry. *International Journal of Computations, Information and Manufacturing, 1*(1).

Morales, E., Sheu, G., & Zahler, A. (2011). *Gravity and extended gravity: estimating a structural model of export entry.* Mimeo.

Morrison, W. M. (2019). China's economic rise: History, trends, challenges, and implications for the United States. *Current Politics and Economics of Northern and Western Asia*, *28*(2/3), 189–242.

Morton, H. (n.d.). *Summary blockchain 2022 legislation*. National Conference of State Legislatures. https://www.ncsl.org/financial-services/blockchain-2022-legislation

Motia, K., Kumar, R., & Luthra, S. (2023). Role of cyber-physical system and Industry 4.0 in smart manufacturing industries for business excellence. *International Journal of Business Excellence*, *31*(2), 258–271. doi:10.1504/IJBEX.2023.134499

Mukherjee, S., Kumar, R., & Banerjee, S. (2022). Smart Healthcare Remote Monitoring System Using Internet of Things. In *Intelligent Systems for Social Good: Theory and Practice* (pp. 99–115). Springer Nature Singapore. doi:10.1007/978-981-19-0770-8_9

Nadkarni, S., Kriechbaumer, F., Rothenberger, M., & Christodoulidou, N. (2019). The path to the hotel of things: Internet of things and big data converging in hospitality. *Journal of Hospitality and Tourism Technology*, *11*(1), 93–107. doi:10.1108/JHTT-12-2018-0120

Nagy, J., Oláh, J., Erdei, E., Máté, D., & Popp, J. (2018). The role and impact of Industry 4.0 and the internet of things on the business strategy of the value chain—The case of Hungary. *Sustainability (Basel)*, *10*(10), 3491. doi:10.3390u10103491

Nagy, S. G., & Stukovszky, T. (Eds.). (2023). *Smart Business and Digital Transformation: An Industry 4.0 Perspective*. Taylor & Francis. doi:10.4324/9781003390312

Nahavandi, S. (2019). Industry 5.0-a human-centric solution. *Sustainability (Basel)*, *11*(16), 4371. Advance online publication. doi:10.3390u11164371

Nahr, J. G., Nozari, H., & Sadeghi, M. E. (2021). Green supply chain based on artificial intelligence of things (AIoT). International Journal of Innovation in Management. *Economics and Social Sciences*, *1*(2), 56–63.

Najafi, S. E., Nozari, H., & Edalatpanah, S. A. (2022). Artificial Intelligence of Things (AIoT) and Industry 4.0–Based Supply Chain (FMCG Industry). *A Roadmap for Enabling Industry 4.0 by Artificial Intelligence*, 31-41.

Narayanan, S., Jayaraman, V., Luo, Y., & Swaminathan, J. M. (2011). The antecedents of process integration in business process outsourcing and its effect on firm performance. *Journal of Operations Management*, *29*(1-2), 3–16. doi:10.1016/j.jom.2010.05.001

Nayeri, S., Sazvar, Z., & Heydari, J. (2023). Towards a responsive supply chain based on the industry 5.0 dimensions: A novel decision-making method. *Expert Systems with Applications*, *213*, 119267. doi:10.1016/j.eswa.2022.119267

Nayyar, A., & Kumar, A. (Eds.). (2020). *A roadmap to industry 4.0: smart production, sharp business and sustainable development* (pp. 1–21). Springer. doi:10.1007/978-3-030-14544-6

Neuhofer, B., Buhalis, D., & Ladkin, A. (2013). High tech for high touch experiences: a case study from the hospitality industry. In L. Cantoni & Z. Xiang (Eds.), *Information and Communication Technologies in Tourism 2013*. Springer. doi:10.1007/978-3-642-36309-2_25

Nozari, H., & Szmelter-Jarosz, A. (2022). *IoT-based Supply Chain For Smart Business* (Vol. 1). ISNET.

Nozari, H., Fallah, M., Szmelter-Jarosz, A., & Krzemiński, M. (2021). Analysis of security criteria for IoT-based supply chain: a case study of FMCG industries. *Central European Management Journal, 29*(4).

Nozari, H., Ghahremani-Nahr, J., & Najafi, E. (2023). The Role of Internet of Things and Blockchain in the Development of Agile and Sustainable Supply Chains. In Digital Supply Chain, Disruptive Environments, and the Impact on Retailers (pp. 271-282). IGI Global.

Nozari, H., Ghahremani-Nahr, J., & Najafi, E. (2023). The Role of Internet of Things and Blockchain in the Development of Agile and Sustainable Supply Chains. In Digital Supply Chain, Disruptive Environments, and the Impact on Retailers (pp. 271-282). IGI Global. doi:10.4018/978-1-6684-7298-9.ch015

Nozari, H., Ghahremani-Nahr, J., & Szmelter-Jarosz, A. (2023). AI and machine learning for real-world problems. *Advances In Computers.*

Nozari, H., Ghahremani-Nahr, J., Fallah, M., & Szmelter-Jarosz, A. (2022). Assessment of cyber risks in an IoT-based supply chain using a fuzzy decision-making method. *International Journal of Innovation in Management, Economics and Social Sciences, 2*(1).

Nozari, H., Tavakkoli-Moghaddam, R., Ghahremani-Nahr, J., & Najafi, E. (2023). *A conceptual framework for Artificial Intelligence of Medical Things (AIoMT)*. Academic Press.

Nozari, H., Fallah, M., Kazemipoor, H., & Najafi, S. E. (2021). Big data analysis of IoT-based supply chain management considering FMCG industries. *Бизнес-информатика*, *15*(1, 1 (eng)), 78–96. doi:10.17323/2587-814X.2021.1.78.96

Nozari, H., & Ghahremani-Nahr, J. (2022). Assessing Key performance indicators in Blockchain-Based Supply Chain Financing: Case Study of Chain Stores. *International Journal of Innovation in Engineering*, *2*(3), 42–58. doi:10.59615/ijie.2.3.42

Nozari, H., Ghahremani-Nahr, J., & Szmelter-Jarosz, A. (2023). A multi-stage stochastic inventory management model for transport companies including several different transport modes. *International Journal of Management Science and Engineering Management*, *18*(2), 134–144. doi:10.1080/17509653.2022.2042747

Nozari, H., Ghahremani-Nahr, J., & Szmelter-Jarosz, A. (2023). AI and machine learning for real-world problems. *Advances In Computers*.

Nozari, H., Najafi, E., Fallah, M., & Hosseinzadeh Lotfi, F. (2019). Quantitative analysis of key performance indicators of green supply chain in FMCG industries using non-linear fuzzy method. *Mathematics*, *7*(11), 1020. doi:10.3390/math7111020

Nozari, H., & Sadeghi, M. E. (2021). Artificial intelligence and Machine Learning for Real-world problems (A survey). *International Journal of Innovation in Engineering*, *1*(3), 38–47. doi:10.59615/ijie.1.3.38

Nozari, H., Szmelter-Jarosz, A., & Ghahremani-Nahr, J. (2021). The Ideas of Sustainable and Green Marketing Based on the Internet of Everything—The Case of the Dairy Industry. *Future Internet*, *13*(10), 266. doi:10.3390/fi13100266

Nozari, H., Szmelter-Jarosz, A., & Ghahremani-Nahr, J. (2022). Analysis of the challenges of artificial intelligence of things (AIoT) for the smart supply chain (case study: FMCG industries). *Sensors (Basel)*, *22*(8), 2931. doi:10.339022082931 PMID:35458916

Ochoa, W., Larrinaga, F., & Pérez, A. (2023). Architecture for managing AAS-based business processes. *Procedia Computer Science*, *217*, 217–226. doi:10.1016/j.procs.2022.12.217

Ocicka, B., Baraniecka, A., & Jefmański, B. (2022). Exploring supply chain collaboration for green innovations: Evidence from the high-tech industry in Poland. *Energies*, *15*(5), 1750. doi:10.3390/en15051750

Ogudo, K. A., Muwawa Jean Nestor, D., Ibrahim Khalaf, O., & Daei Kasmaei, H. (2019). A device performance and data analytics concept for smartphones' IoT services and machine-type communication in cellular networks. *Symmetry*, *11*(4), 593. doi:10.3390ym11040593

Okoroafor, I. B., Okechukwu, C. N., & Anuonye, R. C. & Uka, C. O. (2020). Application of Least Square Dummy Variable (LSDV) In Estimation Of Compensation Of Employée. *European Journal of Statistics and Probability.*, *8*(3), 35–38.

Oladinrin, O. T., Arif, M., Rana, M. Q., & Gyoh, L. (2023). Interrelations between construction ethics and innovation: A bibliometric analysis using VOSviewer. *Construction Innovation*, *23*(3), 505–523. doi:10.1108/CI-07-2021-0130

Olawumi, T. O., Chan, D. W., Saka, A. B., Ekundayo, D., & Odeh, A. O. (2023). Are there any gains in green-tech adoption? Unearthing the beneficial outcomes of smart-sustainable practices in Nigeria and Hong Kong built environment. *Journal of Cleaner Production*, *410*, 137280. doi:10.1016/j.jclepro.2023.137280

Olynec, N. (2023). *13 sustainability trends driving business in 2023*. IMD. https://www.imd.org/ibyimd/sustainability/13-sustainability-trends-driving-business-in-2023/

Omidi, F., Hosseini, S.A. and Rekabdar, G. (2023), Designing a Model for the Application of IoT in Export Businesses Using the Grounded Theory (A Case Study of Agricultural Machinery Exporter Companies), *Journal of Business Administration Researches*. doi. doi:10.22034/JBAR.2023.19577.4268

Oubrahim, I., Sefiani, N., & Happonen, A. (2022). Supply Chain Performance Evaluation Models: A Literature Review. *Acta logistica, 9*(2), 207-221.

Oudani, M., Sebbar, A., Zkik, K., El Harraki, I., & Belhadi, A. (2023). Green Blockchain based IoT for secured supply chain of hazardous materials. *Computers & Industrial Engineering*, *175*, 108814. doi:10.1016/j.cie.2022.108814

Ozdemir, V., & Hekim, N. (2018). Birth of industry 5.0: Making sense of big data with artificial intelligence, "the internet of things" and next-generation technology policy. *Omics A J. Integrative Biology*, *22*(1), 65–76. doi:10.1089/omi.2017.0194

Pan, S. L., & Nishant, R. (2023). Artificial intelligence for digital sustainability: An insight into domain-specific research and future directions. *International Journal of Information Management*, *72*, 102668. doi:10.1016/j.ijinfomgt.2023.102668

Park, H. M. (2009). *Linear Regression Models for Panel Data Using SAS*. Stata, LIMDEP, and SPSS, University Information Technology Services Center for Statistical and Mathematical Computing Indiana University.

Park, H., Kline, S. F., Kim, J., Almanza, B., & Ma, J. (2019). Does hotel cleanliness correlate with surfaces guests contact? *International Journal of Contemporary Hospitality Management*, *31*(7), 2933–2950. doi:10.1108/IJCHM-02-2018-0105

Pathak, P., Pal, P. R., Shrivastava, M., & Ora, P. (2019). Fifth revolution: Applied AI & human intelligence with cyber physical systems. *International Journal of Engineering and Advanced Technology*, *8*(3), 23–27.

Pedro, F. (2023). Foundational Aspects of Smart Cities Leading the Digital Economy-An Review. *Journal of Computing and Natural Science, 3*(1), 35-45.

Perkins, D. H. (2023). Structural challenges to sustained economic growth in China. *China & World Economy*, *31*(1), 22–43. doi:10.1111/cwe.12457

Pesch, P.J., & Sillaber, C. (2017). *Distributed ledger, joint control? Blockchains and the GDPR's transparency requirements*. Academic Press.

Petit, A., & Cambon, L. (2016). Exploratory study of the implications of research on the use of smart connected devices for prevention: A scoping review. *BMC Public Health*, *16*(1), 1–13. doi:10.118612889-016-3225-4 PMID:27401769

Petrillo, A., Felice, F. D., Cioffi, R., & Zomparelli, F. (2018). *Fourth Industrial Revolution: Current Practices, Challenges, and Opportunities*. https://www.intechopen.com/boo ks/digital-transformation-in-smart-manufacturing/fourth-industrial-revolution-current-practices-challenges-and-opportunities

Peugeot. (n.d.-a). *History: an incredible story since 1810*. Peugeot. https://www.peugeot.co.nz/brand/peugeot-universe/history.html

Peugeot. (n.d.-b). *Our competitive advantage and value-added services*. https://www.peugeot.co.ke/about-us/our-competitive-advantage-and-value-added-services.html

Poon, T., Choy, K.L., Chow, H.K., Lau, H.C., Chan, F.T., & Ho, K. (2009). *A RFID case-based logistics resource management system for managing order-picking operations in warehouses*. Academic Press.

Popkova, E. G., Sergi, B. S., & Bogoviz, A. V. (2023). Evolution of environmental economics and management in the age of artificial intelligence for sustainable development. *Frontiers in Environmental Science*, *11*, 545. doi:10.3389/fenvs.2023.1176612

Pradabwong, J., Braziotis, C., Tannock, J. D., & Pawar, K. S. (2017). Business process management and supply chain collaboration: Effects on performance and competitiveness. *Supply Chain Management*, *22*(2), 107–121. doi:10.1108/SCM-01-2017-0008

Prieto, N. P., & Martín-Peña, M. L. (2023). The smart supply chain: A conceptual cyclic framework. *Journal of Industrial Engineering and Management*, *16*(1), 54–77. doi:10.3926/jiem.4018

Qi, B., Shen, Y., & Xu, T. (2023). An artificial-intelligence-enabled sustainable supply chain model for B2C E-commerce business in the international trade. *Technological Forecasting and Social Change*, *191*, 122491. doi:10.1016/j.techfore.2023.122491

Quasim, M. T., Khan, M. A., Abdullah, M., Meraj, M., Singh, S. P., & Johri, P. (2019, December). Internet of things for smart healthcare: a hardware perspective. In *2019 First International Conference of Intelligent Computing and Engineering (ICOICE)* (pp. 1-5). IEEE. 10.1109/ICOICE48418.2019.9035175

Rafique, W., Qi, L., Yaqoob, I., Imran, M., Rasool, R. U., & Dou, W. (2020). Complementing IoT services through software defined networking and edge computing: A comprehensive survey. *IEEE Communications Surveys and Tutorials*, *22*(3), 1761–1804. doi:10.1109/COMST.2020.2997475

Rainer, R. K., & Prince, B. (2022). *Introduction to information systems: Supporting and transforming business*. John Wiley & Sons.

Raja Santhi, A., & Muthuswamy, P. (2022). Influence of blockchain technology in manufacturing supply chain and logistics. *Logistics*, *6*(1), 15. doi:10.3390/logistics6010015

Rajasekaran, A. S., Azees, M., & Al-Turjman, F. (2022). A comprehensive survey on blockchain technology. *Sustainable Energy Technologies and Assessments*, *52*, 102039. doi:10.1016/j.seta.2022.102039

Ralston, P. M., Richey, R. G., & Grawe, S. J. (2017). The past and future of supply chain collaboration: A literature synthesis and call for research. *International Journal of Logistics Management*. Advance online publication. doi:10.1108/IJLM-09-2015-0175

Ramanathan, U. (2017). How Smart Operations Help Better Planning and Replenishment? Empirical Study–Supply Chain Collaboration for Smart Operations. In Supply Chain Management in the Big Data Era (pp. 25-49). IGI Global.

Ramanathan, U. (2012). Supply chain collaboration for improved forecast accuracy of promotional sales. *International Journal of Operations & Production Management*, *32*(6), 676–695. doi:10.1108/01443571211230925

Ramanathan, U., & Gunasekaran, A. (2014). Supply chain collaboration: Impact of success in long-term partnerships. *International Journal of Production Economics*, *147*, 252–259. doi:10.1016/j.ijpe.2012.06.002

Ramesh, A., Banwet, D. K., & Shankar, R. (2010). Modeling the barriers of supply chain collaboration. *Journal of Modelling in Management*, *5*(2), 176–193. doi:10.1108/17465661011061014

Ra, N., Ghosh, A., & Bhattacharjee, A. (2023). IoT-based smart energy management for solar vanadium redox flow battery powered switchable building glazing satisfying the HVAC system of EV charging stations. *Energy Conversion and Management*, *281*, 116851. doi:10.1016/j.enconman.2023.116851

Rana, S. K., Kim, H. C., Pani, S. K., Rana, S. K., Joo, M. I., Rana, A. K., & Aich, S. (2021). Blockchain-based model to improve the performance of the next-generation digital supply chain. *Sustainability (Basel)*, *13*(18), 10008. doi:10.3390u131810008

Rasekhi, S., & Sheidaei, Z. (2019). An Empirical Analysis of Strategic Competition and Exchange Rate Pass-through. *Iranian Journal of Economic Studies*, *8*(1), 119–136.

Rasi, M., & Mohammadi Dolat-Abadi, H. (2022). Proposing a framework for identifying the competitive advantage of small and medium-sized manufacturing organizations under uncertainty conditions. *Journal of Decisions and Operations Research*, 7(4), 515-529.

Rath, C. K., Mandal, A. K., & Sarkar, A. (2022). An Event-B based Device Description Model in IoT with the Support of Multimodal System. *Advanced Computing and Systems for Security*, *13*, 3–19. doi:10.1007/978-981-16-4287-6_1

Rejeb, A., Keogh, J. G., & Treiblmaier, H. (2019). Leveraging the internet of things and blockchain technology in supply chain management. *Future Internet*, *11*(7), 161. doi:10.3390/fi11070161

Rejeb, A., Rejeb, K., Treiblmaier, H., Appolloni, A., Alghamdi, S., Alhasawi, Y., & Iranmanesh, M. (2023). The Internet of Things (IoT) in Healthcare: Taking Stock and Moving Forward. *Internet of Things*, 100721.

Richey, R. G., Adams, F. G., & Dalela, V. (2012). Technology and flexibility: Enablers of collaboration and time-based logistics quality. *Journal of Business Logistics*, *33*(1), 34–49. doi:10.1111/j.0000-0000.2011.01036.x

Rothaermel, F. T. (2021). *Strategic Management* (4th ed.). McGraw Hill Education.

Şahin, H., & Topal, B. (2019). Examination of effect of information sharing on businesses performance in the supply chain process. *International Journal of Production Research*, *57*(3), 815–828. doi:10.1080/00207543.2018.1484954

Salama, R., Al-Turjman, F., & Culmone, R. (2023, March). AI-Powered Drone to Address Smart City Security Issues. In *International Conference on Advanced Information Networking and Applications* (pp. 292-300). Cham: Springer International Publishing. 10.1007/978-3-031-28694-0_27

Salam, M. A. (2017). The mediating role of supply chain collaboration on the relationship between technology, trust and operational performance. *Benchmarking*, *24*(2), 298–317. doi:10.1108/BIJ-07-2015-0075

Salih, S., & Mhlanga, D. (2023). Blockchain for Food Supply Chain: Trust, Traceability, and Transparency Enhancement, How Can Africa Benefit? *The Fourth Industrial Revolution in Africa: Exploring the Development Implications of Smart Technologies in Africa*, 311-325.

Samadi-Parviznejad, P., & Soltani, Z. (2022). Identifying and evaluating smart city marketing parameters (Case study: Tabriz). *International Journal of Innovation in Marketing Elements, 2*(1), 35-50.

Samadi-Parviznejad, P. (2022). The role of big data in digital transformation. *Journal of Data Analytics*, *1*(1), 42–47. doi:10.59615/jda.1.1.42

Sanchez, M. A., & Zuntini, J. I. (2018). Organizational readiness for the digital transformation: A case study research. *Revista Gestão & Tecnologia*, *18*(2), 70–99. doi:10.20397/2177-6652/2018.v18i2.1316

Sanders, N. R. (2014). *Big data driven supply chain management: A framework for implementing analytics and turning information into intelligence*. Pearson Education.

Sangave, N. A., Aungst, T. D., & Patel, D. K. (2019). Smart connected insulin pens, caps, and attachments: A review of the future of diabetes technology. *Diabetes Spectrum*, *32*(4), 378–384. doi:10.2337/ds18-0069 PMID:31798296

Sarmah, S. (2018). *Understanding blockchain technology*. Academic Press.

Seydoux, N., Drira, K., Hernandez, N., & Monteil, T. (2016). IoT-O, a core-domain IoT ontology to represent connected devices networks. *Knowledge Engineering and Knowledge Management: 20th International Conference, EKAW 2016, Bologna, Italy, November 19-23, 2016 Proceedings*, *20*, 561–576.

Seyitoglu, F., & Ivanov, S. (2020). A conceptual framework of the service delivery system design for hospitality firms in the (post-)viral world: The role of service robots. *International Journal of Hospitality Management, 91*(July), 102661. Advance online publication. doi:10.1016/j.ijhm.2020.102661

Shambayati, H., Shafiei Nikabadi, M., Khatami Firouzabadi, S. M. A., Rahmanimanesh, M., & Saberi, S. (2022). Optimization of virtual closed-loop supply chain under uncertainty: Application of IoT. *Kybernetes.*

Shamim, S., Cang, S., Yu, H., & Li, Y. (2017). Examining the feasibilities of Industry 4.0 for the hospitality sector with the lens of management practice. *Energies, 10*(4), 499. Advance online publication. doi:10.3390/en10040499

Sharma, A., Sharma, A., Bhatia, T., & Singh, R. K. (2023). Blockchain enabled food supply chain management: A systematic literature review and bibliometric analysis. *Operations Management Research*, 1-25.

Sharma, P. K., Kumar, N., & Park, J. H. (2019). Blockchain-based distributed framework for automotive industry in a smart city. *IEEE Transactions on Industrial Informatics, 15*(7), 4197–4205. doi:10.1109/TII.2018.2887101

Shen, H. (2021). *Alibaba: Infrastructuring Global China.* Routledge. doi:10.4324/9781003169055

Shin, H., & Kang, J. (2020). Reducing perceived health risk to attract hotel customers in the COVID-19 pandemic era: Focused on technology innovation for social distancing and cleanliness. *International Journal of Hospitality Management, 91*, 102664. doi:10.1016/j.ijhm.2020.102664

Simatupang, T. M. & Sridharan, R. (2018). Complementarities in supply chain collaboration. *Industrial Engineering and Management Systems, 17*(1), 30-42.

Simatupang, T. M., & Sridharan, R. (2005). The collaboration index: A measure for supply chain collaboration. *International Journal of Physical Distribution & Logistics Management, 35*(1), 44–62. doi:10.1108/09600030510577421

Singhal, B., Dhameja, G., Panda, P.S., Singhal, B., Dhameja, G., & Panda, P.S. (2018). *How blockchain works.* Academic Press.

Singla, D., & Rana, S. (2023). Blockchain-Based Platform for Smart Tracking and Tracing the Pharmaceutical Drug Supply Chain. In *Examining Multimedia Forensics and Content Integrity* (pp. 144–172). IGI Global. doi:10.4018/978-1-6684-6864-7.ch006

Sobin, C. C. (2020). A survey on architecture, protocols and challenges in IoT. *Wireless Personal Communications, 112*(3), 1383–1429. doi:10.100711277-020-07108-5

Sodiq, A., Baloch, A. A., Khan, S. A., Sezer, N., Mahmoud, S., Jama, M., & Abdelaal, A. (2019). Towards modern sustainable cities: Review of sustainability principles and trends. *Journal of Cleaner Production, 227*, 972–1001. doi:10.1016/j.jclepro.2019.04.106

Solaimani, S., & van der Veen, J. (2022). Open supply chain innovation: An extended view on supply chain collaboration. *Supply Chain Management*, *27*(5), 597–610. doi:10.1108/SCM-09-2020-0433

Son, T. H., Weedon, Z., Yigitcanlar, T., Sanchez, T., Corchado, J. M., & Mehmood, R. (2023). Algorithmic urban planning for smart and sustainable development: Systematic review of the literature. *Sustainable Cities and Society*, *94*, 104562. doi:10.1016/j.scs.2023.104562

Srivastava, P., Srinivasan, M., & Iyer, K. N. (2015). Relational resource antecedents and operational outcome of supply chain collaboration: The role of environmental turbulence. *Transportation Journal*, *54*(2), 240–274. doi:10.5325/transportationj.54.2.0240

Steenwinckel, B., De Brouwer, M., Stojchevska, M., Van Der Donckt, J., Nelis, J., Ruyssinck, J., . . . Ongenae, F. (2022). Data analytics for health and connected care: Ontology, knowledge graph and applications. *EAI PervasiveHealth, the 16th EAI International Conference on Pervasive Computing Technologies for Healthcare.*

Stellantis. (n.d.). *About Us*. Stellantis. https://www.stellantis.com/en/company/about-us

Stix, C. (2021). *Actionable principles for artificial intelligence policy: Three pathways*. Academic Press.

Stroia, O. V., Kirsch, K., Kline, S., Neal, J., Sirsat, S., & Almanza, B. (2012). *Empirical study on the cleanliness of hotels – cleanest and dirtiest spots.* Paper Presented at the 17th Annual Graduate Conference. 5–7 January, Auburn, AL. http://humsci.auburn.edu/hrmt/hospitality/GradConference2012/POSTERpresentations. pdf

Su, J., Wei, Y., Wang, S., & Liu, Q. (2023). The impact of digital transformation on the total factor productivity of heavily polluting enterprises. *Scientific Reports*, *13*(1), 6386. doi:10.103841598-023-33553-w PMID:37076699

Su, L., Hsu, M. K., & Boostrom, R. E. Jr. (2020). From recreation to responsibility: Increasing environmentally responsible behavior in tourism. *Journal of Business Research*, *109*, 557–573. doi:10.1016/j.jbusres.2018.12.055

Sundram, V. P. K., Bahrin, A. S., Abdul Munir, Z. B., & Zolait, A. H. (2018). The effect of supply chain information management and information system infrastructure: The mediating role of supply chain integration towards manufacturing performance in Malaysia. *Journal of Enterprise Information Management*, *31*(5), 751–770. doi:10.1108/JEIM-06-2017-0084

Surdua, I., Mellahi, K., Glaister, K. W., & Nardella, G. (2018). Why wait? Organizational learning, institutional quality and the speed of foreign market re-entry after initial entry and exit. *Journal of World Business*, *53*(6), 911–921. doi:10.1016/j.jwb.2018.07.008

Taherdoost, H. (2023). Smart Contracts in Blockchain Technology: A Critical Review. *Information (Basel)*, *14*(2), 117. doi:10.3390/info14020117

Talan, G., & Sharma, G. D. (2020). From business goals to societal goals via sustainable investment: An integrative review and research agenda. *World Review of Entrepreneurship, Management and Sustainable Development*, *16*(1), 108–124. doi:10.1504/WREMSD.2020.105530

Tang, C. S., & Veelenturf, L. P. (2019). The strategic role of logistics in the industry 4.0 era. *Transportation Research Part E, Logistics and Transportation Review*, *129*, 1–11. doi:10.1016/j.tre.2019.06.004

Tan, Y. (2011). *Chinnovation: How Chinese innovators are changing the world.* John Wiley and Sons.

Tawalbeh, L. A., Muheidat, F., Tawalbeh, M., & Quwaider, M. (2020). IoT Privacy and security: Challenges and solutions. *Applied Sciences (Basel, Switzerland)*, *10*(12), 4102. doi:10.3390/app10124102

Teece, D. J. (2019). China and the reshaping of the auto industry: A dynamic capabilities perspective. *Management and Organization Review*, *15*(1), 177–199. doi:10.1017/mor.2019.4

Teng, T., Tsinopoulos, C., & Tse, Y. K. (2022). IS capabilities, supply chain collaboration and quality performance in services: The moderating effect of environmental dynamism. *Industrial Management & Data Systems*, *122*(7), 1592–1619. doi:10.1108/IMDS-08-2021-0496

Terzidis, O., Oberle, D., Friesen, A., Janiesch, C., & Barros, A. (2012). The Internet of services and USDL. In Handbook of Service Description. Springer. doi:10.1007/978-1-4614-1864-1_1

Tew, P. J., Lu, Z., Tolomiczenko, G., & Gellatly, J. (2008). SARS: Lessons in strategic planning for hoteliers and destination marketers. *International Journal of Contemporary Hospitality Management*, *20*(3), 332–346. doi:10.1108/09596110810866145

Thakare, V., Khire, G., & Kumbhar, M. (2022). Artificial Intelligence (AI) And Internet Of Things (IoT) In Healthcare: Opportunities And Challenges. *ECS Transactions*, *107*(1), 7941–7951. doi:10.1149/10701.7941ecst

Tijan, E., Aksentijević, S., Ivanić, K., & Jardas, M. (2019). Blockchain technology implementation in logistics. *Sustainability (Basel)*, *11*(4), 1185. doi:10.3390u11041185

Toth-Peter, A., de Oliveira, R. T., Mathews, S., Barner, L., & Figueira, S. (2023). Industry 4.0 as an enabler in transitioning to circular business models: A systematic literature review. *Journal of Cleaner Production*, *393*, 136284. doi:10.1016/j.jclepro.2023.136284

Tourk, K., & Marsh, P. (2016). The new industrial revolution and industrial upgrading in China: Achievements and challenges. *Economic and Political Studies*, *4*(2), 187–209. doi:10.1080/20954816.2016.1180769

Travizano, M., Sarraute, C., Ajzenman, G., & Minnoni, M.. (2018). *Wibson: A decentralized data marketplace*. Academic Press.

Treiblmaier, H., & Pollach, I. (2011). *The influence of privacy concerns on perceptions of web personalisation*. Academic Press.

Treiblmaier, H., & Sillaber, C.. (2021). *The impact of blockchain on e-commerce: a framework for salient research topics*. Academic Press.

Treiblmaier, H., Rejeb, A., & Ahmed, W. A. (2022). Blockchain technologies in the digital supply chain. *The Digital Supply Chain*, 127-144.

Treiblmaier, H. (2018). The impact of the blockchain on the supply chain: A theory-based research framework and a call for action. *Supply Chain Management*, *23*(6), 545–559. doi:10.1108/SCM-01-2018-0029

Treiblmaier, H., & Sillaber, C. (2021). The impact of blockchain on e-commerce: A framework for salient research topics. *Electronic Commerce Research and Applications*, *48*, 101054. doi:10.1016/j.elerap.2021.101054

Trevisan, L. V., Eustachio, J. H. P. P., Dias, B. G., Filho, W. L., & Pedrozo, E. Á. (2023). Digital transformation towards sustainability in higher education: State-of-the-art and future research insights. *Environment, Development and Sustainability*, 1–22. doi:10.100710668-022-02874-7 PMID:36624732

Trivedi, S. (2023). An Umbrella Review of the Literature on Blockchain and Distributed Ledger Technology and Their Roles in Future Banking. *Perspectives on Blockchain Technology and Responsible Investing*, 29-57.

Tuni, A., Rentizelas, A., & Duffy, A. (2018). Environmental performance measurement for green supply chains: A systematic analysis and review of quantitative methods. *International Journal of Physical Distribution & Logistics Management*, *48*(8), 765–793. doi:10.1108/IJPDLM-02-2017-0062

Turjo, M. D., Khan, M. M., Kaur, M., & Zaguia, A. (2021). Smart supply chain management using the blockchain and smart contract. *Scientific Programming*, *2021*, 1–12. doi:10.1155/2021/6092792

Uddin, M. B., & Akhter, B. (2022). Investigating the relationship between top management commitment, supply chain collaboration, and sustainable firm performance in the agro-processing supply chain. *Operations Management Research : Advancing Practice Through Research*, *15*(3-4), 1399–1417. doi:10.100712063-022-00257-9

Udokwu, C., Kormiltsyn, A., Thangalimodzi, K., & Norta, A. (2018). The state of the art for blockchain-enabled smart-contract applications in the organization. *2018 Ivannikov Ispras Open Conference (ISPRAS)*, 137-144. 10.1109/ISPRAS.2018.00029

Ullah, F., & Al-Turjman, F. (2023). A conceptual framework for blockchain smart contract adoption to manage real estate deals in smart cities. *Neural Computing & Applications*, *35*(7), 5033–5054. doi:10.100700521-021-05800-6

Ullah, F., Shen, L., & Shah, S. H. H. (2023). Value co-creation in business-to-business context: A bibliometric analysis using HistCite and VOS viewer. *Frontiers in Psychology*, *13*, 1027775. doi:10.3389/fpsyg.2022.1027775 PMID:36710832

UNCTAD. (2022). *Circular economy*. https://unctad.org/topic/trade-and-environment/circular-economy

UNECE. (2023). *UNECE adopts two new regulations to improve the safety of vulnerable road users*. https://unece.org/sustainable-development/press/unece-adopts-two-new-regulations-improve-safety-vulnerable-road-users

Ungureanu, P. (2023). Putting Space in Place. Multimodal Translation of the Grand Challenge of Regional Smart Specialization from Policy to Cross-sector Partnerships. *Journal of Business Ethics*, *184*(4), 895–915. doi:10.100710551-023-05359-3

Vagadia, B. (2020). *Digital Disruption*. Springer Nature. doi:10.1007/978-3-030-54494-2

Vaigandla, K. K., Karne, R., Siluveru, M., & Kesoju, M. (2023). Review on Blockchain Technology: Architecture, Characteristics, Benefits, Algorithms, Challenges and Applications. *Mesopotamian Journal of CyberSecurity*, *2023*, 73–85.

Valeonti, F., Bikakis, A., Terras, M., Speed, C., Hudson-Smith, A., & Chalkias, K. (2021). Crypto collectibles, museum funding and OpenGLAM: Challenges, opportunities and the potential of Non-Fungible Tokens (NFTs). *Applied Sciences (Basel, Switzerland)*, *11*(21), 9931. doi:10.3390/app11219931

Veile, J. W., Schmidt, M. C., Müller, J. M., & Voigt, K. I. (2022). The transformation of supply chain collaboration and design through Industry 4.0. *International Journal of Logistics Research and Applications,* 1-29.

Vervest, P. H., Van Liere, D. W., Zheng, L., Vervest, P. H., & Zheng, L. (2009). *The network experience—New value from smart business networks*. Springer Berlin Heidelberg. doi:10.1007/978-3-540-85582-8

Vijayan, V., Connolly, J. P., Condell, J., McKelvey, N., & Gardiner, P. (2021). Review of wearable devices and data collection considerations for connected health. *Sensors (Basel)*, *21*(16), 5589. doi:10.339021165589 PMID:34451032

Villar, A., Paladini, S., & Buckley, O. (2023, July). Towards Supply Chain 5.0: Redesigning Supply Chains as Resilient, Sustainable, and Human-Centric Systems in a Post-pandemic World. *Operations Research Forum*, *4*(3), 60. doi:10.100743069-023-00234-3

Viriyasitavat, W., Bi, Z., & Hoonsopon, D. (2022). Blockchain technologies for interoperation of business processes in smart supply chains. *Journal of Industrial Information Integration, 26*, 100326. doi:10.1016/j.jii.2022.100326

Volza. (2023). *Directory of automotive suppliers & manufacturers in the world*. https://www.volza.com/p/automotive/manufacturers/

von Garrel, J., & Jahn, C. (2022). Design Framework for the Implementation of AI-based (Service) Business Models for Small and Medium-sized Manufacturing Enterprises. *Journal of the Knowledge Economy*, 1–19.

Wang, G., Li, S., & Yang, L. (2022). Research on the pathway of green financial system to implement the realization of China's carbon neutrality target. *International Journal of Environmental Research and Public Health, 19*(4), 2451. doi:10.3390/ijerph19042451 PMID:35206639

Wang, H., & Yang, H. (2019). Ridesourcing systems: A framework and review. *Transportation Research Part B: Methodological, 129*, 122–155. doi:10.1016/j.trb.2019.07.009

Wang, Q., & Su, M. (2020). Integrating blockchain technology into the energy sector—From theory of blockchain to research and application of energy blockchain. *Computer Science Review, 37*, 100275. doi:10.1016/j.cosrev.2020.100275

Wang, S., Yuan, Y., Wang, X., Li, J., Qin, R., & Wang, F.-Y. (2018). An overview of smart contract: architecture, applications, and future trends. *2018 IEEE Intelligent Vehicles Symposium (IV)*, 108-113. 10.1109/IVS.2018.8500488

Webb, W. (2023). The smart city and COVID-19. In Beyond the Pandemic? Exploring the Impact of COVID-19 on Telecommunications and the Internet (pp. 121-133). Emerald Publishing Limited. doi:10.1108/978-1-80262-049-820231005

Wenhua, Z., Qamar, F., Abdali, T. A. N., Hassan, R., Jafri, S. T. A., & Nguyen, Q. N. (2023). Blockchain technology: Security issues, healthcare applications, challenges and future trends. *Electronics (Basel), 12*(3), 546. doi:10.3390/electronics12030546

Whig, P., Velu, A., & Nadikattu, R. R. (2022). Blockchain Platform to Resolve Security Issues in IoT and Smart Networks. In AI-Enabled Agile Internet of Things for Sustainable FinTech Ecosystems (pp. 46-65). IGI Global. doi:10.4018/978-1-6684-4176-3.ch003

Whittington, R., Regnér, P., Angwin, D., Johnson, G., & Scholes, K. (2022). *Exploring Strategy* (12th ed.). Pearson.

Williams, P. A., & McCauley, V. (2016, December). Always connected: The security challenges of the healthcare Internet of Things. In *2016 IEEE 3rd World Forum on Internet of Things (WF-IoT)* (pp. 30-35). IEEE.

World Bank. (2023). *Sharp, Long-lasting Slowdown to Hit Developing Countries Hard.* https://www.worldbank.org/en/news/press-release/2023/01/10/global-economic-prospects

World Health Organization. (n.d.). *Sustainable development goals.* https://www.who.int/europe/about-us/our-work/sustainable-development-goals

Wu, X., & Gereffi, G. (2018). Amazon and Alibaba: Internet governance, business models, and internationalization strategies. In International business in the information and digital age (Vol. 13, pp. 327-356). Emerald Publishing Limited.

Wu, L., & Chiu, M. L. (2018). Examining supply chain collaboration with determinants and performance impact: Social capital, justice, and technology use perspectives. *International Journal of Information Management, 39*, 5–19. doi:10.1016/j.ijinfomgt.2017.11.004

Wu, L., Yue, X., Jin, A., & Yen, D. C. (2016). Smart supply chain management: A review and implications for future research. *International Journal of Logistics Management*, *27*(2), 395–417. doi:10.1108/IJLM-02-2014-0035

Wu, Q., Yan, D., & Umair, M. (2023). Assessing the role of competitive intelligence and practices of dynamic capabilities in business accommodation of SMEs. *Economic Analysis and Policy*, *77*, 1103–1114. doi:10.1016/j.eap.2022.11.024

Xia, L., & Liu, S. (2021). Intelligent IoT-based cross-border e-commerce supply chain performance optimization. *Wireless Communications and Mobile Computing*, *2021*, 1–13. doi:10.1155/2021/9961925

Xiao, B., & Benbasat, I. (2011). Product-Related Deception in E-Commerce: A Theoretical Perspective. *Management Information Systems Quarterly*, *35*(1), 169–195. doi:10.2307/23043494

Xie, J., & Chen, C. (2022). Supply chain and logistics optimization management for international trading enterprises using IoT-based economic logistics model. *Operations Management Research : Advancing Practice Through Research*, *15*(3-4), 711–724. doi:10.100712063-022-00254-y

Xie, K., Wu, Y., Xiao, J., & Hu, Q. (2016). Value co-creation between firms and customers: The role of big data-based cooperative assets. *Information & Management*, *53*(8), 1034–1048. doi:10.1016/j.im.2016.06.003

Xu, G., & Gutiérrez, J.A. (2006). *An exploratory study of killer applications and critical success factors in m-commerce*. Academic Press.

Yang, C., & Chan, D. Y. T. (2021). Market Expansion of Domestic Gaming Firms in Shenzhen, China: Dilemma of Globalisation and Regionalisation. *Tijdschrift voor Economische en Sociale Geografie*, *112*(3), 256–273. doi:10.1111/tesg.12459

Yildiz Ozenc, S. C., Er, M., & Firat, S. U. (2023). Risks in Supply Chain 4.0: A Literature Review Study. In *Global Joint Conference on Industrial Engineering and Its Application Areas* (pp. 163-177). Springer. 10.1007/978-3-031-08782-0_13

Yin, R. K. (2009). Case Study Research: Design and Methods. *Sage (Atlanta, Ga.).*

Yli-Huumo, J., Ko, D., Choi, S., Park, S., & Smolander, K. (2016). *Where is current research on blockchain technology? A systematic review*. Academic Press.

Yu, P., Chang, X., & Mandizvidza, K. (2023). Development of New Energy Vehicles in Entrepreneurial Ecosystem Under the Carbon Neutrality Policy in China. In Corporate Sustainability as a Tool for Improving Economic, Social, and Environmental Performance (pp. 55-84). IGI Global. doi:10.4018/978-1-6684-7422-8.ch004

Zeng, S.-Q., Huo, R., Huang, T., Liu, J., Wang, S., & Feng, W. (2020). *Survey of blockchain: principle, progress and application*. Academic Press.

Zhang, A., Duong, L., Seuring, S., & Hartley, J. L. (2023). Circular supply chain management: A bibliometric analysis-based literature review. *International Journal of Logistics Management*, *34*(3), 847–872. doi:10.1108/IJLM-04-2022-0199

Zhang, G., Yang, Y., & Yang, G. (2023). Smart supply chain management in Industry 4.0: The review, research agenda and strategies in North America. *Annals of Operations Research*, *322*(2), 1075–1117. doi:10.100710479-022-04689-1 PMID:35531562

Zhang, X., Nutakor, F., Minlah, M. K., & Li, J. (2023). Can Digital Transformation Drive Green Transformation in Manufacturing Companies?—Based on Socio-Technical Systems Theory Perspective. *Sustainability (Basel)*, *15*(3), 2840. doi:10.3390u15032840

Zhao, Z., Li, X., Luan, B., Jiang, W., Gao, W., & Neelakandan, S. (2023). Secure Internet of Things (IoT) using a Novel Brooks Iyengar Quantum Byzantine Agreement-centered Blockchain Networking (BIQBA-BCN) Model in Smart Healthcare. *Information Sciences*, *629*, 440–455. doi:10.1016/j.ins.2023.01.020

Zhong, L., Sun, S., Law, R., & Zhang, X. (2020). Impact of robot hotel service on consumers' purchase intention: A control experiment. *Asia Pacific Journal of Tourism Research*, *25*(7), 780–798. doi:10.1080/10941665.2020.1726421

Zhu, H., Wu, C. K., Koo, C. H., Tsang, Y. T., Liu, Y., Chi, H. R., & Tsang, K. F. (2019). Smart healthcare in the era of internet-of-things. *IEEE Consumer Electronics Magazine*, *8*(5), 26–30. doi:10.1109/MCE.2019.2923929

Zreik, M. (2022). Contemporary geopolitics of Eurasia and the Belt and Road Initiative. *Eurasian Research Journal*, *4*(1), 7–26. doi:10.53277/2519-2442-2022.1-01

Zreik, M. (2023a). From Boom to Bust: A Study of China's Economy in the Wake of COVID-19 Outbreak in H1 2020. *BRICS Journal of Economics*, *4*(1), 147–171. doi:10.3897/brics-econ.4.e101050

Zreik, M. (2023b). China's Economic Development: Digital Transformation, Energy Efficiency, and Climate Change. In M. Okur Dinçsoy & H. Can (Eds.), *Optimizing Energy Efficiency During a Global Energy Crisis* (pp. 51–64). IGI Global. doi:10.4018/979-8-3693-0400-6.ch004

Zreik, M., & Abunamous, M. O. (2021). Human thinking at the time of Covid-19 and the role of swot analysis: A case study on the Chinese and Palestinian societies. *Psychology Research on Education and Social Sciences*, *2*(1), 31–40.

About the Contributors

Hamed Nozari is a research assistant in Industrial engineering at the Iran university of science and technology. He holds a Ph.D. in Industrial Engineering with a focus on Production Management and Planning and PostDoc in Industrial Engineering from the Iran University of Science and Technology. He has taught various courses in the field of Industrial Engineering and has published many books and papers as well. Now he is a researcher in the field of digital developments and smart systems and optimization.

* * *

Belem Barbosa received her PhD in Business and Management Studies – Specialisation in Marketing and Strategy from the University of Porto, Portugal. She is Assistant Professor at the School of Economics and Management of the University of Porto. She is full researcher at GOVCOPP, the Research Unit of Governance, Competitiveness, and Public Policies, and Invited Researcher at cef.up Center for Economics and Finance at the University of Porto. Her research interests lie primarily in the areas of digital marketing and consumer behavior.

Gabriela Bessa is a junior researcher interested in the economics of business and strategy, currently pursuing her Master's degree at the University of Porto.

Mariana Ferreira is a junior researcher interested in the economics of business and strategy, currently pursuing her Master's degree at the University of Porto.

Dinesh Kumar is a highly accomplished professional with extensive expertise in the military, academia, business and charity sectors. He holds a PhD from the highly regarded Indian Institute of Technology (IIT) Roorkee. He is the founder of Pomento, and Mission Dost-E-Jahan.

Sunil Kumar is working as associate professor in the department of human resource management, Lovely Professional University, Phagwara, Punjab, India. He has received his/ her Ph.D. degree from Central university of Himachal Pradesh, Dharamshala, India in 2019. His/ her research areas include leadership, e-training, AI, entrepreneurship and resilience. He has published 20 number of publications, and 4 number of copyrights.

Rafaela Martins is a junior researcher interested in the economics of business and strategy, currently pursuing her Master's degree at the University of Porto.

Melisa Ozbiltekin-Pala is a Research Assistant in Yaşar University and PhD Student in Ege University.

Inês Ricardo is a junior researcher interested in the economics of business and strategy, currently pursuing her Master's degree at the University of Porto.

Agnieszka Szmelter-Jarosz is an assistant professor at the Department of Logistics, Faculty of Economics, University of Gdansk, Poland. She is an author of over 80 scientific papers. She has been a principal investigator in two national projects about the urban mobility and a co-investigator and team member in 14 international and national projects. Her major scientific interests are urban logistics and urban mobility. She is a Lean Six Sigma Black Belt, SAP Certified Application Associate and Design Thinking Moderator. She is working as a project director and senior analyst in Polish Railways companies and runs her own consulting company.

Catarina Teixeira is a junior researcher interested in the economics of business and strategy, currently pursuing her Master's degree at the University of Porto.

Meenakshi Yadav completed her PhD in domain Human resource management from lovely professional university, and presently working in Phillaur.

Mohamad Zreik, a Postdoctoral Fellow at Sun Yat-sen University, is a recognized scholar in International Relations, specializing in China's Arab-region foreign policy. His recent work in soft power diplomacy compares China's methods in the Middle East and East Asia. His extensive knowledge spans Middle Eastern Studies, China-Arab relations, East Asian and Asian Affairs, Eurasian geopolitics, and Political Economy, providing him a unique viewpoint in his field. Dr. Zreik is a proud recipient of a PhD from Central China Normal University (Wuhan). He's written numerous acclaimed papers, many focusing on China's Belt and Road Initiative and its Arab-region impact. His groundbreaking research has established him as a leading expert in his field. Presently, he furthers his research on China's soft power diplomacy tactics at Sun Yat-sen University. His significant contributions make him a crucial figure in understanding contemporary international relations.

Index

G

H

I

M

O

P

S

T

Ensure Quality Research is Introduced to the Academic Community

Become an Evaluator for IGI Global Authored Book Projects

The overall success of an authored book project is dependent on quality and timely manuscript evaluations.

Applications and Inquiries may be sent to:
development@igi-global.com

Applicants must have a doctorate (or equivalent degree) as well as publishing, research, and reviewing experience. Authored Book Evaluators are appointed for one-year terms and are expected to complete at least three evaluations per term. Upon successful completion of this term, evaluators can be considered for an additional term.

If you have a colleague that may be interested in this opportunity, we encourage you to share this information with them.

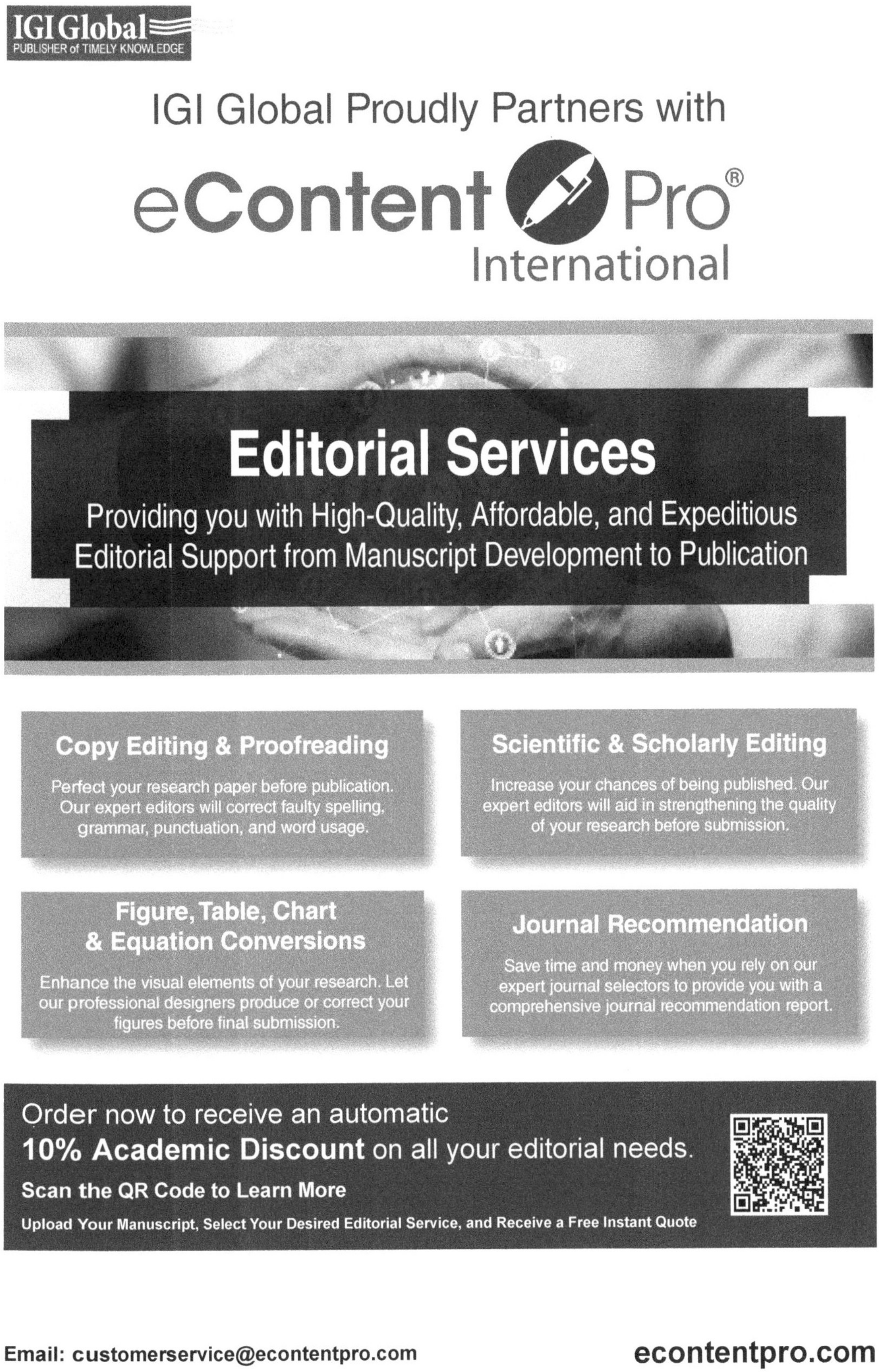
IGI Global
PUBLISHER of TIMELY KNOWLEDGE
IGI Global Proudly Partners with
eContent Pro®
International
Editorial Services
Providing you with High-Quality, Affordable, and Expeditious Editorial Support from Manuscript Development to Publication
Copy Editing & Proofreading
Perfect your research paper before publication. Our expert editors will correct faulty spelling, grammar, punctuation, and word usage.
Scientific & Scholarly Editing
Increase your chances of being published. Our expert editors will aid in strengthening the quality of your research before submission.
Figure, Table, Chart & Equation Conversions
Enhance the visual elements of your research. Let our professional designers produce or correct your figures before final submission.
Journal Recommendation
Save time and money when you rely on our expert journal selectors to provide you with a comprehensive journal recommendation report.
Order now to receive an automatic
10% Academic Discount on all your editorial needs.
Scan the QR Code to Learn More
Upload Your Manuscript, Select Your Desired Editorial Service, and Receive a Free Instant Quote
Email: customerservice@econtentpro.com
econtentpro.com

www.ingramcontent.com/pod-product-compliance
Lightning Source LLC
LaVergne TN
LVHW081335300926
849161LV00008B/1977